American Public Opinion toward Israel and the Arab-Israeli Conflict

American Public Opinion toward Israel and the Arab-Israeli Conflict

Eytan Gilboa
The Hebrew University of Jerusalem

Lexington Books
D.C. Heath and Company/Lexington, Massachusetts/Toronto

Library of Congress Cataloging in Publication Data

Gilboa, Eytan.
American public opinion toward Israel and the Arab-Israeli conflict.

Bibliography: p.
Includes index.
1. Israel—Foreign opinion, American. 2. Jewish-Arab relations—1949– —Public opinion. 3. Jews—United States—Attitudes toward Israel. 4. Public opinion—United States. I. Title.
E183.8.I75G54 1986 956′.04 86-45436
ISBN 0-669-13426-0 (alk. paper)

Published simultaneously in Canada
Printed in the United States of America
International Standard Book Number: 0-669-13426-0
Library of Congress Catalog Card Number: 86-45436

The paper used in this publication meets the minimum requirements of American Nationa Standard for Information Sciences—Permanence of Paper for Printed Library Materials, ANSI Z39.48-1984. ∞™

The last numbers on the right below indicate the number and date of printing.

10 9 8 7 6 5 4 3 2 1

95 94 93 92 91 90 89 88 87 86

To My Parents, Hanna and Yehuda Gilboa

Contents

Figures and Tables

Figures

Tables

Acknowledgments

Several distinguished scholars reviewed sections of my book and offered valuable comments. I especially would like to thank professors Seymour Martin Lipset, Steven L. Spiegel, Herbert Kelman, William V. O'Brien, Michael Mandelbaum and Chaim I. Waxman. Intellectually I owe a great debt to my former teacher and present colleague Nissan Oren, a rare individual of honesty and integrity. Any faults or limitations herewithin are obviously entirely my own responsibility.

A great debt is owed several students of mine who assisted me in the preparation of this book. Shelley Von Berg not only provided thoughtful and analytical insight, but also expertly and painstakingly edited the entire manuscript. My research assistant Yael Nachmias contributed to the conceptual construction and initial phases of the book. She was succeeded by Gil Marom who provided valuable research assistance and designed and drew most of the figures. Matthew Hirshberg and Ann Weisman also assisted in various research capacities.

I am grateful to the Leonard Davis Institute for International Relations at the Hebrew University for providing several research grants. The Eshkol Institute also contributed financial assistance. I owe a special thanks to Dr. George Kuntz, M.D. and his wife Ruby for their moral and material assistance.

Several libraries and organizations, both in the United States and Israel, were helpful in making valuable documents, reports and materials available to me. I would especially like to thank Geraldine Rosenfield and Milton Himmelfarb from Information and Research Services of the American Jewish Committee in New York; Toby Dershowitz and Sara M. Averick from the American Israel Public Affairs Committee in Washington; and Karlyn H. Keene from the American Enterprise Institute for Public Policy Research. In Israel I would like to thank Christine Rimon and Michel Konstantyn of the American Cultural Center Library in Jerusalem; Dr. Moshe Yegar, Deputy Director General of the Ministry of Foreign Affairs and Zvi Amitai from the ministry's archives; Ellen Infeld and Michele Morowitz of the American Jewish Committee Library and Information Center in Jersualem; and Yossi Harroch of the Central Library of the Hebrew University at Mount Scopus.

My greatest debt is to my family—my wife Irit and my children Orna, Amir and Ella—without whose support, patience and love this book never would have been completed.

Introduction

In December 1962, President John F. Kennedy privately told Israeli Foreign Minister Golda Meir "The U.S. has a special relationship with Israel in the Middle East, really comparable only to that which it has with Britain over a wide range of world affairs."[1] Kennedy acknowledged a unique characteristic of American-Israeli relations that has developed since the establishment of Israel in 1948. Fifteen years later, President Jimmy Carter publicly voiced the same sentiments:

> We have a special relationship with Israel. It's absolutely crucial that no one in our country or around the world ever doubt that our number one commitment in the Middle East is to protect the right of Israel to exist, to exist permanently and to exist in peace.[2]

Despite the absence of formal written commitments or a defense treaty, American-Israeli relations are closer than U.S. relations with most of its other allies. This phenomenon has intrigued politicians and scholars alike.

Israel is an extremely small country in population and territory. It lacks natural resources and has been entangled in myriad serious economic, military, and social problems. In contrast, the Arab world is large in population and territory and rich in natural resources, markets, and political power. The United States has significant strategic and commercial interests in the Arab world and, since 1967, has been the leading mediator in the Arab-Israeli peacemaking process. Yet these interests have not adversely affected the special relationship, and the United States has continued to support Israel politically, economically, and militarily.

The special relationship has been attributed to various factors and similarities between the United States and Israel, including Israel's military might and mutual strategic interests in the Middle East, Judeo-Christian roots of American society, similar democratic systems and historical pioneering spirit, common values, the presence of a large Jewish community, and the powerful Israeli lobby in Washington.[3] Each of these factors has contributed to unremitting congressional support of Israel, even in times of crisis between the United States and the Jewish state. On numerous occasions, the Congress has taken action on behalf of Israel in the form of statements, resolutions, legislation, and letters to the White House.[4]

It is widely assumed that the special relationship, the success of the Israeli lobby, and the congressional attitude toward Israel would be untenable were it not for highly favorable American public opinion. American, Israeli, and Arab leaders acknowledge the significance of these sentiments. Former Israeli ambassador to the United Nations and incumbent president of Israel Chaim Herzog commented on the Arab-Israeli conflict in 1975: "The main battlefield now is the theater of opinion in the United States."[5] The late president of Egypt, Anwar Sadat, informed his aides two weeks before his historic visit to Jerusalem that his mission would prove to Americans and the world public "who really wants peace in the Middle East."[6] For close to a decade, American-Arab allies have invested enormous resources in an attempt to improve the Arab image in the United States. Well-known public relation firms were contracted for that purpose, and Americans of Arab origin established lobby organizations emulating those of American Jewry.[7]

Purposes of This Book

In the last decade, the Arab-Israeli dispute has undergone dramatic shifts in structure and process—from a long and highly destructive war in 1973, through an Israeli-Egyptian peacemaking process, to another controversial war in Lebanon. Israeli and Arab-Israeli affairs have attracted considerable attention in public forums and the media, and Americans have increasingly expressed their views on this volatile arena.

Israelis and Arabs alike highly value the importance of American public opinion on their respective causes. However, no study has yet been conducted on the evolution of this issue. Numerous books on American-Israeli relations and U.S. policy in the Middle East have ignored public opinion altogether, and several articles written on this intriguing subject have dealt only with brief periods and have provided fragmented and partial views.[8] Thus, the central purpose of this book is to construct basic long-term trends in American opinion on Israel and the Arab-Israeli conflict within appropriate historical contexts and perspectives. It then seeks to identify opinion alterations over time, from the establishment of Israel and the inception of the Arab-Israeli conflict to the present. Public opinion is a very complex phenomenon; the exact processes and variables that mold it are not yet adequately understood.[9] Nevertheless, this book attempts to identify the factors and sources that probably have had the greatest bearing on the evolution of American public opinion on Israel.

An additional issue is whether public opinion affects policymaking. Numerous facets comprise the decision-making process, and the weight of public opinion varies among leaders and situations. In general, public opinion will affect policy only if leaders perceive it to be important and know, or think they know, its nature. This book questions not only whether public opinion affects American policy on the Middle East but also whether it affects the policies of Israel and other Middle Eastern countries.

Public opinion was a significant factor in the American decision to withdraw from Vietnam. Yet it has been argued that this was an exception, that public opinion generally plays only a marginal role in U.S. foreign policy.[10] Theodore C. Sorensen, special counsel to President Kennedy, wrote:

> In foreign affairs, the issues are frequently so complex, the facts so obscure, and the period of decision so short, that the American people have from the beginning—and even more so in this century—delegated to the President more discretion in this vital area; and they are usually willing to support any reasonable decision he makes.[11]

However, ten years later, another member of the Kennedy team argued:

> all the Presidents of the postwar period spent an extraordinary amount of time and energy attempting to build public support for their policies and to counter opposing views.[12]

In a more recent study on the formulation of U.S. foreign policy, an astute observer and scholar devoted an entire chapter to the role of public opinion. He suggested that a democracy "positively needs the undergirding of broad popular support for great national decisions, particularly those calling for a major sacrifice from the citizenry."[13] This suggestion applies to the domestic contexts of both American and Israeli foreign policy. However, since U.S. support is crucial to Israel, it is possible that American public opinion plays a role in Israeli policies as well. This hypothesis is tested here. An effort has been made to identify the approaches of various American, Israeli, and Arab leaders to American public opinion. This effort, based primarily on memoirs of principal policymakers and other direct testimony, is subjected to the obvious limitations of these sources.

Definitions and Methodology

The term *public opinion* has been defined in various ways. Each definition determines a particular approach and entails a different research method. For example, in the eyes of Hennessy, public opinion is "a complex of beliefs";[14]

for Lemert, it is "a perception imposed by the perceiver" on certain information;[15] and for Hovland, Janis, and Kelley, it is "an implicit verbal response or answer."[16] Very few scholars have offered definitions of *foreign policy opinion,* but in 1961, James Rosenau defined it as "any set of ideas, either informational or judgmental, about any concept of the world scene."[17] For Rosenau, then, public opinion is a set of ideas. According to Trice, however, "The term 'public opinion' denotes the general climate or distribution of opinions among the population at large on a given issue or set of issues."[18] The Rosenau and Trice definitions accurately describe the phenomenon investigated in this book.

Public opinion in the United States is expressed and monitored through several mediums but most frequently appears in the form of public opinion polls, organized interest-group activities, newspaper editorials, and letters to public officials and editors. Of all these mediums, polls are the central measure of public opinion and constitute, in the words of Bernard Cohen, "the major contribution of social science to the objective and accurate study of mass opinion."[19] This book investigates public opinion as expressed and measured by polls. To do so, it presents a history of polling on Israel and the Middle East and identifies and examines the issues that have intrigued pollsters at specific times. It also analyzes polling approaches and techniques.

Charles Roll, Jr., and Albert Cantril explain: "What a poll provides is a picture of the public's view at only one point of time and only on questions being asked."[20] Thus, polls are most useful when they include a large number of questions and when they are conducted over time. The use of several questions on a particular issue allows comparisons of responses, yielding a much more sophisticated view of public opinion. The repetition of a specific question over time allows the construction of long- or short-term trends. Most polls employed in this study include either a series of questions on the same issue or a particular question repeated over time.

Research for this book was beset by several serious methodological problems that required innovative answers. Academic and professional pollsters have employed so many different questions and have approached issues from such diverse angles that the first step required the introduction of order into the chaotic, raw data. Vast quantities of polling data were collected, compiled, and integrated into meaningful patterns and trends. The presentation of data here follows a basic format. In addition to results and scores, detailed information is provided on the polling agency, the dates of interviews, and the exact formulation of questions and answers. When necessary and available, information is also provided on the size of the sample and other relevant technical matters.

Dates of polls are frequently confused. Occasionally, poll dates indicate when the interview was conducted; at other times, they indicate when results were reported or published. Thus, the same score could be attributed to two different dates. Both types of dates are cited in this book, but each serves a different purpose. Dates of interviews are employed to identify public opinion at a particular time, whereas dates of publication or reporting, especially in the mass media, are used in connection with the possible impact of opinions on policymaking.

Public opinion is created and shaped within particular environments and contexts. Yet most current research on the role of public opinion in foreign policy concentrates on technical analysis of polls and ignores the environments in which opinions develop. The mere analysis of responses to a particular survey or series of surveys is seriously inadequate if the political context of the time, the nature of the problem, and the roles of leaders are overlooked. Therefore, this book places opinion data within the context of significant events, statements, and actions of principal policymakers in the United States, Israel, and the Arab world. The presentation is obviously limited and is restricted to the most important details, but it suggests original insights based on independent research.

The mass media play a significant role in the context of opinion formation.[21] Obviously, they do not only represent public opinion. Reporters and commentators have definite opinions of their own. Occasionally, too, a newspaper or television network adopts, consciously or unconsciously, a basic attitude or ideology toward a process or personality. This attitude, in turn, determines the thrust of reports, editorials, and commentaries. Therefore, it is both useful and necessary to identify developments in the approach of the American media to Israel and the Arab-Israeli conflict. Analysis of the media's opinions and coverage of the Middle East is restricted in this book to the "elite" or "prestige" press and the major television networks.[22] The elite press is an important source of news and commentaries to leaders and opinion makers, and television is a prime source of information to the general public. The analysis of specific media approaches is based on both existing and independent research.

In addition to news coverage, the American media are also heavily involved in the polling business.[23] In the last decade, both the print and the electronic media have become the major producers and disseminators of public opinion polls. The prestige press and the major television networks, such as the *Washington Post* and ABC News or the *New York Times* and CBS News, have established joint polling agencies. Others receive and publish poll results through syndication or subscriptions to poll reports. The mass media are interested in polls because results tend to be a source of news that the public eagerly consumes. This book reviews the manner in which the mass media interpret and report poll results.

In most cases, the presentation and discussion of opinion data in this book are preceded by analysis of the various contextual factors. Thus, when reviewing public opinion data, historical background, policy statements of leaders, and media coverage and opinions are presented first. The analysis of polls and other indicators of opinion follow.

Sources and Limitations

Research of past public opinion is inherently limited by the availability and reliability of data. Academic and commercial pollsters do not necessarily conduct polls with the future in mind. Hence, on many occasions, an investigator is both perplexed and frustrated to discover that no polls were conducted on certain issues at specific, critical times. Occasionally, important and relevant polls are conducted but their results remain unpublished. Since such polls are commissioned by various American and foreign organizations for private use only, it involves an enormous effort to determine their existence and an even greater effort to obtain their results.

Poll results for this book were collected from many sources, including official publications of polling agencies—Gallup; Harris; Roper; Yankelovich, Skelly and White; and others—plus public organizations, such as the American Jewish Committee and the Council on Foreign Relations. Reports and articles from newspapers and magazines and original reports of media polling organizations were also utilized (see appendix A). In general, only polls based on national samples are included; polls of specific regions or groups are used in only a few pertinent cases.

Research based on public opinion polls is also inhibited by other difficulties and limitations.[24] Polls are always based on samples and thus are subject to problems of accuracy and validity. Developments in statistics have improved sampling accuracy, but for various reasons, not all polling agencies are willing to divulge detailed descriptions of sample construction. A certain margin of error always exists, depending on the sample size (see appendixes B and C).

Although the statistical construction of a sample might be valid, the composition of survey questionnaires or the administration of interviews might be faulty or inadequate. Poll studies have revealed that slight alterations in the wording of questions are liable to cause the person being interviewed to impart radically different responses.[25] This book documents and critically analyzes numerous examples of this problem.

Additional factors—such as the interview format (face to face, in writing, or over the telephone), the response rate (the number of individuals who answer the questionnaire), the saliency of certain issues in a poll, and the number of questions and responses—could affect the distribution of opinion. Complete and comprehensive information is not always available on these variables, but most polls employed in this book were screened for statistical and operational accuracy. Survey results that did not include the exact questions and answers were discarded. All results reported in this book are presented with the original responses and the questions or statements that preceded them.

Structure

This book is divided into two sections. The first chronologically traces the development of basic attitudes from the establishment of Israel to the war and crisis in Lebanon. The second deals with three significant issues: the Palestinian question, American economic and military aid to Israel, and attitudes of various groups, including American Jewry.

In part I, chapter 1 deals with the development of opinions during the period from the establishment of Israel until the Six-Day War. The two major events that attracted pollsters were Jewish immigration to Palestine, followed by the creation of Israel, and the Suez-Sinai crisis and war of 1956.

The Arab-Israeli conflict was relatively subdued in the decade between 1957 and 1967. Consequently, very few polls were conducted on Israeli or Arab issues. However, the 1967 Six-Day War radically changed this trend. It became a watershed in the history of Arab-Israeli relations and in the history of poll-taking on American opinions on the Middle East. Chapter 2 examines the period between the Six-Day War and events that led to Egyptian President Anwar Sadat's historic visit to Jerusalem, including the War of Attrition, the October 1973 Yom Kippur War, and Henry Kissinger's mediation attempts in the Arab-Israeli conflict.

Three major events merged in 1977 to produce a historic divergence in the pattern of the Arab-Israeli conflict: the new strategy of American President Jimmy Carter toward the Arab-Israeli conflict; Menachem Begin's rise to Israeli prime minister in May 1977; and Sadat's visit to Jerusalem. Chapter 3 briefly analyzes these events and examines how Americans viewed these leaders and their respective roles in the peace process following Sadat's visit. While the Egyptian southern front of the Arab-Israeli conflict was moving toward a state of peace, the northern front deteriorated toward a state of war. Chapter 4 analyzes Israel's clashes with Syria and the Palestine Liberation Organization (PLO) in 1981, the 1982 Israeli war in Lebanon, U.S. military involvement in Lebanon, and ensuing terrorism directed against the United States in that country.

In part II, chapter 5 further examines the development of American attitudes toward the PLO and the Palestinians, demonstrating the complexity of American attitudes toward the Arab-Israeli conflict. The chapter explores in detail public perceptions of the PLO and the Palestinian question over time and identifies significant differences in the respective images of the PLO and the Palestinians. Chapter 6 examines attitudes toward various forms of American aid to Israel—economic and military, actual and hypothetical. To gain a better perspective, these opinions are contrasted with American attitudes toward aid to other countries in general and aid to Arab countries in particular.

The next two chapters deal with specific group attitudes toward Israel and the Middle East. Chapter 7 examines trends in the opinions of American Jewry toward Israel since the inception of the Jewish state, addressing such issues as the nature of American-Jewish attachment to Israel and Jewish attitudes toward the Arab-Israeli conflict. Chapter 8 analyzes attitudes of other groups, including blacks, young adults, Republicans and Democrats, men and women, Catholics and Protestants.

The conclusion, chapter 9, presents a summary of long-term trends on general issues, such as sympathy for Israel and Arab countries, and specific issues, including Arab and Israeli uses of force. It also identifies the most powerful variables that appear to shape American opinion on the Middle East. In addition it discusses several major weaknesses and methodological and ethical polling problems.

Notes

1. The conversation was held in Palm Beach, Florida. Its record was declassified in 1978; see Mordechai Gazit, *President Kennedy's Policy Toward The Arab States and Israel* (Tel Aviv: Tel Aviv University, Shiloah Center for Middle Eastern and African Studies, 1983), 46.

2. *New York Times*, May 13, 1977.

3. Bernard Reich, *The United States and Israel: Influence in the Special Relationship* (New York: Praeger, 1984), 177–223.

4. Cecil V. Crabb, Jr., and Pat M. Holt, *Invitation to Struggle: Congress, the President and Foreign Policy* (Washington, D.C.: Congressional Quarterly Press, 1980), 89–112; Robert H. Trice, "Congress and the Arab-Israeli Conflict: Support for Israel in the U.S. Senate, 1970–1973," *Political Science Quarterly* 92(Fall 1977): 443–63; and David Garnham, "Factors Influencing Congressional Support for Israel during the 93rd Congress," *Jerusalem Journal of International Relations* 2(Spring 1977): 23–45.

5. Cited in William C. Adams, "Middle East Meets West: Surveying American Attitudes," *Public Opinion* 5(April-May 1982): 51.

6. Shmuel Segev, *Sadat—The Road to Peace* (Tel Aviv: Massada, 1978; Hebrew), 49.

7. Mary A. Barberis, "The Arab-Israeli Battle on Capitol Hill," *Virginia Quarterly Review* 52(Spring 1976): 203–23; and Christopher Madison, "Arab-American Lobby Fights Rearguard Battle to Influence U.S. Mideast Policy," *National Journal* (August 31, 1985): 1934–39.

8. See, for example, Seymour Martin Lipset and William Schneider, "Carter vs. Israel: What the Polls Reveal," *Commentary* 64(November 1977): 21–29; George E. Gruen, "Arab Petropower and American Public Opinion," *Middle East Review*

7(Winter 1975–76): 33–39; and William C. Adams, "Blaming Israel for Begin," *Public Opinion* 5(October-November 1982): 51–55.

9. Paul Abramson, *Political Attitudes in America: Formation and Change* (San Francisco: Freeman, 1983); and Susan Welch and John Comer, eds., *Public Opinion: Its Formation, Measurement and Impact* (Palo Alto, Calif.: Mayfield, 1975).

10. Doris A. Graber, *Public Opinion, the President, and Foreign Policy* (New York: Holt, Rinehart and Winston, 1968); Hadley Cantril, *The Human Dimension: Experience in Policy Research* (New Brunswick, N.J.: Rutgers University Press, 1967); and Ernest May, "An American Tradition in Foreign Policy: The Role of Public Opinion," in W.H. Nelson, ed., *Theory and Practice in American Politics* (Chicago: University of Chicago Press, 1966).

11. Theodore C. Sorensen, *Decision-Making in the White House* (New York: Columbia University Press, 1963), 46.

12. Roger Hilsman, *The Politics of Policy Making in Defense and Foreign Affairs* (New York: Harper & Row, 1971), 104.

13. Lincoln P. Bloomfield, *The Foreign Policy Process: A Modern Primer* (Englewood Cliffs, N.J.: Prentice-Hall, 1982), 128.

14. Bernard C. Hennessy, *Public Opinion* (Belmont, Calif.: Wadsworth, 1970), 22.

15. James B. Lemert, *Does Mass Communication Change Public Opinion After All?* (Chicago: Nelson Hall, 1981).

16. Carl I. Hovland, Irving L. Janis, and Harold H. Kelley, *Communication and Persuasion: Psychological Studies of Opinion Change* (New Haven: Yale University Press, 1953), 6.

17. James N. Rosenau, *Public Opinion and Foreign Policy* (New York: Random House, 1961), 16.

18. Robert H. Trice, "Foreign Policy Interest Groups, Mass Public Opinion and the Arab-Israeli Dispute," *Western Political Quarterly* 31(June 1978), 241.

19. Bernard C. Cohen, *The Public's Impact on Foreign Policy* (Boston: Little, Brown, 1973), 122.

20. Charles W. Roll, Jr., and Albert H. Cantril, *Polls: Their Use and Misuse in Politics* (New York: Basic Books, 1972), 109.

21. David Paletz and Robert Entman, *Media, Power, Politics* (New York: Free Press, 1981); Doris A. Graber, *Mass Media and American Politics* (Washington, D.C.: Congressional Quarterly Press, 1980); and Paul A. Smith, Jr., "Media and the Making of U.S. Foreign Policy," *Washington Quarterly* 7(Spring 1984): 135–141.

22. See John C. Merrill, *The Elite Press* (New York: Pitman, 1968).

23. Albert H. Cantril, ed., *Polling on the Issues* (Cabin John, Md.: Seven Locks Press, 1980), 13–55.

24. See John P. Robinson and Robert Meadow, *Polls Apart* (Cabin John, Md.: Seven Locks Press, 1982); and Michael Wheeler, *Lies, Damn Lies, and Statistics: The Manipulation of Public Opinion in America* (New York: Dell, 1976).

25. Seymour Martin Lipset, "The Wavering Polls," *Public Interest* 43(Spring 1976): 70–89; and Howard Schuman and Stanley Presser, *Questions and Answers in Attitude Surveys: Experiments on Question Form, Wording and Context* (New York: Academic Press, 1981).

Part I
Basic Trends

1
The First Twenty Years

In the wake of the Holocaust, the U.S. government was confronted by two increasingly disturbing Jewish issues: the fate of the Jewish survivors in Europe and the future of the Jewish national homeland in Palestine. The Jews in Palestine were determined to establish an independent Jewish state but were opposed by the Arabs. Britain, which had ruled the area since 1920 under a mandate from the League of Nations, was struggling to maintain the status quo and collaborated mainly with the Arabs.

British policies toward Jewish survivors of the Holocaust and the Jewish community in Palestine became a source of tension and disagreement between Britain and the United States. The United States emerged from World War II as a superpower and leader of the entire Western world and became increasingly interested and involved in critical regions, including the Middle East. In this area it confronted the Soviet Union, the new rival superpower, which challenged traditional Western strongholds and sought strategic bases and spheres of influence. Britain maintained that the West must win the support of the Arabs in the battle against the Soviet Union, even at the expense of the Jews. But the United States pointed to the plight of the Jewish refugees in Europe and the violence in Palestine, which Britain could not control.[1] The British government needed American support for its policy in Palestine and therefore had to abide by American concerns and positions.

The administration of Harry Truman was divided on solutions to the two Jewish issues of the post–World War II era. His secretaries of state and defense, George C. Marshall and James Forrestal, opposed Jewish immigration to Palestine and the establishment of an independent Jewish state.[2] However, his advisers at the White House held the opposite view. In a rare demonstration of presidential leadership and authority, Truman rejected the recommendations of the Departments of State and Defense and decided to support the establishment of Israel. He also extended de facto recognition to Israel immediately after its birth.

Several senior officials of Truman's administration, British politicians, and a few scholars suggested that the president's support of the creation of Israel was primarily a stratagem for selfish political considerations.[3] In 1948 Truman faced an uphill battle against his Republican opponent, Thomas E. Dewey, the popular governor of New York. In his own party he suffered defections from both the left and the right. The American people seemed tired of the long rule of the Democrats and were looking for a change in the White House. To win the presidential elections of 1948, Truman needed all of the votes he could get, and therefore, adopted a pro-Jewish policy allegedly to secure the Jewish vote, especially in the state of New York.[4]

Yet Truman argued on several occasions that his actions taken toward the establishment of Israel were supported by the bulk of the American public. On October 4, 1946, he said in a famous speech:

> This proposal [to establish a viable Jewish state in Palestine] received widespread attention in the U.S., both in the press and in public forums. From the discussion which has ensued, it is my belief that a solution along these lines would command the support of public opinion in the U.S.[5]

This chapter investigates whether Truman's impression was correct and sheds light on the development of American opinion toward the founding of Israel in the crucial years of the immediate post–World War II period. President Truman also stated in his speech that the issue of an independent Jewish state in Palestine received widespread attention in the American press. He was right. Polls of editors found substantial attention accorded the Palestinian question.[6] Likewise, general public opinion polls revealed relatively high interest and familiarity with major developments in the Middle East.[7]

Public opinion polls on Israeli and Arab-Israeli issues conducted during the first 20 years of Israel's existence clustered around two major events: the creation of Israel and the Suez-Sinai crisis and subsequent 1956 war. Very few polls were conducted between these events, and those that were contained only one or two questions. This chapter investigates the initial formation of American public opinion toward Israel, beginning with the first polls conducted on the Middle East. It initially presents and analyzes the U.N. debate on the future of Palestine. It later explores the limits of American willingness to participate actively in efforts to create an independent Jewish state. The next section deals with American sympathy toward the Arabs and Israelis and perceptions of their relative importance to the United States. The final section of the chapter presents and examines opinions of the Israeli involvement in the Suez-Sinai war and the American policy toward that involvement.

The Founding of Israel

The Holocaust left European intern camps overflowing with hundreds of thousands of Jewish refugees—most expressing the wish to immigrate to Palestine, but the gates to this country were closed.[8] Britain, which controlled the area, was caught between its commitment to establish a Jewish national home in Palestine (given in the Balfour Declaration of November 1917) and its maintenance of strategic and political interests in the Arab world.[9] During the 1930s, Britain retreated from its commitment to the Jews and tended to adopt a pro-Arab position. This policy culminated in the 1939 white paper, which severely restricted Jewish immigration to Palestine.[10] This document authorized Jewish immigration at a maximum rate of 10,000 per year for 5 years beginning in 1939. At this point, further immigration was to cease unless agreed to by the Arabs.[11]

Jewish organizations strongly condemned and opposed the 1939 restrictions. A special Zionist conference held in May 1942 at the Biltmore Hotel in New York called the 1939 white paper "cruel and indefensible in its denial of a sanctuary to Jews fleeing from Nazi persecution."[12] The Biltmore conference demanded that Britain withdraw from Palestine and allow unrestricted Jewish immigration and called for the establishment of an independent Jewish state in Palestine.

American opinions on the conflicting Jewish and Arab demands on Palestine were first examined by the National Opinion Research Center of Chicago (NORC) in December 1944. The same poll was repeated a year later. Table 1–1 indicates that on both occasions, more Americans favored than opposed the establishment of a Jewish state. In November 1945, when news of the mass extermination of millions of Jews began to sweep the world, the ratio in favor of the Jewish cause increased by 11 percent. The number of respondents who held no opinion remained almost identical to that of 1944.

In May 1945, the Jewish Agency demanded from Britain an immediate admission of 100,000 displaced Jewish refugees to Palestine, but the British government refused to relax the 1939 white paper restrictions.[13] President Truman, deeply moved by the plight of the Jewish refugees, opened the chapter on Palestine in his memoirs: "The fate of the Jewish victims of Hitlerism was a matter of deep personal concern to me."[14] In June 1945, Truman sent a special emissary to investigate the conditions of the refugee camps in Europe. The emissary, Earl Harrison, a former immigration commissioner and dean of the University of Pennsylvania Law School, reported two months later that the conditions at the camps were disgraceful and that most of the displaced Jews wished to immigrate to Palestine.[15] He recommended that 100,000 refugees be allowed to go there immediately.

Table 1–1
Opinions on the Proposed Jewish State in Palestine, 1944–45

Question

There are over a million Arabs and over half a million Jews in Palestine. Do you think the British, who control Palestine should do what some Jews ask and set up a Jewish state there, or should they do what some Arabs think and not set up a Jewish state? (NORC)

Response	*Dec. 1944 (n = 2,500)*	*Nov. 1945 (n = 2,540)*
The British should:		
1. Set up a Jewish state	36%	42%
2. Not set up a Jewish state	22	17
3. Follow neither side, other solutions	10	10
4. Don't know	32	31

Source: Charles H. Stember, "The Impact of Israel on American Attitudes," in C. Stember et al., *Jews in the Mind of America* (New York: Basic Books, 1966), 175.

Truman followed Harrison's proposal and officially asked Churchill's successor, Prime Minister Clement Attlee, to facilitate the plan. Attlee refused because he feared that such a large influx of Jews would upset the Arabs. However, to avoid an open conflict with the United States, he suggested the establishment of a joint Anglo-American Committee of Inquiry (AACOI) to study the conditions of the uprooted Jews in Europe and the feasibility of immigration to Palestine. Truman agreed, and in November 1945, the committee began to work on its mission.[16]

All these dramatic developments were reported in the American press. A Gallup poll of December 1945 found that 55 percent of the American public followed the news.[17] An overwhelming majority (80 percent) of those who did favored Jewish immigration to Palestine. Only 7 percent opposed it.

The AACOI completed its mission in August 1946 and recommended an immediate admission of 100,000 Jewish refugees to Palestine and resettlement of the remainder in other appropriate places.[18] The committee called for the continuation of the British mandate in Palestine but stipulated principles for possible independence in the future. One principle specified that Palestine should be neither an Arab nor a Jewish state.

In May 1946, President Truman, ignoring all other recommendations, publicly endorsed the proposal on the 100,000 refugees. He also stressed that the political future of the land must be determined by the United Nations. Attlee, however, was only ready to implement the committee's recommendations as one comprehensive package. The prime minister assured the House of Commons that the British government would accept the recommendation on the 100,000 refugees only if the United States assumed full financial responsibility for their resettlement and only after anti-British, Jewish, armed organizations were dismantled in Palestine.[19]

While Truman was exerting pressure on Britain to allow the entry of 100,000 Jewish refugees to Palestine, Gallup asked a representative national sample of Americans for its view on the controversial issue. As in his poll of December 1945, Gallup found in May 1946 that half of the sample was familiar with the problem.[20] Again, more than three quarters of the respondents (78 percent) thought that the idea of admitting 100,000 Jews to settle in Palestine was a good one, while 14 percent believed it to be poor. A few months later, Truman responded to this sentiment in American public opinion by strongly advocating Jewish statehood in Palestine.[21]

The British were very disappointed by Truman's stand. They felt his statements favoring the Jews were made to capture the Jewish vote in the 1946 congressional elections, which were to be held a month later.[22] They were also forced to reconsider their policy in view of the serious breakdown in order and security in Palestine and the rising costs of their presence in that country.[23] On February 14, 1947, the British government placed the Palestine issue before the United Nations.[24]

The U.N. General Assembly convened to discuss the events in Palestine in a special session, the first of its kind, on April 28, 1947. The assembly quickly appointed a special committee (U.N. Special Committee on Palestine—UNSCOP) to study the problems and suggest solutions.[25] UNSCOP unanimously recommended the termination of the British mandate and the recognition of the urgent need to solve the problem of Jewish refugees in Europe. However, UNSCOP members were divided on the basic political solution for the Arab-Jewish conflict. The majority (seven states) recommended partition of Palestine into two separate and independent states, one Jewish and one Arab. The minority (three states) was in favor of an independent federal state.[26]

As the 1947 regular session of the General Assembly was about to vote on UNSCOP's recommendations, officials of the Truman administration discussed the various issues and options, most of them opposing the partition resolution.[27] The media's position was unclear. According to the November 1947 NORC survey of newspaper editors, 43 percent ran editorials on UNSCOP's recommendations. Sixteen percent of these editorials either took no stand or stressed the need for a peaceful solution; 14 percent expressed sympathy for the plight of the Jewish refugees and favored the partition resolution; 5 percent advocated U.N. action; and the rest took other stands. The same NORC poll also surveyed the opinions of the editors on solutions to the Jewish-Palestine question and found that 44 percent of the sample favored "a Palestine which shall be neither a Jewish nor an Arab state, in which the rights

Table 1–2
Attitudes toward the U.N. Partition Resolution, 1947–48

Questions

(a) The UN has recommended that Palestine be divided into two states—one for the Arabs and one for the Jews—and that 150,000 Jews be permitted now to enter the Jewish state. Do you favor or oppose this idea?

(b) Have you heard or read anything about the United Nations recommendation that Palestine be divided into two countries—one for the Jews and one for the Arabs? *Seventy-two percent of the sample that was familiar with the subject* (Feb. 1948) *was asked:* Under the circumstances, do you approve or disapprove of dividing Palestine into these two countries?

(c) The United Nations recently proposed a plan to divide Palestine into two separate states, one for the Jews and one for the Arabs. Do you approve of that plan; do you think the UN should try to work out some other solution; or haven't you thought about it one way or the other?

Q	*Date*	*Poll*	*For Partition*	*Against Partition*	*Don't Know*	*(n)*
(a)	Oct. '47	Gallup	65%	10%	25%	(2,685)
(b)	Feb. '48	NORC (aware group)	53	26	21	(915)
(b)	Mar. '48	NORC	49	27	24	(1,289)

Q	*Date*	*Poll*	*Approve Partition*	*Try Other Solution*	*Haven't Thought About It*	*No Opinion*	*(n)*
(c)	Apr. '48	*Fortune-*Roper	26	31	31	12	(3,623)

Sources: Public Opinion Quarterly 12(Spring 1948): 161; 12(Fall 1948): 549–50, Charles H. Stember, "The Impact of Israel on American Attitudes," in C. Stember et al., *Jews in the Mind of America* (New York: Basic Books, 1966), 178–9.

and interests of all people will be guaranteed internationally." Thirty percent supported the partition resolution, and only 10 percent approved of UNSCOP's minority recommendation for an independent federal state. The American public, however, was not in agreement with the prevalent mood of the media and the administration.

Table 1–2 indicates that throughout the United Nation's debate on UNSCOP's proposals, the American public supported partition by a substantial ratio—65 to 10 percent. Despite strong reservations voiced by his chief Middle Eastern and strategic experts, Truman decided in favor of partition and instructed his delegation at the United Nations to vote for this proposal.[28] American diplomats in Arab countries were instructed to provide the following explanation for the American propartition stance at the United Nations:

> After reviewing statements and expressions of policy by responsible American officials, resolutions of Congress and party platforms of the last thirty years, [the American government] came to the conclusion that unless there was some unanticipated factor in [the] situation the trend of *public opinion and policy based thereon practically forced it to support partition.*[29] (emphasis added)

The General Assembly approved the partition plan by the required two-thirds majority on November 29, 1947.[30] About a month earlier the British government had decided to surrender the mandate, and following the vote at the United Nations, it announced that British forces would evacuate Palestine by May 14, 1948.[31]

The Arabs strongly criticized the U.N. resolution and threatened to foil it even by force.[32] Violence erupted in Palestine, and American officials worried about the chaos and prospects for an all-out Arab-Jewish war. Yet as indicated in table 1–2, in February 1948, a bit more than half (53 percent) of those who read or heard about the U.N. resolution supported partition, while a quarter of the aware group (26 percent) opposed it.

As indicated in table 1–3, the editorials in the elite press that chose sides were much more pro-Israel. However, all the editorials that took a stand in the *Detroit Free Press* were either anti-Israel or pro-Arab. The features in the elite press that took sides were mainly pro-Israel, while those in the *Detroit Free Press* were evenly divided between Israel and the Arabs. The cartoons in the *New York Times* and the *Washington Post* were mainly anti-Arab. The general pro-Israeli tone in the elite press could be attributed to the Arabs' rejection of the U.N. partition resolution and their attacks on Jewish communities in Palestine.

American policy on the implementation of the partition resolution was far from firm and consistent. Frequent vacillations in the Truman administration confused the parties directly concerned, the American public, and even the president himself. For example, on March 19, 1947, Warren Austin, the U.S. representative at the United Nations, informed the Security Council that in view of the violence in Palestine, the United States had ceased to consider the partition plan as a viable solution.[33] He called for another special session of the General Assembly to consider the possibility of placing Palestine under a temporary U.N. trusteeship. This was a surprise to Truman, who did not recall any authorization of a change in U.S. policy on partition.[34] A day earlier he had reaffirmed the U.S. commitment to the partition plan when conferring with prominent Zionist leader Chaim Weizmann.[35] Apparently, Truman had seen the trusteeship proposal but had not authorized Austin or the State Department to announce it on any particular day.[36] Truman's understanding was that a U.N. trusteeship would have to be adopted only if it became clear that partition could not be implemented.

Table 1–3
Media Attitudes toward Israel and the Arabs, 1948

Type of Coverage and Attitude	*N.Y. Times*		*Washington Post*		*Detroit Free Press*	
	No.	*Percent*	*No.*	*Percent*	*No.*	*Percent*
Editorials	54[a]	100	31[a]	100	11[a]	100
Pro-Israel	21	38.9	12	38.7	—	—
Anti-Israel	—	—	—	—	2	16.7
Pro-Arab	—	—	1	3.2	1	8.3
Anti-Arab	10	18.5	6	19.4	—	—
Total[b]	31	57.4	19	61.3	3	25.0
Features	70[a]	100	12[a]	100	10[a]	100
Pro-Israel	20	28.6	9	75.0	2	20.0
Anti-Israel	—	—	—	—	—	—
Pro-Arab	3	4.3	—	—	2	20.0
Anti-Arab	3	4.3	—	—	—	—
Total[b]	26	37.2	9	75.0	4	40.0
Cartoons	25[a]	100	10[a]	100	6[a]	100
Pro-Israel	1	4.0	1	10.0	—	—
Anti-Israel	—	—	—	—	—	—
Pro-Arab	—	—	—	—	—	—
Anti-Arab	6	24.0	4	40.0	—	—
Total[b]	7	28.0	5	50.0	—	—
News Articles	586[a]	100	190[a]	100	135[a]	100
Pro-Israel	62	10.6	4	2.1	—	—
Anti-Israel	1	0.2	—	—	1	0.7
Pro-Arab	1	0.2	—	—	1	0.7
Anti-Arab	3	0.5	—	—	—	—
Total[b]	67	11.5	4	2.1	2	1.4

Source: Janice Terry, "A Content Analysis of American Newspapers," in Abdeen Jabara and Janice Terry, eds., *The Arab World from Nationalism to Revolution* (Wilmette, Ill.: Medina University Press International, 1971), 102–7.

[a]Total number of items on the Middle East.

[b]Total number of items choosing sides.

Americans were unaware, of course, of the debates and bureaucratic in-fighting within the Truman administration, but the difficulties surrounding the partition plan were known to all those who followed events in Palestine. In March 1948, NORC still found substantial public support for the establishment of a Jewish state in Palestine. The survey queried whether it should be the policy of the U.S. government to encourage a state that the Jews might set up on their own, presumably without the backing of the United Nations and the United States. No less than half of the sample approved of such a policy, and only 10 percent opposed it.[37]

In April 1948, the Fortune-Roper poll asked a representative national sample of Americans whether it still approved of the partition plan or thought that the United Nations should try to work out an alternative solution. The poll also provided an "escape" answer—"or haven't you thought about it" (see table 1–2). The structure and wording of this poll yielded much less support for partition; only a quarter of the respondents still supported the U.N. resolution, one-third thought the United Nations should attempt another solution, and another third chose the escape answer.

Stember argued that American opinion on the Palestine issue failed to crystallize and largely followed the shifts of American policy.[38] When the U.S. government approved partition, the public also supported it, but when the United States retreated from partition, the public followed suit. As evidence of this trend, he presented the results shown in table 1–2, including the results of a poll taken by NORC in March 1948, after Austin's statement at the United Nations. The results revealed a drop in the percentage of those who supported partition against a rise in the number of those who opposed it (49 to 27 percent in comparison to the earlier distributions of 65 to 10 percent or 53 to 26 percent). However, the 49-to-27 ratio represented the views of only the one-third of the sample that was aware of Austin's statement.

Stember also counted the distribution of answers to question (c) in table 1–2 as evidence of the erosion in public approval of partition. But the results of question (c) are not comparable to those of questions (a) and (b) because of the significant difference in structure and wording of the two categories of questions. Finally, contrary to Stember's arguments, the White House was informed that American public opinion strongly disapproved of the indecisiveness of American policy toward partition.[39]

Polls taken from 1944 to 1948 revealed strong support in American public opinion for free Jewish immigration to Palestine and the establishment of an independent Jewish state in that country. President Truman recognized this trend in public opinion and cultivated and strengthened it. He used the favorable sentiment toward the Jewish cause in his dealings with both his own bureaucracy and Britain's leaders. On the evening of May 14, 1948, while the British high commissioner and his remaining staff were preparing to depart from Palestine, the leaders of the Jewish community proclaimed the establishment of the state of Israel, commencing at midnight. Exactly 11 minutes after midnight (or 6:11 P.M. Washington time) Truman extended de facto recognition to the new state, thus making the United States the first country to recognize Israel.[40]

Opinions on Active Military Involvement

Although a great majority of the American public supported Jewish immigration to Palestine and the creation of Israel, only a minority was willing to endorse U.S. involvement in efforts to realize these goals. Even a relatively mild action such as officially calling on Britain to allow the establishment of the Jewish state was supported, in December 1944 and November 1945, by only a fifth of the sample.[41] About a quarter of the respondents did not have an opinion on this issue. President Truman emphasized this attitude upon his return from the Potsdam conference:

> The American view on Palestine is that we want to let as many of the Jews into Palestine as it is possible to let into that country. Then the matter will have to be worked out diplomatically with the British and the Arabs, so that if a state can be set up there they may be able to set it up on a peaceful basis. *I have no desire to send 500,000 American soldiers there to make peace in Palestine.*[42] (emphasis added)

The Arabs vowed to prevent the implementation of the U.N. partition resolution by force, and their threats worried American policymakers. Theoretically, if a full-scale war were to break out between the Arabs and the Jews, the balance of power clearly leaned in favor of the Arabs. American officials were fearful of a war that would require U.S. intervention to save the Jews from another Holocaust. To avoid this scenario, the United States suggested to the United Nations, before the vote on partition, the establishment of a special constabulary or police force to ensure the implementation of the U.N. resolution.[43] In which capacity did the American public view the prospects of U.S. military involvement in Palestine—alone or as a part of a U.N. or other international force?

Several polls conducted in 1946 and 1948 revealed strong opposition to hypothetical U.S. military involvement in the Arab-Jewish conflict. Table 1–4 indicates that in 1946, a clear majority of Americans opposed any use of American forces in Palestine, even if only to help Britain maintain law and order there. This result is hardly surprising. Only a year and a half had passed since the end of World War II; America had demobilized and was not yet prepared to assume new military commitments abroad.

Table 1–4 presents two different results for May 1946. This probably stemmed from the introduction of different wording and information in the questions used in the polls. Question (b) mentions President Truman's stand, while question (c) specifically mentions the word "troops." The citing of Truman's endorsement of the proposal to allow the admission of 100,000 Jews to Palestine probably yielded a higher rate of support for American involvement, while the mention of troops in question (c) apparently reduced this rate. When offered a choice between U.S. or U.N. troops in Palestine, most Americans

Table 1–4
Opinions of American Involvement in the Jewish-Arab Conflict, 1946–48

Questions

(a) Would you approve or disapprove of sending United States soldiers to maintain peace there [in Palestine]?

(b) The report of the Anglo-American Committee recommends that 100,000 Jewish refugees be admitted to Palestine in spite of protests by the Arabs there. President Truman has said that he thinks this ought to be done. Now England says that the United States ought to help her keep order in Palestine if trouble breaks out between the Jews and the Arabs. Do you think we should help keep order there, or should we keep out of it?

(c) England has suggested that we send troops to Palestine to help keep order there if the Arabs oppose letting 100,000 Jews enter Palestine. Do you approve of our sending troops to Palestine to help England keep order there?

(d) Well, suppose the United Nations cannot agree on sending an international police force [to Palestine]. Do you think the US itself should go ahead and send American troops to Palestine?

(e) It has been suggested that the UN send an international police force to keep order in Palestine. Suppose the UN does decide to send such a police force to Palestine, would you approve or disapprove of having American soldiers take part in it?

(f) As you know, there has been fighting going on in Palestine between the Jews and the Arabs, and the UN Security council has asked both sides to accept an agreement to stop fighting. If the fighting continues, would you approve or disapprove of the UN's sending a police force to help keep order there? *Those who approved the idea of a police force were asked:* Would you approve or disapprove of having American soldiers take part in this police force?

(g) Do you think the big powers should or should not use force if necessary to back up whatever the UN recommends for Palestine?

			U.S. Military Involvement			
Q	*Date*	*Poll*	*For*	*Against*	*D.K., N.O.*[a]	*(n)*
(a)	Jan. '46	Gallup[b]	12%	83%	5%	(3,000)
(b)	May '46	NORC	28	61	11	(1,292)
(c)	May '46	Gallup	21	74	5	(3,000)
(d)	Feb. '48	NORC	9	83	8	(1,271)
			Within U.N. Force			
(e)	Feb. '48	NORC	43	50	7	
(f)	Apr. '48	NORC	51	37[c]	12	(1,280)
(f)	June '48	NORC	47	43[c]	10	(1,295)
(f)	Oct. '48	NORC	46	41[c]	13	(1,257)
			With Other Big Powers			
(g)	June '48	*Fortune*-Roper	62	16	22	

Sources: (a)(b)(c)—Charles H. Stember, "The Impact of Israel on American Attitudes," in C. Stember et al., *Jews in the Mind of America* (New York: Basic Books, 1966), 177; (d)(e)(f), (Apr. 1948), (g)—*Public Opinion Quarterly* 12(Fall 1948): 550–51; (f), (June and Oct. 1948)—*Public Opinion Quarterly* 15(Summer 1951): 391.

[a]Don't know or no opinion.

[b]Asked of the 58 percent of total sample who say they have followed news about disorders in Palestine.

[c]Those who disapproved of both a U.N. police force and American participation in it.

favored U.N. troops. In October 1947, Gallup asked a national sample: "If England pulls her troops out of Palestine and war breaks out between Arabs and Jews, do you think the U.S. should send troops to keep the peace or should this be done by a U.N. volunteer army?" Only 3 percent of the sample thought the United States should send troops to Palestine; 65 percent preferred the U.N. option; 18 percent rejected both the U.S. and the U.N. options, and 14 percent held no opinion.[44]

A U.N. force that included an American contingent was also more acceptable to the American public. This conclusion emerged from the second part of table 1–4. Question (e) was addressed to respondents a few months after the United Nations adopted the partition resolution and several months before the outbreak of the Israeli War of Independence. At that time, American participation in a U.N. force was opposed by a ratio of 50 to 43 percent, but later, when the war broke out, U.S. involvement within a U.N. framework was supported by close pluralities. The greatest support for U.S. military involvement in Palestine was recorded in response to question (g), which did not mention the United States specifically but rather "the big powers" and the need to back up U.N. resolutions.

The preceding data indicate that a substantial majority of Americans opposed direct U.S. involvement in Palestine and was much more inclined to support the dispatching of troops as part of a U.N. force. In 1948, the young United Nations was considered the best hope for collective security and conflict resolution by peaceful means. The United States enthusiastically cultivated it, and these circumstances probably contributed to the relatively higher rates of support in American public opinion for U.S. involvement in Palestine within a U.N. force. Similar evidence was obtained in a NORC poll of newspaper editors. The poll, conducted in November 1947, before the U.N. vote on the partition resolution, included a question on preferences for a particular solution to the problems in Palestine. The editors were asked: "Would you still feel that way if it meant that the U.S. would have to share the responsibility for enforcing whatever the U.N. decided?" Eighty-five percent said yes, while only 12 percent said no.[45]

Americans had reservations, not only toward U.S. participation in possible efforts to implement the U.N. partition resolution, but also toward military aid to the Jews. The partition resolution called for the establishment of local "armed militias" in the envisioned Jewish and Arab states to maintain "internal order and to prevent frontier clashes."[46] Since the United States was one of the main sponsors of the U.N. resolution, it presumably should also have been ready to assist in the creation of local forces. However, on December 5, 1947, only a few days after the General Assembly approved the partition resolution, the State Department formally announced "the discontinuance of the licensing of arms shipments to Palestine and neighboring countries."[47]

Apparently, Truman never authorized this action but nevertheless conceded and refused to reverse it despite heavy Jewish pressure.[48] One poll was taken on this issue (by NORC in July 1948), and results reveal strong public approval of the embargo. NORC asked: "The U.S. is refusing to allow either Jews or Arabs to buy arms and ammunition in this country. Do you think this policy should be continued, or should we change and sell them military supplies?" Only 10 percent of the sample was in favor of altering the embargo policy; 82 percent felt that the present policy should continue.[49] Of those in favor of a change, 5 percent thought the United States should sell arms to both sides, 4 percent favored selling arms only to the Jews, and 1 percent was undecided about which side to sell arms. American policy may be contrasted with that of the USSR and the Soviet bloc, which provided Israel with most of its weapons during the War of Independence.[50] From this perspective, it could be argued that the Soviet commitment to the implementation of the U.N. partition resolution and to the establishment of Israel was firmer than that of the United States.[51]

Sympathy toward Israelis and Arabs

Even though the American public held reservations about possible U.S. involvement in the Arab-Jewish conflict, there was a clear tendency toward greater sympathy for the Jews than for the Arabs. Table 1–5 presents results of seven surveys that measured American sympathy toward the Jews and the Arabs from November 1947 to March 1949. About one-third of the respondents consistently sided with Israel, double the number of those who favored the Arabs. It should be noted that when asked about a hypothetical situation—question (a): "If war breaks out . . ."—only 24 percent of the respondents sympathized with the Jews, and the ratio in favor of the Jewish side was two to one. However, when war did break out a few months later, the percentage of those who sympathized more with the Jews rose by 10 to 12 percent, making the ratio in favor of the Jewish side closer to three to one (see question (c)—June, July 1948). It is also interesting to note that from November 1947 through March 1949, the majority of Americans preferred not to take sides ("sympathized with neither or both sides or did not know").

In one particular poll, that of July 1948, NORC asked respondents to explain why they chose to sympathize with one side or the other.[52] Those who expressed sympathy toward the Jews (36 percent of the total sample) cited three main reasons for their choice: "Palestine is their country by religious, historical and legal rights" (31 percent); "Jews are entitled to a home, need a country of their own" (28 percent); and "Jews have been persecuted and mis-

Table 1–5
Sympathies for Jews and Arabs, 1947–49

Questions

(a) If war breaks out between the Arabs and Jews in Palestine, which side would you sympathize with?

(b) The United Nations has recommended that Palestine be divided between the Jews and the Arabs. The Arabs say they will not agree to have Palestine divided, and fighting has broken out between the Jews and Arabs. Do you sympathize with the Jews in this matter?

(c) In the conflict in Palestine, do you sympathize with the Arabs or with the Jews?

(d) On the whole, which do you think has the most right on its side in the war in Palestine—the Jews or the Arabs?

Q	*Date*	*Poll*	*Jews*	*Arabs*	*Both, Neither, D.K.*	*(n)*
(a)	Nov. '47	Gallup	24%	12%	64%	(2,685)
(b)	Feb. '48	NORC	35	16	49	(1,271)
(c)	June '48	NORC	34	12	54	(1,295)
(c)	July '48	NORC	36	14	50	(1,301)
(d)	Sep. '48	Roper	29	16	55	(2,508)
(c)	Oct. '48	NORC	33	11	56	(1,257)
(c)	Mar. '49	NORC	32	13	55	(1,301)

Source: Charles H. Stember, "The Impact of Israel on American Attitudes," in C. Stember et al., *Jews in the Mind of America* (New York: Basic Books, 1966), 179.

treated" (27 percent). Of those who sympathized more with the Arabs (14 percent of the total sample), 43 percent cited the historical, religious, and legal rights of the Arabs in Palestine as the reason for their choice, while 35 percent simply did "not like the Jews."

Although Americans expressed greater sympathy toward the Jews, they rated the importance of American cooperation with the two sides equally. Between 1950 and 1956, NORC conducted five surveys of opinions on the importance of American cooperation with several countries, including Israel and the Arab nations. These surveys reveal that between 31 and 35 percent of the respondents rated cooperation between the United States and Israel as very important. The comparable figures for the Arabs were 30 to 47 percent. In 1953 and 1956 the rates for Israel surpassed those of the Arabs, while in 1950 and 1955, the Arab rates were higher than those of Israel. In the 1953 poll, those who felt it was very important for the United States to cooperate with Israel (34 percent of the total sample) were asked to explain their reasoning.[53] They cited three main motives: "The Israelis are a new nation, need help," "We need them in the Cold War," and "Their trade is useful to us." It should be noted that only 5 percent cited the democratic system of Israel as a reason for its favorable position. Also, it is interesting that almost a third of the respondents did not know why they considered American-Israeli relations very important.

The NORC polls further reveal that Americans considered cooperation with countries such as India and Greece, nontraditional allies of the United States, to be more important than cooperation with Israel. Thus, beyond basic sympathy, Americans were ambivalent about the importance of Israel to the United States. In the 1950s, Israel was very weak, both economically and militarily. The country was recovering from the devastating results of the War of Independence and was absorbing vast numbers of Jewish refugees, most of them from Arab countries.[54] During this period, the Middle East turned into a Cold War zone; thus, the Arab and nonaligned countries were considered more important to the United States than was Israel in the battle against the USSR to gain dominance in the Middle East.[55] However, efforts to organize the Arab world into an anti-Soviet alliance failed while Israel demonstrated its military strength in the Suez-Sinai crisis of 1956. These developments may well have served to improve Israel's perceived importance, at least among the more influential segments of the American public.

The 1956 Suez-Sinai Crisis

The Israeli War of Independence ended with a series of cease-fire agreements.[56] Egypt was the first Arab country to sign this type of agreement and Syria was the last. Iraq, also a participant in the war, did not join the others and has legally and technically remained at war with Israel. Although Israel viewed the cease-fire agreements as a step toward peace, the Arab states, with the exception of Jordan, considered the armistice a period for preparations for another war to destroy Israel and bring Arab rule to the Jewish state.[57] Jordan adopted a different policy and tentatively discussed with Israel terms of a possible peace treaty. However, under tremendous threats from the Arab world, Jordan was forced to back off, and King Abdullah Ibn Hussein, who had negotiated with Israel, was assassinated.[58]

The Arab nations undermined all international efforts to achieve peace agreements between Israel and its Arab neighbors, including the efforts of the United States, which was a member of the Palestine Conciliation Commission.[59] In the early 1950s, the Arabs intensified their campaign against the Jewish state. Gamal Abdul Nasser, the president of Egypt, led the way, organizing and sponsoring acts of terrorism across Israeli borders, barring Israeli shipping from the Suez Canal (in violation of the Egyptian commitment to free

Table 1–6
Blame for the Arab-Israeli Conflict, 1953–57

Question

Have you heard or read about the recent conflict between Israel and the Arab countries? *If yes:* Which side to you feel is more to blame in this dispute—Israel or the Arabs/Egypt? (NORC)

Date	*Israel*	*Arab/Egypt*	*Neither, Both*	*No Opinion*	*(n)*
Dec. '53	8%	11%	14%	67%[a]	(1,233)
		Egyptian-Czechoslovakian (USSR) Arms Deal			
Sep. '55	6	12[b]	14	68[a]	
Nov. '55	5	15	18	62[a]	(1,276)
Apr. '56	7	18	18	57[a]	(1,224)
		Suez-Sinai Crisis and War			
Nov. '56	19	29[b]	14	38	(1,286)
		Israeli Withdrawal from Sinai (1957)			
Apr. '57	12	40[b]	18	30	(1,279)

Source: Hazel Erskine, "The Polls: Western Partisanship in the Middle East," *Public Opinion Quarterly* 33(Winter 1969–70):633–34.

[a]Includes both those who have not heard or read about the conflict and those who have but do not know who is to blame.

[b]Egypt only.

navigation in this waterway), and tightening the pan-Arab economic boycott of Israel.[60]

Despite American support for the establishment of Israel and the record of Arab hostility leading to the Suez-Sinai crisis of October-November 1956, the majority of Americans were uncertain about which side bore more responsibility for the conflict. Nevertheless, in every poll conducted on this issue between 1953 and 1957, the Arabs and Egypt were assigned the greater share of the blame for the conflict.

Table 1–6 demonstrates that until the Suez-Sinai crisis, Israel was blamed for the conflict by 5 to 8 percent of the American public, while the Arabs or Egypt were blamed by 11 to 18 percent. The ratio of Arab culpability rose slightly in September and November 1955, following Nasser's announcement that Egypt had signed a major arms deal with Czechoslovakia. Actually, the deal was negotiated with the Soviet Union, but both Egypt and the Kremlin preferred to cite Czechoslovakia as the weapons supplier.[61] The pact promised Egypt a substantial quantity of modern weaponry, including fighter planes and tanks. Egypt also signed a mutual defense treaty with Jordan and therefore could feasibly threaten Israel from both the southern and eastern fronts. The arms deal, the treaty, and constant verbal threats led Israel to conclude that another war with the Arabs was inevitable and that the Jewish state should preempt Arab plans before they could absorb the new Soviet weapons.[62]

In October 1956, Israel launched a preventive strike against Egypt in collaboration with Britain and France, whose economic and strategic interests were badly hurt by Nasser's nationalization of the Suez Canal earlier in July.[63] The attack commenced October 29, when Israeli paratroopers parachuted deep into the Sinai Peninsula and captured the strategic Mitla Pass. This action was followed by quick land operations that brought the Israeli forces to the Suez Canal. The Anglo-French military moves commenced October 31 with air raids on Egyptian air fields and strategic bases along the Suez Canal. The raids were followed by paratroop landings at key points of the canal.

Both the United States and the Soviet Union denounced the joint military operations of Israel, Britain, and France at the United Nations. The two superpowers called for an immediate cease-fire and the withdrawal of all foreign forces from Egypt. When the three invading countries were reluctant to acquiesce to the superpowers' demands, the Soviet Union threatened them with "nuclear rockets" and proposed a joint American-Soviet military intervention to stop the fighting.[64] President Dwight D. Eisenhower and Secretary of State John Foster Dulles rejected the Soviet threat and demands but, at the same time, applied considerable pressure on Britain and France to pull out of Egypt. The fighting concluded November 7, with the European powers agreeing to withdraw from Egypt.

The Eisenhower-Dulles policy in the Suez-Sinai crisis was somewhat surprising.[65] Washington sided with Moscow, its major foe in the Cold War, and with Egypt, a new Soviet ally in the Middle East, against Britain and France, longtime allies and NATO members, and Israel. One explanation for the American policy concerned the approaching presidential elections, which were held just a few days after the outbreak of hostilities. President Eisenhower had promised the American public an "era of peace," and the Anglo-French-Israeli operations might have embarrassed him.[66] He was also probably angered and offended by the lack of consultation on the part of Britain and France about their military planning.[67] On October 31, President Eisenhower informed Americans in a television address:

> There can be no peace without law. And there can be no law if we work to invoke one code of international conduct for those who we oppose and another for our friends.[68]

Finally, it is quite possible that at the height of the campaign between the United States and the USSR over the Third World, America did not wish to be associated with military intervention of former colonial powers against Nasser, who was one of the leaders of the nonaligned movement. Regardless of

Eisenhower's true reasons for opposing the Suez-Sinai operation, the American public tended to agree with his policy and positions.

Most Americans, even those who sympathized more with Israel, did not justify the Israeli action. At the beginning of November 1956, NORC asked the American public whether "Israel was justified or not in sending armed forces into Egyptian territory." Forty percent replied that Israel was not justified; 26 percent said it was.[69] To put these figures in proper perspective, the identical poll revealed that 54 percent of the public felt that the British and French use of force against Egypt was unjustified. The difference of 14 percent between the attitude toward the Israeli action, on the one hand, and the British and French action, on the other, is perhaps a result of placing Israel's invasion in a historical context. Those who placed the Israeli operation in the Sinai Desert within the context of earlier Arab acts of hostility and violence were probably more likely to justify the Israeli action. Those who isolated the event may have been more likely to condemn the Israeli invasion.

Although NORC employed the terms "justified" and "unjustified" to assess American attitudes toward the Israeli operation, Gallup preferred the terms "approve" and "disapprove." Obviously, the two sets of terms are not identical and implied different criteria. The word *justify* calls forth a higher degree of moral judgment than does *approve*. In view of the factors of time and circumstance, a policy or an action might be justified but mistaken, or correct but unjustified. Between October 30 and November 2, 1956, Gallup examined opinions of the war in three major American cities (New York, Washington, and Chicago) and found that the public disapproved of the Israeli action by a plurality of 43 to 23 percent and of the British-French operation by a majority of 62 to 15 percent.[70] A few days later, a national sample disapproved of Israel's action by a plurality of 47 to 10 percent and of the British-French operation by a slight majority of 51 to 15 percent. A comparison between the NORC and Gallup results may suggest that although more Americans "justified" than "approved" the Israeli action, they nevertheless generally criticized it.

Table 1–6 shows that following the fighting in Egypt, the percentage of those who blamed Israel for the Arab-Israeli conflict rose to 19; yet those who blamed Egypt grew to 29 percent. Despite the fact that Israel initiated the attack on Egypt, more Americans accused Egypt of abetting the conflict. Also, the war and its coverage in the media transformed the Arab-Israeli conflict into a more salient issue among many Americans, and this resulted in an increased tendency to form opinions and take sides on the "blame" issue.

A further poll, conducted by NORC in November 1956, reveals that half of those who tended to cite Egypt as the catalyst in the Arab-Israeli conflict justified the Israeli military operation in the Sinai Desert, while 79 percent who mostly blamed Israel found no justification for the same action. These results inspired Stember to offer the following comment: "Israel's critics were much readier to condemn her than her supporters were to exonerate her."[71]

Although Israel wished to obtain a peace agreement with Egypt in return for withdrawal from the Sinai Peninsula, Eisenhower and Dulles insisted on unconditional withdrawal. Eisenhower's threats and pressure forced Israel's Prime Minister David Ben-Gurion to withdraw Israeli forces from the Sinai area with no reciprocal political concessions from Egypt.[72] The first opportunity to exchange Arab territory for peace had been lost. Apparently, some Americans had reservations about the Eisenhower-Dulles approach. When asked whether they were satisfied with the manner in which Eisenhower and Dulles handled the Israel-Egypt problem, 50 percent expressed satisfaction with the approach, 23 percent were dissatisfied, and 27 percent had no opinion.[73]

After the war, Egypt was still assigned the greater share of blame for the Arab-Israeli conflict, according to table 1–6. Upon the Israeli withdrawal from the Sinai Desert, this share rose substantially to 40 percent, while Israel's share dropped to 12 percent. The gap between the Israeli and the Egyptian share rose from 6 percent in September 1955 to 10 percent during the crisis, and then, in April 1957, it almost tripled to 28 percent. It appears that the Israeli withdrawal, which concluded the Sinai-Suez crisis, contributed to the increased tendency to blame Egypt for the conflict and the widening gap between perceived Israeli and Egyptian shares of blame. A Roper poll of July 1957 also showed that several months after the war, Americans displayed "sympathetic understanding" toward the Israeli attack on Egypt.[74] Roper found that 55 percent of the respondents had a high opinion or generally thought well of Israel, while only 19 percent held an opposing viewpoint after the Suez-Sinai crisis.

Additional insight into the relative images of Israel and Egypt in American public opinion during and after the war is provided by the Gallup polls. In April 1957, Gallup asked a national sample of Americans for its forecast of another possible Arab-Israeli war. Responses to this query were almost equally divided: 36 percent estimated another war was likely to break out, while 34 percent held the opposite opinion.[75] However, when asked which side was more likely to instigate a new war, 33 percent cited Egypt, while 26 percent named Israel.

Another Gallup poll, conducted during the crisis, on public opinion toward foreign nations also accorded Israel a more favorable rating than it did Egypt. According to table 1–7, exactly twice as many respondents held favorable feelings toward Israel (33 percent) than toward Egypt (17 percent). These and the results of preceding Gallup polls reflected a basic negative attitude toward Egypt, which, in the eyes of Americans, attacked American and Western interests and aligned with the Soviet Union.

Table 1–7
Favorability Rating of Israel and Other Countries, December 1956

Question

How would you rate your feelings toward the following countries?

Country	*Highly Favorable*	*Mildly Favorable*	*Neutral*	*Mildly Unfavorable*	*Highly Unfavorable*
England	23%	34%	27%	7%	9%
France	16	36	34	9	5
W. Germany	16	30	41	6	7
Israel	12	21	53	8	6
India	8	21	56	10	5
Egypt	4	13	52	17	14
USSR	1	2	15	8	74

Source: The Gallup Poll, December 14–19, 1956, 1464–65.

The Dormant Years: 1957–67

In the wake of the Suez-Sinai crisis, President Eisenhower, who had criticized the European and Israeli military intervention in Egypt, created his own American doctrine for the Middle East (the Eisenhower Doctrine) and even used it in May 1958 to intervene militarily in the Lebanese civil war.[76] The Arab-Israeli conflict, however, assumed a relatively low profile. Israel's superior military performance convinced Nasser and the Arabs that they would not easily be able to defeat Israel. United Nations forces, which entered the Sinai Peninsula as part of the agreement to end the Israeli occupation of that area, effectively kept the peace along the Israeli-Egyptian border. Israel also enjoyed free Red Sea navigation to Eilat, its most southern port.

Judging by poll-taking, the Arab-Israeli conflict did not generate much interest in the United States in the post–Suez-Sinai years. American attitudes toward the Middle East were measured in only one national survey, conducted by NORC in 1964 on anti-Semitism.[77] The survey included only two questions concerning the Arab-Israeli conflict, and the responses appear to show a lack of knowledge and interest in this conflict. When asked, "Suppose there were a war between the Arab nations and Israel, which side do you think you would probably sympathize with?" only one-third of the respondents chose sides—25 percent for Israel and 7 percent for the Arabs. Forty percent held no opinion, and 28 percent expressed sympathy toward neither side. Compared to the data on American sympathies toward Jews and Arabs for the 1947–49 period (table 1–5), the number of those who did not choose a side (68 percent) was relatively high. This is probably due to the differences between the two periods. In 1948, Israel and the Arabs were engaged in a massive war, while in 1964, they maintained a stable cease-fire.

The second question in the 1964 survey dealt with attitudes toward the Israeli treatment of Arab refugees in Israel. The responses to this question were as follows: three-quarters of the respondents claimed they had not "heard or read about the relations between the Jews in Israel and the Arab refugees there," or, if they had heard of the issue, they did not know how the refugees were treated (11 percent). Under normal circumstances these results would have represented a considerable lack of interest in the Arab-Israeli conflict. However, the question that produced these results was misleading because there were no Arab refugees inside Israel in 1964. The Arab refugees were those who left Israel during the 1948 war and who, since then, have lived in Arab countries. The authors of the survey might have meant to examine American attitudes toward Israel's treatment of Israeli Arabs; if so, their question was incorrectly formulated. In this light, it is unclear if these results represent a lack of interest and knowledge about the conflict or if they stem from the confusion in the question. In any event, American pollsters were quite indifferent to Arab-Israeli issues. This suddenly changed in June 1967, when another major war broke out between Israel and its Arab neighbors.

Conclusions

The emergence of the state of Israel attracted the attention of several pollsters. Surveys conducted between 1944 and 1948 reveal limited American public awareness and knowledge of the critical events that took place in the Middle East and of U.S. policy on these events. NORC found, in December 1945, that only one-third of the national sample correctly identified the name of the country that ruled Palestine at that time.[78]

Another survey of a national cross section of newspaper editors conducted in November 1947 by the same pollsters found that only 42 percent of the editors could recall the solution that the majority of UNSCOP had recommended to the United Nations.[79] Other polls found that while most Americans claimed they had heard or read about the "trouble in Palestine" (83 percent in February and April 1947) or about "the problem of permitting Jews to enter Palestine" (80 percent in August 1946), relatively smaller groups had heard or read about specific issues, such as the report of the AACOI (28 percent in May 1946) or "the United Nations Committee's proposal to partition Palestine" (56 percent in November 1947).[80] However, it should be noted that these figures are high compared to the American public's overall awareness of foreign affairs.

In general, Americans were touched by the Holocaust and the plight of the Jewish refugees. They overwhelmingly supported Jewish immigration to Palestine, particularly the admission of 100,000 Holocaust survivors interned in Europe. The majority of Americans also favored the establishment of a Jewish state in Palestine.

American sympathy toward Jewish refugees and the creation of Israel can be attributed in part to the U.S. government's reluctance to admit the Jewish refugees into its own territory.[81] From this perspective, Israel seemed to offer the simplest solution to the problem. However, sympathy and support for the Jewish cause stopped at the point at which direct American military involvement in Palestine would have been required to allow Jewish immigration and the creation of Israel. The majority of Americans opposed such involvement and even military aid to Israel. American participation in a U.N. force was much more acceptable, probably because it was linked to the prestige of the United Nations and its place in the international system of the post–World War II era.

President Truman's decisions on Palestine have been found to be controversial at that time and in recent academic research. However, the opinion data indicate that his words and deeds coincided with the wishes of most Americans. As president he had many opportunities to shape public opinion, but at the same time, as this chapter clearly demonstrates, he also expressed American opinions and preferences. Unlike his chief advisers on foreign policy, but reflecting the general sentiments of the public, he identified with the plight of the Jewish refugees. He genuinely searched for a reasonable solution to the refugee problem and to the developing Arab-Jewish conflict in Palestine.[82]

Very few polls were conducted in the United States on Israel and the Arab-Israeli conflict from the establishment of Israel until the outbreak of the Suez-Sinai war, and these surveys dealt with only two issues: blame for the Arab-Israeli conflict and the importance of U.S. cooperation with Israel and the Arab countries (compared to other countries). These surveys reveal some ambivalence in American public opinion toward Israel. Only about one-third of the public rated cooperation between the United States and Israel as very important, and this rate was similar to that accorded the Arabs. As for the culpability issue, until the Suez-Sinai crisis, the majority of Americans did not know which side to blame, but those who did have an opinion cited the Arabs, particularly Egypt, as the greater instigators of the conflict.

The Suez-Sinai crisis renewed the interest of pollsters in the opinions of Americans on Israel and the Arab-Israeli conflict. A greater number of Americans took sides and, despite the Israeli attack, still assigned Egypt a greater share of fault for the conflict. Most of those individuals placed the Israeli military operation in Sinai within the context of earlier Arab provocations and hostile activities. Yet a substantial number of Americans, even those who sympathized more with Israel, were critical of its attack. This attitude might have been based on moral considerations or on the views and policies of President Eisenhower, who strongly condemned the joint Israeli-British-French operation. On the whole, however, the data gave more weight to the conclusion of Lipset and Schneider, which claimed that Israel was seen more as a victim than as an aggressor in the Suez-Sinai crisis.[83]

Following the 1956 war, the Arab-Israeli conflict subsided, at least for a decade, and academic and commercial pollsters were no longer interested in this area. Only one survey dealt with the conflict, but it included just two questions, which failed to reveal much about American attitudes toward this issue. Such attitudes remained largely unexplored until a giant wave of polls exposed them following the eruption of the Six-Day War.

Notes

1. Two books on U.S. policy toward the Palestine problems that were written shortly after the establishment of Israel include valuable information and insights. Both were reprinted in the 1970s. J.C. Hurewitz, *The Struggle for Palestine* (New York: Norton, 1950); and Frank E. Manuel, *The Realities of American-Palestine Relations* (Washington, D.C.: Public Affairs Press, 1949).

2. See James Forrestal, *The Forrestal Diaries*, ed. Walter Millis (New York: Viking Press, 1951).

3. See Kenneth R. Bain, *The March to Zion: United States Policy and the Founding of Israel* (College Station: Texas A&M University Press, 1979); John Snetsinger, *Truman, the Jewish Vote, and the Creation of Israel* (Stanford, Calif: Hoover Institution Press, 1974).

4. Robert Divine, *Foreign Policy and U.S. Presidential Elections, 1940–1948* (New York: New Viewpoints, 1974).

5. U.S. State Department, *Foreign Relations of the United States, 1946* (hereafter referred to as *FRUS*). (Washington, D.C.: Government Printing Office, 1971,) 703. See also Zvi Ganin, *Truman, American Jewry, and Israel, 1945–1948* (New York: Holmes and Meier, 1979), 104.

6. In November 1947 the National Opinion Research Center of Chicago (NORC) conducted a national survey of newspaper editors. Forty percent said they ran editorials on the Palestinian question. The word *editor* was used to include all newspaper representatives interviewed. Actually, 28 percent of the interviews were obtained with owners or publishers, 50 percent with the chief editors, and 22 percent with assistant editors or other staff members. "The Quarter's Polls," *Public Opinion Quarterly* 12(Spring 1948): 160–61.

7. See Charles H. Stember, "The Impact of Israel on American Attitudes," in C. Stember et al., *Jews in the Mind of America* (New York: Basic Books, 1966). 174.

8. Paul W. Massing and Maxwell Miller, "Should Jews Return to Germany?" *Atlantic Monthly* 176(July 1945): 87–90.

9. The British rule of Palestine was discussed in numerous books. See, for example, Bernard Wasserstein, *The British in Palestine: The Mandatory Government and the Arab-Jewish Conflict, 1917–1929* (London: Royal Historical Society, 1978); and Nicholas Bethell, *The Palestine Triangle: The Struggle for the Holy Land, 1935–1948* (New York: Putnam, 1979).

10. Christopher Sykes, *Crossroads to Israel, 1917–1948* (Bloomington: Indiana University Press, 1965), ch. 10; and Michael Cohen, *Palestine: Retreat from the Mandate* (London: Elek, 1978), ch. 5.

11. On the implementation of the 1939 White Paper, see Daphne Trevor, *Under the White Paper: Some Aspects of British Administration in Palestine from 1939 to 1947* (Munich: Kraus, 1980, first published in 1948).

12. Walter Laqueur, ed., *The Israel-Arab Reader* (New York: Bantam Books, 1970), 79. See also Yehuda Baur, *From Diplomacy to Resistance* (New York: Atheneum, 1973), ch. 6.

13. Sykes, *Crossroads*, ch. 12.

14. Harry S. Truman, *Years of Trial and Hope* (New York: Signet, 1965), vol. II, 158. See also Herbert Parzen, "President Truman and the Palestine Quandary: His Initial Experience, April–December, 1945," *Jewish Social Studies* 35(January 1973); 42–72.

15. Earl G. Harrison, "The Last Hundred Thousand," *Survey Graphic* 34(December 1945); 73–77.

16. On the work of the Anglo-American Committee of Inquiry, see Michael J. Cohen, *Palestine and the Great Powers, 1945–1948* (Princeton, N.J.: Princeton University Press, 1982), ch. 5; John Marlowe, *The Seat of Pilate: An Account of the Palestine Mandate* (London: Cresset Press, 1959); and Evan M. Wilson, *Decision on Palestine: How the U.S. Came to Recognize Israel* (Stanford, Calif: Hoover Institution Press, 1979).

17. *The Gallup Poll*, December 7–12, 1945, p. 554.

18. See Anglo-American Committee of Inquiry on Jewish Problems in Palestine and Europe, *Report to the U.S. Government and the U.K.*, Lausanne, Switzerland, April 20, 1946 (Washington, D.C.: Government Printing Office, 1946).

19. Edward Francis-Williams, *A Prime-Minister Remembers* (London: Heinemann, 1961), 195.

20. *The Gallup Poll*, May 17-22, 1946, 584.

21. See note 5.

22. Prime Minister Attlee complained that there "is no Arab vote in America, but there is a very heavy Jewish vote and the Americans are always having elections." Francis-Williams, *Prime-Minister Remembers*, 181.

23. Howard M. Sachar, *Europe Leaves the Middle East, 1936–1954* (New York: Knopf, 1972), 484; F. Northedge, *British Foreign Policy: The Process of Readjustment, 1945–1961* (London: Allen and Unwin, 1962), 117. See also Bruce Hoffman, *The Failure of British Military Strategy within Palestine, 1939–1947* (Tel Aviv: Bar Ilan University Press, 1983).

24. The background for this decision can be found in Hurewitz, *Struggle for Palestine*, 284, Elizabeth Monroe, *Britain's Moment in the Middle East, 1914–1956* (London: Chatto and Winders, 1963), 165–66 and Cohen, *Palestine and the Great Powers*, ch. 9.

25. Wilson, *Decision on Palestine*, ch. 8; Hurewitz, *Struggle for Palestine*, ch. 22; Marlowe, *The Seat of Pilate*, ch. 15, and Dan Tschirgi, *The Politics of Indecision* (New York: Praeger, 1983), 220–25.

26. One country, Australia, abstained.

27. Two officials, Loy Henderson, head of the Near East Division, and George Kennan, director of the Policy Planning Staff, strongly opposed the partition solution. See Wilson, *Decision on Palestine*, 116–21, and also Loy Henderson, "American Political and Strategic Interests in the Middle East and Southwestern Europe," *Proceedings of the American Academy of Political Science* 22, no. 4(1948). Kennan expressed his views in a special report: U.S. State Department, "Report by the Policy Planning Staff on Position of the United States with Respect to Palestine" in *FRUS* 1948, 546-54.

28. President Truman wrote in his memoirs: "I was of the opinion that the proposed position of Palestine could open the way for peaceful collaboration between the Arabs and the Jews. Although it was difficult under the present circumstances to bring the Arabs and the Jews together, I could foresee that under the proposed plan of the United Nations, calling for an economic union of the partitioned areas, the Jews and the Arabs might eventually work side by side as neighbors." Truman, *Years of Trial and Hope*, 184.

29. Tschirgi, *Politics of Indecision*, 240.

30. See Herbert Feis, *The Birth of Israel* (New York: Norton, 1969), ch. 3, and Cohen, *Palestine and the Great Powers*, ch. 11.

31. Michael J. Cohen, "Why Britain Left: The End of the Mandate," *Wiener Library Bulletin* 31 (1978): 74-86; Monroe, *Britain's Moment*, 161–70;; Northedge, *British Foreign Policy*, p. 117.

32. Wilson, *Decision on Palestine*, 130.

33. *U.S. Department of State Bulletin*, March 28, 1948, 407.

34. Truman, *Years of Trial and Hope*, 191–92. Margaret Truman also argued that the trusteeship was a State Department idea that Truman never accepted: *Harry S. Truman* (New York: Morrow, 1973), 387–89.

35. Truman, *Years of Trial and Hope*, 189–90; Chaim Weizmann, *Trial and Error* (New York: Harper and Brothers, 1949), 472.

36. On the academic controversy over the origins of the Austin's trusteeship proposal, see Manuel, *Realities*, 345–50, Wilson, *Decision on Palestine*, 134–36; and Snetsinger, *Truman*, 89–94.

37. Stember, "Impact of Israel," 179.

38. Ibid, 178.

39. Tschirgi, *Politics of Indecision*, 251.

40. Wilson, *Decision on Palestine*, 143–44. Joseph B. Schechtman, *The U.S. and the Jewish State Movement* (New York: Herzl Press, 1966), ch. 11; see also Clark Clifford, "Recognizing Israel," *American Heritage* 28(April 1977): 4–11.

41. Stember, "Impact of Israel," 176.

42. Truman, *Years of Trial and Hope*, 162.

43. UN General Assembly, Ad-Hoc Committee on the Palestine Question, *Summary Records*, 2nd session, 1948, 64.

44. *The Gallup Poll,* October 24-29, 1947, 686.

45. See note 6.

46. U.N. General Assembly, *Official Records of the Second Session of the General Assembly, Resolutions,* September 16–November 29, 1947, 131.

47. *U.S. Department of State Bulletin,* December 14, 1947, p. 1197.

48. Shlomo Slonim, "The 1948 American Embargo on Arms to Palestine," *Political Science Quarterly* 94(Fall 1979): 498. See also Schechtman, *The U.S. and the Jewish State*, ch. 12.

49. "The Quarter's Polls," *Public Opinion Quarterly* 12(Fall 1948): 551.

50. Yaacov Ro'i, *Soviet Decision Making in Practice: The USSR and Israel, 1947–1954* (New Brunswick, N.J.: Transaction, 1980), 149–61.

51. However, it should be noted that many Americans, mostly Jews, volunteered to fight the Arabs during the Israeli War of Independence. See A. Joseph Heckelman, *American Volunteers and Israel's War of Independence* (New York: Ktav, 1974).

52. Stember, "Impact of Israel," 180.

53. Ibid, 182.

54. See Nadav Safran, *Israel—The Embattled Ally* (Cambridge, Mass: Harvard University Press, 1978), chs. 11, 19.

55. See Robert W. Stookey, *America and the Arab States: An Uneasy Encounter* (New York: Wiley, 1975), 127–39; and John C. Campbell, *Defense of the Middle East: Problems of American Policy* (New York: Praeger, 1961).

56. Meron Medzini, ed.,*Israel's Foreign Relations: Selected Documents, 1947–1974.* (Jerusalem: Ministry for Foreign Affairs, 1976), vol. 1. ch. 5.

57. See David Brook, *Preface to Peace: The United Nations and Its Arab-Israeli Armistice System* (Washington, D.C.: Public Affairs Press, 1964); and Fred J. Khouri, *The Arab-Israeli Dilemma* (Syracuse, N.Y.: Syracuse University Press, 1968), 182–204.

58. Nadav Safran, *From War to War: The Arab–Israeli Confrontation, 1948–1967* (New York: Pegasus, 1969), 37.

59. Walter Eytan, *The First Ten Years: A Diplomatic History of Israel* (New York: Simon and Schuster, 1958); and Earl Berger, *The Covenant and the Sword* (London: Routledge and Kegan, 1965), ch. 4.

60. See Berger, *The Covenant,* ch. 10; Khouri, *Arab-Israeli Dilemma,* 204–10; Chaim Bermant, *Israel* (London: Thames and Hudson, 1967), ch. 7; Trevor N. Dupuy, *Elusive Victory: The Arab-Israeli Wars, 1947–1974* (New York: Harper & Row, 1978), book 1; and Ernest Stock, *Israel on the Road to Sinai, 1949–1956* (Ithaca, N.Y.: Cornell University Press, 1967).

61. Uri Ra'anan, *The USSR Arms the Third World* (Cambridge, Mass.: MIT Press, 1969), part 1; and Jon Glassman, *Arms for the Arabs: The Soviet Union and War in the Middle East* (Baltimore, Md.: Johns Hopkins University Press, 1975), ch. 2.

62. See David Ben-Gurion, *The Restored State of Israel* (Tel-Aviv: Am Oved, 1969), 492–95, 520–24. See also Moshe Dayan, *The Diary of the Sinai Campaign* (New York: Schocken, 1967), chs. 1–4; and Michael Brecher, *Decisions in Israel's Foreign Policy* (New Haven, Conn.: Yale University Press, 1975), ch. 6.

63. On the Suez-Sinai crisis and war, see Chester Cooper, *The Lion's Last Roar, Suez 1956* (New York: Harper & Row, 1978); and Hugh Thomas, *Suez* (New York: Harper & Row, 1966).

64. Carsten Holbraad, *Superpowers and International Conflict* (New York: St. Martin's, 1979), ch. 1.

65. The U.S. policy toward the Suez-Sinai crisis is discussed in Townsend Hoopes, *The Devil and John Foster Dulles* (Boston: Little, Brown, 1973), chs. 23, 24; Robert R. Bowie, *Suez 1956* (New York: Oxford University Press, 1974); and Donald Neff, *Warriors at Suez: Eisenhower Takes America into the Middle East* (New York: Linden Press, Simon and Schuster, 1981).

66. Robert A. Divine, *Foreign Policy and U.S. Presidential Elections, 1952–1960* (New York: New Viewpoints, 1974).

67. Richard E. Neustadt, *Alliance Politics* (New York: Columbia University Press, 1970), ch. 5.

68. Cited in John Donovan, ed., *U.S.-Soviet Policy in the Middle East, 1945–1956* (New York: Facts on File, 1972), 255–56.

69. Stember, "Impact of Israel," 187.

70. *The Gallup Poll,* November 13, 1956, 1454, and November 23, 1456.

71. Stember, "Impact of Israel," 185–86.

72. David Ben-Gurion, *The Restored State,* 532–33.

73. *The Gallup Poll,* April 6–11, 1956, 1484–85. It is also interesting that President Eisenhower won two more percentage points of the Jewish vote in the 1956 elections than he did in the 1952 elections. See Mark R. Levy and Michael S. Kramer, *The Ethnic Factor: How America's Minorities Decide Elections* (New York: Simon and Schuster, 1973), 241.

74. National Newspaper Syndicate, Chicago, July 20, 1957.

75. *The Gallup Poll,* April 6–11, 1957, p. 1485.

76. See Campbell, *Defense of the Middle East,* ch. 9, and Stookey, *America and the Arab States,* 148–57.

77. The findings of this survey were reported and analyzed in Gertrude J. Selznick and Stephen Steinberg, *The Tenacity of Prejudice* (New York: Harper & Row, 1969), and in Seymour M. Lipset and Earl Raab, *The Politics of Unreason* Second edition (Chicago: University of Chicago Press, 1978).

78. Stember, "Impact of Israel," 173.

79. See note 6.

80. Stember, "Impact of Israel," 174.

81. Tschirgi, *Politics of Indecision,* 148–49. See also Saul S. Friedman, *No Haven for the Oppressed: U.S. Policy toward Jewish Refugees, 1938–1945* (Detroit: Wayne State University Press, 1973).

82. See Cohen, *Palestine and the Great Powers,* 46–55, and Safran, *Israel—the Embattled Ally,* 39–42.

83. Seymour M. Lipset and William Schneider, *Israel and the Jews in American Public Opinion* (New York: American Jewish Committee, 1977, Mimeographed), 8.

2
From the Six-Day War to Sadat's Breakthrough

Following the Suez-Sinai crisis, President Nasser of Egypt successfully converted his military defeats into political victories and established himself as leader of the entire Arab world. Throughout the next decade, he determined the main course of political and military developments in the region. Although the Israeli-Egyptian border was relatively quiet because of the deployment of the United Nations Emergency Force (UNEF) along the borders and other strategic positions, Nasser had not reduced his hostility toward Israel, nor did he desert his plan to lead an all-out Arab war against it. However, in the early 1960s, he outlined several conditions that he felt must be met before the Arabs could defeat Israel. These conditions included Arab unity and an equal military balance between the two adversaries.[1]

In the early months of 1967, the Arab world was far from united, and Egypt was heavily and unsuccessfully embroiled in Yemen's civil war. Israel, on the other hand, had expanded and upgraded its military strength, thus, a major Arab-Israeli war appeared unlikely. However, in June 1967, the unexpected occurred: Israel and three of its immediate Arab neighbors—Egypt, Syria, and Jordan—fought a short but major war with far-reaching consequences. Upon the conclusion of the war, the Arabs, for the first time in the history of the Arab-Israeli conflict, were confronted with tangible incentives to negotiate peace with Israel. These incentives consisted of Arab territories captured by Israel during the war. Israel hoped to exchange these territories for durable peace agreements, a hope epitomized in a much quoted statement by Israel's Minister of Defense Moshe Dayan, who declared immediately after the war that he was waiting for a phone call from King Hussein of Jordan. Unfortunately, it took another major war (in 1973) and ten years of soul-searching before this peace potential evolved into an Israeli-Egyptian peace treaty. In November 1977, President Anwar Sadat of Egypt made a historic journey to Jerusalem, inaugurating an era of recognition and direct negotiations between Israel and Egypt.

This chapter deals with American opinion on Israel and the Middle East from the Six-Day War to the end of the Kissinger era in American foreign policy and the first meaningful steps toward Israeli-Egyptian peace. Between 1967 and 1973, Israel and the Arabs waged three wars: the Six-Day War, the War of Attrition, and the 1973 Yom Kippur War. The War of Attrition lasted more than a year and drew the Soviet Union into direct, but limited, military involvement on behalf of Egypt. The war was concluded, however, through American diplomacy and mediation. The Yom Kippur war inflicted enormous casualties and damage to both sides, accelerated the energy crisis, and brought the two superpowers to a direct and dangerous confrontation. Following this war, Secretary of State Henry Kissinger mediated several agreements between Israel and its neighbors, opened promising new avenues for conflict resolution, and increased the standing of the United States in the Middle East.

The 1967–77 period witnessed major changes in the leadership of all countries involved, and this chapter examines the effects of these alterations on American public opinion toward the Middle East. Three very different presidents served in the White House during this decade: Lyndon B. Johnson, Richard M. Nixon, and Gerald R. Ford. Israel was also governed by three prime ministers: Levy Eshkol, Golda Meir, and Yitzhak Rabin. Rabin served as Israeli ambassador to the United States from 1968 to 1973. He represented the new generation of Israeli leaders who had been born in Israel and were free of the burden of the past and the enormous task of nation-building. A major government alteration also occurred in Egypt. In 1970, Nasser died of a heart attack after 18 years of uninterrupted rule. He was succeeded by Anwar Sadat, who later defied all expectations and became a highly accomplished statesman.

The 1967 Six-Day War, which was a turning point in so much of the domestic and regional politics of Israel and the Arabs, also proved to be a turning point in the history of poll-taking of public opinion on Israel and the Arab nations. Since 1967, many more pollsters have conducted surveys more frequently on a wider variety of issues. A few attempts have also been made to gauge the sources and depth of opinion.

The Six-Day War—The Apex of Sympathy for Israel

The Six-Day War broke out on June 5, 1967, when Israel resorted to the use of force against Egypt, Syria, and Jordan. In just six days, Israel heavily damaged the armies of those three countries and captured strategic territories: the Sinai Peninsula and the Gaza Strip from Egypt, the West Bank from Jordan, and the Golan Heights from Syria.[2] A grave and lengthy international crisis preceded the war. The Kremlin had informed Nasser that Israel had mobilized forces in preparation for a massive attack against Syria. This information was false and Nasser knew so; yet, he chose to act as if it were true and, on May 14, ordered his troops to move across the Suez Canal into the Sinai Peninsula. At this time Nasser apparently did not seek a war with Israel, but he was later overwhelmed by events and took actions that rendered a full-scale war inevitable.[3]

Nasser's first decisive step was his demand that UNEF leave the Sinai Peninsula. He apparently did not expect the United Nations to comply with his demand, at least not without debate or discussion. United Nations Secretary General U. Thant, however, acted quickly and ordered his forces to withdraw from the Sinai Peninsula.[4] Nasser felt compelled to fulfill his earlier commitments to his people and the Arab world by closing the straits of Tiran to Israeli shipping. Therefore, he ordered the Egyptian army to occupy the areas evacuated by UNEF, including the strategic point of Sharm el Sheikh, from which it is possible to control the straits of Tiran and the passage to Eilat. Israel responded through highly cautious moves.[5] Israeli Prime Minister and Minister of Defense Levy Eshkol ordered partial mobilization of the Israeli Defense Forces (IDF) yet strongly denied plans to attack any Arab country. On May 23, 1967, Eshkol informed the Israeli Knesset:

> Any interference with freedom of passage in the gulf and the straits constitutes a gross violation of international law, a blow at the sovereign rights of other nations, and an act of aggression against Israel.[6]

With the bitter lessons of the 1956 Suez-Sinai war in mind, the Israeli government refrained from immediate military action and called upon the United States, the United Nations, and other major powers to exert pressure on Egypt to reinstate the right of free navigation through the straits of Tiran.[7]

On the same day, May 23, President Johnson stated in a nationally televised address, "The United States considers the gulf to be an international waterway and feels that a blockade of Israeli shipping is illegal and potentially disastrous to the cause of peace."[8] One day later, Israeli Foreign Minister Abba Eban arrived in Washington for talks with Johnson. He had learned from Israeli Ambassador to the United States Avraham Harman that the "Congress and the American people would insist on exhausting this procedure [action by the U.N. Security Council] before considering action outside the United Nations."[9] The following day, Eban met with Johnson, who insisted on Israeli patience with pending international action to solve the crisis. Johnson told Eban: "I am fully aware of what three past presidents have said, but that is not worth five cents if the people and the Congress do not support the president."[10]

Johnson knew that Israel might attempt to use force and warned Eban against a premature attack before all other avenues had been exhausted. Johnson reminded Eban: "The central point is that your nation not be the one to bear the responsibility for any outbreak of war. . . . Israel will not be alone unless it decides to act alone."

The U.S. position was communicated to the Israeli government, but within three days the crisis took on dynamics of its own and the straits issue became irrelevant. Israel's caution was misinterpreted by the Arabs as a sign of weakness, and the entire region became enthusiastic over the prospect of dealing Israel a mortal blow.

In this atmosphere, on May 29, Nasser informed the Egyptian National Assembly that "the issue today is not the question of Aqaba or the straits of Tiran or UNEF. The issue is the rights of the people of Palestine."[11] He clearly implied that the Arabs were prepared for a full-scale war against Israel. Indeed, by the end of May 1967 war had become inevitable. King Hussein of Jordan, a bitter enemy of Nasser, suddenly signed a mutual defense treaty with Egypt and placed his armed forces under Nasser's command. Syria was already involved in frequent military clashes with Israel, and therefore, in just three days, Israel found itself surrounded and threatened by the three fully mobilized armies of Egypt, Jordan, and Syria.[12] This grave situation produced a novelty in the Israeli political system—a government of national unity. Moshe Dayan, chief of staff throughout the 1956 Suez-Sinai war, was appointed minister of defense.

The clouds of war grew thicker, yet Israel wanted to ensure that a preemptive strike would be acceptable to the United States. A special envoy, Meir Amit, was sent to assess the mood in Washington. On June 1 he reported:

> A strong tide of public feeling was now running in Israel's favor. Many Americans were becoming resigned to the feeling that if the U.S. was unable to act quickly, it would not be able to demur strongly should Israel take independent initiative.[13]

The Israeli official recommended waiting a few days to give the plan to open the straits a chance and added, "Public opinion was on our side. . . . the time left to us should be used to prepare public opinion and to plow a deeper furrow."

On June 4, Iraq formally joined the Egyptian-Jordanian defense agreement and Egypt commenced airlifting equipment and personnel to Jordan. Other Arab countries either sent or committed forces to the upcoming war, and in Damascus, representatives of Arab oil-producing countries met to discuss use of the "oil weapon" against countries expected to support Israel. All these developments were seen by Israel as a clear sign of an approaching, major

Arab assault. On June 5, Israel decided to preempt the Arab plans and attacked Egyptian military airfields, destroying the Egyptian air force. Jordan and Syria soon joined the warfare. Within three days, Israel captured the entire expanse of the Sinai Peninsula from Egypt and the West Bank from Jordan. Jordan agreed to a cease-fire June 8, and Egypt followed June 9. Israeli forces were now free to contain the Syrian assault on the northern part of the country and they conquered the Golan Heights. Syria agreed to a cease-fire June 10. The Arab nations had suffered a major military defeat, and the crisis was finally over.

The stunning Israeli victory, especially the devastating attack on the Egyptian air force, led Nasser to accuse the United States of actively participating in the warfare. The United States vehemently denied Nasser's charges, and these denials were confirmed by the USSR. In a way, however, American soldiers were affected by the war, albeit through an ironic and unforeseen accident. On June 7, Israeli airplanes and ships mistakenly attacked the American espionage vessel *Liberty,* which sailed just 13 miles off the coast of the Sinai Desert. When war broke out, the *Liberty* was ordered to move away from the coast, but the order was mishandled and failed to reach the ship in time. Israel assumed that the *Liberty* was an Egyptian naval vessel and attacked it.[14] Thirty-four American lives were lost and many marines were wounded. The incident raised some criticism in the United States, but the quick Israeli apology and explanation, plus the offer to compensate the families of the deceased marines, soon reduced the negative implications of the incident.

Throughout and after the Six-Day War, the American media reported the public outpouring of support for Israel. The *New York Daily News* wrote on June 7, "Most Americans seem likely to sympathize with Israel, a small nation . . . and a brave one." *Time* also reported on June 16, "There was little doubt as to where the majority of Americans stood." Janice Monti Belkaoui investigated Arab and Israeli images in two newspapers, the *New York Times* and the *New York Daily News,* and three magazines, *Newsweek, Time,* and *U.S. News and World Report,* from 1966 to 1974.[15] She found that, in 1967, the Israeli image in these publications was highly positive. Israeli leaders were cast as heroes and winners and characterized as "strong," "decisive," and "confident." Israeli cities and citizens were described as "peaceful and serene." Pro-American Arab leaders, such as King Hussein, were also portrayed in a positive manner, but Nasser was cited as a "typical villain."[16]

The war substantially heightened the American media's interest in the Arab-Israeli conflict. Robert H. Trice examined editorials in 11 elite newspapers from 1966 to 1974 and found an increase in "editorial attention" to the conflict during and immediately after the Six-Day War.[17] He also measured editorial support for several parties and found that editorials printed during

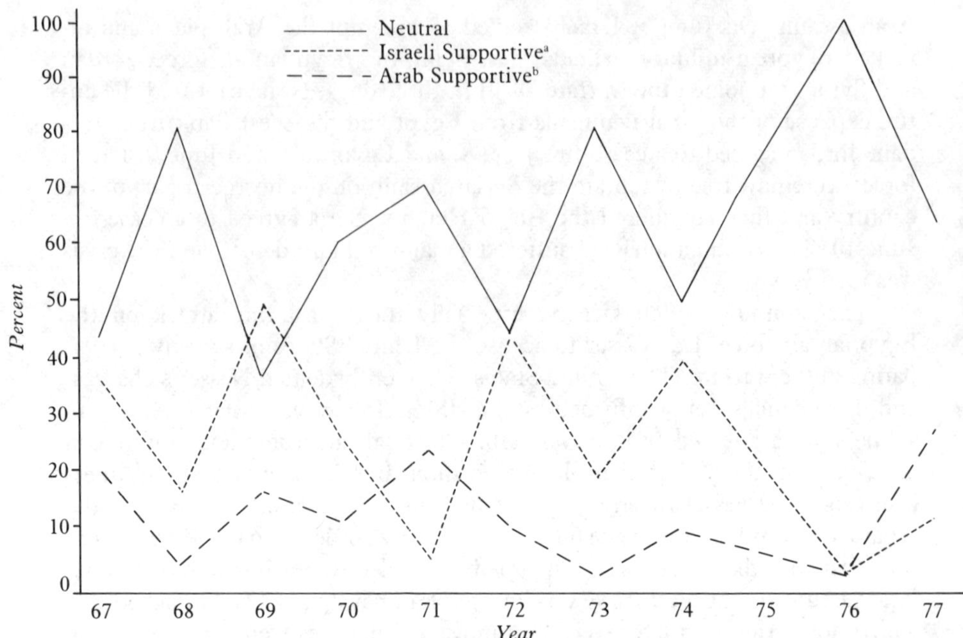

Source: David Daugherty and Michael Warden, "Prestige Press Editorial Treatment of the Mideast During 11 Crisis Years," *Journalism Quarterly* 56(Winter 1979): 781.

[a]Includes "supportive of Israel" and "critical of Arab nations"

[b]Includes "supportive of Arab Nations" and "critical of Israel"

Figure 2–1. Editorial Support for Israel and the Arabs, by Year, 1967–77

the Six-Day War were somewhat supportive of the United States, neutral to Israel, and critical of the Arab states and the USSR.

David Daugherty and Michael Warden also examined the contents and slant of editorials on the Arab-Israeli conflict during the same period, but covered only four elite newspapers and employed a different classification system.[18] The newspapers were the *New York Times,* the *Washington Post,* the *Wall Street Journal* and the *Christian Science Monitor.* According to their study, about 60 percent of all editorials written on the Middle East during the Six-Day War were neutral, about 30 percent supported Israel, and the remainder supported the Arabs (see figure 2–1).

The war created an unprecedented wave of U.S. public sympathy for Israel.[19] Public support for Israel in the United States rose to its highest level since 1948, while the percentage of those favoring Arab nations shrank to its lowest level in the history of the conflict (see tables 1–4 and 2–1). On June 7, Gallup found that 56 percent of Americans expressed sympathy toward Israel, while only 4 percent sympathized with the Arabs. Harris found, on June 10, a pro-Israeli margin of 41 to 1 percent.

The reasons for the dramatic shift in favor of Israel are easily discernable. Israel attacked first, but in view of the prewar crisis the Jewish state was seen as a victim of Arab aggression. On June 10, 1967, Harris asked, "Who do you think has more right on their side—the Arabs or Israel?" Forty-six percent said that Israel had more right on its side; only 4 percent said the Arabs had more right on their side.[20] When asked which side had instigated conditions for the war, 63 percent cited the Arabs and 16 percent blamed Israel. These results correlate with responses to another question in a poll released by Harris on July 10. Respondents were asked how they felt about Russian efforts to have the United Nations condemn Israel as an aggressor. An overwhelming majority of 79 percent rejected such a condemnation; only 7 percent favored it and 14 percent were unsure.

Americans traditionally have expressed special sympathy for the underdog, and Israel epitomized such an image during the crisis and war of May–June 1967. The Arab armies substantially outnumbered the IDF, and during most of the prewar crisis there was a real fear, both in Israel and abroad, that this time the Arabs might succeed in their attempt to annihilate Israel. However, the opposite occurred, and three huge Arab armies were swiftly and decisively defeated. Furthermore, from global and regional perspectives the Israeli success was also seen as an American success. Egypt and Syria were close

Table 2–1
Sympathies for Israel and the Arab Nations, 1967–77

Question

(a) Have you heard or read about the situation in the Middle East? *If yes:* In the Middle East situation are your sympathies more with Israel or more with the Arab nations? (Gallup)

(b) In the latest war between Israel and the Arab states, do you feel more sympathetic to the Israelis, the Arabs, or don't you have any strong feelings either way? (Harris, 1967 and 1973)

(c) As far as the Middle East is concerned, do you feel more sympathy with Israel or with the Arab countries? (Harris, 1970–71)

(d) In the dispute between Israel and the Arabs, which side do you sympathize with more—Israel or the Arabs? (Harris, 1974–75)

(e) Turning to the situation in the Middle East, at the present time do you find yourself *more* in sympathy with Israel, or *more* in sympathy with the Arab nations? (Roper, 1973–77)

(f) If war should break out in the Middle East, with whom would you identify the most—Israel or the Arab nations? (Yankelovich, 1974–76)

Table 2–1 continued

Q	Date	Poll	Israel	Arab Nations	Neither	D.K., N.O.[a]
		Six-Day War (June 5–10, 1967)				
(a)	June 7, '67	Gallup	56%	4%	25%	15%
(b)	June 10, '67	Harris	41	1	40	18
(a)	Feb. '69	Gallup	50	5	28	17
		War of Attrition (April 1969–August 1970)				
(a)	Feb.–Mar. '70	Gallup	44	3	32	21
(c)	Aug. '70	Harris	47	6	25	22
(c)	Oct. '70	Harris	47	6	26	21
(c)	June '71	Harris	46	7	24	23
(c)	July '71	Harris	44	7	22	27
		Yom Kippur War (October 6–25, 1973)				
(a)	Oct. 6–8, '73	Gallup	47	6	22	25
(a)	Oct. 19–22, '73	Gallup	48	6	21	25
(b)	Oct. '73	Harris	39	4	16	41
(e)	Nov. '73	Roper	48	7	28[b]	17
(a)	Dec. 7–10, '73	Gallup	54	8	24	14
(a)	Dec. '73	Gallup	50	7	25	18
(e)	Dec. '73	Roper	41	6	38[b]	15
(f)	Oct. '74	Yankelovich	55	9	22[b]	14
(d)	Dec. '74–Jan. '75	Harris	52	7	30	11
(a)	Jan. '75	Gallup	44	8	22	26
		Reassessment (March–August 1975)				
(a)	Apr. '75	Gallup	37	8	24	31
(e)	Apr. '75	Roper	43	7	36	14
		Israeli-Egyptian Interim Agreement (September 1975)				
(d)	Jan. '76	Harris	52	6	30	12
(f)	Jan. '76	Yankelovich	56	9	24[b]	11
(e)	Jan. '77	Roper	47	6	32[b]	15

Sources: George Gallup, *The Gallop Poll: Public Opinion, 1935–1971,* Vol. 3, (New York: Random House, 1972), 2068, 2071–72, 2149, 2181, 2242; *1972–1977,* Vols. 1, 2 (Wilmington, Del.: Scholarly Resources, 1978), 196, 204, 220, 408, 458, 1121, 1220, 1222; Seymour Martin Lipset and William Schneider, *Israel and the Jews in American Public Opinion* (Mimeographed, 1977), 14–16, 24–29; Michael W. Suleiman, "American Public Support of Middle Eastern Countries 1939–1979," in Michael C. Hudson and Ronald G. Wolfe, eds., *The American Media and the Arabs* (Washington D.C.: Georgetown University, Center for Contemporary Arab Studies, 1980), 18, table 2; Louis Harris and Associates, *A Study of the Attitudes of the American People and the American Jewish Community toward Anti-Semitism and the Arab-Israeli Conflict in the Middle East,* Study No. 804011 (August 1980), 13.

[a]Don't know or no opinion.

[b]Neither and both.

Table 2–2
Israel's Favorability Ratings, 1967–77

Question

You will notice that the boxes on this card go from the highest position of plus 5—for someone or something you have a very favorable opinion of ["like much"—NORC]—all the way down to the lowest position of minus 5 for someone or something you have a very unfavorable opinion of ["dislike very much"—NORC]. How far up the scale or how far down the scale would you rate . . .

Country	*Gallup 1967*	*Gallup 1973*	*NORC 1974*	*NORC 1975*	*Gallup 1976*	*NORC 1977*
Israel	74%	N.A.	68%	62%	65%	63%
Egypt	39	38	48	44	49	51
England	85	82	85	84	87	81
Japan	72	70	70	66	75	62
USSR	19	34	N.A.	N.A.	21	31

Sources: The Gallup Poll: 1935–1971, Vol. 3, 2094; *1972–1977,* Vols. 1, 2, 129, 917; NORC: Lipset and Schneider, 42–43; *World Opinion Update* 1(September 1977).

allies of the Soviet Union, and their defeat was interpreted as a major blow to the Kremlin's prestige in the entire region. This blow was all the more important in view of the concomitant American failures in Vietnam and the psychological need for Americans to identify with a winning cause. It is no wonder that under these circumstances, Israel also enjoyed a high favorability rating in 1967. Table 2–2 shows that after the Six-Day War, Israel's favorability rating stood at 74 percent. It was the highest rate for Israel during the entire 1967–77 period. The Egyptian rating was only 39 percent, the second lowest recorded for Egypt during this period.

During the prewar crisis, the United States took action to avert war through a variety of means: presidential statements and warnings, action at the U.N. Security Council, coordination of efforts with allies, and bilateral contacts with Egypt and Israel. Unfortunately, America's efforts to defuse the crisis were unsuccessful, and when Israel was forced to initiate the attack, the United States accepted its reasoning. On the first day of the war, the spokesman for the State Department announced that the United States was "neutral in thought, word and deed."[21] President Johnson used the "hot line" and demanded from the Soviet Union complete neutrality.[22] At the United Nations, the United States worked for an immediate and unconditional cease-fire but was opposed by the Soviets, who insisted on an immediate evacuation of Israeli forces from the occupied Arab territories. On June 10, 1967, while the Israeli forces were advancing on the Golan Heights, the Kremlin threatened to intervene in the war. President Johnson warned against such a move and, to back up his words, ordered the Sixth Fleet to move closer to the Syrian coast.[23]

Table 2–3
Opinions on U.S. Policy in the Middle East, 1967–70 and 1975

Question

Have you heard or read about the troubles between Israel and the Arab nations in the Middle East? *If yes:* What would you like to see the U.S. government do about this situation? (Gallup)

Policy	*June 1967*	*June–July 1968*[a]	*Jan. 1969*	*Feb.–Mar. 1970*	*Jan. 1975*[b]
Stay out of conflict	41%	61%	52%	58%	55%
Support Israel (aid, etc.)	16	10	13	13	16
Support Israel (troops)	5	—[c]	1	1	2
Support Arab nations	—[c]	—[c]	1	1	—[c]
Work through U.N.	11	3	2	2	—[c]
Negotiate for peace	14	8	11	10	7
Don't know, other	13	20	20	15	29
Total	100	102[d]	100	100	109[d]

Source: The Gallup Poll, 1935–1971, Vol. 3, 2068, 2149, 2181, 2242; *1972–1977,* Vol. 1, 460.
[a]"In the event of a war . . ."
[b]"If a full-scale war were to start there . . ."
[c]Less than 0.5 percent.
[d]Adds up to more than 100 percent because of multiple responses.

President Johnson's management of the situation in the Middle East before and during the initial three days of the war was approved of by less than half of the American public. Between June 2 and 7, 1967, Gallup asked those who had "read or heard about the crisis in the Middle East" (59 percent of the national sample): "Do you approve or disapprove of the way President Johnson is handling the situation in the Middle East?" Forty-seven percent of the respondents approved, 14 percent disapproved, and 39 percent offered no opinion.[24] However, responses to specific questions provided a somewhat different picture.

In the same Gallup poll of June 2–7, the "aware" group was asked what the U.S. government should do about the situation in the Middle East. As revealed in table 2–3, 41 percent of the sample said the United States ought to stay out of the conflict, 25 percent thought the United States should help resolve the conflict on its own or through the United Nations, and 21 percent favored some type of support to Israel. On the day the war ended, Harris also asked a question about U.S. policy in the Middle East. He found that 77 percent of the respondents felt that the United States should work through the

United Nations.[25] Although this result differs from that of Gallup, it still indicates an aversion to direct, independent American involvement.

Thus, although less than half of the public approved of the handling of the 1967 crisis and war by Johnson, a greater percentage of respondents supported his basic approach. This apparent discrepancy could be attributed to the negative effects of the American failures in Vietnam on the general popularity of President Johnson. Although his handling of the situation in the Middle East was approved by a plurality of 47 to 14 percent, at the same time, his handling of the situation in Vietnam was disapproved by a majority of 52 to 33 percent.[26] It is possible, then, that the positive rating of Johnson's policy in the Middle East stood below 50 percent because of the highly negative rating of his performance in Vietnam.

Although the removal of UNEF forces, the deployment of a considerable number of Egyptian troops in the Sinai Desert, and the closure of the straits of Tiran were casus belli from the Israeli perspective, Israel held its fire until it was established that all other avenues for crisis resolution had been exhausted. The delay in the use of force against the Arabs proved beneficial, and Israel won the sympathy of U.S. and world public opinion. Most Americans were concerned about the fate of Israel and clearly cited the Arab nations as instigating the war.

Attitudes toward Postwar Diplomacy

The results of the Six-Day War created a new situation in the Arab-Israeli conflict. Israel's major military victory was expected to convince the Arabs that the conflict could not be resolved by force. In addition, the newly occupied territories were seen as providing Israel with assets for future negotiations. These assumptions also guided U.S. policy in the immediate postwar period. Unlike President Eisenhower, Johnson thought that any Israeli withdrawal from the occupied territories should be exchanged for just peace agreements. However, according to Foreign Minister Eban:

> President Johnson had let us know bluntly that the American attitude on withdrawal would be strongly influenced by the reaction of public opinion to Israel's case. If he were to hold firm against pressure for our withdrawal, he could only do so on the foundation of strong public support for Israel.[27]

On June 19, 1967, President Johnson addressed a national foreign policy conference of educators and declared that a return to the situation of June 4, 1967, as demanded by Arabs and the Soviets, was not "a prescription for peace but for renewed hostilities." He added:

> Certainly troops must be withdrawn, but there also must be recognized rights of national life, progress in solving the refugee problem, freedom of innocent maritime passage, limitation of the arms race and respect for political independence and territorial integrity.[28]

President Johnson argued that the "parties to the conflict must be the parties to the peace," and thus accepted the Israeli appeal for direct negotiations with the Arabs.

Congressional sentiment was in line with the president's basic approach. Several days after the war, the Associated Press sent all U.S. senators and members of Congress a questionnaire on the Middle East crisis. Of the 438 legislators who answered the questionnaire, 364 (42 senators and 322 representatives) expressed the unqualified opinion that Israel should get assurances for its national security and access to the Suez Canal and the Gulf of Aqaba-Eilat before withdrawing troops from the captured Arab territories.[29] Forty-one of the remaining members gave qualified answers, and 33 declined to offer any view.

The American media and U.S. public opinion shared the presidential and congressional views on the necessary linkage between Israeli withdrawal and resolution of the Arab-Israeli conflict. Trice found in his study that the elite press editorials substantially supported the Israeli policy on peace talks and national boundaries.[30] A Harris poll of July 10, 1967, found that 62 percent disagreed with the following statement: "Israel should withdraw all its forces from Arab territory before the other issues can be settled."[31] The public also agreed with other official Israeli and American positions on the ways and means to resolve the conflict.

A Gallup poll of June 22–27, 1967, found that 57 percent of a national sample thought that the Israelis and the Arabs ought to work out their own formula for peace, and 36 percent felt that the United Nations should have a final say in the peace plans.[32] A Harris poll of July 10, 1967, revealed that an overwhelming majority (87 percent) agreed with the statement: "The Arabs and Israel should work out a peaceful settlement without interference." The same Harris poll revealed substantial support for the Israeli peace conditions. Eighty-eight percent agreed that "Israel should be guaranteed the right to send ships through the Gulf of Aqaba"; 86 percent agreed that "Israel should be given the right to use the Suez Canal"; and 82 percent thought that "Israel should be recognized as a state by the Arab nations." These results indicate that American public opinion fully supported the American and Israeli approach to a process of potential conflict resolution.

Jerusalem has always occupied a central, emotional place in Judaism. From 1948 to the Six-Day War, the city was divided, with the eastern side occupied by Jordan. In violation of the 1949 ceasefire agreement, Jordan denied the Jews access to their holiest site—the western wall of the ancient temple.[33] During the Six-Day War, Israel unified East and West Jerusalem and, on June 28, 1967, announced the creation of a "unified administration" for the entire city. Israel also declared that in any future negotiations, it would insist on keeping the city unified under its control. After the Six-Day War, the issue of Jerusalem was brought before the United Nations, where the United States abstained on resolutions that condemned the Israeli unification of the city. The United States did, however, register opposition to any unilateral Israeli changes in the status of Jerusalem and its vicinity.[34] According to Trice, editorials in the elite press were also critical of the Israeli actions in Jerusalem.

A Harris poll of July 10, 1967, included the following question on the status of Jerusalem:

> [As you know], Israel has occupied all of Jerusalem but has opened the city to all people who want to visit there, including all the religious shrines. Do you think Israel should be allowed to keep Jerusalem, or do you think the city should become an international city?

Seventy percent of the national sample favored internationalization, while only 10 percent supported the Israeli claim to the city.[35] However, several months later, in September 1967, the same question was repeated, and this time the results differed greatly. The number of respondents who advocated internationalization dropped from 70 to 33 percent, while the number of those who supported Israeli control over the city rose from 10 to 43 percent.[36] It is possible that immediately after the war, the public did not realize the meaning of "internationalization" and was later influenced by the Israeli arguments for keeping the city.[37]

All hopes for a quick breakthrough in the Arab-Israeli conflict faded away two months after the war. A conference of Arab heads of state, convening in Khartoum, Sudan, at the end of August 1967, decided to coordinate diplomatic and military moves to eliminate what they called the "consequences of aggression." The Khartoum summit conference also adopted the formula: "No peace with Israel, no negotiations with Israel, no recognition of Israel, and maintenance of the rights of the Palestinian people in their nation."[38] Yet on November 22, 1967, the U.N. Security Council unanimously adopted Resolution 242, which outlined principles for a possible process of conflict resolution. This resolution called for the establishment of an Arab-Israeli peace in return for Israeli withdrawal from Arab territories captured in the Six-Day War. It also provided for the appointment of a special United Nations mediator to help the parties negotiate on the basis of Resolution 242.[39] A Swedish diplomat, Gunnar Jarring, was selected by the Security Council to serve as special mediator.

Resolution 242 later became a springboard for all peacemaking initiatives. Still, it was recognized only by Israel and two Arab countries—Egypt and

Jordan. Furthermore, Israel and the Arab nations interpreted the resolution in conflicting manners.[40] Since 1968 was an election year in the United States, this also delayed the rapid implementation of Resolution 242. According to a Gallup poll of June–July 1968, the American public expressed skepticism toward the peace prospects for the Arab-Israeli conflict. When asked whether "full-scale war between the Israelis and the Arabs is likely to occur during the next five years," 62 percent said that such a war was likely, while only 13 percent felt it was unlikely.[41] This finding is remarkable, not only because it accurately predicted the future, but also because it was markedly different from results obtained on a similar issue just one year earlier. At that time, immediately after the Six-Day War (June 22–27, 1969), 70 percent of the national sample thought "a peaceful settlement of the differences between Israel and the Arab countries can be worked out," and only 21 percent held the opposite view.[42] Thus, despite the general view of the Middle East as a region in which war between Israel and the Arab states might break out at any time, following the Six-Day War the issue in the polls was peace, and the public was optimistic about its chances. One year later, with nary a peace settlement in sight, the public was asked about the chances for war (rather than peace) and was considerably pessimistic. The contrast between responses to the two surveys, then, is explained by the historical context that affected the biases of both the questions and the respondents.

In 1968, the trend opposing U.S. involvement in the Arab-Israeli conflict continued. Table 2–3 shows that 61 percent of the respondents to a Gallup poll preferred the United States to stay out of the Middle East "in the event of a war." Only 11 percent thought that in such a case the United States should work for peace on its own (8 percent) or through the United Nations (3 percent). The tendency to avoid involvement in the conflict was also reflected in responses to several separate questions on sending arms or troops to Israel or the Arabs in case of renewed warfare. (A comprehensive analysis of opinion data on the issue of U.S. aid to Middle Eastern countries is presented in chapter 6.) Some opposition to American involvement in the Middle East during this period was identified in elite American newspapers by Charles H. Wagner.[43] He attributed this opposition to the negative effects of the war in Vietnam, which led to strong reservations about any American involvement abroad, even nonmilitary involvement.

Effects of the War of Attrition

Richard M. Nixon won the 1968 presidential election and almost immediately adopted a new policy on the Arab-Israeli conflict. In his first press conference at the White House he announced:

> I believe we need new initiatives and new leadership on the part of the United States in order to cool off the situation in the Mideast. I consider it a powder keg, very explosive. It needs to be defused.[44]

The new initiatives included bilateral talks with the Soviet Union and the parties involved and action at the United Nations. These efforts were not successful, though, and a new round of limited warfare began.[45]

In April 1969, Nasser broke the cease-fire along the Suez Canal and initiated a war of attrition against Israel. He wished to exploit two major Israeli weaknesses: high sensitivity to casualties and static warfare. The Israeli army is designed to achieve a quick, decisive victory through constant movement and maneuvers. A static war nullified its main advantages over the Arab armies. Israel responded to Nasser's massive use of artillery by air strikes deep inside Egypt.[46] In return, Nasser called upon the Kremlin to supply him with additional modern weapons, and Soviet personnel. The Soviet Union responded favorably to the Egyptian request and became directly involved in the war.[47]

The events leading to the outbreak of the War of Attrition and the heavy Soviet involvement on behalf of Egypt increased criticism of the Arabs in the American media. Figure 2–1 reveals that at the beginning of 1969, the number of pro-Israeli editorials in the prestige press considerably surpassed the number of neutral editorials, reaching a record of 50 percent. However, as the war dragged on without an end in sight, the number of pro-Israeli editorials sharply declined. The pro-Arab editorials also declined, but by a lower ratio.

Prior to the outbreak of the War of Attrition, Gallup found that half of the public sympathized more with Israel and only 5 percent sympathized more with the Arabs (see table 2–1). During the War of Attrition, both sides lost points—Israel 6 percentage points, the Arabs 2. However, the sympathy figure for the Arabs, 3 percent, was the lowest ever recorded for them, and the ratio between the two sides was almost 15 to 1 in favor of Israel. In comparison, in February 1969, the equivalent ratio was 10 to 1, and during the Six-Day War, 14 to 1. In February–March 1970, the American public continued to oppose U.S. involvement in the Middle East. Fifty-eight percent advocated that the United States stay out of the region; 14 percent supported aid to Israel; and 12 percent thought that the United States should help negotiate for peace on its own or through the United Nations (see table 2–3).

The issue of American aid to Israel became critical during the War of Attrition because Israel lost equipment, particularly combat aircraft. In view of the developments in the Middle East and the war, Nixon promised in January 1970 to consider Israel's request for 25 Phantom and 100 Skyhawk combat planes, but on March 23, Secretary of State William Rogers announced that the president had decided to delay action on the Israeli request.[48] Congress, however, opposed this decision and, in May, issued a declaration signed by 70 senators and 280 representatives that included criticism of the Nixon policy on military aid to Israel:

> It would not be in the interest of the United States or in the service of world peace if Israel were left defenseless in face of the continuing flow of sophisticated offensive armaments to the Arab nations.[49]

The White House could not ignore the congressional attitude but sought to delay the weapon supplies in hope of encouraging both sides to conclude a cease-fire. The war inflicted heavy damage on both Egypt and Israel, motivating both sides to look for reasonable ways to end it. Secretary of State Rogers sensed this possibility and submitted to Israel and Egypt a draft proposal for a cease-fire.[50] After deliberations and consultations, Nasser and the new Israeli prime minister, Golda Meir, accepted the American proposal. This proposal was unique in that it provided for "standstill" zones close to the Suez Canal, in which movement of weapons was not allowed. Israel insisted on this clause because, in case of renewed hostilities, Egyptian deployment of ground-to-air missiles closer to the canal would have seriously limited the ability of the Israeli air force to knock out the Egyptian artillery. The cease-fire–standstill agreement commenced August 7, 1970.[51] However, Egypt violated the standstill provision in less than 12 hours by moving missiles into the forbidden zones.[52] This violation was critical to the next attempts at conflict resolution, since Israel lost trust in Egypt, an essential for any further progress.

The Egyptian violation of the cease-fire agreement caused a general quarrel between Jerusalem and Washington. The United States mediated the agreement and Israel naturally complained to Washington about the violation. Initially, the United States did not confirm the Israeli allegation, but when presented with clear evidence, it accepted the Israeli complaint; yet it did very little to rectify the violation. Nixon was concerned about renewed hostilities. On August 17, 1970, he met with the Israeli ambassador to Washington and later recalled:

> I pointed out that American public opinion would be very important if another war began in the Middle East. This was why I wanted America to be the prime mover of a cease-fire proposal, and why I wanted Israel to be scrupulously careful in observing it. "If our peace initiative fails, everyone should be able to recognize who is at fault," I said, "and I hope that it will not be Israel."[53]

The end of the War of Attrition led to an internal crisis in Jordan. Various Palestinian factions wished to continue the war and feared the new cease-fire might be a possible step toward a comprehensive Israeli-Arab peace agreement. They therefore decided to conduct a spectacular act of terrorism to protest the termination of the war and to warn Arab countries, especially Jordan, against any conciliation with Israel. On September 12, 1970, Palestinian terrorists hijacked three passenger planes to Jordan and destroyed them. King Hussein, already concerned about growing Palestinian autonomous behavior inside his kingdom, ordered his armed forces to destroy the semi-independent Palestinian bases in Jordan. This operation was successful, and many leaders and members of Palestinian organizations were killed and wounded or expelled from Jordan.[54] During the crisis, which the Palestinians called "Black September", Syria partially intervened in the war, and Hussein asked for American and Israeli assistance. Israel responded favorably, which contributed to the Syrian retreat.[55] The United States and Israel shared an important strategic interest in the crisis and demonstrated considerable ability to cooperate in an effort to protect Western interests in the region.[56]

President Nasser helped negotiate an end to the Jordanian-Palestinian feud, but on September 28, 1970, he died of a heart attack. He was succeeded by Anwar Sadat, seen by many as only an interim leader who would soon be replaced by a greater and more persuasive politician. The end of the War of Attrition and the Jordanian crisis reduced the tension in the Middle East and moved it lower on the list of the American priorities in world affairs. The Nixon administration embarked on ambitious breakthroughs with the Soviet Union on détente and nuclear arms control and with China on recognition and cooperation. It was also involved in an effort to end U.S. involvement in Southeast Asia. From the end of the War of Attrition until the surprise Arab attack on Israel in October 1973 (the Yom Kippur War), Israel and the Arab-Israeli conflict were of little interest to American pollsters. Of the few polls taken in this period, those of Harris, which examined American sympathies for Israel and the Arabs, indicate a stable trend in favor of Israel by an average ratio of seven to one (see table 2–1).

The Yom Kippur War and the Oil Embargo

In 1972, President Anwar Sadat eliminated his major opponents and established himself as the undisputed leader of Egypt. He warned several times that Egypt would not tolerate the "no war-no peace situation," and it would use force if Israel did not unconditionally withdraw from occupied territories. On several occasions, he declared 1972–73 as "a year of decision," but his threats were accorded little credibility in Israel and the United States.[57] Israel calculated that Sadat would not initiate a full-scale war in 1972 or 1973 because of Israel's air superiority.[58] This estimate was based on the rational assumption that states do not initiate wars unless they are fully confident of a decisive victory. Winning an Arab-Israeli war, however, had become a very elusive proposition. Israel decisively won the wars of 1956 and 1967 but was unable to convert its military victories into political gains. Sadat calculated that starting a war and capturing some territory in the Sinai Peninsula would be sufficient to allow him to negotiate with Israel from a more "equal position."[59]

At the beginning of October 1973, Egypt and Syria assembled substantial forces along their borders with Israel. Several months earlier, in May, they had taken a similar action. At that time, Israel had mobilized its forces and the Arabs had dispersed. Israeli military intelligence determined in May that the Egyptian and Syrian troops were called for maneuvers and that these countries had no intention of starting a war with Israel. An identical evaluation of the troops' concentration in October was presented to the Israeli government and to the United States. Both estimates were wrong. In May 1973, Egypt and Syria intended to attack Israel, but following a Soviet veto, they retracted at the last moment. Brezhnev was scheduled to visit Washington to reap the fruits of détente. He did not wish any Middle East war to endanger his promising prospects, but the visit disappointed Brezhnev, and in September he removed his veto over the Arab plan to wage war on Israel.

In the early morning of October 6, Israeli intelligence reversed its previous estimates and determined that on that day, Yom Kippur, the holiest day in the Jewish calendar, Egypt and Syria would commence a war.[60] Israeli Chief of Staff David Elazar requested authorization for a preemptive air strike, but Prime Minister Meir and Minister of Defense Dayan denied this request. Meir told Elazar:

> We don't know now, any of us, what the future will hold, but there is always the possibility that we will need help, and if we strike first, we will get nothing from anyone.[61]

The same thoughts occurred to Kissinger. During the months preceding the war, he had repeatedly warned Israel to avoid a preemptive strike at all costs:

> If you fire the first shot you won't have a dogcatcher in this country supporting you. You won't have presidential support. You'll be alone, all alone. We wouldn't be able to help you. Don't preempt.[62]

Kissinger told Israeli charge d'affairs in Washington Mordechai Shalev and U.S. ambassador to Israel Kenneth Keating to clarify this position to the Israeli government, but as mentioned earlier, Meir had already anticipated the possible adverse repercussions of a preemptive strike and had decided against it. Thus, the need to convince the American public that the Arabs started the war prohibited any Israeli military move prior to the Arab attack.

On October 6, 1973, at noon, Egypt launched a massive surprise attack across the Suez Canal on the Israeli positions. Simultaneously, Syria attacked the Israeli forces on the Golan Heights. The war lasted about three weeks and ended on October 25.[63] After suffering initial losses in the Sinai Peninsula and the Golan Heights, the IDF regrouped, moved across the canal, captured Egyptian territory, trapped the Egyptian Third Army and reached a point just 60 miles from Cairo. On the Golan Heights, Israel drove back the Syrian forces and captured additional territory. However, the war was very costly to Israel in human lives and material, and it was interpreted by the Arabs as a victory for their side.[64]

The Yom Kippur War was dangerous to world peace because it drew the United States and the Soviet Union close to a direct conflict.[65] First, on October 10, the Soviet Union began a massive airlift of weapons and equipment to Egypt and Syria. On October 13, the United States responded with a similar airlift to Israel. Later, between October 22 and 24, Israel and Egypt failed to implement the cease-fire agreement. Sadat blamed Israel for this failure and called on the superpowers to directly impose the cease-fire. Apparently, the Soviet Union alerted airborne troops, moved nuclear weapons to the Mediterranean, and took other actions interpreted by American policymakers as leading to a possible direct intervention in the war. The United States reacted by placing its own troops and nuclear forces on a precautionary alert.[66] Fortunately, the Soviets did not intervene and the alerts were quickly called off, but at no other time in the history of the Arab-Israeli conflict were the two superpowers so close to a direct engagement in a highly tense situation.

Another significant aspect of the Yom Kippur War was the acceleration of the energy crisis. Contrary to popular belief, this crisis did not begin with the war.[67] Two years earlier, oil prices had begun to rise, and talk of an energy crisis was heard frequently during the summer of 1973. Prior to the war, Sadat had communicated with King Feisal of Saudi Arabia on the possibility of using an oil embargo to turn the entire West, particularly the United States, against Israel.[68] This plan was activated during the war. The embargo and the mismanagement of the oil market by American oil companies created long lines at American gas stations and substantially increased oil prices.

The war caught the U.S. presidency in a serious crisis. Vice-President Spiro T. Agnew had resigned on October 10, following a plea of no-contest to a tax-evasion charge. President Nixon was troubled by the Watergate scandal. The court of appeals ruled that he turn over his Watergate tapes for inspection, and on October 19, his counsel, John W. Dean, pleaded guilty to charges of covering up the truth about the Watergate break-in. Under these circumstances, Secretary of State Kissinger assumed the setting of U.S. policy on the war. He did not make many public announcements, other than calling on the parties to halt the war and on the Kremlin to cooperate with the United States to stop the warfare.

The Soviets would not cooperate. On the contrary, they commenced a massive sea- and airlift of weapons to Egypt and Syria. Israel asked the United States to respond with a similar airlift. Nixon approved the request, but execution was delayed. Kissinger blamed Secretary of Defense James Schlesinger for the delay, but Schlesinger argued that the United States must maintain a low profile to avoid a negative Arab backlash.[69] Israeli ambassador to the United States Simcha Dinitz finally lost his patience and threatened to seek public support for Israel's urgent arms needs. According to Marvin and Bernard Kalb, this threat was highly credible. They quoted a National Security Council insider:

> The Congress was behind the Israelis. The press was behind them. And to judge from the polls, the public was behind them. If the Israelis had gone public at that time, it could have been the end of the Nixon administration.[70]

This assessment finally moved Kissinger and Schlesinger to end their bureaucratic infighting and start the U.S. airlift to Israel.

The Battle for Public Opinion

The surprise attack, oil embargo, and superpower involvement all contributed to substantial coverage of the Yom Kippur War and its effects by the American media. Between October 8 and November 8, the three major television networks—ABC, CBS, and NBC—aired about 230 reports.[71] It should be noted that most of the coverage, both live reports from the battlefields and countries involved and commentaries, were balanced. Gordon even claimed that CBS "kept the balance in reporting from the war fronts and often neglected good journalistic practice for the sake of balance." It is also interesting that most television coverage of the war concentrated heavily on the battlefield drama and very little on the lives and feelings of the affected civilian population. Of the 230 reports, no more than four dealt with the civilians of either side.

The print media, especially the prestige press, also devoted considerable space to the war. According to one study, the *New York Times* published 259 news articles, the *Washington Post* 373, and the *Detroit Free Press* 146.[72] Most of the articles and editorials were neutral, although some features and cartoons were more pro-Israeli. Figure 2–1 also demonstrates that during the war, 80 percent of the elite press editorials remained neutral; almost none were pro-Arab, and about 20 percent were pro-Israel. All evidence on the media's attitude toward the war—electronic and print—demonstrates that coverage was mainly neutral and balanced.

American sympathy during and immediately after the war was highly in favor of Israel (see table 2–1). During the first days of the war, Americans sympathized more with Israel by a majority of 47 to 6 percent. Toward the end of the war, this majority grew to 48 versus 6 percent and several weeks later stood at 50 to 7 percent. However, compared to the ratio of the Six-Day War and the War of Attrition, 14 to 1, Americans sympathized more with Israel throughout the Yom Kippur War by a ratio of only eight or seven to one (see table 2–1).

Part of the unfaltering public support for Israel during the Yom Kippur War was probably related to the surprise element. From the time of the Japanese surprise attack on Pearl Harbor in 1941, many Americans have been very sensitive to this type of war initiation and have perceived it in a negative light.[73] The fact that Egypt and Syria selected Yom Kippur as the particular day for their surprise attack might also have contributed to the lack of sympathy toward the Arabs.

Beyond the general emotional element, Americans did not accept the Arab explanation for the attack on Israel. Shortly after the war, Harris found that only about a quarter of the respondents agreed with the Arab argument that they were "justified in fighting this war to try to get back the territory Israel has occupied since 1967."[74] Half of the respondents disagreed with the Arab argument. In response to another question—who is more right, the Arabs or Israel—39 versus 6 percent said that Israel was more right.[75] However, the most interesting effects of the war on American public opinion are found in responses to queries concerning the energy crisis. This was the issue that directly affected the pocketbooks and daily lives of every American.

The public apparently recognized the existence of the energy crisis before the Yom Kippur War. The issue appeared for the first time on the Gallup list of the most important problems facing the United States in May 1973.[76] A month later, 83 percent of a national sample said it had heard or read about the energy crisis. Shortly after the war, the energy crisis climbed to the first place on the list of important issues.[77] The energy crisis caught the American economy unprepared and confused. The Arabs had conspired to use the oil embargo to make the crisis even worse and, by doing so, sought to swing American policy and public opinion to their side and away from Israel.[78] The Arabs' basic assumption was that if presented with a choice between "hard interest"—oil—and "soft interest"—Israel—most Americans would choose oil and would even blame Israel for the crisis.

The Arab position on the link between Israel and the energy crisis was represented by a full-page advertisement that appeared in the *Wall Street Journal* March 14, 1974, titled, "Do Arms for Israel Mean No Gasoline for Americans?" The ad was placed by Alfred M. Lilienthal, a well-known anti-Zionist and anti-Israeli Jew, who at the time served as president of the pro-Arab Middle East Perspective, Incorporated. The ad stated, among other things:

> The simple inescapable fact is that today we would have all the gasoline we need for our cars, all the heat for our homes, all the oil for our industrial machinery—and would not be threatened with a serious recession—were it not for our "Israel-First Policy," which has brought us into a virtual war with the Arab world.

The ad also attributed the energy crisis to the Jewish lobby in Washington.

It is perhaps surprising that similar views were expressed by General George Brown, chairman of the Joint Chiefs of Staff. On October 10, 1974, he said in an informal talk at Duke University Law School that if Americans suffered enough because of the energy shortage, "they might get tough-minded enough to stop the Jewish influence in this country and break that [Jewish] lobby."[79] This remark clearly implied that the Jewish lobby in the United States, and presumably Israel, was mainly responsible for the energy crisis. General Brown also made a typical anti-Semitic slur by repeating the false accusation that Jews owned the banks and media in America and used this power only for their own sectarian benefit.

Brown's remarks raised considerable controversy at the time and were severely criticized by members of Congress and the American-Jewish community. The public also rejected them. Several weeks after the general's remarks became public, Harris found that 47 versus 22 percent of the non-Jewish national sample rejected the statement that linked Israel and the Jewish lobby to the oil shortage.[80] Thus, only about a fifth of the non-Jewish public agreed with Brown, despite his prestigious and authoritative position as chief of staff.

Further data on public attitudes toward the energy crisis indicate an even stronger rejection of Brown's arguments. Gallup queried between December 7 and 10, 1973, "Who or what do you think is responsible for the energy crisis?" The public blamed, in descending order of importance, the following groups: oil companies (25 percent), the federal government (23 percent), the Nixon administration (19 percent), American consumers (16 percent), Arab nations (7 percent), United States exporting too much oil (3 percent), ecologists (2 percent), and Israelis (less than 1 percent).[81] In April 1974, Yankelovich asked a national sample, "Do you feel any of the following groups are responsible at all for the present gasoline and fuel shortage?" By far the largest percentage (70 percent) held the oil companies "mainly responsible" for the oil shortage.[82] Arab nations were held mainly responsible by 28 percent and "partially responsible" by 49 percent. The next place on the list was occupied by the president, who was held mainly responsible by 22 percent and partially responsible by 48 percent. Israel was sandwiched between the president and the Congress and was held mainly responsible by only 10 percent and partially responsible by 42 percent.

At the end of 1973 and during 1974, Harris found that three out of four Americans blamed the oil shortage on the Arab embargo, and two out of three blamed the Arab embargo for the rise in oil prices.[83] In the winter of 1973–74, Harris discovered that 76 percent of the American public singled out "foreign oil-producing countries" as the leading cause of inflation, and 63 percent held "Arab oil producers responsible for the recession." In another Harris poll of October 1974, 64 percent said that Arab oil-producing countries were the major cause of inflation.

Although the public held the Arabs more responsible for the energy crisis than Israel, the question remains whether the oil embargo and the crisis affected attitudes toward Israel. Table 2–4 shows that responses to questions that pitted support and aid to Israel directly against Arab oil favored Israel by larger margins and ratios. From 1973 until 1980, the statement in question (a) was rejected by an average majority of 61 to 26 percent, and the statement in question (b), which specifically singled out military aid, was rejected by an average majority of 60 to 25 percent.

During the years of the energy crisis, several Arab countries, especially Saudi Arabia, hinted that if the United States were to become less pro-Israel and more pro-Arab in its policy on the Arab-Israeli conflict and the Middle East, they would be much more flexible and considerate in oil-pricing decisions.[84] Responses to question (c) in table 2–4 reveal that the public would not have approved of such a trade. No country likes blackmail, and the United States is no exception. Question (c) included a connotation of blackmail, which could explain the large margin; yet compatible results were found in responses to a less biased question.

In January 1975, Gallup found little support in American public opinion for accommodation with the Arabs on their terms. He asked, "If the Arab nations impose another oil embargo on the U.S., what policy do you think the U.S. should follow?" The highest number of respondents (35 percent) favored self-sufficiency, 24 percent wished the United States to retaliate with economic sanctions, and 10 percent even called for military intervention. Only 4 percent supported negotiations with the Arabs, and 2 percent would have liked the United States to have met the Arab demands and conditions.[85]

On the eve of the Yom Kippur War, considerations of U.S. public opinion affected a major Israeli military decision. Because of these considerations, Israel refrained from a preemptive strike when it learned that the Arab attack was imminent. The Yom Kippur War and the energy crisis brought the realities of the Arab-Israeli conflict to the fore of American public opinion. Opinion data reveal that Americans sympathized more with Israel and rejected the Arab explanation for its resort to force. According to several polls, the Arab oil embargo did not hurt Israel's standing and did not improve the Arab image in

Table 2–4
Attitudes toward Arab Oil, Israel, and American Foreign Policy, 1973–80

Question

(a) We need Arab oil for our gasoline shortage here at home, so we had better find ways to get along with the Arabs, even if this means supporting Israel less. (Harris)

Date	*Agree*	*Disagree*	*Not Sure*
Oct. '73	26%	50%	24%
Jan. '74	23	61	16
Dec. '74	20	68	12
Mar. '75	26	61	13
Jan. '76	23	65	12
Jan. '77	24	60	16
Mar. '79	39	55	6
Oct. '79	33	60	7
July '80	22	69	9

Question

(b) Now, if it came down to it and the only way we could get Arab oil in enough quantity would be to stop supporting Israel with military aid, would you favor or oppose such a move by this country? (Harris)

Date	*Agree*	*Disagree*	*Not Sure*
Dec. '74	18%	64%	18%
Mar. '75	23	55	22
Jan. '76	20	61	19
Mar. '79	31	57	12
Oct. '79	29	60	11
July '80	19	63	18

Question

(c) If we yield to Arab restrictions over oil, we will soon find the Arabs dictating much of U.S. foreign policy, and that is wrong. (Harris)

Date	*Agree*	*Disagree*	*Not Sure*
Oct. '73	58%	20%	22%
Dec. '74	76	13	11
Mar. '75	79	11	10
Jan. '76	77	13	10
Mar. '79	74	21	5
Oct. '79	79	18	3
July '80	82	11	7

Sources: Index to International Public Opinion, 1979–80, 94; *ABC News–Harris Survey*, Vol. 1, No. 137, November 6, 1979; and Louis Harris and Associates, Study No. 804011 (August 1980).

American pubic opinion.[86] The evidence suggests that if any change occurred, it was negative. It also suggests that if the Arabs wanted to convey a message to the American public that its real interests were with them, they failed.[87]

Evaluations of American Mediation

Following the Yom Kippur War, the United States found itself in an excellent diplomatic position in the Middle East. Both Egypt and Israel were prepared to engage in serious negotiations for peace. Egypt discovered that even under the best of circumstances—surprise attack and oil embargo—Israel could not be subdued. Israel found that wars could be very costly and that more efforts should be made to resolve the Arab-Israeli conflict by peaceful means. After the war, Egypt trusted the United States and expected it to assume a mediating role in the conflict.

In November 1973, Secretary of State Kissinger proposed an international conference to discuss the Arab-Israeli conflict. The conference convened the following month in Geneva, under the auspices of the two superpowers and the United Nations.[88] Israel attended the meeting, but only Egypt and Jordan participated on the Arab side. Kissinger did not see the large forum as an effective arena in which to negotiate peace agreements, but he wished to neutralize potential Soviet obstructions. The convening of the conference and the granting of ostensibly equal status to the Soviets in the peacemaking process were designed to achieve this purpose. Indeed, the real negotiations were conducted exclusively under American auspices.

In January 1974, Henry Kissinger mediated an agreement between Israel and Egypt to disengage their forces along the Suez Canal.[89] This agreement was seen by both sides as a first, vital step on the long road to peace. It also led to the lifting of the Arab oil embargo on the United States and the restoration of full diplomatic relations between the United States and Egypt. A similar disengagement agreement was concluded in May 1974, by Israel and Syria.[90] To capitalize on this newly acquired American diplomatic strength in the Middle East, and perhaps to alleviate some of the Watergate pressure, President Nixon made an official visit to the Middle East. From June 12 to 18, 1974, he visited Egypt, Saudi Arabia, Israel, and Jordan. The visit not only afforded Nixon some prestige, it also produced a few tangible results, including the reestablishment of U.S. diplomatic relations with Syria. Israeli concerns over the tightening American-Arab relations were somewhat mitigated by Nixon's statement during his visit to Israel: "Under no circumstances does the fact that the United States is seeking better relations with some of Israel's neighbors mean that the friendship of the United States and the support for Israel is any less."[91]

Polls on the degree of sympathy in American public opinion for Israel and the Arabs were taken only toward the end of 1974. They demonstrated, in

October 1974, a pro-Israeli margin of 55 to 9 percent. Harris found, in his December 1974 to January 1975 survey, a similar ratio of 52 to 7 percent in favor of Israel. Harris also found a higher ratio of sympathy (56 to 5 percent) among a national leadership group drawn from government and political, business, labor, communications, education, religious, and voluntary organizations. In January 1975, Gallup found a ratio of only 44 to 8 percent in favor of Israel. Although his figures for the Arab side were similar to those of Yankelovich and Harris, those for Israel were lower by 8 to 11 percentage points. This difference could have been the result of the Gallup screening and the differences in the wording of questions.

On the favorability index (table 2–2), Israel's score in 1974 was down 6 percent in comparison to the 1967 record, but the Egyptian rate rose 9 percent in comparison to the 1967 figure and 10 percent in comparison to the pre–Yom Kippur War rating. The rise in the Egyptian score was probably related to the reorientation of Egypt from close ties with the Soviet Union to close ties with the United States and the new peace prospects opened by the disengagement agreement. Even so, on the list of countries in table 2–2, the Egyptian favorability rating was the lowest, far behind those of Israel and Japan.

Secretary of State Henry Kissinger believed that the Arab-Israeli conflict could be resolved only in stages—step by step.[92] He felt that the disengagement agreements, which dealt primarily with pressing military issues, should be followed by a series of agreements on selected political issues. Like Egypt and Syria, Jordan was now interested in a disengagement agreement with Israel on the West Bank, but Israeli reluctance to negotiate such an agreement, plus the Rabat Arab summit decision (October 28, 1974) to appoint the Palestine Liberation Organization (PLO) as the sole representative of the Palestinians, stripped Jordan of the mandate to negotiate on the West Bank.[93] Under these circumstances, Kissinger sought another possible agreement between Israel and Egypt.

In January 1975, half of a national sample felt that the United States should stay out of the Arab-Israeli conflict, and only 7 percent thought that the United States should negotiate for peace in the Middle East (see table 2–3). But Henry Kissinger thought otherwise and revived his "shuttle diplomacy." In a few weeks, he learned that the differences between the two sides were too wide; consequently, in March 1975, he was forced to terminate his mission. Kissinger implied that his failure was primarily caused by Israeli intransigence, and he persuaded President Gerald Ford to announce a reassessment of United States policy in the Middle East.[94] This "reassessment" was, in reality, a code word for pressure on Israel.[95] For approximately six months, from March to September, the United States delayed its new arms deal with Israel. President Ford recalled: "Since Kissinger's unsuccessful mission to the Middle East in March, we had been engaged in a war of nerves with Israel."[96] The public and Congress played a significant role in this "war." In June 1975, the new Israeli Prime Minister Rabin paid an official visit to Washington and held talks with Ford and Kissinger. He presented a few new ideas, but Kissinger did not feel that they were sufficient to produce an agreement. On June 13, President Ford called Rabin at his hotel in New York:

> Henry [Kissinger] came to my office and we went over the subjects you discussed. I must tell you, in all frankness, that you have not moved far enough to make me feel that we have indeed made any progress toward an agreement. I am disappointed, and I am concerned about *Israel's image in the eyes of the American people.*[97] (emphasis added)

Was Ford's concern justified? The public disagreed with Kissinger's accusation that Israel had quashed the possibilities of an interim agreement. The Congress also strongly opposed the policy of reassessment. According to a Gallup poll of April 4–7, 1975, Americans who had heard or read about Kissinger's failure to achieve a settlement between Israel and Egypt (79 percent of the sample) tended to blame, in descending order of importance: the Arab states and Israel (26 percent); no one, nothing in particular (8 percent); Arab states (8 percent); Israel (5 percent); Kissinger (5 percent); and the United States (5 percent).[98] These results do not indicate any particular assignment of blame to Israel for Kissinger's failure to achieve an agreement between Israel and Egypt. In fact, more Americans held the Arabs responsible for the suspension of the talks, and the percentage that held Israel responsible was identical to the one that blamed Kissinger.

Congress strongly objected to the reassessment policy. On May 21, 1975, President Ford received a letter signed by 76 senators. The senators expressed regret over the suspension of the talks between Israel and Egypt but emphasized that "withholding military equipment from Israel would be dangerous, discouraging accommodation by Israel's neighbors and encouraging a resort to force." The letter concluded with the following statement:

> We urge you to make it clear, as we do, that the United States acting in its own national interests stands firmly with Israel in the search for peace in future negotiations, and that this premise is the basis of the current reassessment of United States policy in the Middle East.[99]

Although the Congress continued to support Israel in face of criticism and sanctions by the Ford administration, the media tended to side with the White House. As figure 2–1 reveals, in 1974 and 1975, elite press editorials grew much less supportive of both Israel and the Arabs, but the decline in the number of pro-Israeli editorials was much sharper. A record of sorts was registered at the end of 1975, when all editorials were neither pro-Arab nor pro-Israeli. The study by Janice M. Belkaoui also identifies a change in the images of Israel and Arabs in the prestige press. According to Belkaoui, after the Yom Kippur War, the Arab image in the prestige press grew more positive and that of Israel more negative. She attributes these changes to the influence of corporate oil interests on the press.[100]

During the period of reassessment Americans were not asked directly for their opinions on this policy, but in August 1975, the Patrick Caddell poll found 42 to 26 percent concurring with the statement that "America's support of Israel in the Middle East is the proper policy and should be continued." In the fall of 1974, a plurality of 44 to 26 percent agreed with the same statement.[101] However, it appears that the cue word in this statement, "proper policy," could have led to the positive response.

The sympathy index indicates some erosion in general American attitudes toward Israel following the announcement on reassessment. A poll conducted by Gallup in April 1975 revealed a drop of 7 percent in the rate of sympathy for Israel compared to his previous poll of January 1975 (see table 2–1). The Arabs, however, did not pick up those percentage points; their rate remained the same. Unlike Gallup, Roper found, in his April 1975 poll, very little change in the distribution of American sympathy for Israelis and Arabs—43 versus 7 percent, compared to 41 versus 6 percent in the previous poll. The favorability index reveals some decline between 1974 and 1975 in both the Israeli and Egyptian ratings. Israel lost six percentage points and Egypt lost four. This result correlates with the Gallup finding of April 1975, in which the highest number of respondents blamed both Egypt and Israel for Kissinger's failure to mediate an agreement between them.

Moving again from Israel and Egypt to the more general context of Israel and the Arabs, even during the reassessment period, Americans tended to blame the Arabs more than Israel for the conflict. Caddell found in August 1975 that Americans held the Arab states more responsible than Israel for the "continuing crisis in the Middle East" by a ratio of three to one (33 versus 10 percent).[102] At about the same time, Yankelovich identified even more negative judgments of Arab attitudes toward peace. He asked: "In the current situation, do you feel that the Arab nations are really interested in making peace with Israel, or do you feel that they are not interested in making peace, but rather in destroying Israel?" Less than a fifth of the sample (17 percent) thought that the Arabs were interested in peace, and more than half (53 percent) felt the Arabs were intent on destroying Israel.

Even after the achievement of the 1974 disengagement agreements, the American public was quite skeptical about the possibility of comprehensive peace in the Arab-Israeli conflict. In 1974, Harris asked: "How would you rate the chances of working out a total peace settlement in the Middle East?" A majority of 73 percent expressed pessimism on such chances; only 18 percent were optimistic.[103] In January 1975, Gallup found that 61 percent thought that "another war between the Israelis and the Arabs is likely to occur this year." Only 19 percent thought otherwise.[104] This forecast failed to materialize, though, and Israel and Egypt made one further, significant step toward peace.

In August 1975, following meetings between President Ford, President Sadat, and Prime Minister Rabin, Kissinger felt that the parties had sufficiently modified their earlier positions on a possible new agreement and were ready to negotiate. He therefore decided to renew his efforts, traveled to the Middle East, and was able to negotiate a new, major agreement between Israel and Egypt.[105] The agreement, known as the "interim agreement," was signed September 1, 1975; it provided for an Israeli withdrawal from the strategic passes in the Sinai Desert and from the rich oil fields of Abu Rudeis, in return for Israeli passage through the Suez Canal and American political and economic commitments. The interim agreement also included a three-year nonbelligerency pledge and an authorization to build an early-warning system in the Sinai Peninsula for both sides.[106]

Apparently, the interim agreement affected the opinion of the elite press on both Israel and the Arabs. According to figure 2–1, from the beginning of 1976 and throughout the year, the number of pro-Arab editorials was greater than the number of pro-Israeli editorials. At the end of 1976, the ratio between pro-Arab and pro-Israeli editorials was almost two to one.

Public opinion, however, did not change. Both Harris and Yankelovich conducted polls on American sympathies for Israel and the Arabs at the beginning of 1976. The Harris results of January 1976 (52 to 6 percent in favor of Israel) were almost identical to those of his January 1975 poll (52 to 7 percent; see table 2–1). The same is true for the Yankelovich results—56 to 9 percent in favor of Israel in January 1976, compared to 55 to 9 percent in his earlier poll of October 1974. The Roper results of January 1977 were even higher for Israel than those of his previous poll of April 1975. Although the sympathy index failed to show any changes in sympathies for Israel and the Arabs at the conclusion of the interim agreement, the favorability index, which provides data for Israel and Egypt, did register a slight change. In 1976, both Israel and Egypt gained a few points compared to the 1975 results; Israel gained three percentage points and Egypt gained five (see table 2–2).

A comparison between the sympathy index and the favorability index reveals that American public opinion gave some credit to Egypt's new peace intentions but did not consider them representative of the overall Arab attitude toward Israel. As if to substantiate this observation, Palestinian terrorists continued to strike at Israelis. In June 1976, a group of Palestinian and German terrorists hijacked to Uganda an Air France jetliner en route from Tel Aviv to Paris.[107] Uganda's President Idi Amin collaborated with the terrorists, who separated about a hundred Israelis from the other passengers and threatened to execute them. On the night of July 3, 1976, an Israeli special commando unit flew approximately 2,500 miles and conducted a daring raid on Entebbe airport, where the hostages were being held. The raid was successful; seven terrorists were killed, but the hostages were freed.

The raid on Entebbe coincided with bicentennial celebrations in the United States and was received with amazement and admiration. No polls were conducted on Israel's standing in American public opinion after the raid, but the outpouring of congratulations, official and unofficial, in government and public circles and the messages sent to the Israeli diplomatic legations testified to the enormous American approval of Israel's courage and determination in dealing with international and Palestinian terrorism. The Entebbe operation probably enhanced the image of Israel as an able and worthwhile ally of the United States.

The Israeli-Egyptian interim agreement contributed to an atmosphere of optimism and stability in the Arab-Israeli conflict. The American public shared this optimism. Although, in January 1975, 61 versus 19 percent of a national sample thought another war between Israel and the Arabs was likely to occur during the next year, in September 1975, after the conclusion of the interim agreement, only 28 percent thought so, while 56 percent held the opposite view.[108] The interim agreement solidified the U.S. position as the sole credible mediator in the Arab-Israeli conflict. In 1976, it became clear that American initiative and involvement would also be required to facilitate the next steps. However, a period of time was needed to test the implementation of the interim agreement, and in any event, 1976 was an election year in the United States and the parties were waiting for the results of the presidential race. Also, it was clear that any progress beyond the interim agreement would require a more extensive Israeli withdrawal, and this condition brought to the fore the complex territorial aspect of the Arab-Israeli conflict.

Opinions on the Territorial Issue

During the Six-Day War, Israel captured territories on all three war fronts. The Sinai peninsula was the largest occupied area, stretching over 23,622 square miles. The other captured territories were much smaller: the Golan Heights—444 square miles; the West Bank—2,270; and the Gaza Strip—140 square miles. Immediately after the war, Israel was prepared to negotiate for the return of all the occupied territories, with the exception of East Jerusalem and a few border areas, in return for a comprehensive peace agreement. In 1957, after the Suez-Sinai crisis, the Eisenhower administration had insisted on complete and unconditional withdrawal of the Israeli forces from the Sinai Desert. In 1967, however, U.S. policy was different, and the Johnson administration supported Israel's insistence on negotiations toward a peace agreement as a condition for the return of the occupied territories.[109]

On November 22, 1967, the U.N. Security Council unanimously adopted Resolution 242, which called for the establishment of a just and lasting peace in the Middle East on the basis of "withdrawal of Israeli armed forces from territories occupied in the recent conflict" in exchange for the "termination of all claims of belligerency and respect for and acknowledgment of the sovereignty, territorial integrity and political independence of every state in the area and their right to live in peace within secure and recognized boundaries free from threats or acts of force."[110]

Although the resolution emphasized the "inadmissibility of the acquisition of territory by war," it allowed for territorial changes in two references. First, Resolution 242 called for Israeli withdrawal from "territories," not from all the territories. Second, it emphasized the right of each state to live in peace "within secure and recognized boundaries." The authors of the resolution assumed that the parties would negotiate permanent borders on the basis of the principles of the resolution. Egypt and Jordan accepted the resolution but interpreted it in a way that placed all emphasis on complete and unconditional Israeli withdrawal. They added the word "the" before the word "territories," upsetting the delicate balance between the Israeli and the Arab demands, which had been so carefully introduced into the resolution.

American pollsters approached the occupied-territories issue in several ways. Shortly after the Six-Day War, Harris asked a national sample of Americans whether it agreed with the statement that Israel should unconditionally withdraw all its forces from Arab territories (see table 2–5). Sixty-two percent disagreed with this proposition, while 21 percent agreed. Between 1970 and 1980, Harris examined the same issue through a different question—question (b) in table 2–5—which omitted the required action of withdrawal before settling the other issues. The new question simply asked whether "Israel should give back the territory gained from the war in 1967." Responses to question (b) show that, throughout an entire decade, Americans rejected the Arab demand for a complete Israeli withdrawal by a ratio of two to one.

Immediately after the war, Gallup also surveyed American opinions on the Israeli approach to the occupied territories and provided three possible options: "keep all," "give back part" or "give back all." The same question was repeated three times a decade later. Responses to question (c) in table 2–5 reveal that in 1967 and 1977, a clear majority supported the Israeli positions ("keep all" and "give back part"), while only 13 to 16 percent advocated the Arab position. Also, question (c) indicates that support for the two extreme positions, "keep all" and "return all," remained almost constant. The only significant change was the increase in the number of respondents who had no opinion, apparently at the expense of support for the middle-of-the-road position.

A different approach to the territorial issue was adopted by Caddell and Roper, who added to the question a condition for Israeli withdrawal. In the

Table 2–5
Attitudes toward the Territorial Issue, 1967–80

Question

(a) Israel should withdraw all its forces from Arab territory before the other issues can be settled. (Harris)

Date	*Agree*	*Disagree*	*Not Sure*
July '67	21%	62%	17%

Question

(b) Israel should give back the territory it gained from the war of 1967. (Harris)

Date	*Agree*	*Disagree*	*Not Sure*
July '70	24%	43%	33%
Jan. '75	25	49	26
Jan. '76	25	49	26
July '80	23	55	22

Question

(c) As a result of the 1967 War, Israel now controls land that was formerly controlled by Arab nations. What do you think Israel should do—give back part of this land, give back all of this land, or keep all of this land?[a] (Gallup)

Date	*Keep All*	*Give Back Part*	*Give Back All*	*N.O.*
July '67	24%	49%	15%	12%
June '77	24	35	16	25
Oct. '77	26	36	13	25
Dec. '77	30	34	16	20

Question

(d) The Israelis ought to give up all the territory they have captured since 1967 if the Arab states agree to peace. (Caddell)

Date	*Agree*	*Disagree*	*D.K.*
Fall '74	36%	36%	28%
Summer '75	36	34	30

Sources: Harris 1967: H. Erskine, "The Polls: Western Partisanship in the Middle East," *Public Opinion Quarterly* 33(Winter 1969–70), 639. Harris 1970, 1975, 1976, and Caddell 1974, 1975: Lipset and Schneider, pp. 31–32. Harris 1980: Study No. 804011, 17. Gallup 1967, 1977: *The Gallup Poll: 1935–1971*, Vol. 3 2072; *1972–1977*, Vols. 1, 2, 1120, 1122.

[a]Asked of those who had read or heard about the issue (aware group).

Table 2–6
Attitudes toward the Future of the Occupied Territories, 1973–77

Question

Ever since the Six-Day War Israel has occupied territory that formerly belonged to the Arab nations. Which one of these statements comes closest to expressing how you feel about this? (Roper)

Statement		*Dec. 1973*	*June 1974*	*June 1975*	*June 1977*
(a)	Israel should keep all of the territory she has won in the last two Arab-Israeli wars.	14%	13%	14%	16%
(b)	It is time for Israel to make *some* concessions, but it is important that she keep what territory is essential for her defense.	27	31	30	34
(c)	Israel should give up all or most of the territory she has taken in the last two wars—but only if a satisfactory treaty can be negotiated with the Arabs that will guarantee her existence as a state.	25	25	25	23
(d)	The territory Israel has taken in the last two wars didn't belong to her and she should not be allowed to keep it under any circumstances.	6	7	7	7
(e)	Don't know	28	24	24	20
	Total	100%	100%	100%	100%

Sosurce: Lipset and Schneider, 35.

fall of 1974 and 1975, Caddell found that his national sample was almost equally divided on the question of whether "Israelis ought to give up all the territory they have captured since 1967 *if* the Arab states agree to peace" (emphasis added; see question (d) in table 2–5).

Between 1973 and 1977, Roper conducted four polls on the future of the occupied territories. As demonstrated in table 2–6, he provided four possible answers. Two represented the extreme positions, keep all and return all. The other two options included a qualifying condition: retain only territory needed for defense—question (b)—or return all or most territory if a satisfactory treaty can be negotiated that will guarantee Israel's existence—question (c). Table 2–6 demonstrates considerable stability in the responses in the period between 1973 and 1977. Between 13 and 16 percent supported the keep-all option, and 6 to 7 percent was in favor of the return-all option. Correlating with Harris and the Gallup polls, those who favored Israeli retention of all the territories outnumbered those favoring a full return of the territories by a ratio of two to one. The majority of respondents supported retention of some territory as a means of defense or as part of a peace agreement.

Results in tables 2–5 and 2–6 point to a pattern of opinion on the future of the occupied territories that developed between 1967 and 1977. In general, most Americans rejected the Arab demand for an unconditional Israeli withdrawal from all the occupied territories. They demonstrated concern for Israel's security and therefore supported Israeli retainment of some territory for the purpose of defense, and if necessary, even within the context of a peace treaty.

Conclusions

Twice during the 1967–77 period, American public opinion played a significant role in major Israeli military decisions. Considerations of this variable delayed Israeli action against the Arabs during the 1967 crisis and prevented a preemptive strike hours before the outbreak of the Yom Kippur War. American presidents and officials and Israeli leaders were aware of this factor and gave it considerable weight. American public opinion also played an important role in less dramatic events, such as the War of Attrition and the Ford-Kissinger reassessment policy.

Few public opinion polls were conducted on Israel and the Middle East in the 10-year period between the Suez-Sinai crisis and the 1967 Six-Day War. But the turbulent events of the next decade, particularly the major wars and the beginning of conflict resolution, produced waves of polls. Table 2–1 shows that throughout the 1967–77 period, American sympathies toward Israel and the Arabs were examined on a more regular basis—and not only during periods of crisis and war. Pollsters such as Harris, Yankelovich, and Caddell joined the veterans, Gallup and Roper, in conducting more frequent and diverse polls on Israel and the Middle East.

Evidence presented in this chapter revals that the opinion of the American media, as expressed in editorials, was supportive of United States policy, especially on the issue of peace talks. Editorials covering Israel were the most supportive during the War of Attrition and after the Yom Kippur War. Elite press editorials specifically supported Israel's policy on the peace talks and territorial boundaries but were critical of actions taken on Jerusalem and of certain military reprisals. Editorials on the Arab countries were critical on the use of force, the oil embargo, and the treatment of Jews. Trice concluded:

> As a group, America's prestige newspapers were more supportive of most Israeli policies and actions than those of the Arab states. However, we were a bit surprised to find that both support for Israel and criticism of the Arab states were considerably weaker than we had anticipated."[111]

In the 1967–77 period, the Gallup sympathy index displayed considerable stability. Rates for Israel moved from a high of 56 percent during the Six-Day War to a low of 37 percent during the Ford-Kissinger policy of reassessment, but between these and other events they shifted only between 50 and 44 percent (table 2–1). Rates for the Arabs moved on the Gallup index from a high of 8 percent, which was recorded several times after the Yom Kippur War, to a low of 3 percent, which was registered during the Egyptian-initiated War of Attrition. In every sympathy poll, Israel enjoyed a substantial margin of favor, although the ratios in favor of its position dropped slightly after the Yom Kippur War. Also, in comparison to the sympathy index of the first period (see table 1–5) many more people chose to side either with Israel or with the Arab nations.

Sympathy for Israel exceeded 50 percent in the Gallup index during the major wars of the period—the Six-Day War and the Yom Kippur War. These scores were partly related to an actual increase in the size of American support for Israel and partly to the increase in the saliency of the issue. Polls that questioned American attitudes on the circumstances of the wars revealed strong reservations on the Arab stands and motives. The Israeli attack on Arab armies during the Six-Day War was probably seen in the context of the crisis that preceded it and, unlike the 1956 Israeli operation in the Sinai, was largely perceived as a legitimate means of defense. Furthermore, the Arabs' argument that they had attacked Israel in October 1973 to free their occupied territories was rejected.

The major wars of the 1967–77 decade were followed by various unsuccessful trials of conflict resolution. Both sides adhered to tough positions. Between the Six-Day War and the Yom Kippur War, the Arabs opposed any open and direct dialogue with Israel and insisted on total Israeli withdrawal from all occupied territories, including East Jerusalem, without offering any reciprocal concessions. Israel demanded peace agreements and direct negotiations in return for withdrawal from most of the occupied territory. Israel also insisted on retaining a united Jerusalem under its control. In general, American public opinion, along with the government and the media, supported the Israeli position on the resolution of the Arab-Israeli conflict. They probably held this view because the Israeli demands for negotiations, recognition, and peace agreements seemed more reasonable than the Arab hostility, rhetoric, and rejection of Israel. The pattern of these opinions altered somewhat after the Yom Kippur War, at least with regard to Egypt, which modified its prewar position and demands.

Despite the high American stakes in the Middle East, a substantial segment of the American public opposed active U.S. involvement in the area, even as mediator and peacemaker. This attitude was detected in responses to general questions such as "What would you like the U.S. government to do . . ." (see table 2–3) as well as in responses to specific questions on aid and energy. At most, the public supported American initiatives at the United Nations and in other international frameworks. It is quite plausible that America's failure in Vietnam had negative effects on attitudes toward any type of American involvement in the Middle East.

The Yom Kippur War and the Arab oil embargo accelerated the energy crisis and exposed weaknesses in the economic infrastructure of the United States and other Western countries. The Arabs, who owned a substantial percentage of the world's proven oil reserves, hoped to capitalize on their new fortunes to alter the basic American attitudes toward Israel and themselves. However, as this chapter illustrates, the oil embargo boomeranged and added negative elements to the Arab image in the United States. Conversely, the Israeli image and standing in American public opinion remained undamaged.

After two full-scale wars separated by the lengthy War of Attrition, all of which took place within a 6-year period, Egypt and Israel decided to embark on a different path. The interim agreement of September 1975 was the first significant sign of a possible shift in the course of the Arab-Israeli conflict, because it included major political concessions from both sides. The agreement provided time for new assessments and plans, but the next steps hinged on the result of the 1976 presidential elections in the United States and the 1977 elections in Israel. Both elections produced somewhat surprising faces and strategies.

Notes

1. Nadav Safran, *From War to War: The Arab-Israeli Confrontation, 1948–1967* (New York: Pegasus, 1969), 271-302.

2. For works on the Six-Day War, see Donald Neff, *Warriors for Jerusalem: The Six Days that Changed the Middle East* (New York: Simon and Schuster, 1984); Theodore Draper, *Israel and World Politics: Roots of the Third Arab-Israeli War* (New York: Viking Press, 1968); Walter Laqueur, *The Road to War: the Origin and Aftermath of the Arab-Israeli Conflict, 1967–68* (Baltimore: Pelican, 1969), ch. 3. For a collection of Arab viewpoints, see Ibrahim Abu-Lughod, ed., *The Arab-Israeli Confrontation of June 1967: An Arab Perspective* (Evanston, Ill.: Northwestern University Press, 1970).

3. Charles W. Yost, "The Arab-Israeli War: How it Began," *Foreign Affairs* 46(January 1968): 304–20.

4. Indar Jit Rikhye, *The Sinai Blunder: Withdrawal of the United Nations Emergency Force Leading to the Six-Day War of June 1967* (London: Cass, 1980).

5. Israel's decisions during the prewar crisis were analyzed in Michael Brecher and Benjamin Geist, *Decisions in Crisis: Israel, 1967 and 1973* (Berkeley: University of California Press, 1980); Janice Gross Stein and Raymond Tanter, *Rational Decision Making: Israel's Security Choices, 1967* (Columbus: Ohio State University Press, 1980); and Abraham R. Wagner, *Crisis Decision-Making: Israel's Experience in 1967 and 1973* (New York: Praeger, 1974).

6. Meron Medzini, ed., *Israel's Foreign Relations: Selected Documents, 1947–1974* (Jerusalem: Ministry for Foreign Affairs, 1976), 741.

7. Among other things, Foreign Minister Abba Eban was sent to France and the United States to explain the Israeli position and to explore the reactions of the countries he visited. See Abba Eban, *Abba Eban: An Autobiography* (New York: Random House, 1977), 339–64.

8. *Weekly Compilation of Presidential Documents* (Washington, D.C.: Government Printing Office, May 29, 1967), 776–77.

9. Eban, *Abba Eban,* 348.

10. Lyndon Baines Johnson, *The Vantage Point: Perspectives of the Presidency, 1963–1969* (New York: Holt, Rinehart & Winston, 1971), 293.

11. Safran, *From War to War,* 270.

12. Israel could not tolerate the deployment of large Arab forces (Egypt—100,000 troops and 900 tanks; Syria—50,000 troops and 400 tanks; Jordan—60,000 troops and 300 tanks) around its borders because of the asymmetric nature of the Arab-Israeli military balance. While most of the Arab forces are based on a permanent army, most of the Israeli forces consist of reservists. The deployment of the Arab troops in May 1967 required almost full mobilization of the Israeli forces, which Israel could not afford for economic and social reasons.

13. Eban, *Abba Eban* 384.

14. Hirsh Goodman and Zeev Schiff, "The Attack on the Liberty," *Atlantic Monthly* 254(September 1984): 78–84.

15. Janice Monti Belkaoui, "Images of Arabs and Israelis in the Prestige Press, 1966-1974," *Journalism Quarterly* 55(Winter 1978): 732–38.

16. Ibid. See also Michael Suleiman, "National Stereotypes as Weapons in the Arab-Israeli Conflict," *Journal of Palestine Studies* 3(Spring 1974): 109–21, and Eugene Michael Mensh, *American Images of Arabs: A Data Based Analysis* (Monterey, Calif.: Naval Postgraduate School, 1978).

17. Robert H. Trice, "The American Elite Press and the Arab-Israeli Conflict," *Middle East Journal* 33(Summer 1979): 308.

18. David Daugherty and Michael Warden, "Prestige Press Editorial Treatment of the Middle East During 11 Crisis Years," *Journalism Quarterly* 56(Winter 1979), 776–82.

19. See Walter Laqueur, "Israel, The Arabs and World Opinion," *Commentary* 44(August 1967): 49–59.

20. "American Public Opinion," *American Jewish Year Book* 69(1968), 199; and Hazel Erskine, "The Polls: Western Partisanship in the Middle East," *Public Opinion Quarterly* 33(Winter 1969–1970): 630.

21. *New York Times,* June 6, 1967. President Johnson described this statement as an error and an oversimplified approach to a complicated situation, Johnson, *The Vantage Point,* 298–99.

22. Johnathan Trumbull Howe, *Multicrises, Sea Power and Global Politics in the Missile Age* (Cambridge: MIT Press, 1971), 91; see also note 6 on the same page.

23. Ibid., 104.

24. George H. Gallup, *The Gallup Poll: Public Opinion, 1935–1971,* vol. 3 (New York: Random House, 1972), 2068.

25. "American Public Opinion," *American Jewish Year Book* 69(1968): 199.

26. Gallup, *Gallup Poll, 1935–1971,* vol. 3, 2071.

27. Eban, *Abba Eban* 417.

28. *The Quest for Peace: Principal United States Public Statements and Related Documents on the Arab-Israeli Peace Process 1967–1983* (Washington, D.C.: U.S. Department of State, 1984), 3.

29. "American Public Opinion," 202.

30. Trice, "The American Elite Press," 316.

31. Erskine, "The Polls," 639.

32. Gallup, *Gallup Poll, 1935–1971*, vol. 3, 2071.

33. For historical background on the Jerusalem question, see H. Eugene Bovis, *The Jerusalem Question, 1917–1968* (Stanford, Calif.: Hoover Institution Press, 1971); and Terence Prittie, *Whose Jerusalem?* (London: Muller, 1981).

34. U.S. Department of State, *Quest for Peace*, 5–10, 19–22.

35. Erskine, "The Polls," 639.

36. Seymour Martin Lipset and William Schneider, *Israel and the Jews in American Public Opinion* (New York: American Jewish Committee, 1977, Mimeographed), 10.

37. For more recent views on the fate of the city, see Saul B. Cohen, *Jerusalem: Bridging the Four Walls: A Geographical Perspective* (New York: Herzl Press, 1977) and *Jerusalem Undivided* (New York: Herzl Press, 1980).

38. On the effects of the Khartoum decision on the postwar diplomacy, see Bernard Reich, *Quest for Peace: United States-Israel Relations and the Arab-Israeli Conflict* (New Brunswick, N.J.: Transaction Books, 1977), 86–7.

39. U.S. Department of State, *Quest for Peace*, 11-18.

40. *U.N. Security Council Resolution 242: A Case Study in Diplomatic Ambiguity* (Washington, D.C.: Georgetown University, Institute for the Study of Diplomacy, 1981).

41. Gallup, *Gallup Poll, 1935–1971*, vol. 3, 2150.

42. Ibid., 2071.

43. Charles H. Wagner, "Elite American Newspaper Opinion and the Middle East: Commitment versus Isolation," in Willard A. Beling, ed., *The Middle East: Quest for an American Policy* (Albany: State University of New York Press, 1973), 306–34.

44. *Department of State Bulletin*, February 17, 1969, 142–43.

45. On the Nixon approach to the Arab-Israeli conflict, see William B. Quandt, *Decade of Decisions: American Policy toward the Arab-Israeli Conflict, 1967-1976* (Berkeley: University of California Press, 1977), 76-83; and Reich, *Quest for Peace*, 114–19.

46. Lawrence L. Whetton, *The Canal War: Four Power Conflict in the Middle East* (Cambridge: MIT Press, 1974); and Y. Bar-Siman-Tov, *The Israeli-Egyptian War of Attrition* (New York: Columbia University Press, 1980).

47. On the Soviet involvement in the War of Attrition, see Alvin Z. Rubinstein, *Red Star on the Nile: The Soviet-Egyptian Influence Relationship Since the June War* (Princeton, N.J.: Princeton University Press, 1977).

48. Reich, *Quest for Peace*, 122-123.

49. *Near East Report*, no. 14 (1970), 84–6. See also Robert H. Trice, "Congress and the Arab-Israeli Conflict: Support for Israel in the U.S. Senate, 1970-1973," *Political Science Quarterly* 92(Fall 1977): 443-63.

50. Nadav Safran, *Israel: The Embattled Ally* (Cambridge: Harvard University Press, 1978), 441–47.

51. U.S. Department of State, *Quest for Peace*, 30-33.

52. Quandt, *Decade of Decisions*, 106–10; and Reich, *Quest for Peace*, 167–71.

53. Richard M. Nixon, *The Memoirs of Richard Nixon* (London: Sidgwick and Jackson, 1978), 482.

54. Quandt, *Decade of Decisions*, ch. 4; and Henry Brandon, *The Retreat of American Power* (New York: Doubleday, 1973).

55. Henry Kissinger, *White House Years* (Boston: Little, Brown, 1979), 623–25; and Yitzhak Rabin, *The Rabin Memoirs* (Jerusalem: Steimatzky, 1979), 147–48.

56. Shlomo Slonim, "United States-Israel Relations, 1967-1973: A Study in the Convergence and Divergence of Interests," *Jerusalem Papers on Peace Problems*, No. 8 (Jerusalem: Magnes Press, Hebrew University, September 1974), 25–30.

57. See John Bulloch, *The Making of a War: The Middle East From 1967 to 1973* (London: Longman, 1974).

58. Israel's assumptions were analyzed in Zeev Schiff, *October Earthquake: Yom Kippur 1973*, trans. Louis Williams (Tel Aviv: University Publishing Projects, 1974); Shlomo Nakdimon, *Sevirut Nemucha* (Low probability) (Tel Aviv: Revivim-Yediot Aharonot, 1982); and Avi Shlaim, "Failures in National Intelligence Estimates: The Case of the Yom Kippur War," *World Politics 28(April 1976): 348–80.*

59. See Saad Shazly, *The Crossing of the Suez* (San Francisco: American Mideast Research, 1980).

60. Moshe Dayan, *Story of My Life* (London: Sphere Books, 1977), 463.

61. Golda Meir, *My Life* (New York: Putnam, 1975), 426.

62. Marvin Kalb and Bernard Kalb, *Kissinger* (Boston: Little, Brown, 1974), 460.

63. For details on the war, see Peter Allen, *The Yom Kippur War* (New York: Scribner's, 1982); Walter Laqueur, *Confrontation: The Middle East War and World Politics* (London: Abacus, 1974); Elizabeth Monroe and A. H. Farrar-Hockley, *The Arab-Israeli War, October 1973: Background and Events* (London: International Institute for Strategic Studies, Winter 1974–75); Chaim Herzog, *The War of Atonement: October 1973* (Boston: Little, Brown, 1975); and Mohamed Heikal, *The Road to Ramadan* (New York: Quadrangle, 1975).

64. Edgar O'Balance, *No Victory, No Vanquished* (San Rafael: California Presidio, 1978); Trevor N. Dupuy, *Elusive Victory: The Arab-Israeli Wars, 1947–1974* (New York: Harper & Row, 1978), book 5; and Dankwart A. Rostow, "Who Won the Yom Kippur and Oil Wars?" *Foreign Policy* 17(Winter 1974–75), 166–75.

65. On the Soviet policy during the war, see Fay D. Kohler et al., *The Soviet Union and the October 1973 Middle East War: The Implications for Détente* (Coral Gables, Fla.: Center for Advanced International Studies, University of Miami, 1974).

66. U.S. Congress, House of Representatives, Committee on Foreign Affairs, *Inquiring into the Military Alert Invoked on October 24, 1973*, H. Rept. 970, 93rd Cong., 2nd sess., 1974. See also Henry Kissinger, *Years of Upheaval* (Boston: Little, Brown, 1982), 587-600; and Kalb and Kalb, *Kissinger*, 479–99.

67. Walter J. Levy, "Oil Power," *Foreign Affairs* 49(July 1971): 652–68; and James E. Akins, "The Oil Crisis: This Time the Wolf Is Here," *Foreign Affairs* 51(April 1973): 462–90.

68. Reich, *Quest for Peace*, 204–05; and Robert W. Stookey, *America and the*

Arab States: An Uneasy Encounter (New York: Wiley, 1975), 255.

69. Edward N. Luttwak and Walter Laqueur, "Kissinger and the Yom Kippur War," *Commentary* 58(September 1974): 33-40; Safran, *The Embattled Ally*, 481–82.

70. Kalb and Kalb, *Kissinger*, 475.

71. Avishag Gordon, "The Middle East October War as Reported by the American Networks," *International Problems* 14(Fall 1975): 76–85.

72. Janice Terry with Gordon Mendenhall, "1973 US Press Coverage on the Middle East," *Journal of Palestine Studies* 4(Autumn 1974): 129.

73. This was precisely the reason for the rejection of a "surgical strike" as an option to deal with the 1962 Cuban missile crisis. See Robert F. Kennedy, *Thirteen Days* (New York: Signet, 1969), 38–9; and Arthur Schlesinger, Jr., *A Thousand Days: John F. Kennedy in the White House* (London: Mayflower-Dell, 1965), 620–21.

74. Lipset and Schneider, *Israel and the Jews*, 15. See also George E. Gruen, "U.S. Middle East Policy, American Public Opinion," *American Jewish Year Book* 75(1974–75): 189–98; and Earl Raab, "Is Israel Losing Popular Support? The Evidence of the Polls," *Commentary* 57(January 1974): 26-29.

75. On this issue, see Kenyon N. Griffin, J.C. Martin, and O. Walter, "Religious Roots and Rural Americans' Support for Israel During the October War," *Journal of Palestine Studies* 6(Autumn 1976): 104–14.

76. The question was: "What do you think is the most important problem facing the country today, and what do you think is the next most important problem facing the country today?" George H. Gallup, *The Gallup Poll: Public Opinion, 1972–1977*, vol. 1 (Wilmington, Del.: Scholarly Resources, 1978), 124.

77. Ibid., 230.

78. Fuad Itayim, "Arab Oil—The Political Dimension," *Journal of Palestine Studies* 3(Winter 1974): 90–105.

79. Brown's remarks only became known a month later. Through an official statement by the Defense Department, he expressed regret for these remarks. See *New York Times*, November 14, 1974.

80. William Schneider, *Anti-Semitism and Israel: A Report on American Public Opinion* (New York: American Jewish Committee, December 1978, Mimeographed), 19.

81. Gallup, *Gallup Poll, 1972-1977*, vol. 1, 226.

82. Schneider, *Anti-Semitism*, 20.

83. Louis Harris, "Oil or Israel," *New York Times Magazine*, April 6, 1975, 21-22.

84. A. L. Udovitch, ed., *The Middle East: Oil, Conflict and Hope* (Lexington, Mass: Lexington Books, 1976).

85. Gallup, *Gallup Poll, 1972-1977*, vol. 1, 406–07.

86. George E. Gruen, "Arab Petropower and American Public Opinion," *Middle East Review* 7(Winter 1975–76), 33-39; and David Garnham, "The Oil Crisis and U.S. Attitudes Toward Israel," in Naiem A. Sherbiny and Mark Tessler, eds., *Arab Oil, Impact on the Arab Countries and Global Implications* (New York: Praeger, 1976), 295-304.

87. Michael W. Suleiman, "American Public Support of Middle Eastern Countries: 1939-1979," in Michael C. Hudson and Ronald G. Wolfe, eds., *The American*

Media and the Arabs (Washington, D.C.: Georgetown University, Center for Contemporary Arab Studies, 1980), 22.

88. Theodore Draper, "The Road to Geneva," *Commentary* 57(February 1974): 23-29; Quandt, *Decade of Decisions*, 218–24, and Safran, *The Embattled Ally*, 513–21.

89. "Egypt-Israeli Agreement on the Disengagement of Forces," *International Legal Materials* 13(January 1974): 23–24. For related statements see U.S. Department of State, *Quest for Peace*, 50-4.

90. "Israel-Syria: Agreement on Disengagement," *International Legal Materials* 13(July 1974), 880-87. For related statements see U.S. Department of State, *Quest for Peace*, 55-6.

91. See Reich, *Quest for Peace*, 296-98, and Quandt, *Decade of Decisions*, 245–49.

92. For Kissinger's own version of the step-by-step diplomacy, see *Years of Upheaval*, 614-26; and Amos Perlmutter, "Crisis Management: Kissinger's Middle East Negotiations (October 1973-June 1974)," *International Studies Quarterly* 19(September 1975): 316-43.

93. Safran, *The Embattled Ally*, 536-39, and Quandt, *Decade of Decisions*, 255-58.

94. On the reassessment policy see Edward R. F. Sheehan, *The Arabs, Israelis, and Kissinger: A Secret History of American Diplomacy in the Middle East* (New York: Crowell, 1976); and Matti Golan, *The Secret Conversations of Henry Kissinger: Step-by-Step Diplomacy in the Middle East* (New York: Quadrangle, 1976).

95. Abraham Ben-Zvi, *Alliance Politics and the Limits of Influence: The Case of the U.S. and Israel, 1975-1983*, Paper No. 24, (Tel Aviv: Tel Aviv University, Jaffe Center for Strategic Studies, April 1984), 12-21.

96. Gerald R. Ford, *A Time to Heal* (New York.: Harper & Row, 1979), 308.

97. Rabin, *Rabin Memoirs*, 208.

98. Gallup, *Gallup Poll, 1972-1977*, vol. 1, 460.

99. Marvin C. Feuerwerger, *Congress and Israel* (Westport, Conn.: Greenwood Press, 1979), 45, 206.

100. Belkauoi, 736–37.

101. Lipset and Schneider, 23.

102. Ibid., 38–9.

103. Louis Harris and Associates, *A Study of the Attitudes of the American People and the American Jewish Community Toward Anti-Semitism and the Arab-Israeli Conflict in the Middle East*, study no. 804011 (August 1980), 8.

104. Gallup, *Gallup Poll, 1972-1977*, vol. 1, 407.

105. Reich, *Quest for Peace*, 323-25; and Quandt, *Decade of Decisions*, 271-81.

106. "Egypt-Israel: Agreement on the Sinai and Suez Canal," *International Legal Materials* 14(November 1975): 1450-69; and "New Agreement Between Egypt and Israel Negotiated Through Secretary Kissinger," *Department of State Bulletin* 73(September 29, 1975); 457-70. For statements related to the agreement, see U.S. Department of State, *Quest for Peace*, 57-65.

107. See Yehuda Offer, *Operation Thunder: The Entebbe Raid* (London: Penguin, 1976).

108. Gallup, *Gallup Poll, 1972-1977*, vol. 1, 567.

109. The views of the Joint Chiefs of Staff on Israel's defensible borders were presented in a special memorandum, June 29, 1967. The document was published in the *Wall Street Journal* on March 9, 1983.

110. See notes 39 and 40.

111. Trice, "The American Elite Press," 324.

3
Peacemaking: Israel-Egypt

The late 1970s witnessed dramatic changes in Israel, in the Arab-Israeli conflict, and also in U.S. policy toward the Middle East. U.S. President Jimmy Carter defined the need to resolve the Arab-Israeli conflict as one of the principal goals of his administration. Israel elected a new prime minister, and President Sadat traveled to Jerusalem in search of a breakthrough in Arab-Israeli relations. The visit initiated a peace process under U.S. auspices, and, with Carter's mediation, Israel and Egypt reached a major agreement at Camp David and subsequently signed a formal peace treaty. American public opinion played a significant role in the peace process, and this chapter examines how the public reacted and how its reactions affected this process.

Jimmy Carter had been a relatively unknown politician and the governor of the relatively small state of Georgia, but in 1976, he surprised the American political establishment by winning the Democratic party nomination for president and defeating President Ford. Carter ran against the system and the Washington establishment and turned his obscurity into an asset. He ran a populist campaign and exploited the public revolt against the abuse of power at the White House, so well demonstrated by the Watergate affair.[1]

Carter promised to turn the government back to the people and vowed that he would listen to the public and consider its wishes and aspirations in decision making. He criticized the "secret diplomacy" of Henry Kissinger and offered to consult the public on the sensitive issues of defense and foreign affairs.[2] Perhaps it was symbolic that Carter chose to announce his new policy on the Arab-Israeli conflict in a town meeting in Clinton, Massachusetts. A further issue explored in this chapter is how and to what extent American public opinion affected Carter's Middle East Policy.

Except for brief periods of war and crisis, the Arab-Israeli conflict had not been an urgent priority in American foreign policy. But for reasons that will be explained later, Carter placed the resolution of the Arab-Israeli conflict very high on his list of foreign policy priorities. This change sparked enormous interest among the parties involved in the conflict and prepared the groundwork for the dramatic events that occurred in the area during the Carter years, although in a very ironic and unanticipated manner. Therefore, another issue examined in this chapter is the attitude of the American public on U.S. policy in the Middle East under Carter and his particular role in the Israeli-Egyptian peace process.

Several months after Carter assumed power in the White House, and while he was experimenting with a new plan for Arab-Israeli peace, a change of historical significance occurred in Israel. After almost 30 years of successive, uninterrupted rule, the Labor party lost the 1977 elections to the Likud party.[3] Menachem Begin became the new prime minister. He was known for his tough, highly nationalistic attitudes toward the Arabs and his party's historical and ideological claims to the West Bank. He was perceived both in Israel and in the United States as a leader who, at best, would not make any concessions for peace and, at worst, would lead the Middle East into another all-out war. How, then, did Americans view Israel under Begin's rule? Did Americans change their basic, favorable attitudes toward Israel after Begin's victory in 1977? This chapter discusses and clarifies these questions.

Sadat's visit to Jerusalem was a major breakthrough in the Arab-Israeli conflict. He himself stated that 90 percent of the conflict was psychological, and to a certain degree he was right. One of the fundamental problems of the Arab-Israeli conflict had always been the refusal of the Arab countries to recognize Israel's legitimate existence. Sadat broke this pattern, and for the first time in the history of the Jewish state, an Arab leader of the greatest and most important Arab nation recognized Israel, visited its capital, negotiated directly with its leaders, and offered them a peace agreement.

Sadat's move was the most spectacular peace overture since the reconciliation of Britain and France with Germany and the United States with Japan after World War II. His Jerusalem visit and the peace process altered the Egyptian image in the United States. This chapter explores the nature and depth of this change and also examines the arguments presented by several reporters and scholars that Sadat altered not only the image of the Egyptians but also that of the entire Arab world.[4] The chapter traces the development of the peace process and American attitudes on its different phases—from the initial probing to the signing of the peace treaty and the end of the Carter era.

Carter's Strategy

In December 1975, a study group on the Middle East at the Brookings Institution in Washington, D.C., issued a framework for a comprehensive resolution of the Arab-Israeli conflict.[5] The group, composed of Middle East experts and former officials, questioned Kissinger's step-by-step approach and argued that further progress would require negotiations on all aspects of the conflict, including peace, the Palestinian question, borders, and the status of Jerusalem—preferably to be conducted under one roof.[6] According to the Brookings report, this "roof" might be facilitated within the mechanism of the Geneva Conference. A reactivation of the conference would require Soviet and Palestinian participation, and the study group claimed that durable peace could be achieved only with Soviet cooperation. The Brookings report also emphasized the Palestinian right to self-determination as a condition for a peace agreement:

> For a peace settlement to be viable, indeed for it even to be negotiated and concluded, this right will have to be recognized in principle and, as a part of the settlement, given satisfaction in practice.[7]

The report outlined two possible alternatives to satisfy the principle of Palestinian self-determination—an independent Palestinian state or an entity linked to Jordan.

One prominent member of the Brookings group, political scientist Zbigniew Brzezinski, wrote several articles in 1975 on the energy crisis, linking it closely to the Arab-Israeli conflict.[8] He maintained that the energy crisis threatened the international order and complex north-south relations and that a resolution of the Arab-Israeli conflict was a key to the diffusion of this energy crisis. According to Brzezinski, if this conflict were resolved through an American initiative, Arab oil-producing countries would respond by lowering oil prices. He further argued that the Palestinian problem was the source of the Arab-Israeli conflict and, therefore, that to facilitate an Arab-Israeli peace, the problem must be quickly resolved. Thus, according to Brzezinski's theory, resolution of the Palestinian problem was a key to stability and accommodation in the entire international economic and political order.[9]

However, Brzezinski's approach to the linkage between the energy crisis and the Arab-Israeli conflict was misguided, since it assumed that Arab oil-producing countries made oil-pricing decisions according to the U.S. policy on Israel and the Arab-Israeli conflict. In fact, those decisions were based solely on economic considerations, yet at the time, Brzezinski's theory held some appeal, especially to the presidential candidate, Jimmy Carter.

Carter conferred with Brzezinski in the early meetings of the Trilateral Commission and was impressed by his criticism of Henry Kissinger and his ideas for a new American foreign policy.[10] Therefore, when the Georgia governor won the 1976 presidential elections, he appointed Brzezinski as his national security adviser. Consequently, the Brookings report and Brzezinski's proposals soon guided President Carter's policy on the Middle East.[11] In the early months of his presidency, Carter placed the Arab-Israeli conflict high on his list of foreign policy priorities and devoted much time and energy to it. On March 16, 1977, he spoke at a town meeting in Clinton, Massachusetts, and outlined the following principles for an Arab-Israeli peace agreement:

1. Recognition of Israel by her neighbors and her right to exist permanently in peace—that is, open borders, travel, tourism, culture exchange and trade;
2. The establishment of permanent borders through diplomatic negotiations;
3. A homeland for the Palestinian refugees, the exact nature of which must be first agreed upon by the Arab countries and then negotiated with Israel.[12]

Most Middle East reactions to the Clinton statement were negative. Israel criticized the call for a Palestinian homeland, and the Arab nations denounced the principle of genuine peace. The thirteenth Palestinian National Council, which was in session in Cairo when Carter made his statement, failed to produce any new decisions, and delegates repeated the traditional rejections and extremist positions toward Israel.[13] Despite these reactions, Carter continued his efforts to reconvene the Geneva Conference.

Carter's declaration in favor of a comprehensive solution at the Geneva Conference did not go unnoticed by the USSR. On March 21, just a few days after the speech in Clinton, Soviet President Leonid Brezhnev presented the Sixteenth Congress of the Trades Union of the USSR a Soviet proposal for peace in the Middle East.[14] The proposal was more flexible than earlier similar declarations on issues such as the pace of Israel's withdrawal from occupied territories and the role of the PLO in the peace process. On October 1, 1977, the two superpowers suddenly issued a joint communique on the Middle East that included elements from both the Carter and the Brezhnev addresses.[15] The communique created the impression that the United States and the USSR had reached an agreement on methods to resolve the Arab-Israeli conflict and were ready to impose them on their respective allies. The joint communique created alarm and confusion in the United States and the Middle East and, as indicated later in this chapter, contributed to a very different course of events.

As in the case of most new presidents, Carter received substantial public approval during the first months of his presidency. According to a Gallup poll conducted between March 18 and 21, the American public approved of his performance by a preponderance of 75 to 9 percent.[16] At the end of March, his approval rating stood at 72 to 10 percent; however, within a few weeks, these highly favorable ratings sharply declined. The number of those who disapproved of his management of the presidency had doubled by May, and in October disapproval had reached 29 percent, or triple that of March 1977.[17]

Part of this rapid decline was natural and stemmed from the dissipation of Carter's "honeymoon" with the American public. Heightened disapproval, however, might have been related to Carter's policy on the Middle East. According to table 3–1, although Carter's approval rating on "his working for a peace settlement in the Middle East" was positive in August 1977, it grew negative from September through November.

It should be noted that a CBS–*New York Times* poll (CBS–*NYT*) conducted between October 23 and 26, 1977, found a higher rate of approval for Carter's policy on the Middle East, albeit only among those who claimed that they followed "news reports from the area closely enough to form an opinion" (48 percent of the sample).[18] Slightly more than half of this aware group (53 percent) felt that Carter's efforts to achieve peace in the Middle East were either excellent or pretty good. A similar number of respondents among the same group felt that "the U.S. should give its strongest support to Israel even if it means risking an Arab oil boycott." Only 27 percent took the opposite view: "that the U.S. should pay more attention to the demands of the Arabs—even if it means antagonizing Israel." In a second query, the aware group was asked to compare American support for Israel under the Carter versus the Ford administrations. More than a third of the aware group said that compared to a year earlier, American support for Israel was less strong, while 21 percent said the support for Israel was greater under Carter than under the Ford administration. But these results must be viewed against a historic event that had occurred in Israel several months earlier.

Begin's Victory

During the first 30 years of its existence, Israel was ruled by a coalition government under the leadership of the Labor party. This hegemony terminated, however, in a dramatic way in the general elections of May 1977. Labor fell to the permanent opposition leader, Menachem Begin, and his Likud (Union) party. In the prestate years, Begin led an underground organization, Irgun Zvai Leumi, which fought the British mandatory government in Palestine through methods that were not always acceptable to the leaders of the Jewish community and the more moderate underground Jewish organization, Hagana.[19]

Upon the establishment of Israel, Begin founded and led the Herut (Freedom) party, but was unable to challenge the Labor party's solid grip on Israel's political system until May 1977. Ten years earlier, just before the outbreak of the Six-Day War, Begin had helped form a national unity government and had also pressed for the appointment of Moshe Dayan as defense minister. Begin served for three years in the government of national unity as a minister without

Table 3–1
Carter's Middle East Approval Rating, 1977–80

Question

How would you rate President Carter on his working for a peace settlement in the Middle East: Excellent, pretty good, only fair, or poor? (Harris)

Date	*Excellent, Pretty Good*	*Fair, Poor*	*Not Sure*	*Net Difference*	*(n)*
Aug. '77	51%	40%	9%	+11%	
Sep. '77	34	47	19	−13	
Oct. '77	44	46	10	−2	(1,537)
Nov. '77	44	48	8	−4	(1,200)
		Sadat's Visit to Jerusalem			
Dec. '77	63	29	8	+34	(1,259)
Jan. '78	57	35	8	+22	(1,191)
		Breakdown in Talks			
Feb. '78	46	45	9	+1	
Mar. '78	44	48	8	−4	(1,199)
		Camp David Accords			
Sep. '78	78	18	4	+60	
Jan. '79	63	30	7	+33	(1,498)
		Peace Agreement			
Mar. '79	71	26	3	+45	
Oct. '79	58	39	3	+21	(1,500)
July '80	46	51	3	−5	(1,506)

Sources: August 1977 to March 1978: *New York Post,* April 10, 1978; September 1978 to January 1979; *ABC News–Harris Survey,* Vol. 1, No. 4, January 11, 1979; October 1979: Elizabeth H. Hastings and Philip Hastings, eds., *Index to International Public Opinion, 1978–1979* (Westport, Conn.: Greenwood Press, 1980, 106–10; *1979–1980,* 180; July 1980: Louis Harris and Associates, Study No. 804011 (August 1980), 37.

portfolio, but left in August 1970 because he opposed the terms of the Rogers' proposal to end the War of Attrition.[20]

Begin was known for his tough, nationalistic outlook, and despite his flawless record as a parliamentarian, he was often accused by his critics and opponents of being a dangerous politician with fascist intentions. In 1977, the Carter administration preferred and expected another Labor victory. The position of the Labor party on the Arab-Israeli conflict was perceived to be much more moderate than that of the Likud party, and since Carter wished to advance a comprehensive resolution in Geneva, he preferred a government that, in his eyes, would be more willing to make substantial concessions to the Arabs.

The American media capitalized on government sentiments and tended to concentrate on the international aspects of the elections. It assumed that the Israeli voter ignored all domestic issues and cast his vote solely on the approaches of different parties to the Arab-Israeli conflict. On May 15, 1977, a commentator at ABC television stated, for example, that the Israeli voter must choose between "war and peace." As it happened, the Israeli voter, in May 1977, weary of the long rule of Labor, punished it for corruption and failures in various social and economic fields.[21]

Begin's victory surprised the American media and led to indiscriminate attacks on the new prime minister and his Likud party. Begin was repeatedly cited as a "ruthless terrorist," "fanatic," "zealot," "chauvinist," "extremist" and "fascist." The *New York Times* wrote: "As luck and Israeli democracy would have it, the politics of the Middle East are now dangerously out of synch."[22] *Newsweek* headlined its article on Begin's victory "Day of the Hawks" and reported that Begin had already "turned his country to the right and onto a politically dangerous path."[23] For *Newsweek* and several other newspapers and magazines, the term "hawk" was sufficient. Not to be outdone, however, *Time* magazine called Begin's victory "The Triumph of the Superhawk" and noted, "His first name means 'comforter.' Menachem Begin (rhymes with Fagin) has been anything but that to his numerous antagonists."[24] The reference to Fagin, a highly unsympathetic and cruel Jewish character in the novel *Oliver Twist*, was not simply a display of bad taste; it revealed considerable prejudice and perhaps even anti-Semitism.

The hysteria over Begin's victory in the American media somewhat subsided after the new prime minister appointed Moshe Dayan, a former Labor leader, as foreign minister, and the noted archeologist Yigael Yadin, who ran successfully at the top of the newly established "Democratic Movement for Change," as deputy prime minister. In July, Prime Minister Begin visited Carter and granted numerous interviews to the media. His calls to Sadat and other Arab leaders to negotiate peace with Israel somewhat improved his image.[25] But many American officials and reporters continued to view him as an extremist leader bent on undermining the Carter grand design for a comprehensive resolution of the Arab-Israeli conflict.

Polls on Prime Minister Begin and his policies on the Arab-Israeli conflict commenced several months after the election. But general polls on American sympathies toward the conflict were conducted by Gallup in June and October 1977. Table 3–2 reveals that, initially, the hysteria over Begin and the future of Israel did not affect the general Israeli standing in American public opinion. Shortly after Begin's victory, Gallup found a 44 to 8 percent plurality of sympathy in favor of Israel—identical to the score of January 1975 (see table 2–1). In October, Israel and the Arabs gained points—two and three, respectively.

Efforts to open a new phase in the peacemaking process were intensified in August and September 1977. Israel and Egypt were involved in hectic diplomatic activity, covert and public, across three continents.[26] Several foreign leaders, including Rumanian President Nicolae Ceausescu and the Shah of Iran, met with Begin, Sadat, and Dayan. On September 16, Foreign Minister Dayan flew secretly to Tangier, Morocco, and met with Egyptian Deputy Prime Minister for Presidential Affairs Hassan Tuhamy.[27] Dayan clearly signaled a desire for direct negotiations with Egypt at the highest possible level. President Sadat did not rule out this option.

Sadat's Visit to Jerusalem

The Israeli-Egyptian interim agreement of September 1975 covered a period of three years. Unless renewed, the nonbelligerent pledge of this agreement was to expire in September 1978, and Sadat wished to make additional progress toward further Israeli withdrawal by that date. In the meantime, Carter's courting of the extreme elements in the Arab world—Syria and the PLO—annoyed Sadat. He was also dismayed by the joint U.S.-USSR October communique on the Middle East.[28] Sadat had not gone to such great lengths to rid Egypt of the Soviets just to see them return through the back door. In September 1977, the prospects for a new breakthrough via the Carter strategy were slim. Therefore, prompted by overt Israeli interest in direct negotiations, Sadat decided to take a bold initiative.

On November 7, 1977, Sadat met with his aides and officials and informed them of his proposed mission to Jerusalem. The officials were shaken, but Sadat pacified them by explaining that he intended to expose the true Israeli position toward lasting negotiations and prove to the world which state was genuinely interested in Middle East peace.[29] Two days later, Sadat spoke be-

Table 3–2
Sympathies for Israel and the Arab Nations, 1977–80

Question

(a) Have you heard or read about the situation in the Middle East? *If yes:* In the Middle East situation are your sympathies more with Israel or more with the Arab nations? (Gallup)

(b) With regard to the situation in the Middle East, at the present time do you find yourself *more* in sympathy with Israel, or *more* in sympathy with the Arabs? (Roper)

(c) If war broke out between Israel and the Arab nations, with whom would your sympathies lie—Israel or the Arab nations? (Yankelovich)

(d) At the present time, do you find yourself more in sympathy with Israel or more in sympathy with the Arab nations? (Los Angeles Times)

(e) In the dispute between Israel and the Arabs, which side do you sympathize with more—Israel or the Arabs? (Harris)

Table 3–2 continued

Q	*Date*	*Poll*	*Israel*	*Arab Nations*	*Neither*	*D.K., N.O.*	*Both*
(b)	Mar. '77	Roper	43%	5%	23%	16%	13%
		Begin Wins Israeli Elections (May 1977)					
(a)	June '77	Gallup	44	8	28	20	—
(a)	Oct. '77	Gallup	46	11	21	22	—
		Sadat's Visit to Jerusalem (November 1977)					
(a)	Dec. '77	Gallup	44	10	27	19	—
		Breakdown in Israeli-Egyptian Talks (January 1978)					
(b)	Jan. '78	Roper	37	10	20	17	16
(a)	Feb. '78	Gallup	33	14	28	25	—
(a)	Mar. '78	Gallup	38	11	33	18	—
		Terrorist Attack on Israeli Bus—Litani Operation (March 1978)					
(a)	Apr.–May '78	Gallup	44	10	33	13	—
(b)	May '78	Roper	35	9	22	18	15
(a)	Aug. '78	Gallup	44	10	33	13	—
(a)	Sep. '78	Gallup	41	12	29	18	—
		Camp David (September 1978)					
(a)	Sep. '78	Gallup	42	12	29	17	—
(a)	Nov. '78	Gallup	39	13	30	18	—
(a)	Jan. '79	Gallup	40	14	31	15	—
		Talks on Peace Agreement Stalled (February 1979)					
(a)	Mar. '79	Gallup	34	11	31	24	—
(b)	Mar. '79	Roper	36	9	21	13	20
		Israeli-Egyptian Peace Agreement (March 1979)					
(c)	Apr. '79	Yankelovich	47	11	19	22	—
(d)	Oct. '79	*L.A. Times*	49	12	19	11	9
(c)	Dec. '79	Yankelovich	49	6	16	29	—
(b)	Mar. '80	Roper	37	10	21	16	15
(e)	July '80	Harris	52	12	17	10	9
(a)	Oct. '80	Gallup	45	13	24	18	—

Sources: Gallup: "The Polls: Attitudes Toward the Arab-Israeli Conflict," *Public Opinion Quarterly* 47(Spring 1983): 123; and *Gallup Opinion Index* (March 1979), 18, *Gallup Opinion Index* (August 1981), p. 2. Yankelovich, G. Rosenfield, *Attitudes of the American Public Toward American Jews and Israel,* December 1979, Publication 80/180/1, (New York: American Jewish Committee, March 1980), 9. *Los Angeles Times,* National Survey, No. 18, 1979; Harris: Louis Harris and Associates, Study No. 804011 (August 1980), 13; Roper: *Roper Reports,* (July 1983), 37.

fore the Egyptian National Assembly and declared that he was ready to travel to the ends of the earth, even to the Israeli Knesset, if that would help prevent a single Egyptian soldier from being killed or wounded in battle.[30] Sadat had gone a long distance from the days when he claimed he was ready to "sacrifice a million lives for my independence and liberation of my land."[31] Sadat's new peace policy was received with much enthusiasm in Egypt and Israel. Begin responded with a public invitation to Sadat, and, at this point, the visit became inevitable—the only question was timing.

Sadat's new policy and Begin's response attracted the attention of the American media and the three major television networks. ABC, CBS, and NBC scrambled to interview Sadat and Begin side by side. On the morning of November 14, 1977, Walter Cronkite of CBS interviewed Sadat, who said that he was waiting for a "proper invitation" from Israel and, if invited, that he was ready to proceed to Jerusalem within a week. When Cronkite asked how the invitation might be transmitted, Sadat suggested American diplomatic channels.[32] Cronkite immediately searched for Begin and located him six hours later. From an improvised studio at the Tel Aviv Hilton, Begin declared that he would send a formal invitation to Sadat through U.S. ambassadors in Cairo and Tel Aviv. On the CBS evening news of November 14, Cronkite introduced the interviews with Sadat and Begin by claiming, "Now all obstacles appear to have been removed for peace discussions in Jerusalem between Egyptian President Sadat and Israeli Prime Minister Begin."[33] Five days later, Sadat flew to Israel. He received full honors and was warmly greeted by the public.

Sadat's visit to Jerusalem was not only a breakthrough in the thick walls of the Arab-Israeli conflict, it was also a spectacular media event and an "electronic extravaganza."[34] Sadat's every move in Jerusalem was followed by approximately 2,000 reporters, of whom 580 were Americans. During the visit, the evening news on the American networks originated from Jerusalem, and almost two-thirds of the editions were devoted to the visit. The visit was personally covered by Walter Cronkite, Barbara Walters of ABC, and John Chancellor of NBC. A total of almost 20 hours were broadcast on the three major networks, with perhaps 30 million Americans tuned in.[35] Typical characterizations of the visit were "historic," "stunning," "breakthrough," "daring venture," "bold gamble," "momentous visit," and "dramatic gesture." Harry Reasoner of ABC called it a "sheer drama of the pictures," and a correspondent for the *New York Times* added that this drama continued "as various network commentators rattled on about boggled minds, astonished ears and startled eyes, the images alone—moving and even thrilling—told all."[36]

Throughout Sadat's visit, the American media, notably television, treated Sadat more favorably than it did Begin. Sadat appeared on the television screen at least twice as often as Begin and, according to one study, was presented as more outgoing, open, gregarious, popular, and active.[37] Begin, on the other hand, was portrayed as more aloof and withdrawn. The study of the televised images of Sadat and Begin concluded:

> Sadat's ascension in television news put into place a highly visible, articulate voice that was treated as a credible alternative to Begin. Sadat's image was solidified as a 'Westernized', rational, peaceful, personal leader, sufficiently legitimate to appear on a warm, first-name basis with Cronkite and Walters.[38]

Further studies also reveal that Sadat and Egypt received much more positive coverage than did Begin and Israel.[39] Sadat's visit and its portrayal in the American media set the stage for a major Egyptian-Israeli battle for American public opinion. The starting positions were clearly in favor of Sadat. An overnight media hero in the United States, he was much more popular than Begin and almost as popular as Carter.[40] Sadat clearly altered the Egyptian image in the United States. From this point forward, Egypt was seen as an ally of the United States who was interested in peace.

Table 3–3 reveals that prior to Sadat's visit, only 37 percent of the public believed that Egypt sincerely desired peace in the Middle East. After the visit, 58 percent held this view. However, according to the sympathy index (table 3–2), the visit did not alter the overall Arab image in the United States. The Gallup poll indicates that the Arabs had climbed to a double-digit figure for the first time since 1956 in October 1977—after the Begin victory in Israel but before Sadat's visit to Jerusalem. A poll conducted after the visit demonstrates a marginal slip in the Arab column. It is probable that the criticism originating from many Arab nations against Sadat's visit led American public opinion to distinguish between Egypt and the rest of the Arab world.[41]

Sadat's visit also altered the American public's evaluation of Carter's performance on the Middle East and possibly also of his overall management of the presidency. As table 3–1 reveals, before the visit, Carter received negative marks on his policy in the Arab-Israeli conflict. After the visit, though, the public approved of his policy by a plurality of 63 to 29 percent. Before Sadat's visit, the overall rating of Carter's performance was negative by a ratio of 48 to 52 percent. After the visit, this result reversed; 52 percent approved of his performance, while 48 percent disapproved. Ironically, perhaps, these positive results for Carter were achieved because of a decision that, among other things, registered a protest against Carter's original strategy for peace in the Middle East.

Opinions on Initial Peacemaking Efforts

In his speech to the Israeli Knesset, Sadat reaffirmed the tough Egyptian conditions for peace: complete withdrawal from all territories taken in the Six-Day War, including withdrawal from East Jerusalem, and recognition of the rights of the Palestinians for self-determination.[42] Thus, despite Sadat's goodwill venture, a long process of negotiations was necessary before the two na-

Table 3–3
Opinions on Peace Intentions and Efforts, 1977–79

Egyptian-Israeli Peace Intentions

Question

(a) Do you feel that (*read list*) really wants just peace in the Middle East, only reluctantly wants just peace, or really does not want peace? (*Percentage indicates "really wants peace"*) (Harris)

	Oct. '77	*Nov. '77*	*Dec. '77*	*Jan. '78*	*Mar. '78*	*Aug. '79*
(n)	(1,537)	(1,200)	(1,259)	(1,191)	(1,199)	(1,209)
Egypt	37%	58%	52%	52%	42%	63%
Israel	55	61	47	51	40	59

Sadat and Begin: Handling of Peace Negotiations

Question

(b) What kind of job do you think Sadat/Begin is doing in handling peace negotiations in the Middle East? Do you think he is doing an excellent job, a good job, only a fair job, or a poor job? (*Results represent the combined score for doing an excellent or good job*)

	Nov. '77 NBC	*Jan. '78 NBC*	*Feb. '78 Gallup*[a]	*Feb. '78 NBC*	*Mar. '78 NBC*	*May '78 Roper*[b]	*Aug. '78 NBC*	*Sep. '78 NBC*	*Mar. '79 CBS-NYT*[c]
Sadat	66%	65%	66%	56%	46%	40%	40%	64%	60%
Begin	49	49	41	29	25	28	21	53	53

Egyptian and Israeli Peace Efforts

Question

(c) Do you think Egypt/Israel is or isn't doing all it should to bring about peace in the Middle East? (Gallup)

	Egypt				*Israel*			
Date	*Is*	*Isn't*	*N.O.*	*Total*	*Is*	*Isn't*	*N.O.*	*Total*
Jan. '78	33%	50%	17%	100%	25%	58%	17%	100%
Aug. '78	20	54	26	100	18	57	25	100
Nov. '78	33	44	23	100	26	52	22	100
Jan. '79	30	51	19	100	22	60	18	100
Mar. '79	36	43	21	100	28	51	21	100

Sources: (a) *New York Times*, November 2, 1977; *New York Post*, January 23, 1978; April 10, 1978; *AB[C] News–Harris Survey*, August 27, 1979. (b) *NBC News Poll*, December 3, 1977; February 23, 1978; Marc[h] 23, 1978; September 26, 1978; *Newsweek*, February 27, 1978; *Roper Reports*, October 1982. CBS-NYT Pol[l] March 26–27, 3. (c) *Gallup Opinion Index, Mideast Situation*, March, 1979.

[a]The question was on "efforts to bring peace."

[b]The question was on approval of "handling responsibilities in the Mideast situation."

[c]The question was on approval of "handling peace negotiations."

tions could reach a peace agreement. The first phase of the peacemaking process included the following principal steps:

1. The visit of U.S. Secretary of State Vance to the Middle East (December 9–12, 1977);
2. Cairo Conference—a high-level meeting of Israeli, Egyptian, and American officials in Cairo (December 14–24, 1977);
3. Prime Minister Begin's visit to the United States and presentation of the Israeli plans for peace with Egypt and autonomy for the West Bank and Gaza (December 15–17, 1977);
4. A Sadat-Begin summit meeting in Ismailiya, Egypt, including discussions of frameworks and procedures (December 25–26, 1977);
5. President Carter's visit to Aswan, Egypt, and adoption of the "Aswan formula" for resolution of the Palestinian problem (January 4, 1978).[43]

The initial probings of positions revealed Israeli-Egyptian differences related to the peace treaty with Egypt and the linkage between this treaty and a solution to the Palestinian problem. Under these circumstances, Sadat wanted the United States to be what he defined as an "active partner."[44] He expected the United States to concur with Egypt in cases of disagreement with Israel and asked for American pressure on Israel to accept the Egyptian terms for peace. Israel, on the other hand, hoped to achieve as much as possible through bilateral negotiations, leaving the remaining disputes to neutral American mediation. It is interesting to note that after Sadat's visit to Jerusalem, an NBC poll asked a national sample, "Do you think the U.S. should participate in negotiations or do you think the U.S. should not participate?" The response was 53 to 47 percent against U.S. participation.[45] It was certainly a close result, but the Carter administration had no choice and played a major role in the peace process in subsequent months.

At the Begin-Sadat summit at Ismailiya, Israel and Egypt agreed to create two committees, political and military, to proceed with the process. American representatives were invited to participate in committee discussions. The first meeting of the political committee opened in Jerusalem on January 17, 1978. The Egyptian and Israeli delegations were led by the foreign ministers of the two countries, and Secretary of State Vance represented the United States. The Egyptian delegates submitted a framework for peace that called for complete Israeli withdrawal from territories occupied since 1967 and the establishment of a Palestinian entity in the West Bank and Gaza. Israel submitted its plan for peace with Egypt and an autonomy plan for the Palestinians.[46]

However, on the second day of the proceedings, before the parties had a chance to negotiate these proposals, Sadat abruptly recalled his delegation and suspended the talks. This decision seemed arbitrary, since the talks had not yet begun. In an official statement, Sadat criticized Israel for what he called "partial solutions that cannot lead to achieving a just, lasting and comprehensive peace in the Middle East." An Egyptian spokesman added that the recall was "not a result of today. . . . Things accumulated and the last straw was Begin's toast."[47] In his toast of the opening day of the meeting, Begin had stated the Israeli positions and rejected the Egyptian demands for a total withdrawal and a Palestinian state. Apparently, the new Egyptian Foreign Minister Mohammad Ibrahim Kamel was offended by Begin's remarks, and when he reported them to Sadat the following day, he was ordered to proceed immediately back to Egypt.[48]

The breakdown in Israeli-Egyptian talks caused concern in both Jerusalem and Washington. The Israeli government issued a statement that criticized the Egyptian behavior and mentioned that the Israeli plan, which Sadat had so flatly rejected, had been deemed "a long step forward" by Carter only a few weeks earlier.[49] It had been asserted that Sadat suspended the talks because he wanted the United States to fully support the Egyptian position against Israel. If this was the intended goal, Sadat certainly achieved it. Carter invited Sadat to Washington and later wrote in his diary:

> I think we ought to move much more aggressively on the Middle East question . . . discussing the various elements with Sadat one by one. . . . The plan that we evolve has got to be one that can be accepted by Begin in a showdown if we have the *full support of the American people*. . . . I don't know how much support I have, but we'll go through with this effort."[50] (emphasis added)

In February, Sadat and Dayan conferred separately with Carter and, in March, Carter also met with Begin. Following these meetings, American officials publicly supported the Egyptian stand and criticized Begin and Israel.

The January breakdown and other difficulties that emerged in the first months of 1978 sparked a rash of poll-taking on the peacemaking process and Carter's role in it. Immediately after the breakdown, Harris found that the American public blamed Israel and Egypt equally (22 percent each) for the impasse.[51] But the sympathy index (table 3–2) registered some dissatisfaction with the Israeli position, and a series of other surveys, on more specific issues, revealed the nature of the dissatisfaction. After the breakdown, both Roper and Gallup found a decrease in the Israeli sympathy score and an increase in the Arab sympathy score. In January 1978, Roper found that, in contrast to the results of March 1977, Israel lost six percentage points and the Arabs gained five. Gallup also registered a greater slip in the Israeli score—down from 44 percent in December 1977 to 33 percent in February 1978—and an increase for the Arab side from 10 to 14 percent. The 33 percent figure represented the lowest support accorded Israel since 1964, whereas the Arab gain represented the highest support given them since 1948 (see tables 1–4 and 2–1).

President Sadat and Prime Minister Begin stood at the center stage of the peacemaking process, and several polls examined their attitudes and performance. From November 1977, NBC, Gallup, Roper, and CBS-*NYT* asked Americans to evaluate the handling of the negotiations by the Israeli and Egyptian leaders (see question (b) in table 3–3). Responses demonstrate that Sadat outscored Begin on the management of the negotiations from the beginning of the process. After the January 1978 breakdown in negotiations, both leaders received lower marks, but Begin suffered a large drop. In other polls, covering more specific aspects of the peacemaking process, Sadat outscored Begin, sometimes by large margins. For example, according to an NBC poll of February 1978, 53 percent of the sample agreed that Sadat "made more concessions for peace," while only 11 percent held the same view about Begin. However, when the question, "Whom would you trust in a disagreement concerning the peace settlement?" was asked on two occasions, national samples were equally divided between Sadat and Begin (32 percent in January 1978 and 35 percent in March).

In similar queries, the names of Sadat and Begin were replaced by the countries of Egypt and Israel. The responses to these questions deviated from those dealing with Sadat and Begin. On the question of trust, for example, Israel outscored Egypt by a substantial margin (43 versus 20 percent in January 1978 and 43 versus 24 percent in March 1978), while the results for Sadat and Begin were identical. It is possible that Americans distinguished between Begin and Israel and therefore gave lower marks to the prime minister and higher marks to the state.

The role of the United States and President Carter during the initial steps of negotiations and the first crisis were also present in several polls. Following the January breakdown, the *Newsweek*-Gallup poll asked respondents whether the United States should bring more pressure on Israel and Egypt to compromise. Similar segments of the sample, 52 percent and 55 percent, respectively, rejected pressure on Israel and Egypt.[52] An NBC survey of 321 congressmen on the issue of American pressure, however, yielded a different opinion: 39 percent rejected any pressure, but 44 percent were in favor of American pressure on both Egypt and Israel.[53]

Polls on Carter's performance in the first phase of the peace process produced mixed results. In January 1978, his management of peace negotiations was rated "excellent" or "pretty good" by 57 percent of the respondents (table 3–1). But after the January breakdown in the Israeli-Egyptian talks, this percentage dropped to 46 percent. In February 1978, the net difference between the positive and negative ratings was only +1, compared to +22 a month earlier. In March 1978, Carter received a negative rating. In February 1978, however, Gallup found that 56 percent of its national sample approved of the manner in which Carter dealt with the Middle East situation, while 27 percent disapproved.[54] Gallup also asked whether Carter "is leaning too much in favor of Israel, or of Egypt, or is treating both sides fairly?" The majority, 61 percent, felt that Carter treated both sides fairly; 17 percent thought he unduly favored Israel; and 6 percent said he was too much in favor of Egypt.

After the euphoria of Sadat's visit to Jerusalem had waned, the January breakdown in the talks caused confusion and disappointment in American public opinion. Many polls examined opinions on Sadat, Begin, and Carter; results indicate that Sadat was the only leader who kept his image and standing intact.

Perceptions of Israeli-Egyptian Interest in Peace

Andrew Kohut argued, in an article published in the May–June 1978 issue of *Public Opinion,* that American public opinion had shifted from a completely pro-Israeli orientation to a more balanced view of Israel and the Arabs.[55] He based his conclusion mainly on the drop in the Israeli column of the sympathy index in January and February 1978. However, this conclusion proved to be too hasty.[56] Table 3–2 demonstrates that as early as March 1978, Israel had already gained five more percentage points, while the Arabs had lost three percentage points. In the following months, the rates of sympathy in favor of Israel held steady in the vicinity of four to one.

The impasse in the peace process continued, and in the interim, Israel used retaliatory action against PLO bases in South Lebanon. On March 11, 1978, Palestinian terrorists landed on the Israeli shore of kibbutz Magan Michael, located between Haifa and Tel Aviv. They murdered noted American photographer Gail Rubin, then proceeded to hijack a passenger bus.[57] During the rescue operation, 37 persons were killed and 82 wounded. The American public was outraged and overwhelmingly condemned PLO terrorism by a majority of 93 to 2 percent.[58]

On March 14, Israel responded to the terrorist attack on the bus with a relatively large-scale military operation in South Lebanon (the Litani operation). Israeli forces drove out the PLO and destroyed its bases in the entire area south of the Litani River.[59] The operation was very rapid, and within less than 48 hours, Israel had established a "security belt" some 4 to 6 miles wide, skirting the border area. Prime Minister Begin and Defense Minister Ezer Weizman claimed that Israel's forces would withdraw from Lebanon as soon as security arrangements were established in the area. Egypt strongly denounced the operation, calling it "organized genocide."[60] But the official American response was neutral. Although warning that the operation could impede the peace process, a spokesman for the State Department admitted that the terror emanating from Lebanon constituted a security threat to Israel.

Two polls were conducted on the Litani operation at approximately the same time. Between March 20 and 21, Harris conducted a telephone poll of 1,199 American adults nationwide and found that a plurality of 47 to 40 percent thought that the Israeli operation was justified.[61] A poll by NBC News conducted between March 21 and 22 initially asked a national sample of 1,604 Americans whether they had heard or read about the operation in Lebanon. Those who answered positively (about three-quarters of the sample) were then asked, "Do you think that Israel was justified in invading South Lebanon in an effort to halt terrorist attacks, or do you think the Israeli attack was not justified?" Half of the respondents said that the attack was justified, and 35 percent thought that it was not.[62]

On March 21 and 22, Begin met with Carter in Washington to discuss an approach that might break the deadlock in the peace process. The meeting was unsuccessful, and Carter defined it as a "heart-breaking development." Brzezinski simply called it "unpleasant."[63] Begin also appeared before the U.S. Senate Foreign Relations Committee and the House International Relations committee. These meetings were "unpleasant" as well. Following the official visit, Carter told a group of senators that Begin was uncooperative in efforts to resume the peace process. More specifically, Carter complained that Begin would not allow Egypt or the United Nations to assume control over the Israeli settlements in the Sinai Desert, failed to agree to withdraw from certain areas in the West Bank and Gaza, and refused to permit the inhabitants of these territories to determine their future after 5 years of autonomy. However, upon his return from Washington, Begin's positions were unanimously endorsed by his cabinet and were also approved in the Knesset by a vote of 64 to 32.[64]

In mid-April 1978, the Israeli forces began to withdraw from South Lebanon, and the United Nations Interim Force in Lebanon (UNIFIL) assumed the responsibility of preventing the use of southern Lebanon as a base for Palestinian terrorist attacks against Israel. At the same time, however, the Carter administration accused Israel of using cluster bombs in the Litani operation in violation of an earlier pledge to use such bombs only for "internal security and legitimate self-defense."[65] Obviously, Israel argued that the operation was an act of self-defense, but these justifications were ignored by Carter, who apparently wished to exploit the cluster-bomb issue to criticize Israel—following the failure of the Carter-Begin meeting just three weeks earlier. A few days later, the four-part series "Holocaust" was aired on American television. It portrayed the Jewish plight and despair prior to and throughout World War II.[66]

Thus, despite Carter's accusations, it appears the preceding events had a positive impact on American sympathy toward Israel. The sympathy index, (table 3–2) shows that, compared with the February 1978 figures, Israel gained 11 percentage points in the polls of April-May and August 1978, while the Arabs lost 4 points. According to the Roper poll, however, both sides lost one to two points. In the case of the peace process negotiations, table 3–3 demonstrates that both Israel and Egypt received lower marks for their peace efforts. Question (a) in table 3–3 registers an almost identical drop of 11 and 10 percent, respectively, in the ratings of Israel and Egypt. Question (b) indicates that from February to March 1978, Sadat lost 10 percent and Begin lost 4 percent on the rating of "handling of the peace negotiations." Carter also lost points in the public rating of his peace efforts. According to table 3–1, his score in March 1978 was negative (44 to 48 percent) for the first time since Sadat's visit to Jerusalem.

The IDF completed its withdrawal from South Lebanon on June 13, 1978, but the peace process was still frozen. At the end of June, Vice-President Walter Mondale traveled to Israel and Egypt and returned with a discouraging report. Carter then decided to assess whether "there was enough remaining desire for peace" among the parties and suggested a meeting between the foreign ministers of Israel, Egypt, and the United States on neutral ground.[67] The meeting convened July 18 and 19 at Leeds Castle in England. Israel and Egypt reiterated their old positions, but Dayan broke the deadlock by stating that if Egypt accepted the autonomy plan, Israel would agree to discuss the final status of the West Bank and Gaza after 5 years.[68]

Secretary of State Vance and his aides were encouraged by the progress of the Leeds conference but were convinced that any new advances hinged on the presentation of an American peace plan. Vance expected the talks to resume in the Sinai Desert two weeks later, but Sadat adamantly refused. Vance felt that "Sadat lost his initiative to Begin in the struggle for Israeli and American public opinion."[69] The sympathy index (table 3–2) for this period did not register any significant change in the relative strength of Israel and the Arab countries in American public opinion. The results for August 1978 were identical to those of April-May 1978 and December 1977. A poll by NBC, conducted in mid-June, reveals that most respondents (45 percent) either held both Israel and Egypt, or neither one (19 percent), responsible for the "stalled talks."[70] Question (b) in table 3–3 indicates that the slide in the rating of Sadat's and Begin's handling of the peace negotiations continued. In August 1978, their ratings plummeted to a low of 40 and 21 percent, respectively. In contrast to the previous poll of March 1978, Sadat lost six percentage points and Begin four points, but Sadat still led Begin by a ratio of two to one.

Question (c) in table 3–3 shows that in August 1978, a majority of respondents, 54 percent for Egypt and 57 percent for Israel, thought that those countries were not working hard enough for peace. In February 1978, after the first breakdown in peace talks, responses to the identical question were much more favorable to Egypt. But what probably counted the most to President Carter was pressure from Democratic officials and members of Congress to "back out of the situation and to repair the damage they claimed I had already done to the Democratic party and to U.S.-Israeli relations."[71] Carter decided to take a high-risk initiative. Instead of backing out, he invited Sadat and Begin to a summit meeting at the presidential resort of Camp David.

Breakthrough at Camp David

The unprecedented summit meeting began September 6 and lasted almost two weeks.[72] The U.S. president transferred most of his regular duties to his vice-president and mediated between the two tough leaders. Various American presidents had participated in different summit conferences since the end of World War II, but their duties usually had been limited to the signing of agreements that had already been negotiated and agreed upon. In this case, the meeting called for actual negotiations, and results were by no means certain. Furthermore, the president took it upon himself to negotiate detailed formulations of ideas and principles. The high level of the meeting precluded any appeal option. In most cases, if foreign ministers negotiate and fail to reach an agreement, the matters are transferred to the heads of state. At Camp David, the heads themselves negotiated, and the appeal option did not exist. In an unusual move, no time limit was established for the conference, and the mass media, barred from the site, were left in the dark for most of the summit. Carter's stakes in the conference were very high; failure would have meant a devastating blow to his prestige and his political future.

During the first days of the meeting, the president and his aides received the Israeli and Egyptian proposals. On September 10, Carter presented the American proposal, and from that point all further negotiations revolved around this framework. During the process, no fewer than 23 drafts were prepared and revised until the two sides reached an agreement.[73]

The Camp David summit yielded two important frameworks: one outlined an overall peace in the Middle East; the other projected a peace treaty between Israel and Egypt. The first framework dealt primarily with the Palestinian problem and the future of the West Bank and Gaza. Israel and Egypt agreed to invite specified Jordanian and Palestinian representatives to negotiate an autonomy plan for a period of 5 years. During this period, the parties would determine the final status of the areas. The framework for a peace treaty with Egypt called for a complete Israeli withdrawal from the Sinai Peninsula, including the removal of Israeli settlements and airfields, limitation of force deployment in the Sinai area, and normalization of relations, including recognition and diplomatic relations. Egypt and Israel agreed to conclude a peace treaty on the basis of these principles within a period of 3 months.

Despite the media blackout, the Camp David summit attracted considerable attention in the American media. According to one study, the summit and related developments in the Middle East constituted almost one-fourth of all news coverage on television throughout the month of September.[74] In terms of news content, before and after the meeting, both Sadat and Begin received substantial credit for their participation. President Carter received less attention before and during the summit but garnered a substantial amount after Camp David.

The Camp David Accords awarded Carter a giant personal victory. During the post-summit ceremony at the gold and crystal East Room of the White House, Sadat congratulated Carter for taking a "giant step." Begin added, "It was really the Jimmy Carter conference. . . . The president of the U.S. won the day."[75] Begin first embraced Carter and later Sadat. The polls registered dramatic gains for Carter. Figure 3–1 clearly demonstrates how the Camp David summit reversed the steep slide in Carter's popularity ratings. The *New York Times* poll found that the percentage of the public approval rating of his presidential performance climbed from 38 percent in June 1978 to 51 percent at the end of September. A similar increase was identified by Harris. The Gallup poll found an even higher rise in Carter's popularity, from 39 percent in August to 56 percent after Camp David. As table 3–1 reveals, Carter, after Camp David, received a very high mark for his peace efforts, the highest recorded during the entire period from August 1977 to July 1980. The Roper poll also found that Carter's approval rating on the Middle East rose from 44 versus 33 percent in August 1978 to a soaring majority of 73 versus 11 percent in September.

Sadat and Begin also received high marks for their contributions to the Camp David Accords. According to table 3–3, in August 1978, before the summit, the favorability rating of the peace efforts by Sadat and Begin were 40 percent and 21 percent, respectively. After the summit, these percentages climbed to 64 and 53 percent. For the first time in the peacemaking process, Begin exceeded the 50 percent mark and cut the gap between him and Sadat by half. Also, following the achievements at Camp David, Sadat and Begin were awarded the 1978 Nobel Peace prize.

In November 1978, Gallup conducted a survey for the Chicago Council on Foreign Relations. The survey included a question on the favorability of various countries in the eyes of the American public.[76] Israel and Egypt achieved "warm" ratings; Israel's score, 61 degrees, was surpassed only by Canada (72), Great Britain (67), and France (62). The Egyptian score was 53 degrees, and Saudi Arabia scored only 48 degrees.

Although Saudi Arabia simply criticized the Camp David Accords, other more extreme Arab countries, such as Syria and Libya, took more Draconian measures and broke diplomatic relations with Egypt.[77] Syrian President Hafez Assad called the accords "a phony deal signed by two phony men. It represents American imperialism and a complete sell-out of the Palestinians."[78] In view of this harsh criticism from the Arab world, it is hardly surprising that after

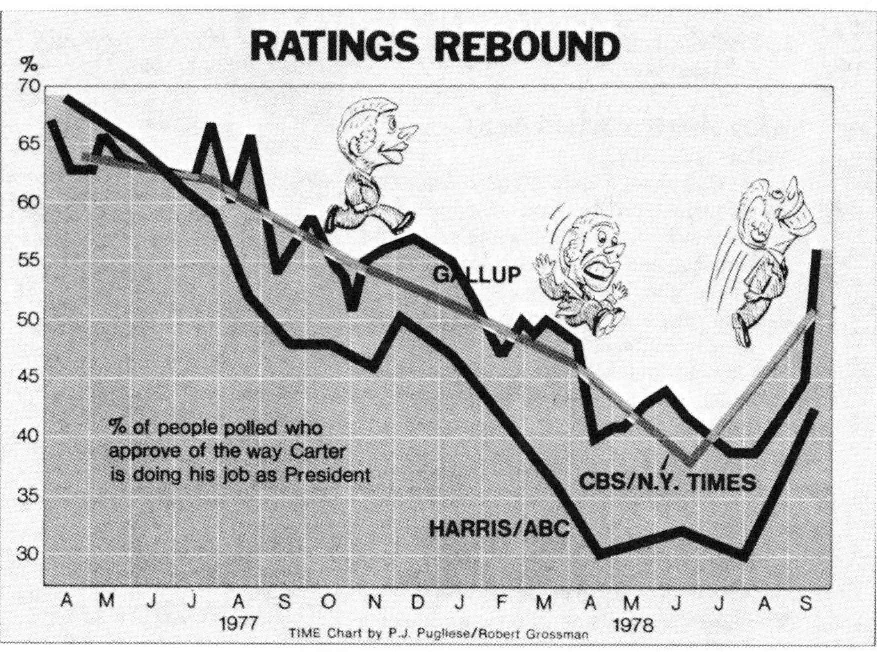

Source: Time, October 2, 1978:8.

Figure 3–1. Carter's Approval Rating

Camp David, the Arabs did not gain any points on the sympathy index (table 3–2.)

Attitudes toward the Israeli-Egyptian Peace Agreement

According to the Camp David Accords, the negotiations between Israel and Egypt toward a peace agreement should have been completed by mid-December 1978. However, the two sides still differed on many critical issues, and the transformation of the Camp David framework into a tangible peace agreement proved to be a very complicated task. The differences between the two countries stemmed mainly from the following issues: Egypt's demand to set a definite date for the completion of the autonomy talks and the beginning of the autonomy arrangement; Egypt's demand for a satisfactory solution to the "priority of obligations" problem, to ensure that the peace treaty would not prevent Cairo from honoring defense agreements with other Arab countries;

Egypt's demand to set a definite duration to the security arrangements in the Sinai Desert; and Israel's demand that Egypt exchange ambassadors one month following the completion of the interim withdrawal.[79] These issues were discussed in several meetings and visits:[80]

1. Blair House conference in Washington, ministers of foreign affairs and defense, for discussions on the peace treaty, beginning October 12, 1978;
2. Secretary of State Vance's visit to the Middle East, December 10–14, 1978;
3. Conference of foreign ministers in Brussels, Belgium, December 23–24, 1978;
4. Visit of Prime Minister Begin to Washington, March 2–4, 1979.

These meetings led to some progress but failed to produce an agreement, and the parties missed the deadline for the finalization of the negotiations. Another snag developed around the Israeli settlement policy in the West Bank. At the end of October, Begin informed the Israeli Knesset that the government would proceed with a program to expand existing settlements in the West Bank.[81] Carter severely criticized this policy, claiming that Begin had promised, at Camp David, to freeze action on settlements. Begin and Foreign Minister Dayan asserted, however, that although Israel had agreed to refrain from forming *new* settlements for the duration of negotiations, it had never consented to suspending expansion of existing West Bank settlements.

American public opinion expressed a deep disappointment in these stalled developments. Question (c) in table 3–3 reveals that in November 1978 and January 1979, the public felt that Israel and Egypt were not doing all they could to achieve peace. In the 1979 poll, the marks of both nations were very similar to those of February 1978, which were recorded after the first major breakdown in the talks. Between December 21 and 26, 1978, a few days after Egypt and Israel failed to meet the peace agreement, the Harris-ABC News poll on the Israeli-Egyptian negotiations presented as follows:

> Talks between Israel and Egypt are now stalemated. Egypt says Israel must give some guarantee about Palestinian self-rule. Israel says that this demand changes the agreement for a separate Egypt-Israel peace made at Camp David. Now, who do you think is more right in the latest breakdown in Middle East talks—Egypt or Israel?[82]

Thirty percent of the respondents said that Israel was more right, while 37 percent sided with Egypt; 6 percent felt neither or both sides were right; and 27 percent were unsure.

In the dispute over the interpretation of the Camp David Accords, Carter clearly sided with Egypt. Noting this partiality, the same ABC News–Harris survey asked whether the president should have backed one side or another. The majority of respondents, 59 percent, thought that Carter should have remained neutral; 22 percent justified the backing of Egypt; and 6 percent felt that Carter should have backed Israel. The public, then, criticized Carter and demanded from him strict adherence to an evenhanded policy. Some criticism of Carter is also evident in the rating of his peace efforts (see table 3–1). In January 1979, this rating was positive, but he lost many points compared to the previous results of September 1978. It is no wonder that under these circumstances, only 21 percent of the late-December 1978 ABC-Harris sample held "a great deal of confidence in the ability of Carter to make peace."

The American public's pessimism toward Carter was probably related to negative evaluations of his overall presidential performance and, in particular, of his foreign policy. It should be noted that in addition to the Israeli-Egyptian peace negotiations, other dramatic events occurred elsewhere in the Middle East that damaged Carter's image even further. During most of 1978, the Shah of Iran had been saddled with rising political and social dissension in his country. The crisis in Iran reached an acute stage in November and December 1978, and the Shah was forced to accept many demands from the opposition.[83] On January 16, 1979, the Shah left Iran and traveled to Egypt, and his 37-year rule came to an end. Two weeks later, the instigator of the revolution against the Shah, Ayatollah Ruhollah Khomeini, returned to Iran after a long period of exile and assumed power over the government. The Shah had been a close ally of the United States and had helped protect American interests in the Persian Gulf area since the departure of the British from that area in 1967. Khomeini and his followers were extremely anti-American, and many groups in the United States and the Middle East accused Carter of not doing enough to help the Shah. Unnerved by Carter's inaction, American allies, including Egypt and Israel, grew concerned with the credibility of the United States in crisis situations.

In the first months of 1979, Carter lost substantial ground in American public opinion. The *New York Times*–CBS poll found that as early as January 1979, only 42 percent approved of Carter's overall management of the presidency and only 34 percent approved of his foreign policy.[84] Five weeks later, his ratings slipped even further—to 37 percent on the overall job and 30 percent on his foreign policy.

Carter was desperate and looked for a major foreign policy achievement that might buoy his image. He recalled:

> Sadat was adamant in his position; I had not been able to penetrate past Begin to his cabinet, the Knesset, or the Israeli people; and the American public was getting weary of our continuing obsession with an apparently futile effort.[85]

Carter chose to take another bold initiative and visit Israel and Egypt in an effort to break the new deadlock. Carter wrote that his press secretary was concerned about the effects of a possible failure on Carter's image, but other officials felt that the president had nothing to lose and that even if he failed, the American public would still appreciate his efforts.[86]

Carter visited Israel and Egypt between March 10 and 13, 1979, and presented Begin and Sadat with an American proposal for the solution of the remaining peace agreement problems. His mission was successful, and the peace treaty was finally approved.[87] It was signed in Washington on March 26, in a ceremony attended by Sadat and Begin. The differences between Israel and Egypt were resolved through the following concessions: Israel agreed to withdraw its armed forces from the Sinai Desert in two phases—the first within 9 months and the second after 3 years. The two sides also agreed on a permanent border—the international border that had existed during the British mandate in Palestine.[88] Egypt agreed to terminate the state of war with Israel and to establish diplomatic relations at the ambassadorial level upon the completion of the interim withdrawal. Egypt also agreed to normalize economic and cultural relations.[89]

The highly disputed linkage between the peace treaty and the autonomy negotiations was resolved through a letter in which the parties agreed to set "the goal of completing the negotiations within one year." The Arab world rejected the peace agreement and representatives from 18 Arab League nations and the PLO met in Baghdad, Iraq, and unanimously agreed to sever diplomatic and economic relations with Egypt.[90]

The achievement of the peace agreement in March 1979 did not produce many spin-off polls on American attitudes toward the Arab-Israeli conflict, but between March 16 and 18, 1979, after Carter's announcement in Cairo that Israel and Egypt had accepted his proposal for a peace agreement, Gallup conducted a poll on the situation in the Middle East.[91] The poll revealed a very high level of interest. The respondents were then asked a few questions on Carter's role in the agreement. The majority, 62 percent, said that Carter "was treating both sides equitably"; 11 percent thought he sided too much with Israel; and 10 percent thought he favored Egypt. Table 3–1 indicates that Carter's Middle East approval rating jumped again to a net difference of +45 percent.

A CBS-*NYT* poll of March 1979 (see question (b) in table 3–3) found high positive marks for Sadat and Begin. But Gallup, who repeated the question on the peace efforts of both sides (see responses to question (c) in table 3–3) still found that 43 percent and 51 percent respectively, thought that Egypt and Israel were not doing all they could to achieve peace. These results are similar to those of November 1978 and probably indicate resentment toward the slow pace of the peace process and the difficulties that had emerged since the Camp David summit. Americans were also skeptical about the future prospects of the agreement. Only a quarter of the sample believed that the agreement would lead to lasting peace between Israel and Egypt; 59 percent thought otherwise.

The sympathy index also registered some dissatisfaction (see table 3–2). The Gallup poll of March 1979 found a slide of 6 percent in the Israeli ratings and 3 percent in the Arab ratings in comparison to its previous results of January 1979. Roper also conducted a poll on American sympathy in March 1979. The results do not greatly differ from those of Gallup and are almost identical to his previous results of May 1978. Thus, according to Roper, the Camp David Accords and the peace process had no effect on American sympathy toward Israel and the Arab nations. The major criticism of Sadat in the Arab world and the actions taken against him may account for this result.

Autonomy Issues: Wrangle over the West Bank and Jerusalem

The implementation of the Israeli-Egyptian peace treaty began immediately after it was officially ratified by the parliaments of both countries. Israel began preparations for the first interim withdrawal and also hosted the first talks on the autonomy plan. However, Jordan and the Palestinians refused to participate, and the Carter administration soon returned to the concept of a comprehensive solution to the Arab-Israeli conflict and took measures to bring the PLO into the process.[92] Therefore, the United States probably encouraged a meeting in Vienna between PLO Chairman Yasser Arafat, Bruno Kreisky, chancellor of Austria, and Willy Brandt, the former chancellor of West Germany and president of Socialist International. The meeting convened July 8, 1979, and, as expected, accorded Arafat high-level legitimacy.[93] On July 26, U.S. Ambassador to the United Nations Andrew Young met with the PLO observer at the United Nations to discuss the upcoming debate on the Palestinian problem in the Security Council. Young first denied then later admitted that he had met with the PLO observer.[94] The meeting violated a pledge given by the United States to Israel in September 1975, which stipulated that the United States would not negotiate with the PLO until this organization accepted U.N. Resolution 242 and recognized Israel. Young was forced to resign from his post.

Polls conducted in August 1979 on the U.S. policy toward the PLO and the Palestinians reveal criticism of Carter's comprehensive approach. In an ABC News–Harris survey, the majority of the public, 54 percent, disapproved of the Young talks.[95] By a substantial ratio, 77 to 13 percent, the public supported the main provisions of the autonomy plan and reaffirmed, by a majority of 65 to 27 percent, the American commitment of September 1975.[96] Concerning a second issue—the vote in the Security Council on Palestinian self-determination in the West Bank—the public favored a U.S. veto on such a resolution by a plurality of 47 to 36 percent. On the other hand, the ABC News–Harris poll found higher ratings for the Israeli and Egyptian interest in a just peace. Question (a) in table 3–3 reveals that the rate for Egypt in August 1979 was 63 percent versus 59 percent for Israel. These figures represent an increase of 21 percentage points for Egypt and 19 percentage points for Israel compared to the results of the pre-Camp David period. Also, the figure for Egypt was the highest and, for Israel, the second highest, following Sadat's visit to Jerusalem.

While Israel and Egypt proceeded with the implementation of the peace agreement, several dramatic events occurred in the northern tier of the Middle East. These events—the hostage crisis in Iran and the Soviet invasion of Afghanistan—bore many repercussions for the Carter administration and for U.S. policy in the Middle East. The hostage crisis began November 4, 1979, when several hundred Iranians seized the U.S. embassy in Tehran and took approximately 60 Americans hostage.[97] The immediate cause of this act of terrorism was the admission of the ailing Shah to the United States for medical treatment. The forces of the Ayatollah Kohmeini demanded the extradition of the Shah, the return of his money to Iran, and other conditions for the release of the hostages. President Carter rejected the Iranian demands and insisted on an immediate release of the hostages. In the initial stages of the crisis, as in most similar cases, the American people united behind the president.[98] As the saga dragged on without solution in sight, however, the public rose against Carter and criticised him for his failure to facilitate the release of the hostages.

Several weeks after the seizure of the U.S. embassy in Tehran, the Carter administration faced another challenge in neighboring Afghanistan. Throughout 1979, the Marxist government in Kabul had attempted without success to subdue an internal Muslim rebellion.[99] At the end of 1979, the rebellion intensified, and the government tottered on the verge of total collapse. On December 27, 1979, the Soviet Union deployed thousands of troops across the border to save the Marxist regime in Afghanistan.[100] The Soviet invasion shocked the United States and the world. In the past, the Soviet Union had used force to quash freedom campaigns in Hungary (1956) and Czechoslovakia (1968), but these countries had been defined and recognized as part of the Soviet sphere of influence in Eastern Europe. The Kremlin had never claimed a similar status for Afghanistan; therefore, military intervention on its southern flank established a new precedent.

The hostage crisis and the Soviet invasion severely damaged the image of the United States as a superpower, particularly in the eyes of Middle East regimes. Carter felt that action was needed to restore American credibility in the region, and in his 1980 State of the Union address, he announced a new American doctrine for the Middle East:

> Let our position be absolutely clear. An attempt by any outside force to gain control of the Persian Gulf region will be regarded as an assault on the vital interests of the United States of America, and such an assault will be repelled by any means necessary, including military force.[101]

American public opinion approved of the Carter doctrine by a ratio of 61 to 30 percent. However, words were insufficient in the Middle East. Countries of the region wished to see words backed up by actions and a new determination.

While the hostage crisis and the Soviet occupation of Afghanistan were attracting considerable attention in the United States, implementation of the first phase of the Israeli-Egyptian peace treaty was completed. By January 23, 1980, Israel finalized the withdrawal of its forces to the interim line and, on February 18, opened its embassy in Cairo. Two weeks later, Egypt inaugurated its embassy in Tel Aviv. The autonomy talks, however, did not proceed well—mostly because of the participants' inability to separate the arrangements for the 5-year autonomy period from the postautonomy status of the West Bank and Gaza. For example, when the parties discussed the number of representatives to be elected to the Autonomy Governing Council, Israel suggested about 20, but Egypt, which envisioned this body as a nucleus for a Palestinian parliament, suggested about 80 members.[102]

The difficulties in the autonomy talks created some tension between the United States and Israel.[103] The preparations for the 1980 presidential elections had started; the economic difficulties at home and the failures abroad made Carter very vulnerable, and he did not want to antagonize any segment of his constituency, including the Jews. Thus, on March 1, the U.S. vote in the Security Council for the anti-Israel resolution surprised everyone. The resolution severely condemned Israeli settlements in the West Bank and the Israeli development and administration of Jerusalem.[104] In the past, the United States had always abstained on such resolutions. On March 3, however, Carter issued a statement in which he claimed the vote was an error that had resulted from a failure in communications between Washington and the U.S. mission to the United Nations:

> The U.S. vote in the United Nations was approved with the understanding that all references to Jerusalem would be deleted. The failure to communicate this clearly resulted in a vote in favor of the resolution rather than in an abstention.[105]

Shortly after the incident, Harris probed American public opinion both on the vote and on the retraction.[106] He first asked: "Do you think the U.S. should have voted for the Arab resolution condemning Israeli settlements on the West Bank and continued Israeli occupation of Jerusalem, or should we have abstained, not voted on it, as we have in the past?" A clear majority, 70 percent, said that the United States should have abstained; 4 percent thought that the vote should have gone against the Arab-sponsored resolution, and 12 percent said that the United States should have voted for it. The second question asked: "Do you think President Carter made a serious mistake or not by saying the U.S. had never intended to vote in favor of the Arab resolution in the first place?" In response to this question, 64 percent said that it was a serious mistake, and only 19 percent held the opposite view. Following the "failure in communications" announcement, the Carter foreign policymaking process was reprimanded, and the responses to the second question could have been influenced by this criticism.

The issue of Jerusalem, one of the problems Egypt and Israel had failed to agree upon at Camp David, emerged again a few months later. On April 1, 1980, Egypt's National Assembly issued a statement asserting that East Jerusalem was sovereign Arab territory and "an integral part of the West Bank which had been occupied by armed force." All steps that had been taken in the city by Israel since the Six-Day War were proclaimed "illegal, null and void and non-binding."[107] On July 1, 1980, the Egyptian parliament adopted a resolution confirming the statement of April 1.[108] President Sadat repeated the same themes on July 22, when he spoke during a ceremony that commemorated the 1952 revolution in Egypt.[109]

In response to the Egyptian resolution, a small, rightist opposition party in the Knesset, Ha-tchiya, argued that the Egyptian parliament decision must be countered by a similar action in the Israeli parliament and proposed the "Basic Law: Jerusalem." The Jerusalem Law was approved by the Knesset on July 30, 1980, by a vote of 65 to 13, with 3 abstentions.[110] It did not add to or change the existing status of Jerusalem. East Jerusalem had been annexed to Israel immediately after the Six-Day War. The new law thus reaffirmed previously passed laws and stated that reunited Jerusalem, in its entirety, is the capital of Israel and the seat of its national institutions. The law also protects the holy places and authorizes the government to develop all parts of the city. The Jerusalem Law was strongly criticized in the United States, in the region, and throughout the world. Egypt reacted to the law by demanding a delay in the autonomy talks, and the Netherlands and several Latin American countries transferred their embassies from Jerusalem to Tel Aviv.[111]

Prior to the Knesset vote on the Jerusalem Law, Harris conducted a comprehensive survey on American attitudes toward the Arab-Israeli conflict. This survey included questions on three possible solutions to the problem of Jerusalem: a unified city under Israeli control and joint Arab-Israeli local government; internationalization; and return to Arab control.[112] Internationalization was rejected by a majority of 52 to 26 percent. (It should be recalled that immediately after the Six-Day War, 70 percent of the public supported internationalization.) The Arab demand to control Jerusalem was also rejected by a similar majority of 56 to 22 percent. On the other hand, the public endorsed, by a sizable majority (63 to 17 percent), the Israeli position, which called for a unified city under Israeli control, with provisions for shared municipal administration and free access to holy places.

Further polls also found strong and clear support for the Israeli stand on Jerusalem. The fall 1980 poll analyzed by Slade revealed that 65 percent of the sample completely or mostly concurred with Israel on the issues of Jerusalem; only 10 percent completely or mainly sided with the Arabs.[113] A Yankelovich poll of February 1981 asked, among other queries, whether Israel "has the right to make Jerusalem the capital of Israel."[114] Almost half of the respondents (48 percent) said yes; only 17 percent said no. All of the preceding data indicate that the American public had firm ideas about the issue of Jerusalem. It rejected the Arab and Egyptian positions, disagreed with the American official stand, and supported the basic Israeli claim to the city.

Jerusalem—or, more specifically, the question of whether the Arab city residents would be allowed to vote in elections for the Autonomy Governing Council—was only one difficult issue in the autonomy talks. These talks were suspended by Egypt after the approval of the Jerusalem Law, but even before the interruption, the proceedings had been hindered by fundamental disagreements. In a July 1980 survey, when Harris asked the major reasons for the lack of progress on the autonomy talks, identical numbers of respondents (47 percent each) cited both the inability of Sadat to "get other Arab countries and groups to join in the peace talks" and the intention of Begin "to set up new Jewish settlements on the West Bank."[115] In a *Newsweek*-Gallup poll of April 1981, a plurality of 44 to 32 percent stated that the United States should "put more pressure on Israel to stop developing Jewish settlements on the mostly Palestinian West Bank."[116] But a Roper poll of August 1980 found only 19 percent supporting and 61 percent opposing "reduction of U.S. military supplies to Israel until it agrees with the idea of a Palestinian homeland."[117] Finally, the sympathy index (table 3–2) also registered improvement in the Israeli ratings. In the July 1980 Harris survey, Americans sympathized more with Israel by a majority of 52 to 12 percent. The Gallup poll of October 1980 found an 11 percent increase for Israel, compared to only a 2 percent increase for the Arabs, since the previous poll of March 1979.

While preparing for his election battle against Republican presidential candidate Ronald Reagan, Carter received only minimal credit for his mediation in the Arab-Israeli conflict. The Harris poll of July 1980 found that only 27 percent of the sample approved of his performance at the White House and 72 percent disapproved.[118] The latter rating was one of the lowest ratios ever accorded an occupant of the White House. On Carter's management of the Middle East crisis (the question probably referred to the hostage crisis and the Soviet occupation of Afghanistan), he received a negative rating of 34 to 64 percent, and, as table 3–1 reveals, the rating on his peace efforts was also negative by a ratio of 46 to 51 percent. Regarding Carter's role in the peacemaking process, he was credited by an overwhelming majority (90 percent) for "trying to keep good U.S. relations with both the Arabs and Israel," but only 49 percent agreed that "he had been evenhanded with both Arabs and Israel." A sizable majority (63 percent) criticized Carter for allowing himself to be influenced too much by Arab oil; a lesser majority (56 percent) complained that "he keeps changing his mind too much about what the U.S. is for or not for in the Middle East." In the 1980 presidential elections, Carter was defeated by Ronald Reagan, who quickly changed US. Middle East policy.

Effects of the Peace Process

Sadat's visit to Jerusalem and the belated, yet successful, peacemaking process caused enormous effects on the Egyptian image in the United States. Positive American attitudes toward Sadat and the Egyptian position in the peace negotiations were discussed earlier. In February 1978, a few months after Sadat's visit, the *Newsweek*-Gallup poll conducted a telephone survey with a national sample of 654 Americans and asked: "Compared with a year ago, would you say you are more sympathetic or less sympathetic to the Egyptian position?" Almost half of the sample (48 percent) said they were more sympathetic.[119]

The favorability rating of Egypt rose dramatically—not so much after the Sadat visit but rather after the Camp David summit and the signing of the peace treaty. The intensity of these feelings also changed. In 1976, only 14 percent of the Gallup sample were highly favorable to Egypt (ratings +5, +4, +3), but in 1980, 34 percent held the same feelings. Table 3–4 demonstrates that the peace process also prompted the increase in the favorability rating of

Table 3–4
Israel and Egypt Favorability Ratings, 1967 and 1977–80

Question

You will notice that the 10 boxes on this card go from the highest position of plus five—for someone or something you have a very *favorable* opinion of—all the way down to the lowest position of minus five—for someone or something you have a very *unfavorable* opinion of. How far up the scale or how far down the scale would you rate Israel/Egypt? (*Percentage indicates favorable ratings only*) (Gallup)

	Jan. '67	*Nov. '77*	*Mar. '78*	*Feb. '79*	*Jan. '80*	*Jan. '81*
Israel	65%	62%	59%	68%	74%	75%
Egypt	49	51	45	63	71	71

Source: "Scalometer Ratings," *Gallup Report,* September 1982, 21.

Israel, from 65 and 62 percent in 1976 and 1977 to 74 and 75 percent in 1980 and 1981.

Sadat's peace policy altered American perceptions of his interest in a Middle East settlement. On several occasions after 1974, Harris probed national samples for views on the approaches of Middle East leaders to Arab-Israeli peace. As indicated in table 3–5, in 1974, after the Yom Kippur War, 45 percent of the sample felt that the Egyptian leadership "will really work for a just peace settlement." This percentage rose to 52 percent after the interim agreement of September 1975 and then jumped to 77 percent after the signing of the Israeli-Egyptian peace treaty. In 1980, the Egyptian score on this issue even surpassed that of Israel.

Following Sadat's visit and throughout most of the peacemaking process, the sympathy index (table 3–2) registered only minor changes in the distribution of American sympathies for Israel and the Arabs. This finding is probably related to American awareness of the severe criticism of Sadat's visit and peace policy from most of the Arab world. Yet table 3–5 reveals that Sadat's policy might have affected, at least to a certain degree, the image in the United States of other Arab countries, especially those considered pro-American. Jordan and Saudi Arabia criticized the Camp David Accords and the Israeli-Egyptian peace treaty, but as table 3–5 demonstrates, in 1980 (compared to the 1974 and 1976 results) they received higher marks for their interest in peace. This was not the case with the leadership of the more radical and anti-American countries, such as Libya and Syria. A somewhat similar pattern emerges from polls conducted on the degree of friendship and alliance between the United States and several Middle East countries.

Responses to questions (b) and (c) in table 3–5 demonstrate the revolutionary change in the Egyptian image. In January 1976, approximately a third of the respondents thought that Egypt was a "close ally" or "friendly to the U.S." In July 1980, though, twice as many respondents held this view, and about a year later, an overwhelming majority considered Egypt an ally of the United States. The second section of table 3–5 also indicates that the ratings of Saudi Arabia and Jordan rose considerably from those in 1976, while those of Syria and Libya fluctuated by a few percentage points.

The ratings of Israel rose by ten percentage points from 1976 to 1981, but the real strength of the Israeli image as an American ally in comparison to all the Arab nations, including Egypt, is revealed on the lower right-hand side of table 3–5. In November 1981, the combined score for the categories "close ally" and "friendly" was identical for Israel and Egypt. But in the "close ally" category, Israel outscored Egypt. Israel also surpassed Egypt and other Arab nations by a large margin in response to the question, "Who is America's strongest ally in the Middle East?"

The overall strength of Israel in American public opinion compared to Egypt and other Arab nations also emerges from polls taken by the Yankelovich organization in April 1979.[120] The question in this poll read: "If war broke

Table 3–5
Opinions on the Effects of Egypt's Peace Strategy

Middle East Leadership Working for Peace

Question

(a) The leadership of (*country*) is reasonable and will really work for a just peace settlement. (Harris)

	1974		*1976*		*1980*	
Country	*Agree*	*Disagree*	*Agree*	*Disagree*	*Agree*	*Disagree*
Israel	57%	13%	60%	10%	69%	16%
Egypt	45	20	52	13	77	9
Saudi Arabia	29	26	33	20	43	25
Jordan	36	17	31	16	42	22
Syria	—	—	21	26	17	33
Libya	—	—	16	22	15	37

Close Ally Ranking

Questions

(b) I am going to read you the names of some countries and groups. For each, tell me if you feel that country is a close ally of the U.S., friendly but not a close ally of the U.S., is not friendly but not an enemy, or is unfriendly and an enemy of the U.S. (Harris)

(c) Which of the following countries would you say is America's strongest ally in the Middle East? (Penn and Schoen)

	(b) "Close Ally" and "friendly"				*(b) "Close Ally"*	*(c) "Strongest Ally"*
Country	*Jan. '76*	*Nov. '77*	*July '80*	*Nov. '81*	*Nov. '81*	*Aug. '81*
Israel	74%	72%	81%	84%	35%	41%
Egypt	35	48	73	84	29	20
Saudi Arabia	32	39	52	69	14	14
Jordan	34	42	47	51	6	1
Syria	17	25	19	22	2	1
Libya	18	21	23	20	1	1

Sources: (a) Louis Harris and Associates, Study No. 804011 (August 1980), 20–22. (b) *Public Opinion* 5(April–May 1982), 52; *USA Today,* November 29, 1982. (c) *Penn and Schoen General Survey,* No. 244, 357, May 1982.

out between Israel and Egypt/Arab nations, with whom would your sympathies lie?" The respondents favored Israel over Egypt by a plurality of 37 to 14 percent and Israel over the Arab nations by a plurality of 47 to 11 percent. These findings and the data in table 3–5 vaguely define the limits of the change that Sadat's peace policy brought about in the relative images of Israel, Egypt, and the Arab world in American public opinion.

Conclusions

The years of the first major peacemaking process in the Arab-Israeli conflict were marked by the rise of three unique politicians and personalities: Sadat, Begin, and Carter. All three were religious in their own way and were strongly motivated by a sense of history. All three, especially Sadat and Carter, saw favorable American public opinion as a key to the success of their actions and moves. Sadat emphasized this point in his speeches and talks, and Carter described, in his memoirs, the substantial weight he assigned to public opinion in the consideration of major decisions. Both believed that only supportive public opinion would force Begin to make the difficult but necessary concessions for Israeli-Egyptian peace, and they manipulated the American media toward that end.

The American media—notably, the television networks—were fascinated and intrigued by the peace process and by Sadat's personality. The peace process became a major news item that greatly increased the coverage of Israel and the Middle East in the American media. Events such as Sadat's visit to Jerusalem, the Camp David conference, Carter's visit to the Middle East, and the signing of the Israeli-Egyptian peace treaty dominated the news for relatively long periods of time.

Sadat certainly was a hero in the eyes of the American media and public. He was perceived as a leader who singlehandedly made a giant, historic step toward peace in the Middle East. The sight of former bitter enemies meeting and conferring is always a thrilling experience, but considering the long record of hostility and violence between the two nations, Sadat's and Begin's mutual visits surprised the public and the media and were considered extraordinary. Sadat changed the Egyptian image in the United States from negative to positive, but he did not alter the overall Arab image in the United States, which remained negative. Furthermore, the improvement in the Egyptian image was not achieved at the expense of Israel.[121]

The change in the Egyptian image was apparent in many aspects. Following Sadat's visit to Jerusalem, the American public sympathized more with Egypt, considered it a U.S. ally and friend, and believed in its peace intentions. Sadat became a very popular leader and received high marks for his handling of the peace negotiations—marks higher than those of Begin and Carter. Changes in the Egyptian image were not followed by a similar alteration in the image of the Arab world. At most, these changes slightly affected the perceptions of the pro-Western Arab countries. The overall Arab image in American public opinion remained low, however, primarily because of the criticism of Sadat and his peace policy by the entire Arab world. Sadat was isolated, and even American allies in the Middle East, such as Jordan and Saudi Arabia, attacked him and condemned his policy.

Throughout the peace process, pollsters compared the performance of Sadat and Begin. In many of these comparisons, Sadat out-scored Begin, but when the conduct of the two countries was compared, the results were different; in several cases, Israel's score surpassed Egypt's. It could be, as suggested by several scholars, that the American public distinguished between Begin and the Israeli public, believing that the Israeli public was more interested in peace than Begin was and thus was more willing to make concessions.[122] This impression was probably created by the activities of antigovernment groups, such as Peace Now, in Israel. However, polls conducted in Israel revealed substantial public support for Begin's negotiating positions.[123]

In the popularity battle, Begin could hardly compete with Sadat. The American media adopted a negative attitude toward him from the day he became Israel's prime minister. In addition, the process necessary for producing peace between Israel and Egypt was destined to be long, difficult, and arduous. Breakdowns and setbacks were inevitable, and although the Carter administration and the media attributed most of them to Begin, the American public was not always convinced. On several occasions, when asked directly to assign blame for the breakdowns, the public blamed Israel and Egypt equally. Other opinion data revealed that despite Sadat's immense popularity, American public opinion continued to sympathize more with Israel, looked upon it very favorably, and considered it a close ally.

No American president was so immersed in Arab-Israeli peace efforts as Carter. This was the major issue and task of his foreign policy. Even after his defeat in the 1980 presidential elections, he continued to speak and write about the Arab-Israeli conflict and organized programs and conferences on this issue.[124] At the beginning of the peace process, Carter maintained strict neutrality between Israel and Egypt, but later, whenever the talks reached a dead end, he mostly sided with Egypt and exerted pressure on Israel to make more concessions. The public wanted Carter to act as a neutral mediator, but it gave him substantial credit for his efforts. Undoubtedly, all of the data demonstrate that his achievements in the Israeli-Egyptian peace process boosted his popularity ratings and public evaluation of his overall presidential performance. However, Carter could not reap all the benefits from the Camp David Accords and the peace treaty. The hostage crisis and the Soviet invasion of Afghanistan overwhelmed the public and, among other things, contributed to his defeat in the 1980 presidential elections. The events also inspired a new American approach to the Middle East and to the Arab-Israeli conflict.

Notes

1. Jules Witcover, *Marathon: The Pursuit of the Presidency, 1972–1976* (New York: Viking Press, 1977).

2. President Carter emphasized this point in one of his first major speeches on U.S. foreign policy: "A Democratic Foreign Policy," delivered at Notre Dame University, South Bend, Indiana, May 22, 1977, published in *U.S. Department of State Bulletin*, June 13, 1977.

3. Don Peretz, "The Earthquake—Israel's Ninth Knesset Elections," *Middle East Journal* 31 (Summer 1977): 254–55. See also Scott Johnston, "The Prospects for New Israeli Politics," *World Affairs* (Spring 1977): 314–17.

4. See, for example the statement by Professor Hisham Sharabi to Mark A. Bruzonsky in his "Straws in the Wind," *Middle East International*, no.86(August 1978): 8; and Meg Greenfield, "Our Ugly Arab Complex," *Washington Post*, November 30, 1977.

5. *Toward Peace in the Middle East*, Report of a study group (Washington D.C.: Brookings, 1975).

6. The members of the Brookings Middle East Study Group were Morroe Berger, Robert R. Bowie, Zbigniew Brzezinski, John C. Campbell, Najeeb Halaby, Rita Hauser, Roger W. Heyns, Alan Horton, Malcolm Kerr, Fred Khouri, Philip Klutznick, William Quandt, Nadav Safran, Steven L. Spiegel, A.L. Udovitch, and Charles W. Yost.

7. *Toward Peace*, 10.

8. "It is impossible to seek a resolution to the energy problem without tackling head on—and doing so in an urgent fashion—the Arab-Israeli conflict," Zbigniew Brzezinski in "Recognizing the Crisis," *Foreign Policy* 17(Winter 1974-75): 67. See also Zbigniew Brzezinski, Francois Duchene, and Kiichi Saeki, "Peace in an International Framework," *Foreign Policy* 19(Summer 1975): 3-17.

9. For an early criticism of Brzezinski's approach, see Shlomo Avineri, and Amos Perlmutter, "An Exchange on the Middle East," *Foreign Policy* 21(Winter 1975–76): 212–17, 219–21.

10. The Trilateral Commission was established to identify joint interests and policies of the United States, Western Europe, and Japan. Zbigniew Brzezinski, *Power and Principle: Memoirs of the National Security Adviser, 1977–1981* (New York: Farrar, Straus and Giroux, 1983), 5.

11. See Bernard Reich, *The United States and Israel: Influence in the Special Relationship* (New York: Praeger, 1984), 41-64. For a critical analysis of the Carter strategy on Israel and the Arab-Israeli conflict, see Steven L. Spiegel, "The Carter Approach to the Arab-Israeli Dispute," in H. Shaked and I. Rabinovich, eds., *The Middle East and the United States* (New Brunswick, N.J.: Transaction, 1980), 93-120; and Harvey Sicherman, *Broker or Advocate? The U.S. Role in the Arab-Israeli Dispute 1973-1978*, Monograph No. 25 (Philadelphia: Foreign Policy Research Institute, 1978).

12. *The Quest for Peace: Principal United States Public Statements and Related Documents on the Arab-Israeli Peace Process, 1967–1983* (Washington, D.C.: U.S. Department of State, 1984), 66–67.

13. See Sabri Jiryis, "Political Settlement in the Middle East: The Palestinian

Dimension," *Journal of Palestine Studies* 7(Autumn 1977): 3-26; and Y. Harkabi's interpretation: *The Palestinian Covenant and Its Meaning* (London: Vallentine, Mitchell, 1979), 149–59.

14. Leonid I. Brezhnev, *Selected Speeches and Writings on Foreign Affairs* (Oxford: Pergamon Press, 1979), 299-300.

15. U.S. Department of State, *Quest for Peace*, 70–71.

16. George H. Gallup, *The Gallup Poll: Public Opinion, 1972-1977* (Wilmington, Del.: Scholarly Resources, 1978), 1036.

17. Ibid; 1225, 1239.

18. *New York Times*, November 2, 1977.

19. On Begin's background, see Eric Silver, *Begin: A Biography* (London: Weidenfeld and Nicolson, 1984); Eitan Haber, *Menachem Begin* (New York: Delacorte Press, 1978); and Yitzhak Ben-Ami, *Years of Wrath, Days of Glory: Memoirs from the Irgun* (New York: Speller, 1982).

20. See chapter 2.

21. Asher Arian, ed., *The Elections in Israel—1977* (Jerusalem: Academic Press, 1980); and Howard Penniman, ed., *Israel at the Polls: The Knesset Elections of 1977* (Washington D.C.: American Enterprise Institute for Public Policy Research, 1979).

22. *New York Times*, May 19, 1977, A-22.

23. *Newsweek*, May 30, 1977, 35.

24. *Time*, May 30, 1977, 27.

25. *Newsweek* titled the report of the visit "A Charmer Named Begin," August 1, 1977, 27. See also favorable reports in the *Washington Post* and the *New York Times*, July 23-24, 1977.

26. Shmuel Segev, *Sadat—The Road to Peace* (Tel Aviv: Massada, 1978), 39-53 (Hebrew).

27. Moshe Dayan, *Breakthrough: A Personal Account of the Egypt-Israel Peace Negotiations* (London: Weidenfeld and Nicolson, 1981), 42–43.

28. Melvin A. Friedlander, *Sadat and Begin* (Boulder, Colo.: Westview Press, 1983), 65, 68; and Saadia Touval, *The Peace Brokers* (Princeton, N.J.: Princeton University Press, 1982) 299.

29. Segev, *Sadat*, 49.

30. Anwar el-Sadat, *In Search of Identity* (London: Collins, 1978), 308; *New York Times*, November 10, 1977; Segev, *Sadat*, 49.

31. Raphael Israeli, *The Public Diary of President Sadat* (Leiden, Netherlands: Brill, 1978), 109.

32. "Behind Cronkite's Coup," *Time*, November 28, 1977; "The Cronkite Summit," *Newsweek*, November 28, 1977; Robert Kaiser, "When World Chiefs Turned to Walter to Trade Greetings," *New York Post*, November 17, 1977.

33. The full transcript of the interviews with Sadat and Begin was published in the *New York Times*, November 15, 1977.

34. "TV Diplomacy and Other Broadcast Quandaries," *Columbia Journalism Review* 18(May–June 1979): 69-80.

35. Ibid. and *New York Times*, November 22, 1977.

36. John J. O'Connor, "TV: Symbolic Event Is Highlighted by 'Sheer Drama of Pictures,'" *New York Times*, November 22, 1977.

37. Magda Bagnied and Steven M. Schneider, "Sadat Goes to Jerusalem: Televised Images, Themes and Agenda," In William C. Adams, ed., *Television Coverage of the Middle East* (Norwood, N.J.: Ablex, 1981), 60.

38. Ibid. 64. See also Steven M. Schneider, "A Content Analysis of Sadat's 1977 Visit to Israel," In Richard L. Cole, ed., *Introduction to Political Inquiry* (New York: Macmillan, 1980), 245–59.

39. See, for example, Douglas J. Feith, "Israel, the Post and the Shaft," *Middle East Review* 12(Summer 1980): 62–66; and Edwin Diamond and Paula Cassidy, "Arabs vs. Israelis: Has Television Taken Sides?" *TV Guide,* January 6, 1979.

40. *The Gallup Opinion Index,* February 27, 1978.

41. Five Arab countries (Libya, Algeria, Iraq, Syria, South Yemen) and the PLO met in Tripoli, Libya, December 2–4, 1977, and formed a "Rejectionist Front" against Egypt and Sadat's initiative.

42. Friedlander, *Sadat and Begin,* 90; *Newsweek,* November 28, 1977; and *New York Times,* November 21, 1977.

43. See Dayan, *Breakthrough,* 110; and Friedlander, *Sadat and Begin,* 146-47.

44. Thomas W. Lippman, "Sadat Wants U.S. to Play a Key Role," *Washington Post,* December 8, 1977. See also Touval, *The Peace Brokers,* 296 and Bernard Lewis, "The Egyptian Perspective," *Commentary* 66(July 1978): 38.

45. Survey by NBC News, November 29-30, 1977, reprinted in "Opinion Roundup," *Public Opinion* 1(March-April 1978): 31.

46. Dayan, *Breakthrough,* 109–14.

47. *New York Times,* January 19, 1978.

48. Cyrus Vance, *Hard Choices: Critical Years in America's Foreign Policy* (New York: Simon and Schuster, 1983), 201–2.

49. For the Israeli response, see *Ha'aretz,* January 19, 1978. For the original Carter praise of the autonomy plan see "The President: Television Interview," *U.S. Department of State Bulletin* (January 1978): 9–11.

50. Jimmy Carter, *Keeping Faith: Memoirs of a President* (New York: Bantam, 1982), 306.

51. *The Harris Survey,* January 18–19, 1978, published January 26, 1978.

52. *Newsweek,* February 27, 1978.

53. *NBC News Poll,* presented on "NBC Nightly News," February 9, 1978.

54. *Los Angeles Times,* February 9, 1978.

55. Andrew Kohut, "American Opinion on Shifting Sands," *Public Opinion* 1(May-June 1978): 15-18.

56. Even at the time, Seymour Martin Lipset had reservations about Kohut's findings, see Ibid., 16-17.

57. *New York Times,* March 12-13, 1978.

58. *New York Post, Washington Post,* April 10, 1978.

59. See Itamar Rabinovich, *The War for Lebanon, 1970-1983* (Ithaca, N.Y.: Cornell University Press, 1984), 107–11; and David Gilmour, *Lebanon: The Fractured Country* (New York: St. Martin's Press, 1983), 148–49.

60. *New York Times,* March 16, 1978.

61. *Washington Post,* April 10, 1978.

62. *NBC News Poll,* March 21-22, 1978.

63. Carter, *Keeping Faith*, 313, and Brzezinski, *Power and Principle*, p. 246.

64. *Ha'aretz*, March 30, 1978.

65. Vance, *Hard Choices*, 207–08.

66. The producer of the series wrote a bestseller about it: Gerald Green, *Holocaust* (New York: Bantam, 1978).

67. Carter, *Keeping Faith*, 315.

68. Dayan, *Breakthrough*, 138–48; and Friedlander, *Sadat and Begin*, 84–90.

69. Vance, *Hard Choices*, 216.

70. Quoted in Seymour Martin Lipset "The Polls on the Middle East," *Middle East Review* 11(Fall 1978), 29.

71. Carter, *Keeping Faith*, 315–16.

72. On the Camp David conference, see William B. Quandt, *Camp David: Peacemaking and Politics* (Washington, D.C.: Brookings, 1986), Chs. 8-9; Carter, *Keeping Faith*, 319-403; Vance, *Hard Choices*, ch. 10; Brzezinski, *Power and Principle*, 252–72; Ezer Weizman, *The Battle for Peace* (New York: Bantam, 1981); Dayan, *Breakthrough*, 149-90; and Reich, *The United States and Israel*, 65-73.

73. E. Rubinstein, *Turning Points in the Peace Process* (Jerusalem: Information Center, 1980), 7 (Hebrew).

74. William C. Spragens with Carole Ann Terwood, "Camp David and the Networks: Reflections on Coverage of the 1978 Summit," in William C. Adams, ed. *Television Coverage of International Affairs* (Norwood, N.J.: Ablex, 1983), 122.

75. *New York Times*, September 18, 1978, and *Time*, September 25, 1978.

76. This survey used a "feeling thermometer." This thermometer, printed on a display card, showed regular gradations ranging from 0 degrees (no feeling one way or the other) to 100 degrees (extremely warm or favorable feeling); John E. Rielly, ed., *American Public Opinion and U.S. Foreign Policy, 1979* (Chicago: Council on Foreign Relations, 1979), 18.

77. Paul A. Jureidini, *Beyond Camp David: Emerging Alignments and Leaders in the Middle East* (Syracuse, N.Y.: Syracuse University Press, 1981); and Fayez A. Sayegh, "The Camp David Agreement and the Palestine Problem," *Journal of Palestine Studies* 8(Winter 1979): 3-40.

78. *Time*, October 2, 1978, 8.

79. The differences between Israel and Egypt were summarized in Vance, *Hard Choices*, 245–46.

80. See Reich, *The United States and Israel*, 74–9.

81. *New York Times*, October 26, 1978.

82. *ABC News-Harris Survey*, vol. 1, no. 4, December 21–26, 1978, released January 11, 1979.

83. On the revolution in Iran, see Barry Rubin, *Paved with Good Intentions: The American Experience and Iran* (New York: Oxford University Press, 1980); and Shaul Bakhash, *The Reign of the Ayatollahs: Iran and the Islamic Revolution* (New York: Basic Books, 1984).

84. *New York Times*, March 6, 1979.

85. Carter, *Keeping Faith*, 415–16.

86. *New York Times*, March 6, 7, 1979; and Vance *Hard Choices*, 245.

87. *New York Times*, March 17, 20, 23, 1979.

88. Later, however, Israel and Egypt could not agree on the southern tip of the border and both claimed the tiny territory of Taba, each arguing that it lies on its side of the international border.

89. "The Egyptian-Israeli Peace Treaty," *Middle East Journal* 33(Summer 1979) 327–47. For various views about the treaty, see "Egypt and Israel: Prospects for a New Era," *Washington Quarterly* (special issue), Georgetown University Center for Strategic and International Studies (Spring 1979); Elie Kedourie, "After the Treaty," *New Republic*, April 7, 1979, 17-18; and Robert W. Tucker, "Behind Camp David," *Commentary* 66(November 1978): 25-33.

90. See Paul A. Jureidini, R.D. Mclaurin and James M. Price, *Arab Reactions to the Egyptian-Israeli Peace Treaty*, Abbott Associates SR 46 (March 26, 1979).

91. *Gallup Opinion Index*, March 16-18, 1979.

92. Abraham Ben-Zvi, *The United States and the Palestinians: The Carter Era*, Paper No. 13 (Tel Aviv: Tel Aviv University, Center for Strategic Studies, November 1981): 20-26; and Reich *The United States and Israel*, 80-81.

93. *New York Times*, July 9, 1979.

94. *New York Times*, August 15, 16, 1979. For more details on the Young Affair, see ch. 5.

95. Elizabeth H. Hastings and Philip Hastings, eds., *Index to International Public Opinion, 1979-1980* (Westport, Conn.: Greenwood Press, 1980), 101, (hereafter referred to as *Index to International Public Opinion*).

96. *ABC News-Harris Survey*, vol. 1, no. 105, August 21-22, 1979, released August 27, 1979.

97. Charles W. Scott, *Pieces of the Game: The Human Drama of Americans Held Hostage in Iran* (Atlanta: Peachtree, 1984); and Warren Christopher et al., *American Hostages in Iran: The Conduct of a Crisis* (New Haven, Conn.: Yale University Press, 1985).

98. *Index to International Public Opinion*, 100-101, Iran: The Early Reaction," *Public Opinion* 2(December-January 1980): 58; and "Opinion Roundup," *Public Opinion* 3(February-March 1980): 29.

99. See Henry S. Bradsher, *Afghanistan and the Soviet Union* (Durham, N.C.: Duke University Press, 1983).

100. Joseph J. Collins, *The Soviet Invasion of Afghanistan* (Lexington, Mass.: Lexington Books, 1986).

101. *Public Papers of the Presidents of the U.S.: Jimmy Carter, 1980–1981* (Washington, D.C.: Government Printing Office, 1981), 197.

102. See Reich, *The United States and Israel*, 74-79.

103. Harvey Sicherman, "The United States and Israel: A Strategic Divide?" *Orbis* 24(Summer 1980): 381–93.

104. *New York Times*, March 3, 4, 5, 1980.

105. Carter's full statement was published in the *New York Times*, March 5, 1980. See also Carter, *Keeping Faith*, 493–94.

106. *Index to International Public Opinion*, 94.

107. *Ha'aretz*, April 2, 1980.

108. *Ha'aretz*, July 2, 1980.

109. *Ha'aretz*, July 23, 1980.

110. *Ha'aretz,* July 24, 1980.

111. *New York Times,* August 3, 1980.

112. Louis Harris and Associates, *A Study of the Attitudes of the American People and the American Jewish Community toward anti-Semitism and the Arab-Israeli Conflict in the Middle East* Study No. 804011, August 1980, 55–56.

113. Shelley Slade, "The Image of the Arab in America: An Analysis of a Poll on American Attitudes," *The Middle East Journal* 35(Spring 1981), 154.

114. Gregory Martire and Ruth Clark, *Anti-Semitism in the United States* (New York.: Praeger, 1982), 78.

115. Harris and Associates, *A Study of the Attitudes,* 39.

116. *Newsweek,* April 21, 1980, 35.

117. *Roper Reports,* no. 8(October 1982), Question 17.

118. Harris and Associates, *A Study of the Attitudes,* 37.

119. *Newsweek,* February 2, 1978.

120. Yankelovich, Skelly and White, Inc., Memorandum, December 28, 1979, 6-7.

121. William Schneider, "Is Israel Losing Public Support?" *Politics Today* (March-April 1979): 14-16.

122. Lipset, "The Polls on the Middle East," 26–28; and William C. Adams, "Middle East Meets West: Surveying American Attitudes," *Public Opinion* 5(April-May 1982): 51-5.

123. See Shmuel Sandler and Hillel Frisch, *Israel, The Palestinians and the West Bank* (Lexington, Mass.: Lexington Books, 1984): 129-30.

124. Jimmy Carter, *The Blood of Abraham: Insights into the Middle East* (Boston: Houghton Mifflin, 1985). See also "Interview with Jimmy Carter," *American-Arab Affairs* 7(Winter 1983–84): 1–10.

4
War and Terror in Lebanon

Ronald Reagan's victory in the 1980 presidential election led to a major shift in U.S. global priorities and policies and consequently to changes in the American approach to the Middle East and the Arab-Israeli conflict. Reagan's assumption of power coincided with the beginning of government alterations in principal Middle Eastern countries throughout 1981.

On May 30, 1981, elections were held in Israel, and Begin was able to continue with his previous coalition. However, his second government varied greatly from the first. Moderate politicians, such as Yigael Yadin, had retired, and Moshe Dayan and Ezer Weizman, who had resigned, were looking for new political avenues. Begin appointed tough-minded Ariel Sharon, a highly controversial figure, as minister of defense. The third change in principal governments was prompted by a tragic event—the murder of Egypt's President Sadat by an extreme Islamic group on October 6, 1981. He was succeeded by his vice-president, Hosni Mubarak. Reagan's victory, the second Begin coalition, and the assassination of Sadat contributed to new, major developments in American policy and Middle Eastern politics.

While the southern front of the Arab-Israeli conflict (Egypt) was edging closer to a state of peace, the northern front (the PLO and Syria in Lebanon) was moving closer to a state of war. The Israeli-Lebanese border presents an interesting case study. From 1948 to 1970, it was Israel's most quiet and stable border. In 1970, following the events of Jordan's "Black September," the PLO penetrated Lebanon and built an independent mini-state of its own in the southern areas adjacent to the Israeli border. These areas were used as bases for attacks on Israeli towns and cities across the border and as training centers for terrorist assaults on Israeli, Jewish, and American targets abroad. Since the 1973 Yom Kippur War, the Israeli-Lebanese border has been the only violent border between Israel and its Arab neighbors.

The PLO's activities in Lebanon presented Israel with a serious challenge. In April 1978, Israel conducted a limited military operation against PLO bases in southern Lebanon and the border stabilized for a time, but the PLO recovered and resumed its attacks on Israel. Despite United States–mediated cease-fires, warfare continued on and off throughout the next 4 years until it erupted into a large-scale confrontation that lasted almost 3 months.

The 1982 Israeli war in Lebanon was very controversial in both Israel and the United States. Never in the history of Arab-Israeli wars was a resort to force by Israel so severely criticized inside and outside the country. The leaders and citizens of the United States followed the war with considerable uneasiness and confusion. This was also the first war in history to be televised by American networks from both sides. It was fought in heavily populated urban areas, and almost every evening, television viewers fixed their gazes on the ugly face of modern warfare.

The war in Lebanon occupies a substantial section of this chapter. Its long- and short-term effects on American attitudes toward Israel and the Arab-Israeli conflict are discussed in great detail. Since the Palestinians and PLO were highly involved, it is both interesting and significant to examine possible effects of the war on American attitudes toward these two groups. This examination is pursued in the following chapter, which deals specifically with long-term trends in American public opinion toward the Palestinian question. The American media played a highly controversial and adverse role in the war, and this issue is also analyzed.

The war in Lebanon led to limited American military involvement in Beirut. A small unit of U.S. Marines was dispatched to Lebanon as part of a multinational peacekeeping force. However, after the IDF partially withdrew, the marines became victims of Shiite suicide bombing attacks. A section of this chapter traces the developments in American public opinion on this involvement.

Various Lebanese factions continued to harass both Israel and the United States, even after the withdrawal of the U.S. Marines and the IDF from Lebanon. In June 1985, Lebanese-Shiite terrorists hijacked a TWA passenger carrier to Beirut and a major crisis ensued. The terrorists presented demands to the United States and Israel, forcing the two traditional allies into an uncomfortable situation. Throughout the second week of the crisis, the media compared the TWA affair to Carter's long hostage crisis in Iran and referred to the president as "Jimmy Reagan." But Reagan's crisis ended in a very different manner; the final section of this chapter examines its effects on American attitudes toward Israel.

Prelude to War

Reagan's victory in 1980 led to a major shift in U.S. foreign policy. He deemed the threats of Soviet expansionism and aggression the major challenge facing the United States, condemned the Soviet military intervention in Afghanistan, announced the battle against international terrorism as his most important goal, and stated that the United States should project military strength and be ready to use it if necessary.[1]

In the Middle East, these principles led to a U.S. effort to contain Soviet threats and subversion by creating a regional alliance of pro-Western Arab countries and Israel. The alliance, Reagan assumed, would naturally emerge from a "strategic consensus" among the countries of the region in response to the Soviet threat.[2] Because of this strategy, the Arab-Israeli conflict was relegated to a much lower level on the list of U.S. global priorities. The Reagan administration simply assumed that the Soviet threats, so devastatingly and brutally demonstrated in the invasion of Afghanistan, would be sufficient to unite rival Arab countries and Israel under the American flag. Consequently, Reagan ignored the Camp David Accords and did not appoint a special representative to the dying autonomy talks.

Within several months, however, he discovered how mistaken these assumptions were. The fragile cease-fire between rival factions in Lebanon collapsed in April 1981. Christians fought Syrians over the town of Zahle, which controls access to both the Bekaa Valley and the Beirut-Damascus highway. Israel, a Christian ally since the PLO invasion of Lebanon in 1970, intervened and, on April 28, 1981, shot down two Syrian assault helicopters.[3] The Syrians responded by introducing SAM antiaircraft missiles to the Bekaa Valley, in violation of a Syrian-Israeli 1976 tacit agreement, and a major missile crisis developed. The United States cited Syria for the crisis but nevertheless offered to mediate and sent a special envoy to the Middle East—Philip Habib.

While Habib was wrestling with the missile crisis, Israel surprised the United States and the world on June 7, 1981, when it attacked and destroyed an Iraqi nuclear reactor near Baghdad.[4] The Begin government defended the action by arguing that the Osirak reactor was built to produce nuclear weapons and was capable of endangering Israel's existence. The Israeli attack on the Iraqi nuclear reactor was strongly criticized in the United States, and it voted with all of the other members of the U.N. Security Council for a resolution condemning the Israeli operation.[5] President Reagan also decided to withhold a delivery of four F-16 combat aircraft to Israel, pending a review of alleged Israeli violations of the American law regarding limitations on the use of American weapons. This punishment of Israel had no precedent, and for the first time in the history of American-Israeli relations, the U.S. government withheld shipment of weapons in violation of signed contracts.[6]

In the meantime, Israel was involved in an election campaign; Labor led the Likud in public opinion polls, and Labor spokesmen hinted that the Iraqi attack was designed to improve the chances of the Likud at the polls. In the Israeli elections of June 30, Begin won just one more seat than Labor, but this slight advantage was sufficient to allow him to proceed with his former coalition.[7] The Syrian missile crisis was not yet resolved, and Syria further exacerbated the problem by encouraging the PLO to attack Israeli cities and towns near the northern border from South Lebanon. By that time, the PLO had accumulated tremendous artillery force and firepower. Two serious attacks were perpetrated by the PLO on July 10 and 15, 1981, causing heavy casualties and damage. Israel retaliated by attacking PLO headquarters in Beirut, drawing further criticism from the United States and the Israeli public, since the assault caused many civilian casualties.[8]

Reagan was about to resume shipment of the F-16s but, in view of the new incident, chose to postpone the delivery. The State Department issued an official declaration that condemned both the PLO attacks on Israeli cities and Israel's bombing of the PLO headquarters in Beirut.[9] The statement called for a cease-fire—which was achieved by Habib on July 24.

How did these events and repercussions affect American attitudes toward Israel and the Arab-Israeli conflict? According to a poll by R.H. Buskin, the public disapproved of Israel's action against the nuclear reactor by a plurality of 38 to 31 percent.[10] However, a CBS-*NYT* poll of an "aware" group (June 22-27) revealed an equal division on the Israeli operation: 39 percent of the respondents thought that it was justified and an identical percentage said that it was not. American opinions on the Israeli bombing of the PLO headquarters in Beirut were examined in two polls. Between July 22 and 23, the *Newsweek*-Gallup poll conducted a telephone survey of 551 adults who said that they were familiar with the Middle East conflict.[11] The poll used the following question: "Was Israel justified to try and stop Palestinian rocket attacks by bombing PLO positions in Beirut although it caused extensive civilian casualties or was the bombing of Beirut not justified?" Half of the sample said that the bombing was not justified and 31 percent thought that it was. A Penn and Schoen poll conducted several days later yielded different results.[12] The question in this poll queries: "As you know, Israel and the Palestine Liberation Organization have been fighting on and off in Lebanon. Generally speaking, would you say Israeli attacks on PLO military installations in Lebanon have been justified or not justified?" Responses to this question were almost the opposite of those given to the *Newsweek*-Gallup question. Forty-nine percent of the sample said the Israeli attacks were justified, and 29 percent thought they were not. These differences might relate to the different samples—aware versus unaware groups—and to the wording of the questions. The question in the *Newsweek*-Gallup poll mentioned civilian casualties, while the Penn and Schoen question was more general and mentioned both Israeli and PLO confrontations.

The July 1981 *Newsweek*-Gallup poll also asked: "Compared to a year ago, would you say you are more sympathetic or less sympathetic to the Israeli position?" Thirty-seven percent said that they were less sympathetic, 29 percent said they were more, and 18 percent indicated no change in sympathies. The same poll included a standard question on American sympathies for Israel and Arab countries, but the query and responses were not published with the other poll responses.[13] They were published only in 1982 and reveal that, in comparison to the previous October 1980 score, on July 22-23, Israel had gained four percentage points and the Arabs had lost three. (See table 4–1.)

A few days later, Gallup conducted another poll on sympathies and found a plurality of 44 to 11 percent in favor of Israel, which is very similar to the score of October 1980—45 versus 13 percent. Also, the Roper results for July 1981, 35 versus 10 percent, were very similar to those of his previous poll of March 1980 (37 versus 10 percent; see table 3–2). Therefore, according to both the Gallup and Roper polls, the events on the northern Israeli front did not affect the distribution of American sympathies for either Israel or the Arabs.

Two specific questions in the July 1981 *Newsweek*-Gallup poll reveal some U.S. public dissatisfaction with Israel's policy. Begin's peace efforts were rated as excellent or good by only 29 percent of the sample in July 1981, a sharp drop from February 1978 when the score for the same question had been 41 percent. Also, in February 1978, a plurality of 52 to 36 percent opposed American pressure on Israel to compromise on its peace conditions, but in July 1981, this ratio reversed—57 to 33 percent favored such pressure.

In the summer of 1981, responding to the missile crisis, the bombing of the Iraqi nuclear reactor, and the Israeli bombing of the PLO headquarters in Beirut, a portion of the media, several members of Congress, and government officials described Israel as a "prickly" and unpredictable ally and criticized Begin for behavior and policy that ignored U.S. interests in the Middle East.[14]

Table 4–1
Sympathies for Israel and the Arab Nations, 1981–85

Question

(a) Have you heard or read about the situation in the Middle East? *If yes:* In the Middle East situation, are your sympathies more with Israel or more with the Arab nations? (Gallup)

(b) With regard to the situation in the Middle East at the present time do you find yourself *more* in sympathy with Israel, or *more* in sympathy with the Arabs? (Roper)

(c) In the Middle East situation, are your sympathies more with Israel or more with the Arab nations? (WP-ABC)

(d) At the present time, do you find yourself more in sympathy with Israel or more in sympathy with the Arab nations? (Los Angeles Times)

(e) In the dispute between Israel and the Arabs, which side do you sympathize with more, Israel or the Arabs? (Harris)

Q	*Date*	*Poll*	*Israel*	*Arab Nations*	*Neither*	*D.K.*	*Both*
		Clashes among Israel, Syria, and the PLO in Lebanon (June 1981)					
(a)	July 22–23, '81	*Newsweek*-Gallup	49%	10%	20%	21%	—
(a)	July–Aug. '81	Gallup	44	11	34	11	—
(b)	July '81	Roper	35	10	22	23	11
(a)	Nov. '81	Gallup	49	12	20	19	—

Table 4–1 continued

Q	*Date*	*Poll*	*Israel*	*Arab Nations*	*Neither*	*D.K.*	*Both*
			Golan Law (December 1981)				
(a)	Jan. '82	Gallup	49	14	23	14	—
(c)	Mar. '82	*WP*-ABC	55	18	13	14	—
			Return of Sinai to Egypt (April 1982)				
(a)	Apr.–May '82	Gallup	51	12	26	11	—
			War in Lebanon (June–September 1982)				
(a)	June 11–14, '82	Gallup	52	10	29	9	—
(b)	June '82	Roper	39	9	23	17	12
(d)	July 4–8, '82	*L.A. Times*	48	17	22	13	—
(a)	July 11–14, '82	Gallup	41	12	31	16	—
(c)	Aug. 17, '82	*WP*-ABC	52	18	16	14	—
(b)	Sep. '82	Roper	40	15	20	16	9
			Sabra-Shatila Massacre (September 16–17, 1982)				
(a)	Sep. 22–23, '82	*Newsweek*-Gallup	32	28	21	19	—
(c)	Sep. 24–26, '82	*WP*-ABC	48	27	12	13	—
(b)	Oct. '82	Roper	38	14	21	18	9
(a)	Jan. '83	Gallup	49	12	22	17	—
(c)	Jan. '83	*WP*-ABC	47	17	15	21	—
			Kahan Report—Sharon's Resignation (February 1983)				
(c)	Feb.–Mar. '83	*WP*-ABC	52	16	13	19	—
(a)	July '83	Gallup	48	12	26	14	—
(b)	July '83	Roper	37	9	21	22	10
(c)	Sep. '83	*WP*-ABC	49	13	14	24	—
(b)	Jan. '84	Roper	44	8	21	14	12
(b)	Mar. '84	Roper	39	8	21	23	9
			TWA Hostage Crisis (June 1985)				
(c)	July '85	*WP*-ABC	49	11	18	22	—
			Achille Lauro Incident (October 1985)				
(e)	Oct. '85	Harris	64	14	10	9	3

Sources: Gallup: C. de Boer, "The Polls: Attitudes Toward the Arab-Israeli Conflict," *Public Opinion Quarterly* 47(Spring 1983): 121–31. Gallup, August 1981: *Gallup Report,* August 1981, 2. Gallup, November 1981: *Attitudes Concerning the American Jewish Community—The Gallup Poll,* November 1981, Publication No. 81/180/15, (New York: American Jewish Committee, Information and Research Services, December 1981), 6. Gallup, January and July 1983, *Gallup Report International,* Vol. 1, no. 6, (August 1983), 6–7. *Newsweek*-Gallup: *Newsweek,* October 4, 1982, 11. *WP*-ABC Poll: *Washington Post,* August 20, 1982, March 9, 1983: *WP*-ABC, 1982–85: Survey Nos. 0196 and 0197, July 1985. *L.A. Times* Poll: *Los Angeles Times,* July11, 1982. Roper: *Roper Reports,* April 1984. Harris: *The Harris Survey,* No. 92, November 14, 1985.

This criticism probably prompted Penn and Schoen to include the following question in their August 1981 poll: "Is Israel a reliable ally of the U.S., or do its actions threaten American interests in the Middle East?" Forty-five percent of the respondents felt that Israel was a reliable ally; 35 percent thought that Israel threatened U.S. interests; and 4 percent said that Israel was both a reliable ally and one that threatened U.S. interests. Yet when the *Newsweek*-Gallup poll asked whether President Reagan should resume shipments of U.S. F-16 fighter planes to Israel, 61 percent said no and only 30 percent said yes. However, when queried several days later in a different poll on whether the United States should keep, increase, or reduce military aid to Israel, 71 percent of the sample was in favor of either keeping or increasing military aid to Israel. In character with responses to the Israeli bombing of PLO headquarters, the more specific question yielded negative responses for Israel, and the more general questions produced positive results.

President Reagan's management of the unstable, July-August 1981 Middle East situation was approved of by a plurality of only 39 to 25 percent (see table 4–2). By comparison, his overall performance at the White House during the same period was rated positively by a majority of 62 to 29 percent. A similar ratio also rated positively his management of foreign affairs.[15]

Prickly Ally?

Following the American-mediated cease-fire in Lebanon, the Reagan administration lifted the combat-aircraft embargo on Israel and sought a return to its major goal in the Middle East—containment of the Soviet Union. The containment strategy included three main elements: (1) commencing American Rapid Deployment Force (RDF) exercises on the soil of countries friendly to the United States, such as Egypt, Sudan, and Oman; (2) the delivery of sophisticated weapons to Saudi Arabia, included Airborne Warning and Control System (AWACS); and (3) the conclusion of a strategic cooperation pact with Israel.

The Saudi and the Israeli elements were related. Israel had opposed the AWACS deal since early April 1981 on the grounds that this system would constitute a serious threat to Israel's security. In September and October 1981, the Reagan administration pushed for congressional approval of the sale, but the House and Senate were not persuaded, and toward the end of September it appeared that the deal would be rejected.[16]

The concept of close Israeli-American strategic cooperation, introduced by Secretary of State Alexander M. Haig, Jr., on September 10, was designed, among other things, to reduce Israel's opposition to the AWACS deal, but the turning point in the controversy was the assassination of Sadat on October 6, 1981.[17] Sadat was murdered by an extremist Islamic group while attending a

Table 4–2
Reagan's Middle East Approval Rating, 1981–85

Question

Do you approve or disapprove of Ronald Reagan's handling of the . . .

Date	*Poll*	*Approve*	*Disapprove*	*N.O.*	*Net Difference*
		Situation in the Middle East			
July–Aug. '81	Gallup	39%	25%	36%	+14%
Mar. 8, '82	*WP*-ABC	49	34	17	+15
	Situation in Lebanon, Israel's War (June–October 1982)				
Aug. 17, '82	*WP*-ABC	48	37	15	+11
Sep. 26, '82	*WP*-ABC	42	45	13	−3
Oct. 11, '82	*WP*-ABC	43	37	20	+6
Oct. '82	Roper	43	33	23	+10
	Situation in Lebanon, U.S. Military Involvement (October 1982–February 1984)				
Mar. 2, '83	Roper	44	39	17	+5
Oct. 26, '83	*WP*-ABC	41	53	6	−12
		Reagan's Speech (October 27, 1983)			
Oct. 28, '83	*WP*-ABC	52	42	6	+10
Nov. '83	Gallup	34	52	14	−18
Dec. '83	*WP*-ABC	43	50	7	−7
Jan. 4, '84	*WP*-ABC	43	46	11	−3
Jan. 30, '84	*WP*-ABC	30	60	10	−30
Feb. '84	Gallup	28	60	12	−32
		TWA Hostage Crisis (June 1985)			
June 17, '85	*WP*-ABC	48	32	20	+16
June 18, '85	CBS	51	23	26	+28
June 19, '85	*WP*-ABC	68	25	8	+43
June 20–21, '85	*Newsweek*-Gallup	59	24	17	+35
June 20–22, '85	*WP*-ABC	69	22	8	+47
July 1, '85	*WP*-ABC	72	21	7	+51

Sources: Gallup: *Gallup Reports,* August 1981, 42; *Baltimore Sun,* March 1, 1984. *WP*-ABC: Survey No. 0114Y, March 1982; Survey No. 0072, March 1983; *WP*-ABC: *Washington Post,* December 15, 1983, January 20, 1983; *WP*-ABC Survey Nos. 0196 and 0197, July 1985; "20/20," January 5, 1984. Roper: *Roper Reports,* October 1982, March 1983. *Newsweek*-Gallup: *Newsweek,* July 1, 1985, 15. CBS: *CBS News Poll,* June 18, 1985.

parade in commemoration of the eighth anniversary of the Yom Kippur War. He was succeeded by his vice-president and former air force commander, Hosni Mubarak, but his sudden death caused concern in both Washington and Jerusalem about the future of the peace process and U.S. positions and influence in the Middle East. Following the assassination, nine senators announced support for the AWACS deal.[18] The American public, however, expressed reservations. At the end of October 1981, the *Los Angeles Times* found that the sale of AWACS to Saudi Arabia was opposed by a majority of 56 to 29 percent,[19] but the Senate nevertheless approved it by a close vote of 52 to 48.[20]

To soften the blow dealt by the AWACS deal, the United States conducted intensive negotiations for the Israeli-American strategic agreement. In Washington on November 30, 1981, Secretary of Defense Caspar Weinberger and Israel's Minister of Defense Ariel Sharon signed a memorandum of understanding on strategic cooperation.[21] The memorandum emphasized Soviet threats and contemplated various measures that the two nations should take to meet and counter these threats. The pact sparked heated debate in Israel. For the first time, the Israeli government officially defined the Soviet Union as an enemy and implied that it would cooperate with the United States against the USSR across the region. Apparently, the Reagan administration had its own reservations about the memorandum and downplayed its importance. In any event, the strategic agreement was short-lived. On December 14, 1981, the Knesset, led by Begin, approved a law that extended Israeli jurisdiction over the Golan Heights.[22]

The "Golan Law" surprised and angered the United States. The legislation took place at a very delicate moment in the Solidarity crisis in Poland, and American officials, particularly Weinberger, severely criticized the Israeli action.[23] The United States concurred with the other 14 members of the Security Council and voted for a resolution that called the de facto annexation of the Golan Heights "null and void without any international legal effect." The United States also suspended the strategic pact and the arms deal with Israel.[24] When U.S. ambassador to Israel Samuel Lewis appeared before Begin and served him with an official protest, the prime minister angrily complained that the United States treated Israel like a "banana republic."[25] Responding to the suspension of the strategic pact, Begin canceled it altogether. American-Israeli relations were marred once again by a serious rift.

The polls, however, did not register any erosion in American opinions of the Israeli image. The sympathy index reveals that in November 1981 and January 1982, Israel enjoyed favorable pluralities of 49 to 12 percent and 49 to 14 percent, respectively (see table 4–1). These scores represent similar increases for Israel and the Arabs compared to the previous Gallup poll taken in July–August 1981. Also, the January 1982 results are higher for Israel than those of October 1980 and substantially higher than those of January 1979—40 versus 14 percent (see table 3–2).

The *Washington Post*–ABC (*WP*-ABC) poll of early March 1982 also reveals highly favorable American opinions of Israel. This was the poll that "ABC News" aired on March 10, 1982, but that the *Washington Post* did not publish.[26] The presentation of poll results commenced with the following statement:

> Despite the widely publicized disagreements between Israel and America in recent months, the American public still strongly backs the state of Israel.

Israel was characterized as a reliable ally of the United States by 54 percent of the sample, and 51 percent thought that Israel was "striving more to bring about peace in the Middle East." Only 20 percent felt the same about the Arab nations. Another 51 percent of the sample felt that the United States "should not lessen our ties to Israel to ensure an adequate oil supply from the Arabs."

American opinions of Begin were more reserved; only 39 percent of the respondents expressed favorable feelings for the prime minister, and 22 percent held the opposite view. When asked, "During the past year, have your feelings about Prime Minister Begin changed?" 64 percent said no and 29 percent said yes. Finally, the *WP*-ABC poll also presented the "sympathy" question and found a majority of 55 to 18 percent in favor of Israel.

At the beginning of 1982, Reagan was forced to revise his basic approach to the Arab-Israeli conflict. He now perceived the conflict as an obstacle to his design for an anti-Soviet alliance in the Middle East. A new plan was needed to remove these obstacles, and it had to recognize the fundamental issues of the conflict. Ironically, perhaps—although under very different circumstances—Reagan had reached the juncture at which Carter had spent most of his presidency. For the time being, however, the United States could not initiate any new mediation efforts, since Israel had not yet completed its withdrawal from the Sinai Peninsula and the implementation of the remaining provisions of the Israeli-Egyptian peace agreement.

On April 25, 1982, Israel completed its withdrawal from the Sinai Desert, but not before the inhabitants of the town of Yamit and other Israeli settlements had been removed by force from the area. Scenes of this removal well demonstrated the heavy price Israel paid for the peace treaty with Egypt. After the withdrawal, Israel's popularity in the United States reached a level that had previously been achieved only after the Yom Kippur War. Gallup found, in April and May 1982, that a majority of Americans (51 percent) now sympathized with Israel; 12 percent sympathized more with the Arabs (see table 4–1). The punctual completion of the Sinai withdrawal restored credibility to Israel and, for a while, lowered American apprehensions about unpredictable Israeli behavior.

Table 4–3 displays the results of polls on perceptions of several Middle

Table 4–3
Evaluations of American Allies, 1981–82

Question

(a) I am going to read you the names of some countries and groups. For each, tell me if you feel that country is a close ally of the U.S., is friendly but not a close ally . . . (Harris)

(b) I'm going to mention the names of some foreign countries. For each, I'd like you to tell me whether you think that country is a reliable ally of the United States—one that can be trusted to cooperate with the U.S. in almost any circumstances—or not. Would you say that (*country*) is a reliable ally of the U.S. or not? (*WP*-ABC)

(c) Which of the following countries would you say is America's strongest ally in the Middle East? (Penn and Schoen)

(d) If U.S. interests were attacked in the Mideast, which of the following countries do you think would be most likely to fight on behalf of the U.S.? (Penn and Schoen)

Country	*(a) Close Ally, Nov. '81*	*(b) Reliable Ally, Mar. '82 (n = 1,672)*	*(c) Strongest Ally, May 1982 (n = 1,007)*	*(d) Fight for U.S., May 1982 (n = 1,007)*
Israel	35%	54%	37%	44%
Egypt	29	52	22	21
Saudi Arabia	14	28	15	12
Jordan	6	24	1	2
Syria	2	14	1	0
Libya	1	6	1	1
Others	—	—	7	4
D.K.	—	—	16	16

Sources: (a) *USA Today,* November 29, 1982; (b) *WP*-ABC Poll No. 0114Y, March 1982, q. 60; (c)(d) Penn and Schoen, Poll No. 244, 357, May 1982.

Eastern countries as allies of the United States. In each poll, Israel's score surpassed that of every Arab country, including Egypt and other moderates. The difference between Israel and other American allies in the Middle East is most evident in questions that asked respondents to rate the countries in relative terms—for instance, "Which . . . is America's strongest ally?" (c), or "Which . . . would be most likely to fight on behalf of the U.S.?" (d). One other notable finding in table 4–3 is the relatively low rating of Saudi Arabia, which several months earlier, during the AWACS sale debate, had been portrayed by Reagan and his aides as one of the closest American allies in the entire Middle East.

Reagan's performance in the Middle East during the first months of 1982 was examined by a *WP*-ABC poll (table 4–2). In March 1982, his performance was approved by a plurality of 49 to 34 percent. Compared to the previous results of July–August 1981, this score represents similar increases in both the positive and the negative columns. It should be noted that in March 1982, Reagan's score for the handling of the Middle East situation was higher than that of his overall performance (48 versus 46 percent) and his handling of foreign affairs (45 versus 43 percent).

The *WP*-ABC poll of March 1982 also asked whether the president was "leaning too much in favor of Israel or in favor of the Arab countries." Less than one third of the sample (30 percent) said that Reagan was neutral; 38 percent thought that he was leaning toward one side or another; and the remainder (32 percent) held no opinion. Of those who felt that Reagan was not neutral, 21 percent thought that he favored the Arabs and 18 percent believed that he favored Israel. The same issue appeared in a different form in the May 1982 Penn and Schoen poll. They asked first whether the "commitment of President Reagan to Israel changed since he was elected," and if so, whether he became more committed to Israel or less. Of a 54 percent response rate, 30 percent thought that he had become less committed and only 9 percent believed that he had become more committed to Israel.

War in Lebanon

The April–August 1981 battles in Lebanon exposed the tremendous growth of the PLO's conventional military capabilities.[27] The Begin government concluded that the PLO was preparing an assault for the purpose of igniting an all-Arab war effort against Israel.[28] In the winter of 1981, Begin and Sharon decided to preempt the PLO's strategic plan by force and presented their intentions to high-ranking American officials. The reactions of Ambassador Philip Habib were critical, but those of Haig were indecisive.[29] Apparently, Sharon envisioned larger goals in confronting the PLO, including expulsion of the PLO and Syrian troops from Beirut, the election of Christian leader Bashir Gemayel to the presidency, and a possible Israeli-Lebanese peace agreement.[30] The Israeli government favored a limited military operation in Lebanon, but never knew, or approved, the larger goals.

On June 3, 1982, a Palestinian terrorist squad from the Abu-Nidal organization attacked the Israeli ambassador in London, Shlomo Argov, and seriously wounded him. On June 6, the IDF crossed its northern border into Lebanon. The war moved through several phases.[31] The first drive occurred primarily along the coast through the towns of Tyre and Sidon to Damour. During this phase, Israel encountered the PLO, whose fighters rapidly withdrew to Beirut. Israeli official announcements set limited goals to the operation and declared that Israel had no intention of fighting Syrian troops.[32] The United States took a cautious position. Reagan, who was attending the Versailles Economic Conference, later told the British Parliament on June 8:

> The fighting in Lebanon on the part of all parties must stop, and Israel should bring its forces home. But this is not enough. We must all work to stamp out the scourge of terrorism that in the Middle East makes war an ever-present threat.[33]

The United States also blocked attempts at the United Nations to impose an early cease-fire on Israel.

By June 9, the IDF had clashed with Syrian troops in the eastern sector of Lebanon. In just two days, Syria lost its antiaircraft missiles, suffered considerable damage to its air force, and its ground troops found themselves caught in a pincer stretching from the Golan Heights to the Bekaa Valley. On June 11, Israel and Syria agreed to a cease-fire. At this stage, according to various sources, the Bashir Gemayel Christian units were to have stormed PLO headquarters in West Beirut.[34] However, this move did not materialize. Instead, Israel demanded the withdrawal of PLO leaders and troops from Beirut—a demand refused by Arafat.

The United States was concerned about the acceleration of the war from a limited operation to large-scale warfare and about the reports of massive destruction and civilian suffering. However, Reagan's officials were divided on immediate U.S. policy. While Haig stressed that Israel should be allowed to continue pressuring the PLO, Weinberger and National Security Adviser William Clark criticized the entire Israeli operation and recommended an American initiative to halt it.[35]

On June 21, Reagan met Begin at the White House and agreed to seek an independent, unified Lebanon and to push for withdrawal of all foreign forces, including those of the PLO and Syria.[36] Immediately after the talks, however, the IDF moved into the eastern sector of the front and blocked the main Beirut-Damascus highway. This move was designed to increase pressure on the PLO and Syrian troops in West Beirut, but it also caused considerable dissension in both Israel and the United States. On June 25, Haig resigned, and Arafat concluded that by holding on to his position, he might save his headquarters.

Habib began negotiations for a peaceful evacuation of the PLO from Beirut, but because of Arafat's refusal to relinquish his base, arbitration was difficult and slow. Israel threatened to break into PLO headquarters, but strong opposition within Israel and the United States ruled out this option. The alternative was harsh siege measures and a war of attrition. In addition, Israel and the PLO exchanged gunfire in residential areas.[37] During this period, American television networks portrayed the difficult conditions in West Beirut and filmed Arafat wandering around hugging and kissing babies. The PLO chairman hoped to mobilize American public opinion against Israel and almost succeeded. On August 12, Israel fiercely bombed West Beirut. Reagan called Begin and asked him to stop, but it was this use of force that finally persuaded Arafat to surrender. On September 1, the PLO completed its withdrawal from Lebanon under the supervision of a multinational force that included about 800 U.S. Marines.[38]

On September 1, Reagan announced a major new American initiative for a comprehensive resolution of the Arab-Israeli conflict.[39] The plan called for Arab acceptance of Israel and for the resolution of the Palestinian problem within a Jordanian context. Reagan discounted both possibilities of establishing an independent Palestinian state in the West Bank or an Israeli annexation of this territory. After a period of autonomy, he said, the area should be returned to Jordan. Israel and the Arab nations rejected the Reagan initiative; only Egypt saw in it "positive elements."[40]

In the meantime, a new internal development occurred in Lebanon. On August 23, Bashir Gemayel was elected president of Lebanon and was expected to assume office 30 days later. Israel hoped that Gemayel would restore order and perhaps even sign a peace agreement. However, on September 14, he was assassinated under Syrian orders.[41] The tension between Beirut's rival factions rose dramatically, and Israel moved several units into the city's western zone. A few days later, Christian Phalangists entered the Palestinian neighborhoods of Sabra and Shatila and murdered between 500 and 800 people.[42]

The alleged Israeli involvement in the tragedy immediately triggered a tremendous wave of antigovernment criticism in Israel and extreme anti-Israel criticism abroad.[43] Reagan issued a blistering statement and sent the marines back to Beirut.[44] In Israel, a huge antigovernment demonstration forced Begin to appoint a special committee of inquiry to investigate Israel's role in the tragedy. The committee issued a report on February 8, 1983, that completely exonerated Israel from any participation in the massacre.[45] Sharon's performance, however, was found faulty, and he was forced to resign.

The war in Lebanon was unlike any previous Arab-Israeli war. First, it was a long, offensive war of choice lasting about three months, and not all Israelis considered it necessary.[46] Also, it was the first war of the Likud. All previous wars had been conducted by Labor governments, which could count on the full support of the right. The war took place on Lebanese territory, but Israel was fighting not the state of Lebanon but the PLO and, to a lesser extent, the Syrians, whose forces had been stationed there since 1975. Furthermore, for the first time, an Arab-Israeli war occurred in an Arab capital during a period of relative Arab-Israeli peace. Finally, it was the first war to be televised from both sides. The American media played a significant role in this war, but this fact requires further analysis.

The American Media's Coverage of the War—Conflict through a Camera

The role of the U.S. media in the 1982 war in Lebanon was controversial and raised serious questions of fairness, objectivity, and accuracy. Several organizations commissioned investigations into the American coverage of the war.[47] All but the *Columbia Journalism Review* study found numerous instances of inaccurate reporting, extreme exaggerations, double standards, imbalanced treatment of sources, exclusion of conflicting points of view, unjustified associations and derogatory comments, ignorance, selective and tendentious interviewing, and significant omissions.[48]

Veteran reporter Frank Gervasi claimed that omissions are as serious a fault as distortions. He concluded that throughout the war, the American media failed to report on many subjects, including subversive PLO activities in Lebanon against the local inhabitants and its attacks from Lebanon against Israel.[49] In addition, items aired or published were not exactly what news correspondents and photographers implied they were.

On August 2, 1982, the *Washington Post* and many other newspapers printed a large photo of a heavily bandaged Lebanese baby being fed by a nurse. Later the same day, Reagan showed the photo to Israel's Foreign Minister Yitzhak Shamir and, according to various reports, told him, "This is an ugly picture. Look what's happening in Beirut."[50] Newly appointed Secretary of State George Shultz said on August 14, "The symbol of this war is a baby with its arms shot off."[51] He referred to the same photograph. Obviously, the photo moved the president and his secretary of state, who probably read the following caption supplied by a United Press International (UPI) photographer:

> Nurse feeds a seven-month-old baby who lost both arms and was severely burned late yesterday afternoon when an Israeli jet accidentally hit a Christian residential area in East Beirut during a raid on Palestinian positions to the West.

This was false. A photographer from the Associated Press (AP) who had taken pictures of the identical baby at the same time in the same place, described the child as "badly injured by a PLO shell" (with no reference to any lost limbs). Later investigations by Israel and UPI found that the baby had not lost both arms but, in fact, had suffered a broken arm and a superficial facial burn. Furthermore, he was hit by a PLO bomb fired from West Beirut, not by an Israeli bomb.[52] UPI confirmed that the original caption was inaccurate and expressed regret. Not all media that published the original photo on page one corrected this distortion, and those that did, such as the *New York Times*, buried the correction in one of the inside pages.

In many ways the UPI photo was symptomatic of other serious, frequent distortions in the American media's coverage of the war. Many Americans justified the right of Israel to hit back at the PLO terror bases in Lebanon but criticized the proportions of the retaliation (the magnitude of the damage to people and buildings). On June 10, Richard Cohen of the *Washington Post* compared Israel's suffering from the PLO's terrorism with Israel's offensive and concluded that the latter was "totally out of proportion." *Time* magazine calculated that the Israeli retribution for the shooting of Ambassador Argov was more than 200 to 1.[53] These feelings were expressed not only by the media;

on June 20, 1982, Secretary of Defense Weinberger stated, "There are tens of thousands of people who have been killed and wounded now in Labanon who had nothing to do with any side of the conflict."[54] These opinions were probably based on a flood of reports and film from correspondents in Beirut that depicted considerable destruction and mentioned heavy civilian casualties. The photographs left no doubts. They depicted destroyed buildings, piles of rubble, smoke, fire, and streams of refugees. On June 14, 1982, for example, CBS correspondent Bob Faw reported on the evening news that he was broadcasting from "Tyre—or what's left of it."[55] ABC's Mike McCourt and many other reporters used similar language.[56] Canadian journalist Ilya Gerol viewed such reports at home and expected to see high-level destruction during his forthcoming visit to southern Lebanon. The first site of his visit was Tyre. Gerol wrote, "For the first few minutes after driving through the streets it looked as if we had missed our road and were maybe in a different country. There was no destruction."[57]

How then, were Faw and his colleagues able to show a city almost totally destroyed? The secret was "Television Alley," the only street in the entire city where 11 buildings belonging to the PLO had been destroyed. When Gerol asked a television cameraman how he had managed to make an apocalyptic destruction out of only 11 houses, the cameraman answered, "We just had to film them from different angles." Similar cases of serious distortions were found in reports on the level of destruction in Beirut and other cities.

But the greatest and most circulated distortion of the war was the reporting on the highly sensitive issue of civilian casualties. This distortion is important because many Americans formed opinions about the war from the perceptions of the loss of human lives. From an early stage in the war and for several weeks, the American media reported that 10,000 had been killed, 40,000 wounded, and 600,000 to 700,000 left homeless. These figures were absurd. The entire population of southern Lebanon in the area of Israel's military operation numbered only 500,000 inhabitants. Approximately a quarter of them lived in areas friendly to Israel and were not affected at all by the war. How then did 375,000 persons become 600,000 homeless?

Any responsible journalist covering an item as serious as civilian casualties should cite a source. Yet as one study found, 17 reports on casualty figures aired on American television networks between June 4 and June 28 failed to cite a source.[58] In cases in which sources were cited, they were not fully identified. The main source of the "phantom statistics" used by other organizations, including the International Committee of the Red Cross (ICRC), was the Palestine Red Crescent. This was a PLO institution headed by Dr. Fahti Arafat, brother of the PLO leader. For years, the PLO has conducted a propaganda effort designed to dehumanize Israel. For obvious reasons this effort intensified during the war.[59] Yet when American reporters in Beirut quoted the Palestine Red Crescent, they neither explained the nature of the organization nor made any effort to question or confirm its figures. Moreover, when the ICRC discovered that it had received and distributed false information and corrected it, most American media ignored the correction and continued to publish the grossly inflated figures.[60]

The foregoing examples are not sporadic and exceptional cases of inaccurate and distorted reporting of the war by the American media. They are *typical* cases of widespread malpractice. On July 14, David Shipler reported on the front page of the *New York Times:*

> It is clear to anyone who has traveled in South Lebanon, as have many journalists and relief workers, that the original figures of 10,000 dead and 600,000 homeless, reported by correspondents quoting Beirut representatives of the International Committee of the Red Cross during the first week of the war, were *extreme exaggerations*. (emphasis added)

On touring South Lebanon, Martin Peretz wrote in *The New Republic* (August 2, 1982, 15): "Much of what you have read in the newspapers and newsmagazines about the war in Lebanon—and even more of what you have seen and heard on television—is simply not true." Frank Gervasi, who arrived in the area after watching the coverage for two weeks, observed; "Much of the coverage, however, especially when it originated from Beirut . . . was remarkable for its distortions of the truth."[61] Canadian correspondent Gerol, who also arrived in Lebanon at a later date, wrote: "but never have real events been so grossly distorted as they have been at the most recent scenes of international turmoil in Lebanon."[62]

Several explanations were suggested for the faulty coverage of the war in Lebanon by the American media.[63] They include access difficulties, PLO and Arab intimidation, double standards, latent anti-Semitism, lack of knowledge and background, Vietnam's legacy, Israel's inefficient information policy, Begin's and Sharon's negative images, and the propensity of television to dramatize and exaggerate violence. It appears that the main explanation might be what one investigator labeled "media on a crusade." Muravchik concluded: "Israel's lack of justification was the 'big picture' that much of the press strove to capture in Lebanon, and too often standards of accuracy, balance, and objectivity were discarded in its favor."[64]

Americans, of course, were unaware of the serious war coverage distortions. Yet in an ABC News poll of October 1982, they expressed reservations about the performance of the American media in the war. Almost half of the respondents did not know whether the network television news reported accurate casualty figures, and 27 percent thought that the networks reported higher casualty figures than there actually were.[65] The majority of the sample, 50 versus 35 percent, felt that the war "has been sensationalized by network television news." Finally, 41 percent thought that television gave too much

Table 4–4
Attitudes toward the War in Lebanon, June–November 1982

Questions

(a) Israel recently began military operations in Southern Lebanon to stop Palestinian artillery attacks on settlements in Israel. Do you approve or disapprove of this action?

(b) Do you approve or disapprove of the Israeli invasion of Southern Lebanon?

(c) Some people say Israel is right to fight in Lebanon in order to stop the PLO. Others say Israel is wrong to go into Lebanese territory. Do you think that Israel is right or wrong to fight in Lebanon?

(d) As you know, Israel moved its troops into Lebanon to try to eliminate the PLO and Syrian military bases there which had been used to shell Northern Israel. If the conflict ends with all foreign military powers—Israeli, Syrian and PLO—finally getting out of Lebanon, do you think the Israeli move into Lebanon was justified or not?

(e) Israel was right to take defensive action by moving into Lebanon, since the PLO bases there were regularly shelling Israel. Agree or disagree?

(f) Israel was wrong to go to war and kill thousands of Lebanese civilians. Agree or disagree?

(g) The Israelis sent their military forces into Lebanon. Do you approve or disapprove of this action?

(h) The Israelis have given the following reasons for sending troops into Lebanon: to stop the rocket attacks on Israeli settlements and to remove PLO military forces from Lebanon. Do you think the Israelis were justified in sending troops into Lebanon for these reasons or not?

(i) Israel is right to crush the military might of the PLO, since the PLO has sworn to destroy Israel and is an international terrorist organization. Agree or disagree?

(j) Some people say Israel was justified in invading Lebanon. Others say Israel was not justified. What do you think?

Q	*Date*	*Poll*	*Approve*	*Justified*	*Right*	*Disapprove*	*Not Justified*	*Wrong*	*Other, D.K.*	(*n*)
(a)	June 11–14	Gallup	40%			35%			25%	(1,504)
(b)	June	NBC	24			41			35	
		(aware)	32			54			14	
(c)	June 22–27	CBS			34%			38%	28	
(d)	July 9–14	Harris		44%			36%		20	(1,250)
(e)	July 9–14	Harris			57			28	15	

(f)	July 9–14	Harris			35			52	13	
(g)	Aug. 4–5	*Newsweek*-	30			60			10	(752)
(h)	Aug. 4–5	Gallup		47			41		12	
(f)	Aug. 5–10	Harris			29			63	8	(1,254)
(i)	Aug. 5–10	Harris			61			28	11	
(d)	Aug. 5–10	Harris		43			42		15	
(b)	Aug. 9–10	NBC	25			51			24	
		(aware)	27			56			17	
(j)	Aug. 18	*WP*-ABC		37			41		21	(913)
		(aware)		52			38		10	(749)
		(unaware)		28			43		29	(164)
(j)	Sep. 24–26	*WP*-ABC		37			46		17	
(i)	Nov. 15	Harris			57			33	10	

Sources: (a) George Gallup, "Americans' Pro-Israel Sentiments Unaffected by Lebanon Incursion," *The Gallup Poll*, July 4, 1982. (b) G. Rosenfield, *Attitudes Toward Israel Since June 1982*, Publication No. 82/180/19 (New York: American Jewish Committee, Information and Research Services, November 1982), 12. (c) C. de Boer, 130. (d)(e)(f) *Washington Post*, July 19, 1982; de Boer, 131. (h) *Newsweek*, August 16, 1982. (i, August 1982) Louis Harris, *Israel Loses Little Public Support in the War: PLO Makes No Gains*, August 23, 1982. (i, November 1982) *How Americans Feel About Israel*, 46–47. (j) *Washington Post*, August 20, 1982, September 28, 1982.

attention to the war, and a similar number of respondents disapproved of the manner in which the networks reported the news about the war.

The effects of the war and its coverage on policymakers and politicians were mentioned earlier—but how did the American public react?

Public Opinion of the War in Lebanon

The unique character of Israel's war in Lebanon led to a rash of poll-taking on both general and specific issues. Many polls included questions on the legitimacy of the war, and others asked the public to convey its feelings toward Begin, Israel, and the Arabs.[66] Several polls examined official U.S. policy on the war and Reagan's performance, but most surveys dealt with issues the media chose to emphasize.

A Just or Unjust War?

The controversial nature of the war was reflected in the number and frequency of public opinion surveys about its legitimacy. Fifteen questions were asked on this issue between June and November 1982. The results of these polls are presented in table 4–4. As table 4–4 indicates, pollsters used three sets of terms in their questions about the war: *approved-disapproved, justified-unjustified*, and *right-wrong*. As mentioned in the discussion of polls on the 1956 Israeli operation in the Sinai Desert, these terms are not identical and may imply different judgments. Yet a leading and experienced pollster used those terms interchangeably. Between July 9 and 14, 1982, Harris asked whether the Israeli move into Lebanon was "justified," but in his interpretation of response, published in the *Washington Post* July 19, 1982, he wrote, "A 44 to 36 percent plurality would grant its *approval* of that invasion" (emphasis added).

The preceding question and interpretation by Harris raises another problem of wording. He used the expression "move into Lebanon" in his question, but the term "invasion" in his interpretation. Table 4–4 shows how these and other terms were used in the various questions. The table reveals that many of the questions about the war solicited moral judgments and included a bias in one direction or another. Accordingly, the results varied considerably from one question to another.

Questions that included reference to PLO attacks on Israeli towns (a, d, e, i) yielded positive attitudes for the Israeli action. The query that referred to civilian casualties (f) yielded negative responses for Israel. Questions that omitted contexts (b, j) produced negative scores. Examination of results over time indicates that criticism of the war grew in August and September, probably because of the cumulative effect of the war, the siege of Beirut, and the Sabra-Shatila massacre. However, public dissatisfaction rose by only a few percentage points.

The NBC and *WP*-ABC polls employed the awareness factor and received interesting results. First, as might be expected, the "aware" groups tended to adopt firmer positions in contrast to other groups. Thus, figures for the aware groups in the "don't know" (D.K.) column are relatively low. Second, at least in the *WP*-ABC poll of August 18 (j), the unaware group thought that the Israeli invasion was "unjustified" by a plurality of 43 to 28 percent, but the aware group said that it was justified by a majority of 52 versus 38 percent. It could be that the more knowledgeable respondents judged the war on the basis of its general context and the events in Lebanon that preceded it. Of the 15 scores in table 4–4, eight yielded negative opinions and seven yielded positive opinions on Israel's initiative. Taking into account the awareness factor and the polls' wording and analyses, the public was quite divided on the question of the war's legitimacy.

Prime Minister Begin's Image

Begin's negative image in American public opinion further deteriorated throughout the war in Lebanon. According to Gallup's "Scalometer," Begin's favorability rating at the beginning of the war stood at 52 to 34 percent—a slight decline from the previous rating of June 1981 (54 to 30 percent). As figure 4–1 indicates, Begin's rating dropped further to 47 versus 44 percent in August.

Two further polls gauged Begin's ratings from 1978 to 1982. According to Roper, as early as August 1978 the public disapproved of the "handling of his responsibilities in the Middle East" by a 36 to 27 percent plurality.[67] But in September 1978, Begin's performance was rated positively by a majority of 55 to 16 percent following the Camp David Accords. By October 1982, however, the pendulum had swung back, and 45 versus 23 percent disapproved of his policy.

In the 1978 Gallup survey for the Chicago Council on Foreign Relations, Begin was regarded quite favorably on the "Thermometer Scale" at 57 degrees.[68] In the October–November 1982 survey, though, his rating slipped to a chilly 45 degrees. The same survey also revealed that Begin's favorability rating was 10 degrees lower than Israel's.

A *Newsweek*-Gallup poll conducted four days after the Sabra-Shatila massacre found that a substantial majority (70 percent) agreed that "Begin's policies are hurting support for Israel in the U.S."[69] This result is hardly surprising in light of the circumstances surrounding the massacre. However, Adams' assertion that Begin's policy also caused a fundamental erosion in American perceptions of Israel requires a closer examination.[70]

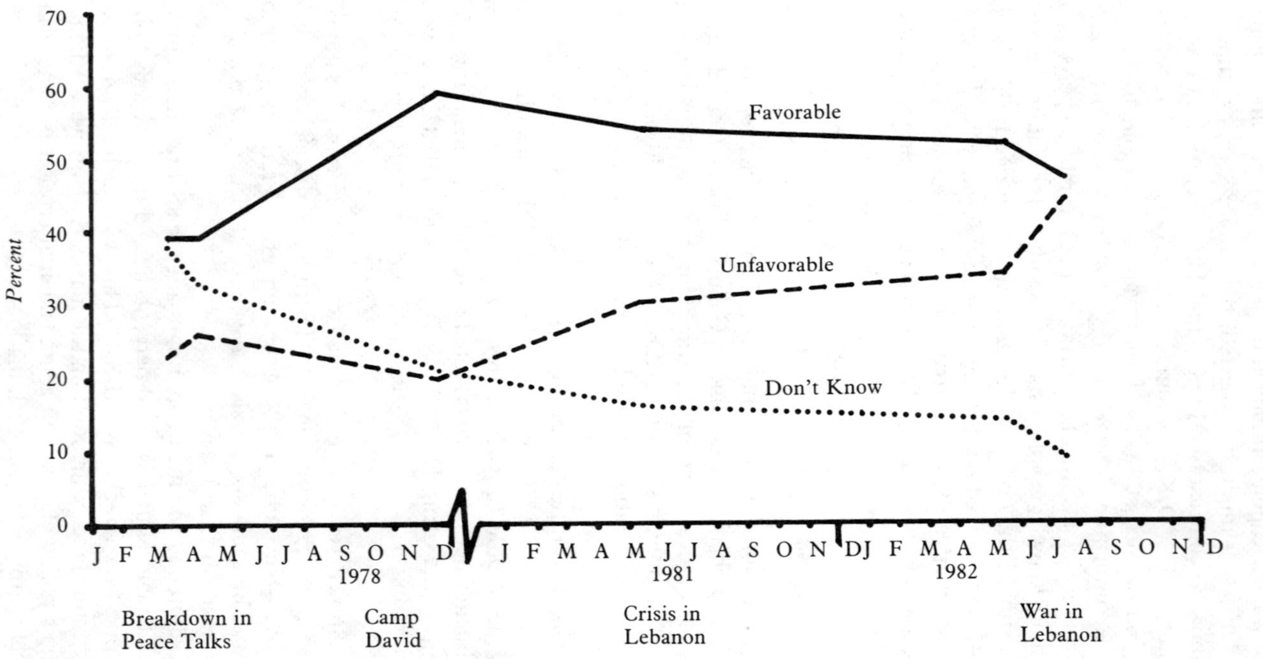

Source: "Scalometer rating," *Gallup Report*, September 1982, 21.

Figure 4–1. Begin's Favorability Rating.
Question (respondents were handed a Scalometer card): You will notice that the 10 boxes on this scale go from the highest position of plus five—for someone or something you have a very favorable opinion of—all the way down to the lowest position of minus five—for someone or something you have a very unfavorable opinion of. How far up or down the scale would you rate the following? . . . Menachem Begin.

American Sympathies for Israel and the Arabs

As indicated in table 4–1, many polls used the standard sympathy question throughout and after the war in Lebanon. At the onset of the war, Roper found a gain in American sympathies for Israel. A comparison of his June 1982 score to the previous score (July 1981) reveals an increase of 4 percent in the Israeli column and a decrease of 1 percent in the Arab column. Gallup conducted a poll of American sympathies during the second week of the war and compared it to his previous results (April–May 1982), also finding a minimal gain of 1 percent for Israel and a loss of 2 percent for the Arabs. But the Israeli gain was short-lived. Exactly a month later, Gallup found a loss of 11 percentage points in the Israeli column and a gain of 2 percent for the Arabs. The length of the war, critical media coverage, and the emerging siege of West Beirut probably contributed to the considerable decline in the pro-Israeli rating.

During the siege of Beirut, *WP*-ABC and Roper conducted further surveys of American sympathies. The *WP*-ABC poll of August 17, 1982, found considerable sympathy for Israel—52 versus 18 percent. Compared to the previous poll on this issue by the same organization (March 1982), these data show that Israel lost just 3 percent while the Arabs' score remained constant. In contrast to Gallup's results, the *WP*-ABC poll recorded a much higher degree of sympathy for both sides, but this difference could be attributed to the Gallup procedure of tabulating only the answers of those respondents who had previously heard or read about the events in question. As of mid-August 1982, the rate of sympathy toward the Arabs had remained almost unchanged, while the Israeli sympathy rate declined substantially according to the Gallup polls but only marginally according to the *WP*-ABC polls.

Following the PLO's expulsion from Beirut and the Israeli and Arab rejection of the Reagan plan, Roper found a negligible increase in sympathy for Israel (one percentage point) and a larger increase for the Arabs (six percentage points); however, the tragedy of Sabra and Shatila altered this trend.

The Gallup-poll of September 22–23 found a substantial drop in the rate of sympathy for both sides. The percentage of those sympathizing with Israel dropped to 32 percent, the lowest rate since 1967. It represents a drop of 9 percent compared to the July 1982 rate and 20 percent compared to the June 1982 rate. The number of those polled in September who sympathized with the Arabs rose by 16 percent to a record level of 28 percent. These results could reflect disapproval of the alleged Israeli involvement in the massacre. In the same 605-person telephone poll, Gallup asked for Americans' views concerning the Israeli involvement. Only 8 percent of his sample felt that Israel should not be held responsible for the massacre. The vast majority (81 percent) said that Israel was either partially or very much responsible.

A September 24–26 poll by *WP*-ABC, conducted a few days after the massacre, shows that the pro-Israel sympathy rate had declined by a smaller margin—only 4 percent compared to the August 1982 poll. The Arabs' rate increased by 9 percent. The Roper poll of October 1982 also identified only a slight change in the ratings for both sides. Compared to his previous poll of early September, results showed that Israel lost 2 percent and the Arabs lost 1 percent. Thus, the Gallup results differed from those of *WP*-ABC and Roper on both the rise of the Arab rate and the decline of the Israeli rate. In any event, the Gallup ratio of 32 to 28 percent did not last long.

In a poll conducted 3 months later, in January 1983, Gallup found a plurality of 49 to 12 percent in favor of Israel. This ratio was very similar to the one reported for January 1982 (49 to 14 percent). A *WP*-ABC survey also taken in January 1983 did not register any changes in the Israeli column but, with the evaporation of the massacre's effects, found a drop of ten percentage points in the Arab column. The special Israeli committee investigating the massacre (Kahan Committee) issued its report February 8, whereupon Minister of Defense Ariel Sharon was forced to resign from his position. At the end of February and the beginning of March 1983, *WP*-ABC conducted another sympathy poll. Their results were now 52 to 16 percent in favor of Israel. This result is very similar to the March 1982 ratio—55 to 18 percent in favor of Israel. A July 1983 Gallup poll yielded a ratio of 48 to 12 percent in favor of Israel.

A Roper survey of the same month produced a score very similar to that registered by the same organization in July 1981 and June 1982. These results clearly demonstrate that as early as the beginning of 1983, American sympathies for Israel and the Arabs had returned to prewar levels, and according to two Roper polls conducted in 1984, they remained at those levels.

Rating Israel as an American Ally

Another interesting issue raised by the war in Lebanon was the possible effects of the Israeli invasion on U.S. public perceptions of Israel as an American ally. Responses to question (a) in table 4–5 indicate that during the war, Israel's rating as an American ally ("close ally" and "friendly") dropped by as much as 12 percentage points below prewar levels. Likewise, the number of respondents who thought Israel was "unfriendly" or "an enemy" of the United States almost doubled from November 1981 to November 1982. The lowest rating for Israel (69 percent) was recorded in February 1983, but the rate for September 1983 shows that Israel had regained most points lost during the war.

Question (b) in table 4–5 examines Israel's standing in a comparative setting with other American allies in the Middle East. It reveals a deterioration of 10 percent in the Israeli rating between March and August 1982. But during the same period, Egypt lost 13 percent and Syria, which fought against Israel in Lebanon, lost 5 percent. By January 1984, Israel had regained all points lost during the war. Its rating was identical to that of the prewar survey of

Table 4–5
Israel's Rating as an American Ally

Question

(a) I am going to read you the names of some countries. For each, tell me if you feel that country is a close ally of the U.S., is friendly but not a close ally, is not friendly but not an enemy, or is unfriendly and an enemy of the U.S." (*Specified country, Israel*)

	Dec. '74	*Nov. '81*	*Jan. '82*	*June '82*	*Aug. '82*	*Nov. '82*	*Feb. '83*	*Sep. '83*	*Nov. '84*	*Oct. '85*
Close ally	26%	35%	29%	35%	24%	32%	24%	35%	35%	34%
Friendly	49	49	46	44	49	40	45	43	46	38
Not friendly	10	8	14	11	13	16	16	12	11	16
Enemy	1	3	3	2	3	4	4	3	3	5
Not sure	14	5	8	8	11	8	11	7	5	7
Total	100%	100%	100%	100%	100%	100%	100%	100%	100%	100%

Question

(b) I am going to mention the names of some foreign countries. For each I'd like you to tell me whether you think that country is a reliable ally of the U.S.—one that can be trusted to cooperate with the U.S. in almost any circumstances—or not. Would you say that (*country*) is a reliable ally of the U.S. or not." (*Responses indicate reliable ally*)

Country	*WP*-ABC *Oct. '81*	*WP*-ABC *Mar. '82*	*WP*-ABC *Aug. '82*	*Gallup Jan. '83*	*Roper Jan. '84*
Israel	64%	54%	44%	41%	54%
Egypt	59	52	39	33	37
Saudi Arabia	33	28	28	NA	NA
Jordan	NA	24	26	16	17
Syria	NA	14	9	5	7

Sources: (a) *USA Today*, November 11, 1982; *How Americans Feel About Israel*, 44, *Index to International Public Opinion, 1982–1983*, 256. *The Harris Survey*, No. 56, July 11, 1985, 2. (b) G. Rosenfield, "U.S. Public Opinion Polls and the Lebanon War," *American Jewish Year Book* 84(1984), 110, table 6; *WP*-ABC Poll No. 0114Y, March 1982; American Jewish Committee's Poll, January 1984 (Roper), table IV.

March 1982. On the other hand, Egypt's and Jordan's scores remained low and fell far behind those recorded in March 1982. The Syrian score in 1984 was exactly half that of its prewar rating. Responses to question (b) indicate that the rating of Israel as a reliable ally of the United States remained high above those of the other American allies in the Middle East, even throughout the war and that, by 1984, the gap between Israel and these countries had widened even further than that recorded in October 1981.

The Public's Evaluation of Reagan and U.S. Policy

Throughout most of the war, official U.S. policy was critical of the Israeli operation in Lebanon. According to various polls, however, it appears that the U.S. public either did not recognize, or was unaware of, such a policy. A *Los Angeles Times* national poll published on July 11, 1982, reveals that 28 percent of the respondents thought that Reagan supported Israel, 17 percent said that he opposed Israel, and 25 percent felt that he was neutral. A *WP*-ABC poll examined Reagan's stand through the following question: "How about Reagan: Would you say he is leaning too much in favor of Israel, too much in favor of the Arab countries, or what?" In the August 1982 poll, 30 percent of the sample said that he leaned too much in favor of Israel and 17 percent felt the same about the Arab nations; 23 percent said that he was neutral; and 30 percent held no opinion on this issue.[71] Similar results were obtained in September 1982 and March 1983.

As revealed in table 4–2, the public was divided on its opinion of Reagan's handling of the war. The overall ratings were still positive, but by smaller ratios compared to those of the prewar period. One rating, obtained after the Sabra-Shatila massacre, was negative. Further polls asked respondents what they thought U.S. policy should be on the Israeli war in Lebanon. Most questions on this issue included answers that emphasized a possible reduction of aid as a means of pressure. For example, in August, Gallup asked the following question:

> In the past few days Israel has sent its military forces into West Beirut to try to expel the PLO military forces. What should the U.S. government do?

He provided five answers and recorded the following results: "Support Israel's action" (16 percent); "Criticize Israel and pressure diplomatically" (16 percent); "Suspend military aid for the time being" (27 percent); "Permanently cut off military aid" (16 percent); and "Do nothing" (15 percent).[72] This structure of responses yielded little support for Israel and considerable support for reducing or permanently cutting military aid. In November 1982, however, Roper asked the following question:

> The United States supports Israel both morally and diplomatically, and also with economic and military aid. In light of the situation that exists now in the Middle East, what do you think the U.S. should do in terms of moral and diplomatic support of Israel—do you think we should increase our support, or decrease our support, or continue it as it is?

In response to this question, 57 percent thought that the United States should either continue or increase American support to Israel.[73]

The preceding data and analysis lead to several conclusions. In general, Americans were divided on the justification of the Israeli war in Lebanon and subsequent U.S. policy. They sympathized with Israel's goals but not with its means. In particular, Americans opposed the siege and constant fighting in and around Beirut and supported reduction of aid to Israel as a means of pressure. In addition, rates of sympathy for Israel decreased. Begin's image further deteriorated, but apparently many Americans distinguished between the prime minister and Israel. Polls conducted after the war clearly demonstrate that the erosion in the Israeli image and standing in U.S. public opinion was short and limited. Ratings of sympathy for Israel as an American ally and other indicators demonstrate that shortly after the war, American attitudes on Israel resumed prewar patterns.

U.S. Military Involvement in Lebanon

The concept and means of facilitating the dispatch of U.S. troops to Lebanon were formulated in three different settings. Early in the war in Lebanon, it was suggested that a non-U.N. multinational military force—including U.S. troops—be sent to southern Lebanon to prevent the PLO from using this area as a base for attacks against Israel. Harris presented this idea to a national sample between June 18 and 22, 1982, and found that Americans rejected it by a majority of 54 to 41 percent.[74] Between July 10 and 17, Roper also examined public opinion on the same idea. He formulated the following question:

> As you know, there has been fighting between Israel and the PLO in Lebanon recently. One of the proposals that has been made to insure a lasting peace in Lebanon is to create a multinational peace-keeping force that would patrol Southern Lebanon. There has been talk about including U.S. troops in such a force. If such a force is created, would you favor or oppose having U.S. troops in it?

A substantial majority of the sample (69 percent) opposed the idea of dispatching U.S. troops; only 19 percent favored it; and 12 percent had mixed feelings.[75] Reagan later offered to dispatch 1,000 marines to Lebanon, but within a very different context and for a different reason. This offer was part of a multinational arrangement to secure the safe evacuation of the PLO leadership and troops from Beirut, and it obviously called for a brief mission lasting less than two weeks. Yet Harris found that the public opposed Reagan's offer by a majority of 54 to 40 percent.[76] It is possible that many Americans did not believe the official explanation of the troops' intended objective and feared that the "short mission" would turn into a protracted involvement.

Nevertheless, on August 25, 1982, the first contingency of 800 marines landed in Beirut and remained there for 16 days with French, Italian, and British troops. The marines left Beirut, as Reagan had earlier promised, but returned on September 29 after the assassination of Bashir Gemayel and the Sabra-Shatila massacre. The day earlier, Reagan had stated that the U.S. troops would remain until the Israeli and Syrian armies left Lebanon. He expected this "mutual withdrawal" to happen soon, and promised the Congress that the marines would stay in Lebanon for a "limited period of time."[77] This limited period of time extended to 16 months, however, and raised serious public debate in the United States.

Table 4–6 reveals that at the beginning of the active American military involvement in Lebanon, the public approved of it by 52 to 40 percent. However, a month later, according to an NBC-AP poll, Americans were more equally divided. The Reagan administration and Israel favored evacuation of all foreign forces from Lebanon and offered to assist the new Lebanese President Amin Gemayel (brother of slain president-elect Bashir Gemayel) in building the Lebanese army. Israel claimed that it was prepared to pull back, provided that it received security agreements.

The United States offered to mediate between Israel and Lebanon, but negotiations were slow and difficult. Resentful of U.S. pressure, Syria refused to relinquish its power bases in Lebanon. On April 18, 1983, a bomb exploded in the American Embassy in Beirut, killing 83 persons, including 17 American citizens.[78] The attack was carried out by the Syrian-backed Shiite terrorist group, Islamic Jihad Organization. Reagan denounced the attack as a "cowardly act" and vowed it would not deter the United States, but he soon discovered that the embassy attack was only the first in a series of assaults against the United States in Lebanon.

On May 17, 1983, Israel and Lebanon concluded an agreement that provided for a complete Israeli withdrawal in return for security arrangements along the Israeli-Lebanese border.[79] Syria opposed the agreement and encouraged its surrogates in Lebanon to sabotage its ratification and implementation. In July, weary of playing policeman among the rival Lebanese factions and disappointed by Gemayel's inability to ratify the May 17 agreement, Israel decided unilaterally to withdraw from the Shouf Mountains overlooking Beirut to a line along the Awali River.[80] The withdrawal took place September 3. One

Table 4–6
U.S. Public Opinion about American Marines in Lebanon, 1982–83

Questions

(a) Do you approve or disapprove of President Reagan's decision to send U.S. Marines to Beirut to help keep the peace and encourage a withdrawal of Israeli, Syrian and PLO forces from Lebanon?

(b) Do you approve or disapprove of President Reagan sending American military troops to Lebanon?

(c) U.S. Marines went to Lebanon as part of an international peacekeeping force to try to prevent fighting there. Do you approve or disapprove of the government sending troops to Lebanon for that purpose?

Q	*Date*	*Poll*	*Approve*	*Disapprove*	*D.K., N.O.*	*(n)*
(a)	Sep. '82	*Newsweek*-Gallup	52%	40%	8%	
(b)	Oct. '82	NBC-Associated Press	44	45	11	
(a)	Aug. '83	*Newsweek*-Gallup	41	54	5	
(c)	Sep. '83	CBS-*New York Times*	36	53	11	(1,587)
(a)	Oct. 27, '83	*Newsweek*-Gallup	48	42	10	(759)
(c)	Oct. 27, '83	CBS-*New York Times*	48	42	10	(545)

Sources: (a) *Newsweek,* November 7, 1983, 19. (b) "Opinion Roundup," *Public Opinion* 6(August–September 1983), 37. (c) Mark F. German with Kirk Brown, *Public Opinion Polls on U.S. Policy in Lebanon* (Washington, D.C.: Library of Congress, February 8, 1984), B-6.

of the rival factions, the Druze, immediately mobilized to capture the vacated area and forced the Christians and the Lebanese army out. In anticipation of this scenario, on September 1, Reagan ordered 2,000 additional troops and naval units to Lebanon to "assure the safety of the 1,370 Marines already on shore."[81]

The American public and Congress again grew suspicious of the marines' presence in Lebanon.[82] Table 4–6 indicates that in August and September 1983, majorities of respondents disapproved of the marines' role in Beirut. A comparison of the *Newsweek*-Gallup results of August 1983 and those of September 1982 reveal a complete turnabout from approval of the marines' mission by 52 to 40 percent in 1982 to disapproval by 54 to 41 percent a year later. The public also opposed Reagan's decision to send 2,000 additional marines to Lebanon. Between September 24 and 28, the CBS-*NYT* poll presented the following question to its sample: "If the Marines who are now in Lebanon cannot achieve their goals without substantial reinforcements, would you favor sending in more Marines, or would you favor withdrawing those who are there now?" A majority of 67 percent versus 23 percent supported withdrawal.[83]

Question (a) in table 4–7 demonstrates that in September 1983, a majority

Table 4–7
Opinions on U.S. Policy on Presence of Marines in Lebanon, 1983–84

Questions

(a) Do you think the U.S. Forces should be brought back home now, or do you think they should stay and continue their peacekeeping mission? (*Newsweek*-Gallup)

(b) Do you think the U.S. should withdraw its troops from Lebanon at this time or not? (Gallup)

	(a) *Sep. 1983*	(a) *Oct. 27, 1983*	(b) *Jan. 1984*	(b) *Feb. 1984*
(n)		(759)	(1,439)	(1,610)
Should withdraw	53%	42%	57%	74%
Should stay	38	49	34	17
D.K., N.O.	9	9	9	9
Total	100%	100%	100%	100%

Questions

(c) Would you say the U.S. should send more troops to Lebanon, leave the number about the same, or remove the troops that are there now? (*WP*-ABC)

(d) What do you think the U.S. should do now in Lebanon—withdraw the Marines, replace those who were killed and continue their current role there, or substantially increase the number of Marines so they can attack hostile forces? (CBS-*NYT*)

	(c) *Oct. 26, 1983*	(c) *Oct. 28, 1983*	(c) *Jan. 4, 1984*	(c) *Jan. 17, 1984*	(d) *Oct. 26, 1983*	(d) *Oct. 27, 1983*	(d) *Jan. 14–21, 1984*
(n)	(729)	(519)		(1,524)	(548)	(545)	(1,433)
Withdraw	45%	37%	57%	58%	36%	35%	49%
Current policy	33	41	29	31	16	26	27
Escalate	16	17	8	7	33	28	11
N.O.	6	5	6	4	15	11	13
Total	100%	100%	100%	100%	100%	100%	100%

Questions

(e) Whether or not you agree with U.S. military involvement in Lebanon, do you feel that U.S. Marine[s] have a clearly defined purpose in Beirut? (*Newsweek*-Gallup)

(f) Do you think that the U.S. government has clear goals for the United States Marine force in Lebanon or not? (*WP*-ABC)

Q	*Date*	*Yes*	*No*	*D.K., N.O.*	*(n)*
(e)	Oct. 26–27, '83	34%	56%	10%	(759)
(f)	Oct. 26, '83	37	50	13	(729)
(f)	Oct. 28, '83	42	48	10	(517)
(f)	Dec. '83	33	52	15	(1,506)
(f)	Jan. '84	30	59	11	(1,524)

Sources: (a)(e) *Newsweek*, November 7, 1983, 19. (b) *Baltimore Sun*, March 1, 1984. (c)(f) *Washington Pos[t]* October 30, 1983, December 15, 1983, January 20, 1984. (d) German with Brown, B-2.

of 53 to 38 percent preferred to bring the marines back home. The motives for this negative stand could stem from the Vietnam legacy of a limited involvement getting out of hand. Two polls taken at the time evoked bitter Vietnam memories. The CBS-*NYT* poll of September 24–28 asked:

> Some people say that what we're doing in Lebanon is like the way we got started in Vietnam. Other people say that the two situations are very different. Do you think this is like the beginning of our involvement in Vietnam, or not?

A majority of 58 to 27 percent said yes. Another poll by Gallup on October 7 and 20, 1983, revealed similar results.[84]

The Congress apparently sensed U.S. public sentiment and began to insist on its authority under the U.S. War Powers Act to supervise the use of the marines in Beirut. Following several debates between the White House and Capitol Hill, a compromise was reached and Congress authorized the presence of the marines in Lebanon for a period not to exceed 18 months.[85] This decision effectively neutralized the issue from debate in the approaching election year.

From the beginning of the U.S. military involvement in Beirut, Syria and its allies in Lebanon viewed the marines as a pro-Western force sympathetic to the Lebanese Christians and Israel. Thus, throughout September and October 1983, U.S. troops were constantly subjected to sniper attacks and shelling. On October 23, the marines suffered a tragic blow. A truck bomb—a favorite terrorist technique in Beirut—exploded inside marine headquarters, killing 241 Americans.[86] The high number of casualties, the horrendous terror technique used to inflict the damage, and the unclarified mission of the marines in Lebanon contributed to heated public debate within the United States.[87]

In two polls conducted on October 26 (questions (e) and (f) in table 4–7) the public said that the Marines had no clear, defined purpose in Beirut. It also disapproved of Reagan's handling of the situation in Lebanon by a majority of 53 to 41 percent (see table 4–2). However, when asked whether the United States should withdraw the marines (question (c) in table 4–7), 45 percent said yes, but a combined 49 percent wished them to stay with or without additional forces. According to a September 24–28 poll by CBS-*NYT* the public also complained, by a majority of 65 to 28 percent, that "the U.S. government has not yet tried hard enough to explain to the American public its reasons for sending the Marines and navy to Lebanon."

On October 27, 1983, Reagan, who was aware of this handicap, publicly addressed the American people. In his national address, he spoke of the American military involvement in Lebanon and Grenada and linked the two by suggesting that if the United States had not acted, the areas would have fallen to hostile powers.[88] Reagan also argued that the involvement in Lebanon was required to assure Israel's security and the prospects for a broader Arab-Israeli peace. He then stated:

> As for that narrower question, what exactly is the operational mission of the Marines, the answer is to secure a piece of Beirut; to keep order in their sector and to prevent the area from becoming a battlefield.

Reagan also rejected the call for American withdrawal, explaining, "If terrorism and intimidation succeed, it'll be a devastating blow to the peace process and to Israel's search for genuine security."

Reagan's address had some impact on American attitudes toward U.S. involvement in Lebanon. According to two polls conducted after the speech, the public turned from disapproval of the marines' presence to approval by 48 to 42 percent (see table 4–6). Prior to the speech, the public supported withdrawal by a plurality of 53 to 38 percent, but after the address, this result was reversed. Forty-nine percent, compared to 42 percent, now said that the marines should stay in Lebanon (question (a) in table 4–7). A similar change of attitude was recorded in response to other questions on the withdrawal issue (questions (c) and (d) in table 4–7). Reagan's management of the situation in Lebanon was rated negatively before the speech by a 53 to 41 percent majority, but after the speech American opinion turned favorable by 52 to 42 percent.

Yet the public was still uncertain about the purpose of the marines in Lebanon. Following the address, a plurality of 48 to 42 percent did not think the United States had clear goals for the marines (question (f) in table 4–7). Despite Reagan's address, another 53 to 40 percent majority did not think "the U.S. government had tried hard enough to explain to the American people its reasons for sending the Marines and navy to Lebanon."

The bombing of marine headquarters in Beirut clearly demonstrated the vulnerability of U.S. troops in Lebanon.[89] Yet Reagan could not simply order the withdrawal, since this would have been interpreted as a surrender to Syrian terrorism. Therefore, the president decided to punish Syria by reviving the dormant U.S.-Israeli strategic cooperation pact.[90] Israel attacked Syrian positions in the Bekaa Valley, and the United States followed suit with a retaliatory attack of its own—losing two planes. One pilot was killed and another captured.[91] In related action, eight marines were killed by artillery fire.

The public again expressed reservations about th U.S. military involvement in Lebanon. In mid-November, a *Los Angeles Times* poll found that 51 versus 34 percent did not think the U.S. involvement "will eventually get us into a full-scale war."[92] But responses to a similar question in mid-December yielded opposite results; a plurality of 48 to 43 percent thought the involvement "will eventually lead to a full-scale war." Respondents to a *WP*-ABC poll also opposed the notion that "U.S. troops should push the Syrians out of Lebanon" by 61 to 31 percent. Opposition decreased slightly—to 53 percent—when the public was asked whether "U.S. and Israeli troops *together*" should push the Syrians out.[93]

Further opinion indicators were also negative. In December 1983, a majority of 52 to 33 percent felt that the purpose of the marines in Lebanon was unclear (question (e) in table 4–7). In November, the public disapproved of Reagan's handling of the situation in Lebanon by 52 to 34 percent and in December by 50 to 43 percent. According to polls conducted by Gallup, at this point, Americans began to perceive the dispatching of the marines to Lebanon as a mistake. In November, the public was equally divided on this issue, and at the beginning of January 1984, a majority of 52 to 39 percent stated that the sending of marines to Lebanon was a mistake.

At the onset of 1984, an election year in the United States, the president increasingly came under fire to pull the U.S. troops out of Lebanon. Republican senators, including Howard Baker and Barry Goldwater, and prominent conservative columnists, called for the early withdrawal of the marines. Most significant was the voice of Secretary of Defense Weinberger, who represented the military's wish to get out of Beirut.[94] By the end of January 1984, the United States was tentatively searching for an honorable way out, but explosive events in Beirut, the death of the Israeli-Lebanese pact, and the collapse of the Lebanese army in the face of Druze and Shiite assaults, imposed the timing of the withdrawal on the president.[95]

On February 7, the White House announced that the marines had been redeployed and, for safety considerations, were evacuated from their ground positions to navy ships offshore.[96] The rhetoric was "redeployment," but the action was withdrawal. Approximately 16 months after their arrival in Beirut, U.S. troops left the area after paying a heavy price for an impossible mission.

The hasty withdrawal confirmed the earlier reservations of the American public, which now overwhelmingly criticized the U.S. involvement. Prior to the withdrawal, the public did not believe that the marines had a clearly defined purpose in Lebanon by a ratio of two to one (question (f) in table 4–7). By similar, unprecedented ratios, the public disapproved of Reagan's management of the situation. These were the highest negative ratings of Reagan's performance since 1981 (see table 4–2). In January 1984, between 57 and 58 percent thought that the marines should be withdrawn (questions (b) and (c) in table 4–7). Shortly after the redeployment, an overwhelming majority of 74 to 17 percent held the same view (question (b) in table 4–7).

Americans had reservations about the U.S. military involvement in Lebanon from the start. The brutal murder of the 241 marines only exacerbated this opposition. Reagan sensed these feelings and, with the presidential elections in sight, decided to pull out. The American failure in Lebanon was not an issue in the 1984 elections, and Reagan won a landslide victory over Democratic candidate Walter Mondale.

The TWA Hostage Crisis

Sixteen months after departing from the Lebanese shore, American naval units were alerted and dispatched back to Beirut waters. On June 14, 1985, two Shiite terrorists hijacked TWA Flight 847 from Athens to Rome.[97] The plane was flown to Beirut, where about a dozen additional terrorists boarded and joined the hijackers. The plane flew back and forth to Algiers twice, during which time the terrorists released women and children. U.S. Navy diver Dean Stethen was murdered, and six more passengers suspected of either being Jewish or military personnel were removed and dispersed to separate locations in several Beirut Shiite neighborhoods. The crew remained on the plane.

The hijackers, members of an extremist Syrian-backed, pro-Iranian terrorist organization, earlier took credit for kidnapping seven Americans and attacking U.S. institutions in Beirut and the Persian Gulf. The terrorists that later joined them belonged to the Shiite Amal militia, whose leader, Nabih Berri, was Lebanon's justice minister. The terrorists' original demands included the release of about 700 Shiites held by Israel, an end to Arab oil sales to the West, withdrawal of Arab money from Western banks, and the release of Shiite terrorists held in Kuwait and Spain.[98]

After the second landing in Beirut, Berri offered to negotiate for the release of the hostages but in fact took control of the situation. Berri added another paradox to the Lebanese quagmire—a justice minister acting as a terrorist spokesman. Berri soon dropped the hijackers' original demands and insisted only on the release of the Shiites, captured by Israel during its withdrawal from Lebanon, in exchange for the American hostages.[99]

Prior to the hijacking, Israel had released several hundred Shiite detainees and announced that the others would be released soon, depending on the security situation along the Israeli-Lebanese border. Therefore, at the onset of the crisis, Israel contemplated three difficult options: to continue to release the Shiites as scheduled; to release all of them immediately, as the hijackers demanded; or to delay action until the crisis was resolved. All three options were risky and problematic. The first two might have been interpreted as a surrender to terrorism; the third could have prolonged the crisis and endangered the lives of the hostages. Israel sought guidance from Washington but was rebuffed.

The United States spoke in two voices. Reagan and his principal advisers denounced the terrorism against TWA Flight 847, declared that the United States would not negotiate with terrorists, would not make any concessions to them, would not ask Israel to release the Shiites it held, and demanded an immediate, unconditional release of all the hostages.[100] Covertly, however, the Reagan administration signaled Israel that Washington would welcome an immediate release of all the prisoners it held.[101]

This two-pronged American position placed Israel in an impossible situation. Release of all the Shiites held in Israel surely would have been interpreted as capitulation to terrorism. Several weeks earlier, on May 20, Israel had released 1,150 Palestinian terrorists in return for three Israeli soldiers taken prisoner during the 1982 war in Lebanon. The U.S. government and the Israeli public criticized this deal and were likely to criticize another inequitable release. In addition, Berri could offer no assurance that he would be able to release all of the American hostages if the Shiites were set free, since six of the hostages were held separately by a more extremist faction. Israel, however, claimed that if high-ranking U.S. officials asked Israel to release the Shiites in return for the hostages, this request would be favorably considered.[102]

Table 4–2 reveals that less than half of the sample approved of Reagan's management of the crisis and 32 percent disapproved. This score is relatively low in contrast to the generally high ratings of presidents in the initial phases of past crisis situations.

Responses to polls questioning the tactics of the president might clarify his relatively low approval rating. Question (a) in table 4–8 reveals that contrary to Reagan's policy, a majority of the U.S. public preferred to negotiate even if it meant a surrender to terrorists' demands. On the other hand, as responses to questions (d) and (e) indicate, the public supported—by a close ratio—the president's refusal to officially ask Israel to release the Shiite prisoners.

Although Americans were closely divided on the question of whether the United States should have asked Israel to release the Shiites, they clearly felt that Israel should have facilitated the release without an official U.S. request (see table 4–9). On June 17, Americans held this view by a majority of 61 to 26 percent. The public, therefore, supported the cat-and-mouse game played by the Reagan administration and the media—talk tough and do not surrender to terrorism, but expect Israel to do so.

The responses to questions (a) and (b) in table 4–9 correlate with the responses to questions (c) and (d). A majority of the public said that Israel should have released the Shiites even in the absence of an American official request. Since Israel did not take such an action, the public did not think it was doing enough to resolve the crisis. Question (e) in table 4–9, included in only the *WP*-ABC poll, contains a misleading assumption. The question suggests a correlation between anti-American terrorism in the Middle East and close U.S.-Israeli ties. This thesis, however, has not been proven. Moreover, the most spectacular anti-American attacks in the Middle East, such as the hostage crisis in Iran, have had nothing whatsoever to do with Israel. The United States has been a victim of terrorism not because of its ties with any country, including Israel, but because of what it represents. In any event, on June 17, a majority of 53 to 31 percent rejected the notion suggested in question (e).

On June 18, 1985, Reagan held a nationally televised press conference and

Table 4–8
Opinions on U.S. Policy on the Hostage Crisis, June 1985

Questions

(a) Which of these two statements do you tend to agree with more: (1) The U.S. should be negotiating for the release of the Americans taken hostage even if that means giving in to the terrorists' demands, or (2) The U.S. should not be negotiating even if some of the Americans taken hostage are injured or killed? (*WP*-ABC)

(b) Which is more important: ensuring the safe release of the American hostages even if it means working out some compromise on terrorist demands or discouraging future hostage taking by refusing to deal with terrorist demands even if it risks the lives of American hostages? (*Newsweek*-Gallup)

(c) Do you think Reagan should have negotiated with the terrorists or not? (*WP*-ABC)

	(a) June 17	*(a) June 19*	*(a) June 20–22*	*(b) June 20–21*	*(c) July 1*
(n)	(508)	(508)	(1,506)	(1,016)	(1,208)
U.S. should negotiate	59%	53%	57%	47%	42%
U.S. shouldn't negotiate	32	40	36	42	51
N.O.	9	8	7	11	7
Total	100%	101%	100%	100%	100%

Questions

(d) The terrorists demand that Israel release between 700 and 800 Lebanese Shiite Moslems now being held prisoner. Israeli leaders have said they will consider releasing the Shiites if the U.S. asks them to. What is your view: Should the U.S. ask the Israelis to release the Shiites or not? (*WP*-ABC)

(e) Israel is holding over 700 Lebanese prisoners. Should the U.S. government ask Israel to release those prisoners as part of a deal with the Lebanese, or should we not ask Israel to do that? (CBS)

	(d) June 17	*(e) June 18*	*(d) June 19*	*(d) June 20–22*	*(e) June 26*
U.S. should ask Israel	41%	35%	40%	42%	27%
U.S. shouldn't ask Israel	47	51	51	48	61
N.O.	12	14	10	10	12
Total	100%	100%	101%	100%	100%

Sources: (a)(c)(d) *WP*-ABC Survey Nos. 0193, 0194, 0195, 0196, 0197, June–July 1985; *Washington Post,* June 26, 1985; (b) *Newsweek,* July 1, 1985, 15; (e) *CBS Poll,* June 1985.

Table 4–9
Evaluations of Israel's Policy in the Hostage Crisis, June 1985

Questions

(a) Suppose the U.S. doesn't ask Israel to release the Shiites. Should Israel release them anyway if that is what it takes to free the American hostages, or not? (*WP*-ABC)

(b) Israel has already promised to free over a period of time all the Shiites that President Reagan says were detained and taken to Israel illegally. Should that process be speeded up to free the current American hostages, or should it not be speeded up so as to deny any terrorist demands for the Shiites' immediate release? (*Newsweek*-Gallup)

	(a) *June 17*	*(a)* *June 19*	*(a)* *June 20–22*	*(b)* *June 20–21*
Yes	61%	65%	68%	56%
No	26	25	26	29
N.O.	13	10	6	15
Total	100%	100%	100%	100%

Questions

(c) Would you say the government of Israel has done what it should to help resolve the hostage situation, or not? (*WP*-ABC)

(d) Is Israel doing all it should to get the hostages released, or should it be doing more?" (CBS)

	(c) *June 17*	*(c)* *June 19*	*(c)* *June 20–22*	*(d)* *June 26*	*(c)* *July 1*
Yes, doing all it should	24%	23%	28%	24%	47%
No, should do more	49	58	53	57	34
N.O.	26	19	19	19	19
Total	99%	100%	100%	100%	100%

Question

(e) The U.S. should reduce its ties to Israel in order to lessen the acts of terrorism against us in the Middle East. (*WP*-ABC)

	June 17	*June 19*	*June 20–22*	*July 1*
Agree	31%	33%	42%	34%
Disagree	53	53	41	48
N.O.	16	15	17	18
Total	100%	101%	100%	100%

Sources: (a)(c)(e) *WP*-ABC Survey Nos. 0193, 0194, 0195, 0196, 0197, June–July 1985; (b) *Newsweek,* July 1, 1985, 15; (d) *CBS Poll,* June 1985.

outlined his administration's policy on the hostage crisis. In his opening statement, he said, "America will never make concessions to terrorists. To do so would only invite more terrorism."[103] Then, in an obvious reference to Israel, he added, "Nor will we ask or pressure any other government to do so. Once we head down that path, there'll be no end to it." When asked why he did not promote the release of the Shiites held by Israel, he answered, "the linkage that has been created makes it impossible for them [Israel] and for us. There was no question but that they were going to [release] in stages . . . but it has now been tied to where such a movement would be in effect giving in to terrorists."

Reagan also expressed his frustrations: "I've pounded a few walls myself," and added that the United States was unable to use force against the terrorists because the enemy could not be pinpointed. He also demanded from the terrorists the unconditional release of the hostages. The president avoided numerous questions on Berri's role and on diplomatic moves to resolve the crisis.

Following the press conference, the media continued to ponder U.S. public opinion on the crisis. The new polls registered a much higher rating of approval of Reagan's handling of the crisis—68 versus 25 percent (see table 4–2). However, the majority of the public opposed his refusal to negotiate for the release of the hostages, albeit by a smaller ratio. On the other hand, as table 4–8 indicates, the number of those who opposed an appeal to Israel grew by several percentage points. Table 4–9 shows that the number of Americans who thought Israel should release the Shiites grew slightly, and the number of those who said that the Israeli government "has not done what it should to help resolve the hostage situation" grew by nine percentage points. The distribution of answers to question (e) remained fairly consistent.

Throughout the first few days of the crisis, Israel kept a low profile. The then Israeli Prime Minister Shimon Peres instructed his ministers to avoid statements or comments on the incident. He hoped that quiet diplomacy would resolve the crisis in a manner that would not compromise the longstanding American and Israeli positions against surrender to international terrorism. But Reagan's cat-and-mouse policy and the media's criticism and manipulation of public opinion required an adequate response from the Jewish state.[104]

On June 19, Israel's Minister of Defense Yitzhak Rabin appeared on ABC News' "Nightline" and reflected the mood in Israel. He said, "Look, what do you expect Israel to do? You say 'we are not going to give in to any blackmail, but we [the United States] want you [Israel] to do so even without asking you to do so.'"[105] Rabin reiterated the Israeli stand: "If there is a desire, if there is a request on the part of the U.S. that this [release of the Shiites] has to be done in relation or as part of a deal for the release of the hostages, come out and say it." Rabin was obviously critical of Reagan's policy, and his comments were not received well.

As the first week of the hostage crisis neared an end, parts of the Reagan administration, the media, and the U.S. public grew impatient with the attempts to secure the release of the hostages. On June 20, the terrorists staged a press conference with five hostages. The hostages asked Reagan to refrain from any military action against the terrorists and expressed sympathy for the terrorists' demands.[106] From this press conference onward, the American television networks, especially ABC, played a highly controversial role in the crisis.[107] *Newsweek* justly deemed it the "network circus."[108] The networks frequently interviewed hostages who said they were treated well (a statement they would later reverse).[109] They also interviewed the hostages' families, who called for an Israeli and American surrender. The terrorists did not have to appear on the screen. The hostages did all of the work for them. The violent kidnapping of innocent passengers metamorphosed into an emotional drama made for Hollywood. The terrorists were cast as the victims, and Israel, of course, as the villain. It is quite possible that the televised "humanizing" of the crisis may have compromised Reagan's bargaining position, prolonging the crisis.[110]

The results of the *WP*-ABC June 19 poll were aired on June 20 and published on June 21. The staged press conference with the five hostages was also aired on June 20. The transcript of the interviews was published on June 21. Leaders of American Jewry viewed and read them with growing concern for Israel's image in the United States and for U.S.-Israeli relations. Subsequently, they made an urgent appeal to Peres to release the Shiites.[111] On June 23, Israel announced that on the next day it would release 31 Shiites. On the same day (Sunday), Peres appeared on NBC News' "Meet the Press" (Berri appeared on the same program) and Rabin appeared on CBS' "Face the Nation."[112] Undoubtedly, the decision to release the 31 Shiites was influenced by the apparent growing discontent of the American public, and the television appearances were designed to alleviate the pressure of the media and public opinion against Israel.

Several polls were conducted between June 20 and 22, prior to the release of the 31 Shiites but during and after the first hostage appearances on television. Gallup conducted polls for *Newsweek* between June 20 and 21, and the *WP*-ABC poll took surveys between June 20 and 22. The two polls used similar questions but received somewhat different results. The general pattern, though, is consistent. As revealed in table 4–2, both polls recorded high, positive approval ratings for Reagan's handling of the crisis (+35 and +47, respectively). A comparison between the *WP*-ABC polls of June 19 and June 20–22 revealed an increase of 4 percent. Table 4–8 indicates public opposition to Reagan's refusal to negotiate with the terrorists, but the *Newsweek*-Gallup ratio is much smaller than that of *WP*-ABC. A similar difference emerged from responses to questions (a) and (b) in table 4–9, but in both cases a majority of respondents thought Israel should have released the Shiites.

Answers to questions (c) and (d) in table 4–9 reveal an interesting finding. According to *WP*-ABC, before the release of the 31 Shiites from Israel, a majority of 53 to 28 percent did not think Israel was doing what it should to resolve the crisis; but according to a CBS-*NYT* poll conducted two days after the actual release, a larger majority of 57 to 24 percent still said that Israel should be doing more to get the hostages released. Finally, answers to question (e) in table 4–9 indicate that between June 20 and 22, for the first time in the crisis, a very close plurality of 42 to 41 percent thought the United States should reduce its ties with Israel.

The results of the preceding polls were aired and published June 25 and 26. At the same time, the media published the contents of a letter sent from Peres to Reagan on June 24. In his letter, Peres wrote:

> I said, as I really feel, that . . . our concern for the safety of the hostages is no different than if they were our own hostages. I see this as a struggle of the entire enlightened and free world against the ugly phenomenon of terror, and, of course, we stand by the U.S.[113]

The letter was interpreted as an offer for Israeli-American cooperation in efforts to free the hostages. In the meantime, the United States had assembled a considerable military force along Beirut's shores and, on June 25 and 26, threatened to blockade Lebanon.[114]

American officials also appealed to Syrian President Assad and asked him to assist with the release of the hostages. Assad had just returned from the Soviet Union, where he had been warned against exacerbating the anti-American provocation in Lebanon.[115] The Soviets were concerned about the U.S. projection of power in Lebanon, which could have advanced American interests in the entire Middle East. Assad quickly intervened and ordered Berri and the leaders of the more extreme Shiite group, Hizbullah, to release the hostages to him. After two days of negotiations and delays, the hostages were released in Damascus on June 30.

The release of the hostages with no apparent American concessions or further bloodshed boosted Reagan's rating to its highest level since the outbreak of the crisis—72 versus 21 percent (see table 4–2). According to the polls, the public, at this point, altered its opinions of U.S. policy on the crisis. Table 4–8 indicates that throughout the crisis, the public advocated negotiations with the terrorists, but after the release of the hostages, it justified Reagan's refusal to negotiate by a majority of 51 to 42 percent (question (c)).

The release of the hostages relieved the media's pressure on Israel and altered basic trends in public opinion on the Jewish state.[116] A *WP*-ABC poll of July 1 revealed that upon the release, a plurality of 47 to 34 percent said that Israel had done what it should have to release the hostages. In all earlier surveys, the public had held the opposite view by a two to one ratio (see table

4–9). Also, on July 1, a plurality of 48 to 34 percent opposed reduction of American ties with Israel. These results reversed findings recorded in the previous poll of June 20–22 and are similar to those of the first polls conducted during the crisis. Finally, as indicated in table 4–1, 49 percent said that their sympathies were more with Israel in the Middle East; only 11 percent sympathized more with the Arabs.

Conclusions

Violence and terror in Lebanon were the main issues covered in this chapter. The most significant erruption was the 1982 Israeli war in Lebanon, followed by U.S. military involvement. The war in Lebanon was controversial in both Israel and the United States and left the American public puzzled and confused. In general, it could be said that Americans sympathized with Israel's goals but not with its means.

As table 4–4 indicates, the public was divided on the legitimacy of the war and was probably affected by the media's reporting of alleged mass destruction and damage. Begin's image in American public opinion was never highly favorable, and it quickly deteriorated throughout the war. It appears that in keeping with the period of peace negotiations between Israel and Egypt, the American public distinguished between Begin and Israel. Contrary to popular belief, analysis of public opinion trends reveals that the image and standing of Israel in American public opinion were not damaged by the war. The sympathy index (table 4–1) indicates a slippage in the Israeli rating and an increase in the Arab rating during the war, but afterwards, the scores returned to normal prewar distributions.

According to the Gallup poll, immediately after the Sabra-Shatila massacre, sympathy for Israel declined to its lowest level since the Six-Day War. But as revealed in table 4–1, just 3 months later, Israel regained all of the lost points. In July 1981, Israel led the Arab countries by 49 to 10 percent. After the massacre, the rating dropped to 32 versus 28 percent, but in January 1983 it rose again to 49 to 12 percent. A similar result was obtained in July 1983. Polls by *WP*-ABC and Roper, which did not use the "awareness filter," registered much lower fluctuations in American sympathies.

The tension in American-Israeli relations during the war and its 1981 prelude probably prompted pollsters to examine perceptions of Israel as a reliable ally of the United States. The polls indicate that although the standing of Israel as a reliable ally declined during the war in Lebanon, after the war it climbed again to the relatively high average of the prewar period. Moreover, when compared to ratings of other American allies in the Middle East, including Egypt, the Israeli rating was much higher, even during the war. It was suggested, particularly during and after the war, that Israel's perceived value as an American ally had been irreparably damaged. The polls do not confirm this assertion. Short-lived criticism of Israel in American public opinion was also found during the TWA hostage crisis. Table 4–9 (questions (c) and (d)) reveals that at the conclusion of the crisis, negative opinions reversed and once again grew favorable to Israel.

The American military involvement in Lebanon during and after the war was not supported by American public opinion. Opposition to this involvement grew after the terrorist attack on marine headquarters in Beirut on October 23, 1983. The public did not think that the marines had clear goals in Lebanon, thought it a mistake to send them there, was concerned that the limited mission would grow into a Vietnam-like entanglement, and called for a quick withdrawal. It is interesting to note that after the withdrawal, U.S. military involvement was criticized even more harshly by the American public.

The TWA hostage crisis exposed certain sensitivities in American attitudes toward Israel. The majority of Americans opposed Reagan's refusal to negotiate with the terrorists but agreed with his reluctance to officially ask Israel to release the Shiites in exchange for the American hostages. The public felt that Israel should have released the Shiites without an official American request and, until the end of the ordeal, did not think that Israel had done all it should have to resolve the crisis. Furthermore, even after the ordeal, about a third of the respondents still agreed that the United States should reduce its ties with Israel "to lessen acts of anti-American terrorism in the Middle East."

These results, the critical media, and the pressure of American Jewry all affected the Israeli position in the crisis. Undoubtedly, the prime minister's decision to release 31 Shiites and to seek close cooperation with the U.S. government was inspired mainly by the perceptions of growing adverse public opinion toward Israel. According to the polls, however, the Israeli decision did little to alter the basic pattern of opinion; only the peaceful release of the hostages restored the generally positive Israeli standing in American public opinion.

In October 1985, barely three months after the TWA hostage crisis, Middle East terror hit the United States again. The Palestine Liberation Front, a Palestinian terrorist group affiliated with the PLO, hijacked an Italian cruise ship, *Achille Lauro*. They killed an elderly, crippled American passenger, Leon Klinghoffer, and were given safe conduct by Egypt. Later, the terrorists were intercepted by U.S. military aircraft and brought to trial. Surveys by Harris found a sharp rise in public hostility to the PLO, and at the same time, a soaring rise in Israel's popularity. The standard question on the distribution of sympathies in the Arab-Israeli conflict yielded a record 64 to 14 percent favorability rate for Israel (see table 4–1).[117]

The media's role in shaping U.S. policy and public opinion on Israel and the Middle East was highly controversial during both the war in Lebanon and the TWA hostage crisis. In the first case, it has been clearly demonstrated that the media's coverage of the war was grossly inaccurate and distorted. This coverage affected the perceptions of policymakers and commentators and probably contributed to critical public opinion. However, the polling data reveal that the effects of the war and the media coverage were brief. The media went far beyond their traditional role of presenting and analyzing events during the hostage crisis and became active players. The terrorists exploited the competition among the various networks and used them to manipulate public opinion.

At the inception of his term, President Reagan did not place the Middle East and the Arab-Israeli conflict high on his list of foreign policy priorities, but successive Middle East crises between 1981 and 1985 forced these issues on the White House. As table 4–2 indicates, except for the months of the ill-fated American involvement in Beirut, Reagan received positive scores for his handling of Middle East issues. The lowest approval ratings (−30 and −32) were recorded at the conclusion of the unsuccessful American involvement in Lebanon. The highest approval ratings (+47 and +51) were obtained during the TWA hostage crisis. However, Reagan's "Teflon syndrome"—the public's separation of Reagan from his policies—was evident, and on several occasions the public accorded him high marks on his management but criticized his policies.

Notes

1. Charles W. Kegley, Jr., and Eugene R. Wittkopf, "The Reagan Administration's World Review," *Orbis* 26(Spring 1982): 223–44.

2. Reagan's approach to the Middle East is discussed in Steven L. Spiegel, *The Other Arab-Israeli Conflict: Making America's Middle East Policy, from Truman to Reagan* (Chicago: University of Chicago Press, 1985), ch. 10; and Bernard Reich *The United States and Israel* (New York: Praeger, 1984), ch. 3. See also Fred Lawson, "The Reagan Administration in the Middle East," *Merip Reports* 14 (November-December 1984): 27–34; and the critique of Robert W. Tucker, "The Middle East: Carterism without Carter?" *Commentary* 72(September 1981): 27–36.

3. See Itamar Rabinovich, *The War for Lebanon, 1976–1983* (Ithaca, N.Y.: Cornell University Press, 1984), 118–20; and Efraim Inbar, "Israel and Lebanon: 1975–1982," *Crossroads*, no. 10(Spring 1983): 60–64.

4. For background on the Israeli attack on the Iraqi nuclear reactor, see Jed C. Snyder, "The Road to Osiraq: Baghdad's Quest for the Bomb," *Middle East Journal* 37(Autumn 1983): 565–93; and Ben Martin, "Iraq's Nuclear Weapons: A Prospectus," *Middle East Review* 13(Winter 1980–81): 43–49.

5. For various official statements, see U.S. Senate Committee on Foreign Relations, *Hearings, Israeli Attack on Iraqi Nuclear Facilities* 97th Cong., 1st sess. (Washington, D.C.: Government Printing Office, 1981). President Reagan, however, expressed sympathy toward the Israeli operation in a press conference held June 16; see

report by Lou Cannon in *Washington Post,* June 17, 1981. See also Haig's letter to Representative Thomas P. O'Neill and Senator Charles H. Percy, *New York Times,* June 11, 1981.

6. Abraham Ben-Zvi, *Alliance Politics and the Limits of Influence: The Case of the U.S. and Israel, 1975–1983,* Paper No. 24 (Tel Aviv: Tel Aviv University, Jaffa Center for Strategic Studies, April 1984), 33–40.

7. Asher Arian, ed., *Elections in Israel—1981* (Tel Aviv: Ramot, 1983).

8. It is not clear how many PLO members, as opposed to civilians, were killed or wounded in this action. Spokesmen for the PLO and the Lebanese government and Western reporters provided different and conflicting figures. On July 19, 1981, the *New York Times* quoted Palestinian sources who put the death toll at 300 killed and 800 wounded. According to Israeli sources, about 100 were killed and 600 wounded; see Zeev Schiff and Ehud Ya'ari, *Israel's War in Lebanon* (Tel Aviv: Schoken, 1984), 29.

9. The official statement was published in *New York Times,* July 18, 1981, 4.

10. Elizabeth H. Hastings and Philip Hastings, eds., *Index to International Public Opinion, 1981–1982,* (Westport, Conn.: Greenwood Press, 1982), 221.

11. *Newsweek,* August 3, 1981, 16.

12. Penn and Schoen Poll, No. 244, 357, May 1982.

13. These results were published in the October 4, 1982, issue of *Newsweek.*

14. See "Troubles with a Prickly Ally," *Time,* July 27, 1981, 22; and Richard Whittle, "American Support for Israel Appears Shaken Following Repeated Raids in Lebanon," *Congressional Quarterly* (July 25, 1981): 1351.

15. *Washington Post*–ABC Poll, Survey Nos. 0196 and 0197, July 1985.

16. Reich, *The United States and Israel,* 105–06; and U.S. Senate Committee on Foreign Relations, *Hearings on the AWACS and F-15 Enhancements Arms Sales Package to Saudi Arabia,* Part 1, 2 — October 1, 5, 6, 14 and 15, 1981 (Washington, D.C.: Government Printing Office, 1981).

17. *Washington Post,* September 11, 1981.

18. *New York Times,* October 9, 1981.

19. Steven J. Rosen and Yosef I. Abramowitz, *How Americans Feel About Israel,* Papers on U.S.-Israel Relations, No. 10 (Washington, D.C.: AIPAC, 1984), 25.

20. *Washington Post,* October 29, 1981.

21. The text of the memorandum was published in *New York Times,* December 1, 1981, 14.

22. For the Israeli considerations, see *Ha'aretz,* December 15, 1981; and *Newsweek,* December 28, 1981, 43. Haig and Larry Speakes, the White House deputy press secretary, criticized the Israeli action on December 14—*New York Times,* December 15, 1981.

23. On June 16, Weinberger called the Israeli move "provocative and destabilizing." See also transcripts of press conferences with Weinberger and Haig in *New York Times,* December 21, 1981, 18.

24. *Washington Post,* December 19, 1981.

25. *New York Times,* December 21, 1981; and Schiff and Ya'ari, *Israel's War,* 97.

26. An editorial source at the *Washington Post* explained that the subject is "dealing with issues most people don't think about" and that "numbers by themselves are not always helpful." See *Jewish Week* (Washington, D.C.), April 8-14, 1982.

27. Schiff and Ya'ari, *Israel's War,* 127–28; *New York Times,* November 10, 1981, and December 5, 1981.

28. See Avner Yaniv and Robert Lieber, "Personal Whim or Strategic Imperative? The Israeli Invasion of Lebanon," *International Security* 8(Fall 1983): 117–42.

29. Habib and Sharon met on December 5, 1981; see Schiff and Ya'ari, *Israel's War,* 81. See also Zeev Schiff, "The Green Light," *Foreign Policy* 50(Spring 1983): 73–85. For Haig's interpretation, see Alexander M. Haig, Jr., *Caveat: Realism, Reagan and Foreign Policy* (London: Weidenfeld and Nicolson, 1984), ch. 15.

30. Schiff and Ya'ari, *Israel's War,* ch. 2. Also see Shimon Shiffer, *Snow Ball* (Tel Aviv: Yediot Aharonot Book, Edanim, 1984); David Gordon, *The Republic of Lebanon—Nation in Jeopardy* (Boulder, Colo.: Westview Press, 1983), ch. 8; and Jonathan C. Randal, *Going All the Way: Christian Warlords, Israeli Adventurers, and the War in Lebanon* (New York: Viking, 1983).

31. The various phases of the war are described in Rabinovich, *War for Lebanon,* 135–45; and Richard A. Gabriel, *Operation Peace for Galilee: The Israeli-PLO War in Lebanon* (New York: Hill and Wang, 1984).

32. The Israeli limited goals were transmitted to Reagan in a special message; Schiff and Ya'ari, *Israel's War,* 146.

33. *Public Papers of the Presidents of the U.S.: Administration of Ronald Reagan, 1982* (Washington, D.C.: Government Printing Office, 1983), vol. 1, 745.

34. Rabinovich, *War for Lebanon,* 138–9. Schiff and Ya'ari, *Israel's War,* ch. 10.

35. *New York Times,* June 21, 28, 1982.

36. The statements of Reagan and Begin were published in *New York Times,* June 22, 1985.

37. Schiff and Ya'ari, *Israel's War,* ch. 11; Rabinovich, *War for Lebanon,* 141–43.

38. *New York Times,* August 26, 1982.

39. Ronald Reagan, *U.S. Involvement in Mideast Peace Effort: "A Moral Imperative,"* United States Policy Statement Series, September 1, 1982, (Washington, D.C.: United States Information Service, 1982).

40. For various evaluations of Reagan's initiative, see Alan J. Kreczko, "Support Reagan's Initiative," *Foreign Policy* 49(Winter 1982-83): 140-53; Avner Yaniv and Robert Lieber, "Reagan and the Middle East," *Washington Quarterly* 6(Autumn 1983): 125–37; Khalil Nakhleh and Clifford A. Wright, *After the Palestine Israel War* (Belmont, Mass.: Institute of Arab Studies, 1983), 67-126; and Robert W. Tucker, "Our Obsolete Middle East Policy," *Commentary* 75(May 1983): 21-27.

41. The details of the assassination are described in Schiff and Ya'ari, *Israel's War,* 308–9.

42. According to official reports from the Lebanese government, 460 people were killed in Sabra and Shatila, of whom 15 were women and 20 were children. The remainder were 328 Palestinian men, 109 Lebanese who were held prisoner by the Palestinians, 7 Syrians, 2 Algerians, 3 citizens of Pakistan, and 21 Iranians. Schiff and Ya'ari *Israel's War,* 350.

43. In contrast to other massacres in Lebanon and elsewhere in the Middle East, or even the world, the death toll at Sabra and Shatila was unusually low. In the Hama massacre of February 1982, Syrian troops killed 10,000 to 20,000 residents of Hama. This incident received very little attention in the American media, let alone criticism.

See David Hirst, "A Hole at the Heart of Hama," *Guardian*, December 9, 1982; and Wolf Blitzer, "The Lessons of Hama," *Jerusalem Post*, September 19, 1983. Another example is the massacre that occurred in the Indian state of Assam in February 1983, which left about 2,500 persons dead. While the *New York Times* devoted 1,050 column inches to the Sabra-Shatila massacre, it devoted only 127 column inches to the Assam massacre. See the report by the Committee for Media Accuracy, Washington, D.C., April 1983.

44. The statement was issued September 18, 1982. See *Public Papers of the Presidents of the U.S., 1982*, vol. 2, 1181.

45. The unclassified portions of the Kahan Commission report were published in a special supplement to the *Jerusalem Post*, February 9, 1983.

46. Prime Minister Begin defended the war in an article published on August 20, 1982, in the *Jerusalem Post*, entitled "Alternatives of War." For academic studies of the war's legitimacy, see Robert W. Tucker, "Lebanon: The Case for the War," *Commentary* 74(October 1982), 19–30, and William V. O'Brien, "Israel in Lebanon," *Middle East Review* 15(Fall-Winter 1982-83): 5–14.

47. Heritage Foundation—Joshua Muravchik, "Misreporting Lebanon," *Policy Review* 23(Winter 1983): 11-66; Center for International Security—Frank Gervasi, *Media Coverage: The War in Lebanon* (Washington, D.C., December 1982); *Columbia Journalism Review*—Roger Morris, "Beirut and the Press under Seige," (November-December 1982), 23-33; The Committee on Media Accuracy—"Lies About Lebanon," *AIM Report* 9(September 1, 1982); Anti-Defamation League of B'nai B'rith—*Television Network Coverage of the War in Lebanon* (New York, October 1982); and the American-Arab Affairs Council—*Split Vision* (Washington, D.C., 1983). In June 1983, Americans for Safe Israel produced a one-hour film entitled *NBC in Lebanon: A Study of Media Misrepresentation*. They later also published a study by Edward Alexander, *NBC's War in Lebanon: The Distorting Mirror* (New York, 1983).

48. See Yoel Cohen and Jacob Reuveny, *The Lebanon War and Western News Media*, Research Report No. 6-7 (London: Institute of Jewish Affairs, July 1984). Considerable additional evidence can be found in Julian Landau, ed., *The Media: Freedom or Responsibility—The War in Lebanon, 1982: A Case Study* (Jerusalem: B.A.L. Mass Communications, 1984).

49. Gervasi, *Media Coverage*, 22-23.

50. Cohen and Reuveny, *The Lebanon War*, 6

51. Muravchik, "Misreporting Lebanon," 11

52. Reed Irvine, "Lies about Lebanon," in Landau, ed., *The Media: Freedom or Responsibility*, 192–93; Cohen and Reuveny, *The Lebanon War*, 6; Gervasi, *Media Coverage*, 22.

53. *Time* June 14, 1982, 45

54. *New York Times*, June 21, 1982; *Media Coverage* 3.

55. Muravchik, "Misreporting Lebanon," 45.

56. Ibid., 51; Geravasi, *Media Coverage*, 25, and *Television Network Coverage of the War in Lebanon*, in Landau, *The Media: Freedom or Responsibility*, 122-169.

57. Ilya Gerol, "TV exaggerates Lebanese Damage," *The Citizen*, Ottawa, October 30, 1982.

58. B'nai B'rith, *Television Network Coverage*. See also letter by Nathan Perlmutter, *Columbia Journalism Review* 21(January-February 1983): 67.

59. See for example, "PLO Propaganda War: Phony Casualty Figures," *New York Post,* July 15, 1982; George F. Will, "Mideast Truth and Falsehood," *Newsweek,* August 2, 1982; and Edward Luttwak, "Playing the Lebanese Numbers Game," *New York Times,* July 18, 1982. Ze'ev Chafets accused the American media of assisting the PLO in its propaganda efforts: *Double Vision: How the Press Distorts America's View of the Middle East* (New York: Morrow, 1985), ch. 6.

60. On June 18, Michael Berlin reported in the *Washington Post* that according to the ICRC, the real number of civilians "affected" by the war was between 100,000 and 300,000. Yet one day later, Jessica Savitch repeated the 600,000-homeless fabrication on "NBC Nightly News" without quoting a source. Ten days after the ICRC correction, ABC's Mike McCourt still reported the false 600,000 figure, and William Farrel did the same thing in the *New York Times* of June 30. See Muravchik, "Misreporting Lebanon," 15, 51, and 61.

61. Gervasi, *Media Coverage,* 1.

62. Gerol, "TV Exaggerates."

63. Cohen and Reuveny, *The Lebanon War,* 11–24. See also Edward Alexander, "The Journalists' War Against Israel," *Encounter* 59(September-October 1982): 87–97; and Daniel Pipes, "The Media and the Middle East," *Commentary* 77(June 1984): 29–34.

64. Muravchik, "Misreporting Lebanon," 66.

65. ABC News Viewpoint Poll, No. 4, Survey 0063, October 11–12, 1982.

66. See Eytan Gilboa, "Effects of the War in Lebanon on American Attitudes Toward Israel and the Arab-Israeli Conflict," *Middle East Review* 18(Fall 1985): 30–43; and Geraldine Rosenfield, "US Public Opinion Polls and the Lebanon War," *American Jewish Year Book* 84(1984), 105–16.

67. *Roper Reports,* October 1982.

68. John E. Rielly, (ed.), *American Public Opinion and U.S. Foreign Policy, 1983* (Chicago: Chicago Council on Foreign Relations, 1983), 19.

69. *Newsweek,* October 4, 1982.

70. William C. Adams, "Blaming Israel for Begin," *Public Opinion* 5(October-November 1982), 51–55.

71. *Washington Post*–ABC Poll, Survey No. 0072, March 1983.

72. *Newsweek,* August 16, 1982.

73. *Roper Reports,* November 1982.

74. Louis Harris, "Majority Backs Israel's Stated Aim of Lebanese Self Rule," *Washington Post,* July 11, 1982.

75. *Public Opinion* 6(August-September 1983): 31.

76. Louis Harris, "Many Now Accept Israel's Move into Lebanon," *Washington Post,* July 19, 1982.

77. For Reagan's statement, see *New York Times,* September 29, 1982. His letter to Congress on this issue was published a day later by the same newspaper (p. 12).

78. For details see *New York Times,* April 19, 1983.

79. The main principles of the agreement were published in *Jerusalem Post* and *New York Times,* May 18, 1983.

80. The official Israeli statement on the pullback was published in *New York Times,* September 5, 1983.

81. See *New York Times,* September 2, 1983.

82. For two views that were published at the time, see Daniel Pipes, "The Real Problem," *Foreign Policy* 51(Summer 1983): 139–59; and Naomi Joy Weinberger, "Peacekeeping Options in Lebanon," *Middle East Journal* 37(Summer 1983): 341–69.

83. Mark F. German with Kirk Brown, *Public Opinion Polls on U.S. Policy in Lebanon* (Washington, D.C.: Library of Congress, February 8, 1984), B-2.

84. Ibid., B-4.

85. Reagan's statement on the congressional resolution (S.J. Res. 159, the Multinational Force in Lebanon Resolution) was published in *New York Times*, October 13, 1982, 7.

86. *New York Times*, October 24, 1983. See also U.S. Department of Defense *Report of the DOD Commission on Beirut International Airport, Terrorist Act, October 23, 1983* (Washington, D.C.: Government Printing Office, December 20, 1983).

87. On October 25, 1983, for example, the *New York Times* published excerpts from administration statements on U.S. objectives in Lebanon beginning in September 1982.

88. The United States invaded Grenada on October 25. Reagan's televised address was published in *New York Times*, October 28, 1983, 10.

89. For an evaluation of Reagan's policy in Lebanon, see William Quandt, "Reagan's Lebanon Policy: Trial and Error," *Middle East Journal* 38(Spring 1984), 237–54.

90. Ibid., 248.

91. This was Lt. Robert O. Goodman, who was later freed by a special mission of Reverend Jesse Jackson to Damascus.

92. German with Brown, *Public Opinion Polls*, B-4.

93. *Washington Post*, December 15, 1983.

94. Quandt, "Reagan's Lebanon Policy," 249.

95. See *New York Times*, February 5, 1984.

96. Reagan's statement on the redeployment of the marines was published in *New York Times* February 8, 1984, 9. Reagan also submitted a report to the Congress on the U.S. military involvement in Lebanon. The report was published in the same paper, February 16, 1984, 14.

97. A brief chronology of the crisis appeared in *New York Times*, July 1, 1985.

98. *Newsweek*, June 24, 1985, 25.

99. The Reagan administration said that Israel held the Palestinians and Lebanese in contravention of international law, as defined in the Fourth Geneva Convention. However, to several well-known experts in international law, this argument was baseless. See, for example, the letter of Leo Gross to the *New York Times*, July 6, 1985.

100. See, for example, Lou Cannon and John Goshko, "US Stands Firm against Demands of Jet's Hijackers," *Washington Post*, June 20, 1982.

101. Thomas L. Friedman, "Israelis Appear Angered by Subtle US Pressure," *New York Times*, June 21, 1985.

102. Edward Walsh, "Israel Says US Has Yet to Request Freeing of Shiite Prisoners," *Washington Post*, June 17, 1985.

103. The transcript of the press conference was published in *New York Times, June 19, 1985.*

104. Thomas L. Friedman, "Israel Ready to Meet Red Cross on Captives," *New York Times*, June 19, 1985.

105. See Edward Walsh, "Israelis' Remarks Show Strain Over Crisis," *Washington*

Post, June 21, 1985; and Jane Eisner, "Israel Sees Hijack Crisis as the U.S.'s Problem," *Philadelphia Inquirer,* June 21, 1985.

106. See excerpts from the news conference in *New York Times,* June 21, 1985.

107. Christopher Dickey, "The ABCs of Getting the Story in Beirut," *Washington Post,* July 8, 1985.

108. *Newsweek,* July 8, 1985, 13. See also David Bar-Illan, "Israel, the Hostages and the Networks," *Commentary* 80(September, 1985): 33–37; and Peter W. Kaplan, "Competition over Hostages Is Fierce for US TV Networks in Beirut," *New York Times,* June 30, 1985.

109. See, for example, Joseph Berger, "Tones of Sympathy in Beirut Turn More Bitter in Freedom," and Bernard Weinraub, "Hostages Tell of Anger and Terror and Ask Justice Against their Captors," *New York Times* July 3, 1985. See also stories in *Newsday* and *New York Post,* July 2, 1985.

110. See, for example, Dorothy Rabinowitz, "TV Understands Our Enemies," *New York Post,* June 28, 1985. Art Buchwald, "How Networks Hijack the Spotlight," *Washington Post,* June 25, 1985; and Alex Jones," TV in the Hostage Crisis: Reporter or Participant," *New York Times,* July 2, 1985.

111. *Ha'aretz,* June 24, 1985; and reports by Charlotte Saikowski in *Christian Science Monitor,* June 25, 1985; and Saul Friedman in the *New York Daily News,* June 25, 1985.

112. Excerpts from these interviews were published in *New York Times,* June 24, 1985.

113. Robert Ruby, "Peres' Letter to US Reportedly Offers Israeli Cooperation in Hostage Crisis," *Baltimore Sun,* June 26, 1985.

114. See reports by Gerald M. Boyd in *New York Times* and Christopher Dickey in *Washington Post,* June 26, 1985.

115. See report by Jonathan C. Randal in *Washington Post,* June 26, 1985.

116. Mitchell Bard, "Israel's Standing in American Public Opinion," *Commentary* 80(October 1985): 58–60.

117. *The Harris Survey,* 92, November 14, 1985.

Part II
Issues and Group Attitudes

5

Perceptions of the PLO and the Palestinians

The Palestinian problem has proved to be one of the central issues in the Arab-Israeli conflict since the 1948 Israeli War of Independence.[1] From 1948 to the end of the 1960s, the problem was primarily defined as a humanitarian issue, involving refugees who fled Israel before and during the 1948 war. From the late 1960s however, the Palestinian problem meshed with the activities of the Palestine Liberation Organization (PLO) and Israeli policy in areas of the West Bank and Gaza, which the Jewish state captured from Egypt and Jordan during the Six-Day War.[2]

The United States has always been concerned with the plight of the Palestinian refugees. Following its own tradition and principles, the American public was willing, to a certain degree, to accommodate some of the national aspirations of the Palestinians in the late 1970s. The PLO, however, recognized by the Arab world as the "sole legitimate representative of the Palestinians," adopted a national covenant that called for the dismantling of Israel. Under the leadership of its chairman, Yasser Arafat, the PLO initiated a campaign of terror against Israel and the United States. A close associate of the Soviet Union and its allies, the PLO frequently criticized U.S. policy in the Middle East and attacked Americans and the American interests, not only within the Middle East but throughout the world. The PLO bases in Lebanon also grew to be the most notorious centers of international terrorism.

Ties with the USSR and the Third World enabled the PLO to achieve political and diplomatic status in many nations and at the United Nations. In 1974, the General Assembly recognized the PLO as the representative of the Palestinians and granted it the status of observer. The General Assembly also invited Arafat to speak at the United Nations, established a special committee on Palestinian rights, and passed numerous resolutions supporting PLO positions.

Israel recognized the plight of the Palestinians and was ready to participate in local and international efforts to solve the problem. However, Israel refuses to negotiate with the PLO because of its extreme ideology and terrorism. Israel also opposes the establishment of an independent Palestinian state in the West

Bank and Gaza and, on national security grounds, insists on alterations in the Israeli-Jordanian borders.

American policy on the Palestinian question and the PLO has been far from coherent and consistent. The Nixon and the Ford administrations adopted a step-by-step approach to the conflict, preferring to leave the most difficult question to the last phase. In September 1975, the United States gave Israel a written commitment stating that it would not negotiate with the PLO until that organization recognizes Israel and accepts Security Council Resolution 242. The Carter administration, on the other hand, viewed the Palestinian question and the PLO as the key to peace in the Middle East. In March 1977, Carter called for the establishment of a homeland for the Palestinians, and officials of his administration negotiated directly and indirectly with representatives of the PLO. One meeting between the U.S. ambassador to the United Nations, Andrew Young, and a U.N. PLO representative exploded and forced Young's resignation from his post. Reagan defined the PLO as a terrorist organization in the Kremlin's service, and, following the war in Lebanon, introduced a plan to solve the Palestinian problem within a Jordanian context.

Until the 1973 Yom Kippur War, the American media portrayed the PLO in a negative light and presented it mainly as a terrorist organization. Since the mid-1970s, however—and even more so after Carter's courting of the PLO and his emphasis on the need to resolve the Palestinian problem—the American media changed their approach and tone on the PLO and the Palestinians. Following Carter's moderate lead, the media portrayed Arafat and the PLO in a much more favorable light, described the Palestinians as helpless, passive victims, and accused Israel of being intransigent and bellicose toward the PLO and the Palestinians.[3]

PLO leaders have often distinguished between the U.S. government—which they consider overly pro-Israel—and the American public—which they believe to be more sympathetic to their cause. American presidents have distinguished between the PLO and the Palestinians, condemning the PLO and demonstrating sympathy for the Palestinians. Public opinion on the PLO and the Palestinians developed within these confusing circumstances, and pollsters have sought to determine how Americans perceive the Palestinian question and the PLO and the extent to which they have supported or opposed the American and Israeli policies on these issues. In the meantime, Israel fought the PLO during the 1982 war in Lebanon and expelled Arafat and his followers from their strongholds in South Lebanon and Beirut. Palestinians were also murdered by Christian Phalangists during the Sabra-Shatila massacres. How, then, did the war and its repercussions affect American attitudes toward the PLO and the Palestinians?

This chapter deals with these questions on the basis of substantial polling data organized in three basic categories: images of the PLO and the Palestinians, the role of the PLO in the political process, and solutions to the Palestinian problem. But first, a brief summary of the issues is provided.

Background of the Palestinian Problem

The first Arab-Israeli war created a serious refugee problem, and the United States, among other countries, sought a reasonable way to resolve it. Most solutions originated from the assumption that the majority of refugees would have to resettle in their respective host countries. Although the territories of the West Bank and Gaza were under Arab control until 1967, the Palestinians and the Arab world never attempted to establish an independent Palestinian state there. Instead, they insisted on the right of the refugees to return to their homes in Israel.[4] Israel argued that a complete return of all the Palestinian refugees to their homes was impossible and impractical, because those homes either had been destroyed or were occupied by Jews. Israel further claimed that between 1948 and 1951, a massive population exchange had occurred in the Middle East, and though between 600,000 and 800,000 Arabs left Israel, a similar number of Jews immigrated to Israel from hostile Arab countries—most of them empty handed.[5] Israel resettled the Jewish refugees and felt that those Arab countries mainly responsible for the 1948 war should do the same with the Arab refugees.

Both the Eisenhower and Kennedy administrations invested time and effort in developing plans directed toward a resolution to the Arab refugee problem.[6] Both sent special emissaries to the Middle East to ascertain which types of economic projects best suited the facilitation of resettlement.[7] These missions failed, mostly because the Arab countries wished to exploit the Palestinian plight for domestic or regional interests.[8] For that purpose, they created various Palestinian organizations, including the PLO.

The PLO was conceived by President Nasser of Egypt and was founded in 1964 under the official auspices of the Arab League.[9] Nasser also appointed Ahmad Shuqairy as the first chairman of the PLO. Although Shuqairy sought to unite all Palestinians under his leadership, he and the PLO were soon challenged by other Palestinian organizations.[10] One rival was the Fatah, under Yasser Arafat, which began ideological activities in 1959 and military operations against Israel in 1965.[11] Fatah and Arafat seized control of the PLO in February 1969 and made it an umbrella organization for all the Palestinian groups.[12]

During its founding conference in 1964, the PLO adopted a National Covenant, which rejected Israel's right to exist and called for the liquidation of the Jewish state by armed struggle.[13] The covenant was amended in 1968, but its essence has remained the same. The PLO National Covenant claims all rights for the Palestinians, including the right of self-determination, and rejects any rights for the Jews. The covenant also claims that the Jews are not one people and describes the Jewish historical and spiritual ties to the land of Israel as deceit and fraud (article 20). Israel must be eliminated because it is only there that the rights of the Palestinians for self-determination can be realized and only there that they can regain dignity, glory, and freedom (articles 2, 3, 15 and 17). PLO goals are stated in the covenant in positive terms, such as "the liberation of Palestine," "return," "realization of self-determination for the Palestinians," "a just solution," and "the establishment of a democratic state." But the practical consequence of these seemingly positive actions is the elimination of Israel, a result that the covenant and Palestinian spokesmen endeavor to conceal.

The Palestinians hoped for an all-out, decisive Arab war that would eliminate Israel. In May 1967, PLO Chairman Shuqairy said, "Zero hour has come. This is the hour our people have been waiting for the last nineteen years. The UAR [Egyptian] army is capable of destroying the Israeli aggressor within a few hours." Shuqairy also estimated that after the war, not many remaining Israelis would survive.[14] Although the results of the Six-Day War were devastating to Egypt, Syria, and Jordan, the Palestinian organizations, especially Fatah, saw new opportunities in the Israeli occupation of the West Bank and Gaza. Immediately after the war and during 1968, Arafat, envisioning himself as a Palestinian version of Che Guevara or Ho Chi Minh, attempted to organize a classic war of national liberation in the occupied territories. His strategy failed, however, and the next step led to international terrorism and violence.[15]

Political terrorism is a highly disputed term and phenomenon in both public and academic circles.[16] Genuine movements for national liberation prefer to call their military operations "guerrilla warfare," but this form of war is usually restricted to attacks on military and strategic targets. Terrorism, on the other hand, does not distinguish between civilians and soldiers, and innocent people are usually the victims of purposeful attacks. Ideologically, guerrilla warfare carries an aura of legitimacy, whereas terrorism has been viewed in more negative terms. Thus, terrorists and their supporters tend to counter critics of terrorism with the dictum, "One man's terrorist is another's freedom fighter." Yet this dictum fails to take into account the nature of the violent acts and their consequences. Regardless of how they are defined, indiscriminate attacks against unarmed civilians, including children and women, and attacks on civilian targets such as schools, markets, and buses, have normally not been used as a *matter of principle* by genuine national liberation fronts that seek independence from colonial powers.[17] Palestinian violence, however, was directed against civilians and civilian targets.[18] Furthermore, the goal of PLO terrorism is not just the replacement of a foreign government but the destruction of an existing state.

The PLO and the Palestinian organizations attacked not only Israelis and

Jews in Israel and abroad but also Americans and American institutions. They violated many traditional norms of international conduct and behavior. The PLO and its member organizations hijacked civilian airliners and killed passengers, attacked embassies, murdered Israeli and American diplomats, and attacked Israeli athletes in the 1972 Olympic Games in Munich. Palestinian international terrorism received international attention and was widely reported in the United States.[19] Attacks on U.S. civilian aviation triggered angry reactions in the Congress and sharp criticism from officials, who denounced the Palestinian terrorists as "international outlaws" and their actions as "air piracy, inhuman and animal-like."[20] The murder of American diplomats and especially the U.S. ambassador to Sudan, Cleo Noel, also raised strong condemnation of Palestinian terrorism.

In the mid-1970s, it became clear that the PLO was the major source of international terrorism in the Western democracies. It supported and collaborated with terrorist organizations from Germany, Italy, Japan, Turkey, France, and Canada.[21] It also had connections to acts of terrorism in Latin America and Africa. But only in the late 1970s did it become clear that Palestinian terrorism was directly connected with Soviet interests and supervision.[22] The Soviet-PLO connection occupied a central role in the Reagan administration's view of the international system. Reagan and his aides defined the PLO as a terrorist organization employed by the Soviet Union to spread revolution around the world.[23]

Throughout the 1970s, the PLO—notably its more Marxist member organizations—developed close, visible ties with the Soviet Union.[24] These ties possibly contributed to the PLO's negative image in the United States. Yasser Arafat traveled to the USSR for the first time in July 1968 and since 1970 has visited there almost annually. At the onset of Arafat's visits, relations between the PLO and the Kremlin were unofficial and at low levels. However, after the 1973 Yom Kippur War, the levels of the meetings elevated, and the ties became official. The Soviet Union provided the PLO with considerable weapons, including various types of antitank and antiaircraft missiles, tanks, and heavy artillery. Many PLO members received military training in Soviet bases.[25] During the détente years, the USSR was more covert and cautious in its dealings with the PLO, rendering them less noticeable. But in the second half of the 1970s, with the shattering of détente and the American monopolization of the peacemaking process between Israel and Egypt, the link between the Kremlin and the PLO became more significant, official, and visible.

The PLO's heightened connection with the USSR (as well as support from the Soviet bloc) and Arab and Third World countries enabled it to win considerable support in the international arena. Even those Western countries primarily affected by Palestinian violence extended recognition to the PLO and allowed it to open bureaus and offices in their capitals.[26] By 1975, the PLO secured some form of diplomatic representation in approximately 40 countries.[27] By 1980, this number had more than doubled to 82.[28] At the United Nations General Assembly, the Soviet bloc combined forces with the Arab nations and the Third World to award the PLO special status and pass resolutions highly favorable to its cause.

On October 14, 1974, the General Assembly, by a vote of 105 to 4, with 20 abstentions, agreed to recognize the PLO as the representative of the Palestinians.[29] In the next few weeks, the PLO ascended to the apex of diplomatic recognition. At the end of October, a summit conference of Arab leaders proclaimed the PLO to be the "sole legitimate representative of the Palestinian people."[30] The PLO and Yasser Arafat scored a major victory on November 13, 1974, when Arafat was invited to present the views of the PLO concerning Israel and the Palestinian problem before the General Assembly.[31] A few days later, the General Assembly awarded the PLO a resolution that "reaffirmed the inalienable rights of the Palestinian people in Palestine" and granted it observer status at the United Nations (Resolutions 3236 and 3237).[32]

The *New York Times* reported that these decisions were an "invitation to disaster." In the eyes of that publication, the support given to an organization that denies Israel's right to exist is an "incredible surrender to a group which has stooped and continues to stoop to unspeakable acts of terrorism."[33] Yet following its achievements in the world arena, the PLO hoped to gain recognition and legitimacy in American public opinion in an attempt to alter the official U.S. policy on itself and on the Palestinian problem.

Images of the PLO and the Palestinians

One of the main goals of terrorism is to attract world public attention, and indeed the PLO hoped to spark U.S. public awareness of the Palestinian cause through spectacular acts of terror. However, terrorism is a double-edged sword that may create a very negative image for those who use it. The PLO was aware of the possible negative backlash of terrorism and attempted to avoid or minimize it. To achieve this goal, the PLO used three principal means: denial; establishment of cover organizations, such as Black September; and public relations moves, such as meetings with sympathetic Western politicians.[34] This strategy usually failed, however, and the PLO was forced to reduce the levels of terrorism and to take remedial measures.

The terrorist acts that damaged the PLO's standing most in the eyes of Americans were the senseless murders of American diplomats, the attack on Israeli athletes in the 1972 Munich Olympic Games, and the more recent murders of innocent passengers aboard the Italian cruise ship *Achille Lauro* and in the airports of Vienna and Rome.[35] A spokesman for the PLO group (Black September) that attacked the athletes in Munich explained that "the operation was aimed at exposing the close relation between the treacherous German authorities and U.S. imperialism on the one hand, and the Zionist enemy's authorities on the other."[36] But Miller suggests that the murder in Munich "was possibly the most devastating public relations catastrophe in the PLO's history. In a single act, the Palestinians thrust themselves into the almost sacrosanct world of international sports, killing unarmed Israeli athletes while millions of people watched the drama unfold. The same multimedia communications network that the PLO tried to exploit to publicize its cause brought the horror of events at Munich into the living rooms of millions."[37]

Arafat's speech at the United Nations General Assembly was specifically designed to improve the PLO image in the world, particularly in the United States. In his speech, Arafat made a direct appeal to American public opinion: "The PLO appeals to the American people, in friendship, to endorse right and justice, to support the heroic Palestinian people, bearing in mind the heroic achievements of Washington, Lincoln and Wilson."[38] Arafat also granted interviews to the major television networks, the *New York Times, Time,* and the *Christian Science Monitor.* In every interview he noted a distinction between the public and the administration and called upon the public to exert pressure on the Ford administration to change what he considered a policy of total American commitment to Israel. But the American public was not impressed. Several polls conducted a few weeks later reveal that the PLO and Arafat still carried a very negative image in the United States.

In the Harris survey of December 1974 to January 1975, the national sample labeled Arafat an "extremist" by a majority of 48 to 7 percent and as a man "responsible for the outrageous slaughter of innocent children" by a plurality of 37 to 10 percent.[39] However, closer ratios were registered in responses to questions concerning Arafat's political stands. A plurality of 29 to 19 percent rejected the notion that he "has become more moderate in his demands lately," and a similar plurality, 30 to 19 percent, disagreed with the statement that "he wants to work out a peaceful settlement in the Middle East." In response to a direct question on Arafat's appearance at the United Nations, 32 to 17 percent rejected the notion that "he made a good impression at the United Nations." A slightly larger margin of the sample, 35 to 18 percent, did not think the PLO "deserves to have a permanent status at the U.N." It should be noted, however, that in response to most of the queries, almost half of the sample selected the "do not know" response.

The Yankelovich organization conducted surveys questioning the image of the PLO in the United States in January 1975 and in later years. The January 1975 survey, conducted about two months after Arafat's appearance at the United Nations, found that the PLO was perceived by substantial majorities as a "terrorist organization" (85 percent), "undemocratic" (92 percent), and "anti-U.S." (92 percent). By lesser ratios, Americans perceived the PLO as "backward" (63 percent), "pro-Communist" (65 percent), and consisting of "people we cannot get along with."[40] An identical survey repeated in 1976 and

1982 yielded very similar, negative results. According to the Yankelovich surveys, the image of the PLO did not change much between 1975 and 1982—despite the dramatic changes that occurred in the Middle East at this time, including the war in Lebanon.

Additional, more varied evidence on the American perceptions of the PLO was uncovered in several polls by Harris. On March 11, 1978, several months after President Sadat's visit to Jerusalem, a group of Palestinian terrorists conducted a raid on a passenger bus near Tel Aviv in which 37 persons were killed and 82 wounded. Harris found shortly afterward that 93 percent of the public thought the attack wrong and only 2 percent thought it justified.[41] In November 1977, Harris found that 53 percent of his sample viewed the PLO as "unfriendly" or an "enemy" of the United States. During and after the war in Lebanon, this percentage substantially increased. In June 1982 and November 1982, 73 and 79 percent of the sample, respectively, said that the PLO was "unfriendly" or an "enemy" of the United States.[42] In October 1985, following the hijacking of the *Achille Lauro,* 86 percent of the sample held the same view.

A comprehensive poll conducted in the fall of 1980 reveals that the PLO ranked the lowest in popularity of all the Arab political entities and that Arafat ranked the lowest in popularity of all Arab leaders.[43] Only 9 percent of the sample held a "high opinion" of the PLO; the vast majority of the sample (72 percent) had either a "fairly low" (26 percent) or "very low" (46 percent) opinion of the PLO. Only 10 percent had a "high opinion" of Arafat; 55 percent had a "low opinion" of him. The poll reveals that even Qaddafi and Libya were more popular in the United States at the time than Arafat and the PLO.

The fall 1980 poll also demonstrates that in comparison to the PLO and Arafat, the Palestinians had a more favorable image in the United States. While only 9 percent of the sample had a "high opinion" of the PLO, 34 percent had the same opinion of the Palestinians. Indeed, other surveys also reveal that Americans differentiated between the PLO and the Palestinians.

Table 5–1 clearly indicates that when pitted against Israel, the score for the Palestinians was much higher than that for the PLO. On the average, Israel enjoyed an advantage of five to one over the PLO and only three to one over the Palestinians. Moreover, a comparison of results in table 5–1 to results of polls that pitted Israel against the Arabs (tables 2–1, 3–2, and 4–1) reveals that the number of Americans who sympathized with the Palestinians was much higher than the number of those who expressed sympathy for either the PLO or the Arabs. In January 1975, for example, 52 percent of the public sympathized more with Israel and 7 percent with the Arabs (see table 2–1). But when "Arabs" was replaced by "Palestinians" in the same question (table 5–1), the results were only 33 to 14 percent in favor of Israel. In July 1980, Harris used an identical question to examine American sympathies for Israel and three different Middle East groups: Arabs, Palestinians, and the PLO. Israel's score surpassed that of the PLO by a majority of 65 to 6 percent and that of the

Table 5–1
Sympathies for Israel, the Palestinians, and the PLO, 1975–82

Question

(a) In the dispute between Israel and the Palestinians, which side do you sympathize with more, Israel or the Palestinians?

Date	*Poll*	*Israel*	*Palestinians*	*Neither*	*Both*	*Not Sure*	*(n)*
Jan. '75	Harris	33%	14%	53%[a]	—	—	(3,377)
Jan. '76	Harris	40	10	21	9	20	
Nov. '78	Gallup	41	13	46[a]	—	—	(1,546)
Dec. '79	Yankelovich	49	15	12	3	22	(1,041)
July '80	Harris	47	14	13	10	16	(1,506)
Fall '80	Slade	57	16	27[a]	—	—	(600)
Aug. '81	Harris	47	15	11	2	25	(1,248)
Oct. '82	Gallup	40	17	43[a]	—	—	(1,546)

Question

(b) In the dispute between Israel and the PLO which side do you sympathize with more, Israel or the PLO?

Date	*Poll*	*Israel*	*PLO*	*Neither*	*Both*	*Not Sure*	*(n)*
Aug. '79	Harris	71%	8%	9%	3%	9%	(1,201)
Oct. '79	Harris	55	14	10	2	19	(1,500)
Dec. '79	Yankelovich	56	11	10	2	22	(1,041)
Jul. '80	Harris	65	6	13	4	12	(1,506)
Aug. '81	Harris	59	14	8	1	18	(1,248)
Jun. '82	Harris	60	16	11	2	11	(1,255)
Aug. '82	Harris	59	15	10	2	14	(1,254)

Sources: (a) Harris: Louis Harris, *The Harris Survey,* (September 10, 1981); Louis Harris and Associates, *A Study of the Attitudes of the American People and the American Jewish Community Toward Anti-Semitism and the Arab-Israeli Conflict in the Middle East,* Study No. 804011 (August 1980), 31; Gallup: *American Public Opinion and U.S. Foreign Policy, 1983* (Chicago: Chicago Council on Foreign Relations, 1983), 22; Yankelovich: Geraldine Rosenfield, *Attitudes of the American Public Toward American Jews and Israel: December 1979* (New York: American Jewish Committee, Information and Research Services, March 1980, mimeographed), 3; Slade: *Middle East Journal* 35(Spring 1981): 155. (b) Louis Harris, "Israel Loses Little Public Support in War: PLO Makes No Gains," *The Harris Survey,* August 23, 1982.

[a]Neither, both, and not sure.

Table 5–2
Feelings about Palestinians versus the PLO and Arafat

Questions

(a) For each of the following (Palestinians, PLO, Arafat) please tell me whether you have a "very high" opinion, a "fairly high" opinion, a "fairly low" opinion or a "very low" opinion. (*Responses of "very high" and "fairly high" and those of "very low" and "fairly low" were regrouped*)

(b) What is your impression of (*read*) as of today?

(c) On a scale of plus-5 (most favorable) to minus-5 (most unfavorable) how far up or down the scale would you rate (*read*)?

(d) Compared with a year ago, would you say you are more sympathetic or less sympathetic to (*read*)?

Q	*Date*	*Poll*	*Definitions*	*Palestinians*	*PLO*	*Arafat*
(a)	Fall '80	Slade	High opinion	34%	9%	10%
			Low opinion	49	72	55
(b)	July '82	*L.A. Times*	Favorable	—	9	15
			Unfavorable	—	83	79
(c)	Aug. '82	Gallup	Favorable	57	11	17
			Unfavorable	30	77	69
(d)	Sep. '82	Yankelovich	More sympathetic	30	11	7
			Less sympathetic	20	37	36
			Net change	+10	−26	−29

Sources: (a) Shelley Slade, "The Image of the Arab in America: Analysis of a Poll on American Attitudes," *Middle East Journal* 35(Spring 1981): 151. (b) *Los Angeles Times,* July 11, 1982; (c) *Gallup Report,* September 1982, 27–29; (d) Yankelovich, Skelly and White, Memorandum, October 1982.

Arabs by a majority of 52 to 12 percent, but the Palestinians were outscored by a plurality of 47 to 14 percent.[44]

During the 1982 war in Lebanon, the American media accorded the PLO and Arafat considerable favorable attention. But apparently, the coverage affected only the image of the Palestinians, not that of the PLO or Arafat. In a November 1982 interview, Harris stated that Arafat's kissing of babies was viewed as "posturing and play-acting, and was resented by Americans who reacted negatively. Most Americans considered Arafat to be a terrorist."[45] Several polls confirmed this observation.

Table 5–2 clearly indicates that although the Palestinians were seen in a favorable, sympathetic light during and after the war, the PLO and Arafat were viewed in a highly unfavorable light and lost considerable sympathy in American public opinion. In a Gallup survey for the Chicago Council on Foreign Relations in October–November 1982, respondents were asked to give favorability ratings of various international figures. Yasser Arafat finished second lowest, with a rating that was better than only that of Ayatollah Khomeini of Iran.[46]

Two other very different polls attempted to identify descriptive clauses associated with the term "Palestinians." In April 1980 a *Time*-Yankelovich poll reported that 30 percent of the U.S. public associated "Palestinians" with "terrorists"; 17 percent thought of them primarily as "displaced persons who will eventually settle in another country"; and 19 percent saw them as "refugees seeking a homeland."[47] In the fall 1980 poll analyzed by Slade, an almost equal number of respondents associated "Palestinians" with "terrorism" and people who are "countryless" or seeking "self-determination" and a "homeland."[48]

Poll results on Palestinian and PLO images in the United States confirm the observation of Seymour Martin Lipset and William Schneider: "The point at which sympathy for the Palestinians ends is the PLO."[49] Also, the data collected from the period of the war in Lebanon and afterward, indicate that following the war, the gap between the image of these two entities widened.

The Role of the PLO in the Political Process

The PLO's demand to be recognized as the sole legitimate representative of the Palestinians was granted at the 1974 Rabat summit. The U.N. General Assembly also recognized the PLO as the representative of the Palestinians. The Arab and U.N. recognition of the PLO might be interpreted as a means of securing a role for the PLO in possible future Israeli-Arab negotiations toward a peace agreement. But, the PLO refused to recognize Israel's right to exist, rejected Security Council Resolution 242, and severely criticized Sadat's visit to Jerusalem and his negotiations with Israel. The PLO violently condemned the Camp David Accords, and Arafat said that "Camp David is a dirty deal and Carter will pay for it." Carter responded to this attack by associating the PLO with the Ku Klux Klan, the Communist party, and the Nazis and added: "It would be nice for us if they would just go away."[50] Under these circumstances, pollsters sought to determine whether the PLO and the Palestinians were viewed by Americans as interested at all in peace and whether Israel or the United States should have recognized the PLO and accepted it as a partner in negotiations.

On several occasions in 1977 and 1978, Harris asked a question about the interest various parties to the Arab-Israeli conflict had in the goal of peace. The number of those who thought the PLO "really wants peace" fluctuated only between 9 and 13 percent.[51] In March 1982, a *WP*-ABC poll asked, "Do you think the PLO is more a force for peace, or more a force for war?" Just 11 percent said it was a force for peace; 75 percent thought it was a force for war. Finally, in the Penn and Schoen comprehensive poll of May 1982, only 2 percent believed that the PLO was "doing the most to bring peace."

The PLO's claim as sole representative of the Palestinians was not accepted by the majority of the American public. Various surveys by Gallup and the *WP*-ABC poll conducted between 1978 and 1982 indicate that the majority of Americans (63 versus 14 percent and 65 versus 25 percent, respectively) who had heard or read about the PLO did not think it represented the "point of view of a majority of Palestinians."[52] After the war in Lebanon, the ratio between those who saw the PLO as representative of the Palestinians and those who did not was the closest in 5 years—but even so, the ratio was still two to one against the PLO (56 versus 28 percent).

Although the majority of Americans felt that the PLO neither represented the Palestinians nor was interested in peace, pollsters nevertheless questioned whether the U.S. government should grant the PLO recognition and meet with its leaders. Polls taken between 1979 and 1982 reveal strong objection to U.S. recognition of the PLO, but a more divided opinion on U.S.-PLO talks.

The general pattern in the first part of table 5–3 is quite clear, but it is interesting to note that question (b), containing an anti-PLO bias, produced results similar to those obtained by more neutral questions, (c) and (d). As strange as it may seem, the highest percentages in favor of American recognition were recorded in responses to the question in which the PLO was described as a "terrorist organization." Recognition could mean approval of the ideology and practice of the PLO, and therefore, perhaps, the majority of Americans opposed such an action. However, talks and meetings are another matter, and on that issue public opinion was undecided.

The results in the second part of table 5–3 reveal that in only two polls was the margin greater than 10 percent—the first in favor of U.S.-PLO talks and the other against such talks. But in these two cases, the relatively larger margin might be the result of question framing. In the fall 1980 poll, the question prompted a favorable response: ". . . meet in an attempt to bring about a settlement of the situation in the Middle East." The September 1981 poll led in exactly the opposite direction by presenting a negative formulation and references to "Russian arms and terrorism." After the war in Lebanon, a close plurality of 48 to 42 percent favored U.S. talks with the PLO, but the question described the PLO as a "representative of the Palestinians" and ignored the debate inside the Arab world on the status of the PLO as well as the discordance within the PLO ranks. This debate intensified after the PLO's expulsion from Lebanon.

The status of the PLO in the peace process was also raised in an Israeli context. The Israeli position on talks with the PLO has remained consistently negative. Israel claims that it cannot and will not negotiate with an organization whose declared goal is to dismantle the Jewish state and that continually employs indiscriminate terrorism against Israel and the Jewish people. Most Israeli leaders rejected negotiations with the PLO under any circumstances, although a few indicated that they might have agreed to talk to the organization if it had abandoned the articles in the Palestinian National Covenant, terminated terrorism, and recognized Israel's right to exist. As mentioned in the

Table 5–3
Attitudes toward American Recognition of and Talks with the PLO

A. Recognition of the PLO

Questions

(a) The PLO is a terrorist organization that murders athletes at olympic games, skyjacks planes, and should not be recognized by the U.S. (*agree = against, disagree = for*)

(b) The PLO terrorists are part of a worldwide terrorist group who hijack planes, kidnap people, and are international outlaws who should not be given any official recognition by the United States or the rest of the world. (*agree = against, disagree = for*)

(c) Do you think the United States should formally recognize and have direct diplomatic relations with the Palestinian Liberation Organization—that is, the PLO—or don't you think so?

(d) Even though they have official status in the U.N., the U.S. is right not to recognize the PLO or talk with them, until they recognize the right of Israel to exist.

Q	*Date*	*Poll*	*For*	*Against*	*Not Sure*	*(n)*
(a)	Aug. '79	Harris	37%	49%	14%	(1,201)
(b)	July '80	Harris	21	57	22	(1,506)
(b)	Sep. '81	Harris	28	61	11	(1,248)
(c)	Oct. '81	NBC	25	60	15	
(c)	Aug. '82	NBC	26	57	17	
(d)	Aug. '79	Harris	27	65	8	(1,201)

B. Talks with the PLO

Questions

(a) Should the United States talk to the PLO?

(b) Some people say we should negotiate with the PLO, even if Israel objects. Do you think the U.S. should or shouldn't negotiate with the PLO?

(c) Do you think the U.S. should or should not meet the PLO in an attempt to bring about a settlement of the situation in the Middle East?

(d) The PLO should not be dealt with, because they are armed by the Russians and are trained in terrorist tactics in Russia and Libya.

(e) Should the United States talk directly with the PLO as the representative of the Palestinian people or not?

Q	*Date*	*Poll*	*Yes*	*No*	*Not Sure*	*(n)*
(a)	Oct. '79	CBS-*NYT*	42%	45%	13%	(1,385)
(b)	Dec. '79	Yankelovich	34	42	24	(1,041)
(c)	Fall '80	Slade	57	31	11	(600)
(d)	Aug. '81	Harris	34	47	19	(1,248)
(e)	Aug. '82	*Newsweek*/Gallup	48	42	10	(752)

Sources: Panel A: (a) (d) ABC News–Harris Survey, Vol. 1. No. 108, September 3, 1979, *San Francisco Examiner*, August 30, 1979; (b, 1980) Louis Harris and Associates, Study No. 804011 (August 1980), 32–33; (b, 1981) *How Americans Feel About Israel*, 46; (c) *NBC Poll*, Middle East, August 9–10, 1982. *Panel B:* (a) *New York Times*, November 8, 1979; (b) *Attitudes of the American Public Toward American Jews and Israel* (New York: American Jewish Committee, Information and Research Services, March 1980, Mimeographed); (c) *Middle East Journal* 35(Spring 1981): 155; (d) *How Americans Feel About Israel*, 46, n. 26; (e) *Newsweek*, August 16, 1982.

Table 5–4
Attitudes toward Israeli-PLO Negotiations, 1975–81

Question

The Israeli government has agreed to negotiate with Egypt, but has refused to negotiate with the PLO. Do you think Israel is doing the right thing or the wrong thing in refusing to negotiate with the PLO?" (Yankelovich)

	Jan. '75	*Jan. '76*	*Mar. '77*	*Dec. '79*	*Feb. '81*
Right	29%	31%	40%	30%	26%
Wrong	36	31	21	41	31
Not sure, no answer, no opinion	35	38	39	29	43
Total	100%	100%	100%	100%	100%

Sources: January 1975: Geraldine Rosenfield, *Attitudes of the American Public Toward Israel and American Jews* (New York: American Jewish Committee, Information and Research Services, April 1975, Mimeographed), 9. January 1976 and March 1977: Seymour Martin Lipset and William Schneider, "Carter vs. Israel, What the Polls Reveal," *Commentary* 64(November 1977): 22. December 1979: Geraldine Rosenfield, *Attitudes of the American Public Toward American Jews and Israel* (New York: American Jewish Committee, Information and Research Services, March 1980, Mimeographed), 8, 9, 10. February 1981: Gregory Martire and Ruth Clark, *Anti-Semitism in the United States* (New York: Praeger, 1982), 81.

Camp David Accords of September 1978, Israel agreed to negotiations among Israel, Egypt, Jordan, and "Palestinians from the West Bank and Gaza or other Palestinians as *mutually agreed*" (emphasis added).

On several occasions after 1975, pollsters tried to ascertain what the U.S. public thought about the Israeli position concerning talks with the PLO. Harris presented his national samples with the following statement: "Israel is right not to agree to sit down with the PLO, because the PLO is a terrorist organization that wants to destroy Israel." In March 1978, the public agreed with this statement by a majority of 70 to 14 percent; in July 1980, the corresponding results were 62 to 23 percent. However, the overwhelming approval of Israel's position might be related to the negative characterization of the PLO in the queries. The Harris survey of August 1979 presented the issue from a different angle: "As the most powerful force among Palestinian Arabs, the PLO should be in on any negotiations about Gaza or the West Bank, even if the PLO are terrorists." This statement was rejected by a plurality of 57 to 34 percent.[53]

Although Harris received different results at different time intervals, his findings reveal substantial support for the Israeli position. The Yankelovich organization's poll, however, conducted on the issue of Israel-PLO negotiations since 1975, differ from those of Harris. Table 5–4 indicates a much closer ratio between the number of those who supported the Israeli position and the number of those who opposed it. The time fluctuations in table 5–4 are also interesting. In January 1975, just a few weeks after Arafat's U.N. appearance, a small plurality of the public thought that Israel was "doing the wrong thing" in refusing to negotiate with the PLO. Exactly a year later, the results were 31 to 31 percent, and in March 1977, after President Carter's statement in favor of a Palestinian homeland, a plurality of 40 to 21 percent supported Israel's refusal to talk to the PLO. On two other occasions following ratification of the Israeli-Egyptian peace treaty, a plurality of the public thought that Israel was wrong in "refusing to negotiate with the PLO," according to Yankelovich. The most consistent figure in table 5–4 is the relatively high number of respondents that held no opinion on the issue.

Following the *Achille Lauro* incident of October 1985, Harris found considerable opposition to PLO participation in the political process. A substantial 82 to 10 percent majority said the PLO has "unreasonable leadership that probably will make it impossible to work out a peace settlement." A majority of 54 to 41 percent opposed the inclusion of the PLO in the peace process, but a greater majority, 64 to 29 percent, favored having Palestinian leaders not affiliated with the PLO at the negotiating table.[54]

Attitudes toward Negotiations with the PLO

Despite the PLO's strong opposition to the peace process and the American standing commitment to refrain from any contacts with the organization until it recognizes Israel and accepts Security Council Resolutions 242 and 338, American officials contacted PLO officials.[55] One particular meeting between the U.S. ambassador to the United Nations, Andrew Young, and the U.N. PLO observer, Zehdi Labib Terzi, created considerable controversy that led to Young's resignation and a wave of poll-taking on his actions and resignation.

On July 26, 1979, Young met Terzi at the apartment of Kuwait's U.N. ambassador, Abdalla Yaccoub Bishara. When he had been invited to the apartment, Young had known that the PLO observer would be present. In his report to the State Department, however, Young did not mention the presence of Terzi nor any talks with him.[56] The story was leaked to the press and exploded on August 15, 1979. Despite earlier claims, it was discovered that the meeting was not a social event and that Young spoke to Terzi about political issues.[57] Young said that he took action on his own and that he did not tell the State Department because "the less they know, the less they could be responsible."

Young was forced to resign from his U.N. post, and this development touched a sensitive nerve in the already tense relations between blacks and American Jews.[58] Black leaders, including Jesse Jackson, strongly supported Young and lamented his resignation. Jewish leaders criticized the Young-Terzi meeting but faulted not Young but President Carter and his Palestinian policy.[59] Many newspaper editorials criticized the Young-Terzi meeting. The *New*

York Times, for example, wrote on August 16, 1979, that the Young affair was "a clumsy, foolish diplomacy that led his government into a lie, violated its policy and broke its promises."

Just a few days after Young's resignation, ABC news and Harris conducted a major survey on the event and also on U.S. policy on the PLO and the Palestinian problem. The survey included the following, rather lengthy question:

> As you know, Andrew Young resigned as the U.S. Ambassador to the United Nations, and President Carter has accepted his resignation. Young resigned because he first denied and then admitted that he had met with a representative of the Palestine Liberation Organization (the PLO). It is U.S. policy not to sit down and talk with the PLO, because they are terrorists, have not agreed to the right of Israel to exist, and want to see Israel destroyed. Young said it is ridiculous for the U.S. to refuse to talk to the PLO because the PLO is a real power in the Arab world. Do you think Andrew Young was right or wrong to sit down and to talk to the representative of the PLO at the U.N.?[60]

Almost half of the respondents (49 percent) felt that Young was wrong, and 37 percent said he was right. Nonblacks disapproved of Young's talks by a plurality of 54 to 33 percent, and blacks approved of his actions 62 to 17 percent. By a 50 to 36 percent plurality, the national sample disagreed with the statement: "Young lost his job at the U.N. because he was the victim of Israeli and American Jewish pressure on the White House." Blacks were equally divided on this statement, 40 to 40 percent. A national poll by the *Los Angeles Times* in October 1979 included a similar query and, like Harris, found that 50 percent of the sample disagreed with the statement: "U.N. ambassador Andrew Young was forced to resign because of pressure from Jews." Only 26 percent of the respondents agreed with this statement.[61]

American public opinion took exception not only to the Young-Terzi meeting but also to other talks between black leaders and representatives of the PLO. In the ABC-Harris survey, the national sample was presented with the following statement: "Several heads of Black organizations met with representatives of the PLO at the U.N., and endorsed the right of Palestinians to self-determination. Do you think such Black leaders are more right or more wrong to seem to be taking up the cause of the PLO?" A majority of the sample (58 percent) said that the black leaders were "more wrong" to meet the PLO; 23 percent said they were "more right."

A completely different indication of public opinion on the PLO's role in the peace process was found in response to a question on the Venice Declaration of the European Community on the Middle East. This declaration of June 13, 1980, emphasized the right of the Palestinians to self-determination "within the framework of a comprehensive peace settlement" and PLO participation in the peace process.[62] Israel flatly rejected the Venice Declaration, claiming that negotiations with Arafat were the equivalent of negotiations with Hitler.[63] The United States also rejected the declaration and repeated its conditions for PLO participation in the peace process.[64] In a poll conducted a month later, Harris found that only 13 percent of his national sample supported the Venice Declaration; the majority (56 percent) sided with the United States, and 16 percent agreed with the Israeli position.[65]

It was noted earlier in this chapter that the image of the Palestinians in U.S. public opinion has been more positive than that of the PLO. But does the public also distinguish between the Palestinians and the PLO in the context of their possible roles in the peace process? In the Harris survey of August 1979, 61 to 28 percent of the national sample endorsed the following statement: "The U.S., Egypt and Israel should work out an arrangement in which Palestinian Arabs, but *not* the PLO, are brought into the Middle East peace negotiations." A similar percentage held this view in October 1985.[66] Slade's poll analysis of fall 1980 also examined this issue. Although 57 versus 31 percent said that "the U.S. should meet with the PLO in an attempt to bring about a settlement of the situation in the Middle East," 71 versus 18 percent advocated such a meeting between the United States and the Palestinians.

The foregoing data demonstrate that the public had reservations toward hypothetical or actual talks between the United States or Israel and the PLO; yet the public acknowledged the right of the Palestinians to participate in the peace process. To reactivate the stalled talks, respondents preferred that the PLO soften its extreme positions and thus qualify for participation in the peace process. Substantial majorities of Americans agreed in 1979 (69 to 19 percent) and in 1980 (66 to 13 percent) that "once the PLO has recognized Israel's right to exist, then the U.S. should move to include the PLO in the negotiations on the Palestinian rights to self-determination in Gaza and on the West Bank."[67]

Solutions to the Palestinian Problem

Numerous solutions to the Palestinian question have been suggested over the years. From 1948 until the 1967 Six-Day War, the issue was primarily defined as a classic refugee problem, and solutions were designed to alleviate the hardship of Palestinians living in refugee camps. But the Israeli occupation of the West Bank and Gaza Strip and the extensive military and political activity of the PLO added a political dimension to the problem. The PLO argues that the Palestinian question persists because of the denial of Palestinian self-determination. Therefore, the solution must be an independent Palestinian state.

This claim raises several incongruencies. First, the PLO has not been satisfied with the concept of an independent state situated only in the West Bank and Gaza. Rather, it has sought the elimination of Israel and the founding of a Palestinian state over the West Bank and Israel.[68] Second, although Jordan lost the West Bank to Israel during the 1967 war, it has never given up its claim to this area.[69] Jordan's claim must be viewed in both historical and demographical contexts. Between 1948 and 1967, Jordan ruled the West Bank and did not allow the establishment of an independent Palestinian state there. Furthermore, the Palestinians constitute between 65 and 70 percent of the population in Jordan; therefore, that country is already essentially Palestinian.[70]

Finally, it seems that most Arab countries have paid only lip service to the concept of an independent Palestinian state. In a press conference, Carter stated:

> I have never met an Arab leader that in private professed a desire for an independent Palestinian state. Publicly, they all espoused an independent Palestinian state, almost all of them, because that is what they committed themselves to do at Rabat. But the private diplomatic tone of conversations is much more proper than is often alleged by the press and others.[71]

Earlier in his administration, Carter's policy on a solution to the Palestinian problem was purposefully vague. In March 1977, he called for the establishment of a "homeland" for the Palestinians.[72] But "homeland" encompasses numerous connotations, and only a few months later, on July 12, 1977, Carter explained that by "homeland," he had meant "an entity linked to Jordan and not an independent state."[73]

Polls on American opinions on solutions to the Palestinian problem mostly appeared during the Carter administration, especially after Sadat's visit to Jerusalem. Table 5–5 presents opinions on several solutions. Questions (a) and (b) contrast two options: an independent state and an entity linked to Jordan with a continuation of the present living conditions of the Palestinians. Responses to these questions show that during 1978, the idea of a state in the West Bank became slightly more popular, but still, only about one-third of the samples supported it. The solution advocated by Carter—an entity linked to Jordan—received the least support. When Carter's option was eliminated, as in the second part of table 5–5, and the independent state was contrasted with only "continue to live as they do now," the state solution attracted more support. During the 1982 war in Lebanon, a 46 to 23 percent plurality preferred the state option over the status quo, but this result might have been affected by the war and the disruptions in the normal living conditions of the Palestinians.

Table 5–5
Possible Solutions to the Palestinian Question, 1978–82

Questions

(a) On the issue of a homeland for the Palestinians, would you favor having Jordan and parts of the West Bank under Jordan made into a Palestinian homeland, or making the West Bank an independent Palestinian state, or having the Palestinians live where they do now in Jordan, on the West Bank, in the Gaza strip and in Lebanon, with full rights in each of those places? (Harris)

(b) Which of these plans would you prefer with regard to the Palestinians?
—separate, independent nation on the West Bank,
—a state on the West Bank not totally independent and linked to Jordan,
—the Palestinians would go on living as they are now in Israel and the existing Arab nations. (Gallup)

Q	*Date*	*Continue to Live as They Do Now*	*State in West Bank*	*State Linked to Jordan*	*N.O.*	*Total*
(a)	Jan. '78	38%	20%	8%	34%	100%
(a)	Mar. '78	32	21	10	37	100
(b)	Jan. '78	28	26	21	25	100
(b)	Apr. '78	30	24	22	24	100
(b)	June '78	22	32	25	21	100
(b)	Sep. '78	22	32	17	29	100

Question

(c) As you may know, one of the major questions in the Middle East situation concerns the Palestinian people. Do you think a separate, independent Palestine nation should be established or do you think the Palestinians should continue to live as they do now in Israel and the neighboring Arab nations? (Gallup, aware group)

Q	*Date*	*Continue to Live as They Do Now*	*Palestinian State*	*N.O.*	*Total*
(c)	Oct. '77	29%	36%	35%	100%
(c)	Jan. '79	28	41	31	100
(c)	Mar. '79	25	37	38	100
(c)	July '82	23	46	31	100

Sources: (a) *The Harris Survey,* January 26, 1978; *New York Post,* April 10, 1978. (b) *Los Angeles Times,* February 9, 1978; *Gallup Opinion Index,* Report 153 (April 1978), Report 156 (July 1978), Report 158 (September 1978). (c) *Public Opinion Quarterly* 47(Spring 1983): 125; *Gallup Opinion Index,* Mideast Situation (March 1979).

The number of options in table 5–5 are not, by any means, exhaustive. Several other solutions, such as resettling the refugees in the areas where they live or the autonomy plan, were omitted. Yet since President Carter advocated a homeland for the Palestinians as one of three principles for peace in the Middle East, it was only natural for at least one veteran pollster to concentrate on this option. In July 1977, the Roper organization started a series of polls on the homeland idea. At that time, Carter had already clarified what he meant by a homeland—an entity linked to Jordan, but Roper preferred to use the original term without any clarifications.

Table 5–6 traces the development of question wording on the homeland idea. Question (a) includes a factual mistake by referring to the West Bank area as "once held by the Palestinians." The Palestinians, though residing in the West Bank, never held power in this area. Prior to 1948, it was part of the British mandate, and from that point until the 1967 Six-Day War, it was occupied by Jordan. This mistake was corrected in question (b), which was included in the Roper polls from October–November 1979 until 1982. But the major difference in wording is found between questions (a) and (b) and question (c). In the first two questions, the homeland idea is mentioned in connection with the PLO, whereas in question (c) it is mentioned in connection with the Palestinians. Since the Palestinians were much more popular than the PLO in American public opinion, it could be anticipated that more positive answers were given in response to question (c).

Questions (b) and (c) were asked in October 1982, after the war in Lebanon, and indeed, in the response to the two main answers—"right" and "wrong"—the Palestinians' score was higher than that of the PLO. Paradoxically, however, the third response—"right but methods wrong"—received fewer negative responses for the PLO than for the Palestinians, both in October 1982 and in comparison to earlier years. The answers to question (c) in 1983 and 1984 were slightly more positive for the homeland idea, compared to responses of earlier years to questions (a) and (b).

All questions in table 5–6 include an escape clause—"Haven't paid much attention to the issue." In most polls, this clause was selected by the greatest number of respondents. Generally, between 37 and 54 percent of the samples did not take a position by selecting the escape clause or the "don't know" answer. Even throughout the highly visible war in Lebanon, approximately a quarter of the respondents said they had not paid much attention to the idea, and another 12 to 13 percent selected the "don't know" option. In general, regardless of exact question formulation, the American public did not endorse the idea of a Palestinian homeland. Even after the war in Lebanon and the mention of the idea in connection with the Palestinians, only about one-third of the public supported it (combined score for "right" and "right but methods wrong").

Table 5–6
Attitudes toward a Palestinian Homeland, 1977–84

Questions

(a) As you know, the *Palestine Liberation Organization* in the Middle East, known as the PLO, wants to establish a homeland for Palestinian refugees in territory once held by the Palestinians but now held by Israel. Do you think the PLO is right or wrong in wanting to establish a Palestinian homeland in Israel, or haven't you paid much attention to it? (1977)

(b) As you may know, the *Palestine Liberation Organization* in the Middle East—known as the PLO—wants to establish a homeland for Palestinians on territory occupied by Israel since 1967. Do you think the PLO is right or wrong in wanting to establish a Palestinian homeland in Israeli occupied territory, or haven't you paid much attention to it? (1979–82)

(c) As you may know, the *Palestinians* in the Middle East want to establish a homeland for Palestinians on territory occupied by Israel since 1967. Do you think the Palestinians are right or wrong in wanting to establish a Palestinian homeland in Israeli occupied territory, or haven't you paid much attention to it? (1982–84)

	(a) *July '77*	*(a)* *Nov. '77*	*(b)* *Oct.–Nov. '79*	*(b)* *Aug. '80*	*(b)* *Aug. '81*	*(b)* *Aug. '82*	*(b)* *Oct. '82*	*(c)* *Oct. '82*	*(c)* *July '83*	*(c)* *Mar. '84*
Right	21%	18%	26%	19%	17%	18%	19%	24%	22%	22%
Wrong	20	19	17	25	24	34	31	24	20	20
Right but methods wrong	9	10	14	8	11	11	12	14	13	13
Haven't paid much attention	33	40	33	31	31	25	25	26	27	28
Don't know	17	14	10	16	17	12	13	13	18	16
Total	100%	101%	100%	99%	100%	100%	100%	101%	100%	99%

Source: Roper Reports, October 1982, April 1984 (sample size between 2,000 and 2,005).

Attitudes toward an Independent Palestinian State

In the 1978 Camp David Accords, Israel and Egypt agreed to negotiate an autonomy plan for the inhabitants of the West Bank and Gaza for a period not to exceed 5 years. However, most surveys conducted after Camp David that contained solutions to the Palestinian problem omitted the autonomy solution and concentrated on the independent state option.[74]

Table 5–7 shows that support for a Palestinian state varied considerably, from 11 to 71 percent, probably because of different query contexts and phras-

Table 5–7
Attitudes toward an Independent Palestinian State

Questions

(a) The Palestinian people are now homeless and deserve their own independent state just as much as th Jews deserved their own homeland after World War II. (*agree = for, disagree = against*)

(b) Israel should give up the occupied Palestinian Arab territory and let Arafat rule it. (*agree = for, disagre = against*).

(c) Arafat and the PLO should be given the West Bank and allowed to form an independent Palestinia state.

(d) The Palestinians have fought for many years with Israel for the establishment of a Palestinian stat Israel says that such a Palestinian state would be a threat to its security. Should the United States fav a Palestinian state or not?

(e) If the PLO agreed to recognize Israel as a Jewish state and also stop its military raids on Israel, do yc think Israel should agree to the idea of a homeland for Palestinian refugees on territory now held t Israel or don't you think they should agree to such a Palestinian homeland?

(f) If Israel can be assured of its security from attack, then it ought to agree to let Palestinian Arabs s up an independent state on the West Bank.

(g) Do you favor or oppose the creation of a separate Palestinian Arab State on Israel's West Bank, or do you know enough about the issue to have an opinion?

Q	*Date*	*Poll*	*Context*	*For*	*Against*	*D.K.*	*Tota*
(a)	July '80	Harris	General rights	71%	12%	17%	100
(b)	Jan. '75	Harris	Under PLO	11	54	35	100
(c)	July '80	Harris		15	53	32	100
(d)	Apr. '80	*Newsweek*-Gallup	Israeli security needs	33	37	30	10
	July '81			31	44	25	100
	Aug. '82			37	45	18	10
(e)	July '77	Roper	Under PLO *if* it recognizes Israel and stops terrorism	42	19	39	10
	Aug. '80			39	21	40	10
	Aug. '81			39	21	40	10
(f)	July '80	Harris	*If* Israeli security can be assured	56	16	28	10
(g)	Oct. '81	NBC-AP	Knowledge of the issue	15	18	68	10

Sources: (a)(b)(c)(f) Louis Harris and Associates, Study No. 804011 (August 1980), 33, 51. (d) *Newsw* August 16, 1982. (e) *Roper Reports*, October 1982. (g) *Public Opinion* 5(April-May 1982), 53.

ing. Question (a) presents the issue in the context of general rights and includes two phrases—"homeless" and "just as much as the Jews deserve"—that probably introduced a bias in favor of a positive response. Thus a substantial majority (71 versus 12 percent) agreed with the statement in question (a). However, when Arafat's name and the PLO were added to questions on the same solution, the idea was rejected by clear majorities (questions (b) and (c)).

In questions (a), (b) and (c), the option of an independent Palestinian state is mentioned only in connection with the Palestinian problem. When the same idea was included in the context of Israeli security needs, very different results emerged. Israel has consistently maintained that the geographical layout of the West Bank creates legitimate defense concerns and that those concerns were recognized by the United Nations in Security Council Resolution 242 and by the United States and Egypt in the Camp David agreements. It seems that most Americans did recognize the Israeli security interests in the West Bank. On three occasions since 1980, when a question referring to an independent Palestinian state included a reference to Israel's security needs, the number of those who opposed the solution outnumbered the supporters (question (d)). This pattern was maintained even during the war in Lebanon.

Questions (e) and (f) in table 5–7 present hypothetical, conditional situations. The American public expressed support for the establishment of an independent Palestinian state, even under representation of the PLO, if that organization recognized Israel and if Israel's security needs were assured. Responses to questions (e) and (f) demonstrate, once again, that in the eyes of the American public, the key for negotiation and resolution of the Palestinian problem is recognition of Israel and her security needs.

The American public, however, was quite skeptical about possible relations between Israel and a Palestinian state. If the state were to be occupied by peaceful Palestinians, then the public agreed, by a majority of 54 to 22 percent, with the scenario presented in another poll: "By use of terror techniques against peaceful Palestinian officials, Arafat and the PLO would quickly take over control of the Palestinian state."[75] A plurality of 40 to 26 percent agreed that "if the West Bank became an independent Palestinian state, other extremist Arab states such as Syria, Libya and Iraq, would use it as a launching pad to destroy Israel." Finally, question (g) in table 5–7 presents an escape clause—"or don't you know enough about the issue to have an opinion." At least 68 percent of the sample selected this answer; only a third took a stand. This result could indicate that the American public was admitting a lack of in-depth knowledge about the Palestinian state solution or, for reasons of convenience, preferred not to take a stand.

On September 1, 1982, the day the PLO evacuated Beirut, President Reagan presented a new initiative for a comprehensive resolution of the Arab-Israeli conflict. This plan rejected two solutions to the Palestinian problem in the areas of the West Bank and Gaza: an independent Palestinian state and

Israeli annexation.[76] Instead, Reagan supported a period of autonomy, after which the disputed areas would be returned to Jordan within the larger context of an Israeli-Jordanian peace agreement. Egypt stated that the Reagan plan included "positive elements," but the remaining Arab countries—as well as Jordan, the PLO, and even Israel—rejected it.

Three weeks after the announcement of the plan, and immediately after the Sabra and Shatila massacre, the *Newsweek*-Gallup poll asked a national sample of Americans for its views on solutions to the Palestinian problem.[77] The answers were distributed in the following manner: a quarter of the sample chose the "don't know" option; 31 percent essentially supported the Reagan proposal; 23 percent favored an independent Palestinian state; and 21 percent supported Israeli sovereignty over the West Bank. Thus, the Reagan plan was not overwhelmingly endorsed by the public, but the Reagan administration repeatedly offered the plan to the relevant parties from 1983 through 1985.

Conclusions

Surveys on American attitudes toward the PLO and the Palestinians began in the mid-1970s and grew more frequent and extensive during the Carter years and during the war in Lebanon. With the increased American media coverage of the PLO and the Palestinians, the public became much more aware of these entities and the conflicts surrounding them. Yankelovich found in January 1975 that only 52 percent of the public had heard of the PLO. But by 1978, 77 percent had heard or read about the PLO, and during the war in Lebanon, this percentage rose to 83. Yasser Arafat also became a familiar figure in the United States; the July 1980 Harris survey found that Arafat was known to at least 58 percent of the national sample. By October–November 1982, he was known to 83 percent of the public.[78]

Analysis of the various polls clearly demonstrates that the American public distinguished between the PLO and the Palestinians. This distinction is visible in the respective images of the two, in attitudes toward the issues of negotiations, and in solutions to the Palestinian problem.

The Palestinians have garnered a more favorable image in the United States than has the PLO, which has been perceived as a terrorist organization, disinterested in peace with Israel and bent on employing every possible means to foil the peacemaking process. The public has also associated the PLO with extremism, communism, and anti-Americanism. The Palestinians, on the other hand, have evoked the image of innocent refugees whose problem must be urgently resolved. The PLO was aware of its negative image in the United States and tried to improve it, but the evidence in this chapter suggests that those efforts failed.

American officials both echoed and reinforced the distinction between the

PLO and the Palestinians. President Reagan, for example, stated on November 6, 1980:

> The PLO is said to represent the Palestinian refugees. It represents no one but the leaders who established it as a means of organizing aggression against Israel. . . . I think that the PLO has proven that it is a terrorist organization. And I have said repeatedly *I separate the PLO from the Palestinian refugees.* No one ever elected the PLO.[79] (emphasis added)

The general distinction between the PLO and the Palestinians might have affected attitudes toward specific issues. For example, the number of Americans who supported U.S. talks with the Palestinians was far greater than the number who supported talks with the PLO. The majority of the American public did not view the PLO as the sole representative of the Palestinians and opposed granting it any form of recognition. But the public was divided in its support of talks between the United States or Israel and the PLO. This division might be related to a traditional American belief in the need to resolve conflicts through negotiations and peaceful means; the United States followed this principle in Vietnam, when it negotiated with the Viet Cong. Therefore, perhaps many Americans, even those who completely rejected the PLO, believed that the United States or Israel should negotiate with PLO leaders. However, when this principle came to test in the Young affair, more Americans criticized Young and other black leaders for meeting with the PLO. Finally, the public clearly opposed any American pressure on Israel to negotiate with the PLO.

During the 1982 war in Lebanon, the fate of the PLO and the Palestinians was dramatically portrayed in the American media. However, the data indicate that media coverage and the war itself did not significantly affect the principal trends in the American attitudes toward the PLO and the Palestinians. The image of the PLO grew more negative, and the public continued to differentiate between this organization and the Palestinians. American sympathies for the Palestinians grew slightly, especially after the massacre in Sabra and Shatila. The majority of the public continued to oppose American recognition of the PLO. Before the war, the public was divided on the issue of U.S.-PLO talks; afterward, according to one poll, a close plurality supported such talks. The public was also divided on the various solutions to the Palestinian problem but continued to oppose the establishment of an independent Palestinian state.

The empirical data in this chapter reveal the perceived key to adequate resolution of the Palestinian problem: Palestinian acceptance of Israel and its right to exist in peace and security. The public clearly supported the longstanding official American position, which requires that the PLO and the Palestinians first recognize Israel's right to exist, cease terrorism, and accept Security Council Resolution 242 as a basis for Israeli-Palestinian negotiations.

Notes

1. Edward Said, *The Question of Palestine* (New York: Vintage, 1980); Joan Peters, *From Time Immemorial: The Origins of the Arab-Jewish Conflict Over Palestine* (New York: Harper & Row, 1984); Gabriel Ben-Dor, ed., *The Palestinians and the Middle East Conflict* (Tel Aviv: Turtledove, 1978); and Y. Harkabi, *Palestinians and Israel* (New York: Wiley, 1974).

2. David P. Forsythe, "The Palestine Question: Dealing with a Long-Term Refugee Situation," *Annals of the American Academy of Political and Social Science* 467 (May 1983): 89–101.

3. See Morad Asi, "Arabs, Israelis, and TV News: A Time-Series, Content Analysis," and Jack Shaheen, "Images of Saudis and Palestinians: A Review of Major Documentaries," in William C. Adams, ed., *Television Coverage of the Middle East* (Norwood, N.J.: Ablex, 1981): 67-75 and 89-105; Rael Jean Isaac, "Time Against Israel," *New Republic* (October 18, 1980): 18-23; Edward Alexander, "The Journalists' War Against Israel, Techniques of Distortion, Disorientation and Disinformation," *Encounter* 12(September-October 1982): 87-97; and Yoel Cohen, "The PLO: 'Guardian Angel' of the Media," *Midstream* 29(February 1983), 7–10.

4. Henry Cattan, *Palestine, the Arabs, and Israel* (London: Longmans, 1969); and Majid Khadduri, ed., *Arab-Israeli Impasse* (Washington, D.C.: Luce, 1968).

5. Maurice M. Roumani, *The Case of the Jews from Arab Countries*,2nd ed. (Tel Aviv: WOJAC, 1978); and George E. Gruen, ed., *The Palestinians in Perspective* (New York: American Jewish Committee, Institute of Human Relations Press, 1982), 1–25.

6. Mohammed K. Shadid, *The United States and the Palestinians* (London: Croom and Helm, 1981), 63-72.

7. They were Eric Johnston from the Technical Cooperation Administration and Joseph Johnson, president of the Carnegie Endowment for International Peace.

8. Barry Rubin, *The Arab States and the Palestine Conflict* (Syracuse, N.Y.: Syracuse University Press, 1981).

9. Jillian Becker, *The PLO: The Rise and Fall of the Palestine Liberation Organization* (London: Weidenfeld and Nicolson, 1984), ch. 6; and Helena Cobban, *The Palestinian Liberation Organization: People, Power and Politics* (Cambridge: Cambridge University Press, 1984), 28-32.

10. For lists and information about the many Palestinian organizations, see Aryeh Y. Yodfat and Yuval Arnon-Ohanna, *PLO: Strategy and Politics* (London: Croom and Helm, 1981), 140–46; and John W. Amos, *Palestinian Resistance: Organization of a Nationalist Movement* (New York: Pergamon, 1980), 325–33.

11. Ehud Ya'ari, *Strike Terror: The Story of Fatah* (New York: Sabra Books, 1970).

12. Cobban, *The Palestinian Liberation Organization*, 42-44; and Becker, *The PLO*, 68-70.

13. Y. Harkabi, *The Palestinian Covenant and Its Meaning* (London: Vallentine, Mitchell, 1979).

14. Walter Laqueur, ed., *The Arab-Israel Reader* (New York: Bantam, 1970), 100; and Theodore Draper, *Israel and World Politics: Roots of the Third Arab-Israeli War* (New York: Viking, 1968), 98.

15. See Yodfat and Arnon-Ohanna, *PLO*, 24-28; and Y. Harkabi, *Fedayeen Action*

and Arab Strategy, Adelphi Papers No. 53 (London: Institute for Strategic Studies, 1968).

16. See Paul Wilkinson, *Political Terrorism* (London: Macmillan, 1974); and Yonah Alexander, David Carlton, and Paul Wilkinson, eds., *Terrorism: Theory and Practice* (Boulder, Colo.: Westview Press, 1979).

17. J. Bowyer Bell, *The Myth of the Guerrilla: Revolutionary Theory and Malpractice* (New York: Knopf, 1971); and Charles Horner, "The Facts about Terrorism," *Commentary* 69(June 1980): 40-45.

18. Hanan Alon, *Countering Palestinian Terrorism in Israel: Toward a Policy Analysis of Countermeasure,* N-1567-FF (Santa Monica, Calif.: Rand, August 1980), 57, fig. 5. In 1978, 79.4 percent of the Palestinian operations inside Israel were directed against civilian targets.

19. A selected list of terrorist attacks on Americans and American targets appeared in Alon, *Countering Palestinian Terrorism,* 41-67; Shadid, *The United States,* 113–18; and Paul A. Jureidini and William E. Hazen, *The Palestinian Movement in Politics* (Lexington, Mass.: Lexington Books, 1975), 77-81.

20. *U.S. Department of State Bulletin* 61(September 15, 1969): 46; and Statement by Senator Russell Long from Louisiana in *U.S. Congressional Record,* 91st Cong., 2nd sess., 1970, XVI, 11(September 1970), 15224.

21. Lester Sobel, ed., *Palestine Impasse: Arab Guerrillas and International Terror* (New York: Facts on File, 1977); and Ovid Demaris, *Brothers in Blood: The International Terrorist Network* (New York: Scribner's, 1977).

22. Uri Ra'anan, et al. *Hydra of Carnage, International Linkages of Terrorism: The Witnesses Speak* (Lexington, Mass.: Lexington Books, 1985); Ray S. Cline and Yonah Alexander, *Terrorism: The Soviet Connection* (New York: Crane and Russak, 1984); Claire Sterling, *The Terror Network: The Secret War of International Terrorism* (New York: Holt, Rinehart and Winston, 1981); Roberta Goren, *The Soviet Union and Terrorism* (London: George Allen and Unwin, 1984), 95–193.

23. Abraham Ben-Zvi, *The Reagan Presidency and the Palestinian Predicament: An Interim Analysis,* Paper No. 13, (Tel Aviv: Center for Strategic Studies, 1981), 6; see also the statement by Secretary of State Alexander Haig, *New York Times,* January 29, 1981.

24. See Yodfat and Arnon-Ohanna, *PLO,* ch. 6; Galia Golan, *The Soviet Union and the Palestine Liberation Organization* (New York: Praeger, 1980); and Herbert Krosney, "The PLO's Moscow Connection," *New York Magazine,* September 24, 1979, 64-72.

25. Cline and Alexander, *Terrorism,* 46; Yodfat and Arnon-Ohanna, *PLO,* 203; Robert Moss, "Moscow Backs Terror, Inc.," *Daily Telegraph* (London), July 16, 1979; and Raphael Israeli, *The PLO in Lebanon* (London: Weidenfeld and Nicolson, 1983).

26. On the standing of the PLO in the international arena from a legal perspective, see William V. O'Brien, "The PLO in International Law," *Boston University International Law Journal,* 2(1984): 349-413.

27. Aaron David Miller, *The PLO and the Politics of Survival* (New York: Praeger, 1983), 35.

28. *Time,* April 14, 1980, 13; but Becker wrote that by 1981, 117 countries had granted official recognition in some degree to the PLO; see Becker, *The PLO,* 160.

29. *Yearbook of the United Nations 1974* (New York: United Nations Office of Public Information, 1977), 218.

30. For the text of the Rabat resolutions, see Yodfat and Arnon-Ohanna, *PLO,* 180. For analysis of these resolutions, see ibid., 37-44, and Shadid, *The United States,* 102-3.

31. Yasser Arafat, "Abu Ammar at the U.N.," *Palestine* 1(January–February 1975): 12-21.

32. "The PLO at the U.N. and in the Future," *Merip Reports* 33(December 1974): 28-30.

33. *New York Times,* November 23, 1974.

34. For a description of Palestinian cover organizations, including Black September, Black June, and Eagles of the Palestinian Revolution, see Yodfat and Arnon-Ohanna, *PLO,* 146.

35. On the Munich massacre see, Serge Groussard, *The Blood of Israel: The Massacre of the Israeli Athletes* (New York: 1975); On the *Achille Lauro* incident see, *Newsweek*, Special Report, October 21, 1985, 12-29.

36. Quoted in Goren, *The Soviet Union,* 116. For a detailed description of Black September, see Christopher Dobson, *"Black September": Its Short, Violent History* (New York: Macmillan, 1974); and John K. Cooley, *Green March, "Black September": The Story of the Palestinian Arabs* (London: Frank Cass, 1973).

37. Miller, *PLO and Politics of Survival,* 92.

38. *U.N. Monthly Chronicle* 11(December 1974): 80-82.

39. Quoted in Seymour Martin Lipset and William Schneider, "Carter vs. Israel: What the Polls Reveal," *Commentary* 64(November 1977): 22-23.

40. Yankelovich, Skelly and White, *Image of the PLO,* Memorandum, October 1982, 10.

41. *New York Post,* April 10, 1978.

42. *New York Post,* November 13, 1977; *Washington Post,* November 18, 1977; and *USA Today,* November 29, 1982; *The Harris Survey,* 92, November 14, 1985.

43. Shelley Slade, "The Image of the Arab in America: Analysis of a Poll on American Attitudes," *Middle East Journal* 35(Spring 1981), 151.

44. Louis Harris and Associates, *A Study of the Attitudes of the American People and the American Jewish Community Toward Anti-Semitism and the Arab-Israeli Conflict in the Middle East,* August 1980, Study No. 804011, 32.

45. *USA Today,* November 29, 1982.

46. John E. Rielly, ed., *American Public Opinion and U.S. Foreign Policy, 1983* (Chicago: Chicago Council on Foreign Relations, 1983), 19.

47. "The Palestinians, Key to a Wide Peace," *Time,* April 14, 1980, 12.

48. Slade, "Image of the Arab," 155.

49. Lipset and Schneider, "Carter vs. Israel," 22. See also Eytan Gilboa, "Trends in American Attitudes Toward the PLO and the Palestinians," *Political Communication and Persuasion* 3(1985): 45-67.

50. *Time,* October 2, 1978, 8.

51. *New York Post, Washington Post,* April 10, 1978.

52. "Opinion Roundup," *Public Opinion* 6(August-September, 1983): 36.

53. *ABC News–Harris Survey* vol. 1, no. 108, September 3, 1979.

54. *The Harris Survey*, 92, November 14, 1985. See also *The Harris Survey*, 94, November 21, 1985.

55. See Doyle McManus, "U.S., PLO: Seven Years of Secret Contacts," *Los Angeles Times*, July 5, 1981; and Bernard Gwertzman, "U.S. Reportedly Had Contact with the PLO for 9 months," *New York Times*, February 19, 1984.

56. See *New York Times*, August 15, 16, 1979.

57. Young supported self-determination for the Palestinians as early as October 1975; see Ben–Zvi, *The Reagan Presidency*, 11.

58. See *New York Times*, August 16, 1979; and "Blacks and the PLO," *New Republic* (September 18, 1979): 5-6.

59. For Carter's remarks on the incident, see Jimmy Carter, *Keeping Faith* (New York: Bantam Books, 1982), 491.

60. *ABC News–Harris Survey*, vol. 1, no. 104, August 24, 1979.

61. *Los Angeles Times*, Poll no. 18, October 1979, Q. 87.

62. The full text of the declaration was published in the *New York Times*, June 14, 1980.

63. The Israeli response was published in *Ha'aretz*, June 16, 1980.

64. See Becker, *The PLO*, 172.

65. Louis Harris and Associates, Study no. 804011, August 1980, 32.

66. *ABC News–Harris Survey*, vol. 1, no. 108, September 3, 1979; and *The Harris Survey*, 94, November 21, 1985.

67. Gilboa, "Trends in American Attitudes," 54.

68. Several Palestinian leaders suggested, as a tactical maneuver, adopting a two-stage policy. In the first stage, a Palestinian state would be established in the West Bank and Gaza, and in the second stage, Israel would be conquered and annexed to the first-stage territory. See Yodfat and Arnon-Ohanna, *PLO*, 61-64.

69. On PLO-Jordanian relations, see Clinton Bailey, *Jordan's Palestinian Challenge, 1948–1983: A Political History* (Boulder, Colo.: Westview, 1984).

70. See *Time*, April 14, 1980, 12; Shadid, 22, *Observer* (London), March 2, 1976; *Washington Post*, September 23, 1981; George Habash, a PLO leader, told *Der Spiegel* on June 22, 1980 that the Palestinians constitute 70 percent of Jordan's population.

71. *Public Papers of the Presidents of the United States, Jimmy Carter, 1979* (Washington, D.C.: Government Printing Office, 1980), vol. 2, 1985.

72. See ch. 3.

73. *U.S. Department of State Bulletin* (August 8, 1977): 176. See also another clarification by Carter, ibid., (October 24, 1977): 571.

74. This solution was discussed in Mark A. Heller, *A Palestinian State: The Implications for Israel* (Cambridge: Harvard University Press, 1983); and Richard Y. Ward, Don Peretz, and Evan M. Wilson, eds., *The Palestine State: A Rational Approach* (London: National University Publications, 1977).

75. "Opinion Roundup," *Public Opinion* 6 (August–September, 1983): 50-51.

76. See ch. 4.

77. *Newsweek*, October 4, 1982, 11.

78. *American Public Opinion and U.S. Foreign Policy, 1983*, 19.

79. *New York Times*, November 7, 1980.

6
Attitudes toward Aid to Israel

Foreign aid has become one of the principal instruments of foreign policy in the nuclear age.[1] Indeed, since the end of World War II, the United States has allocated financial assistance abroad in the range of $250 billion.[2] Despite such massive infusions, foreign aid has never been popular in America. Presidents have had to persuade both public opinion and Congress to allocate taxpayers' money for this purpose.[3] The annual enacting of foreign aid bills always involves a complex and tense process that frequently leads to heated debates between the White House and Congress.

Several types of programs and policies fall under the umbrella term *aid* and may be ranked in order of obligation.[4] The most elementary and humanitarian program has been the Food for Peace program. Direct financial aid to foreign governments for economic development in the form of loans, credits, or grants is next on the scale. Following this is military aid, the supply and sale of weapons and equipment on a continuing basis. Finally, the highest form of aid, and the ultimate test of a credible alliance, is the dispatching of American troops to allies in cases of extreme threat to their survival or well-being. In addition, specific needs of certain countries have called for other forms of aid, such as security supporting assistance, which is economic in theory but is designed to alleviate the burden of defense rather than directly encourage economic development.[5]

Part I of this book demonstrates that Israel has enjoyed considerable general support of American public opinion since its inception. However, it is one matter to convey sympathy and another to make an actual commitment. One measure of U.S. willingness to support Israel beyond goodwill has been the economic and military aid allocated to the Jewish state from Washington over the years. The Arab-Israeli conflict forced Israel to build and maintain a strong army while absorbing great numbers of immigrants and developing its economy. Israel therefore required substantial infusions of aid from abroad. Jewish communities, especially those in the United States, provided such aid. However these contributions met only a portion of Israel's needs, making it dependent upon the aid of friendly governments, mostly the United States.

During the first years of Israel's existence, it received mostly humanitarian aid from the United States through the Food for Peace program (PL 480).[6] In the last decade, however, Israel has become one of the major recipients of U.S. economic and military aid. Despite reservations on foreign aid, the U.S. Congress has strongly supported aid to Israel. In fact, according to a report published in *Congressional Quarterly*, Israel has been the only foreign aid recipient that "politically, has the option of seeking and getting a better deal from Congress than from the administration."[7]

The Congress, of course, cannot act without adequate support from public opinion, and this chapter examines trends in American opinions on various forms of American aid to Israel. Several polls have examined opinions on overall U.S. economic and military aid to Israel. Other surveys have included questions on specific military aid—supply and sales of arms, and American military intervention on behalf of Israel in the event of an Arab invasion or other extreme threats to the survival of Israel.

A comparison of U.S. attitudes toward aid to Israel, aid to other U.S. allies in the Middle East, and aid to foreign countries in general puts the whole issue in a better perspective. The available data allow such comparisons. In this type of survey, the comparative setting is built in and usually leads to interesting results. The comparative setting was found in polls on both the issue of military aid and military intervention in hypothetical crisis situations.

The enormous amount of American aid to Israel naturally rendered it more dependent on the United States. On several occasions, the United States has threatened to suspend or reduce aid and, at times, took such actions to influence Israel policy. The last section of this chapter presents American opinions on actual or potential uses of aid by the administration as a means of pressuring Israel. First, however, a brief analysis of the scope of U.S. aid to Israel is required.

The Scope and Nature of U.S. Aid to Israel

Until 1971, improbable as it may seem, Israel received only about 1 percent of total U.S. foreign aid.[8] Since 1971 however, the amount of aid has increased to a much higher proportion and, in recent years, has accounted for approximately one-quarter of total U.S. aid. But to put this aid in perspective, it should be noted that since the 1979 Israeli-Egyptian peace agreement, Egypt also has received similar amounts of economic and military aid. Total U.S. aid to Israel from 1951 to 1985 was about $29 billion, equally divided between loans and grants. Most aid granted during the period was military, and most of it was spent in the United States on the purchase of weapons. During the same period, U.S. Arab allies received about $27 billion in military aid.

From 1948 until 1962, Israel did not receive weapons from the United

States. From December 1947 until August 1949, the Truman administration imposed an embargo on arms sales to the Middle East.[9] The embargo was lifted later, but arms sales to Israel were still restricted. The Eisenhower administration limited arms sales and allowed purchases of only a few insignificant items.[10] In May 1950, the United States, together with Britain and France, signed the Tripartite Declaration, which was designed, among other things, to regulate arms shipments to the Middle East.[11] This declaration and its rationale became obsolete in 1955, when Egypt concluded a major arms deal with Czechoslovakia.[12] Israel sought to offset the stream of modern Soviet weaponry to the Arab countries by the purchase of weapons from the United States, but Washington did not want to antagonize the Arabs and was reluctant to sell Israel military supplies. Instead, it encouraged other Western countries, such as France, Britain, and Canada, to do so, and from 1956 until 1967, Israel received most of its weapons from France.[13]

The United States began to supply Israel with modern weapons only in 1962, but even then, the approved equipment—antiaircraft Hawk missiles—was of a purely defensive nature.[14] President Johnson approved the first sales of combat aircraft and tanks but declared that the United States would not become the chief weapons supplier to the Middle East. However, the Six-Day War and the subsequent War of Attrition altered this policy. During the Six-Day War, France imposed an embargo on arms sales to Israel, and the United States thus became Israel's chief weapons supplier. Following the War of Attrition and the 1970 crisis in Jordan, the Nixon administration went one step further and committed the United States to a long-range modernization of the Israeli Defense Forces.[15]

In the last decade, the United States has also become the chief supplier of sophisticated weapons to several Arab countries, partially to regain petrodollars. This development worried Israeli policymakers and led to several battles in the Congress over specific arms deals with Arab countries, such as the 1981 AWACS deal with Saudi Arabia.[16] In response to the Israeli concerns, President Reagan wrote Prime Minister Begin in February 1982:

> I want you to know that America's policy toward Israel has not changed. Our commitments will be kept. I am determined to see that Israel's qualitative technological edge is maintained and am mindful as well of your concerns with respect to quantitative factors and their impact upon Israel's security.[17]

American presidents from Kennedy to Carter promised to maintain the balance of military power in the Middle East. Reagan went so far as to say that the United States would provide Israel with a "qualitative technological edge." But these general commitments leave substantial room for the interpretation of "balance" or "qualitative" edge at any particular time. So far as economic aid is concerned, it should be noted that since 1975, most of this aid has been related to security needs and is designed to alleviate the burden of defense on the Israeli economy.

Figure 6–1 depicts four ascending peaks in American aid to Israel. The first peak was prompted in 1971, when the War of Attrition and the Jordanian crisis (1970) moved Nixon to increase military aid to Israel from 30 million to $545 million. The second peak occurred in 1974, following the Yom Kippur War, which cost Israel some $12 billion and stunted economic growth.[18] The aid for 1974 represents the cost of the U.S. airlift and the effort to replenish Israel's stock of weapons and ammunition.[19] The next two peaks are related to peace agreements rather than to wars. The increase in 1976 reflected the requirements of the Egyptian-Israeli interim agreement of September 1975, and the 1979 peak was created by the stipulations of the Israel-Egyptian peace agreement. The peace agreement provided for the construction of two new airfields in Israel, replacing those Israel had built in the Sinai Desert. The U.S. share in the construction of these airfields accounts for the increase of $3 billion in the amount of aid for 1979.

Opinions on Military Aid

Israel's aid requirements have been primarily determined by developments in the Arab-Israeli conflict, such as the arms race, wars, and redeployment of forces following cease-fires and peace agreements. Since the Cold War, the United States and the Soviet Union have competed for positions of power in the Middle East by attempting to lure the states of the region into their spheres of influence through generous economic and military aid programs. The Soviet Union entered the Middle East in 1955 via a major arms deal with Egypt. Since 1955, about 70 percent of total Soviet arms transfers to non-Communist countries have gone to the Middle East and the Arab countries of North Africa.[20] From 1979 to 1983, the USSR transferred arms to the Middle East valued at about $20.3 billion.[21]

The arms race in the Middle East placed a heavy burden on the developing Israeli economy, but until the 1973 Yom Kippur War, Israel did not receive military assistance in the form of grants. By that time, Israeli defense costs had risen to 49 percent of the state budget, and the country could no longer assume the entire burden of its defense.[22] The growth in the Israeli allocations for defense emerged from a fundamental change in the regional arms race.

In the 1950s, the Middle East was a convenient dumping grounds for outdated, unneeded superpower weaponry; after the 1967 Six-Day War, however, and even more after the 1973 Yom Kippur War, the superpowers provided the area with the most sophisticated and expensive weapons in the world. In this situation, the Arab countries held two advantages over Israel. First, they acquired weapons from several sources, not only from the United

States.[23] (It is estimated that since 1974, the Arab countries have acquired more than $110 billion in sophisticated arms—$34 billion from the Soviet Union, $40 billion from the United States, and $36 billion from Europe.)[24] Second, the Arab oil-producing countries have used their new fortune of petrodollars in the purchase of weapons. Israel, on the other hand, lacking high-revenue natural resources, has had to match the extensive Arab acquisitions through heavier dependence on American military aid.

Since 1971, Israel's requests for substantial military aid have been favorably received by successive administrations and the Congress. The rationale for this response, explained Bernard Reich,

> has been framed in terms of promoting peace through the commitment to the security and well-being of Israel, as well as to developing confidence, maintaining a friendly relationship, and helping to maintain Israel's military edge over its hostile neighbors. It is argued that Israel must be sufficiently confident of its ability to defend itself if it is to take the risks necessary to make peace.[25]

These arguments for economic and military aid to Israel have been frequently cited in public forums. Other reasons, perhaps more powerful ones, have also played a role in the shaping of favorable attitudes toward aid to Israel.

Over the years, Israel has provided the United States with important intelligence on the Middle East and has allowed Americans to inspect captured Soviet-made weapons, including combat planes and tanks.[26] Highly valuable information on the performance of American-made weapons has also been conveyed to the U.S. military. Israel has improved U.S.-made weapons, and many of these improvements have been adopted by the U.S. armed forces, thus saving considerable amounts of money. The presence of U.S. troops in Europe costs about $100 billion annually, and another $40 billion is spent on the security of South Korea and the Far East. The United States does not maintain troops on a permanent basis in the Middle East, partly because this role is fulfilled by the Israeli Army. If the United States maintained a permanent presence in the Middle East, it would cost approximately $100 billion a year. Finally, most U.S. military aid to Israel is spent in the United States. All these facts lead to the conclusion that the United States receives considerable return for its aid to Israel. Some of this return is highly visible and can be precisely calculated. Other areas, such as the worth of intelligence or exchange of information on weaponry performance, are more difficult to price but are extremely valuable. To what extent, then, has the highly favorable approach of successive administrations and Congress toward aid to Israel been supported by American public opinion?

Appropriate grasp of American attitudes toward U.S. economic and military aid to Israel entails an examination of the wider context of American

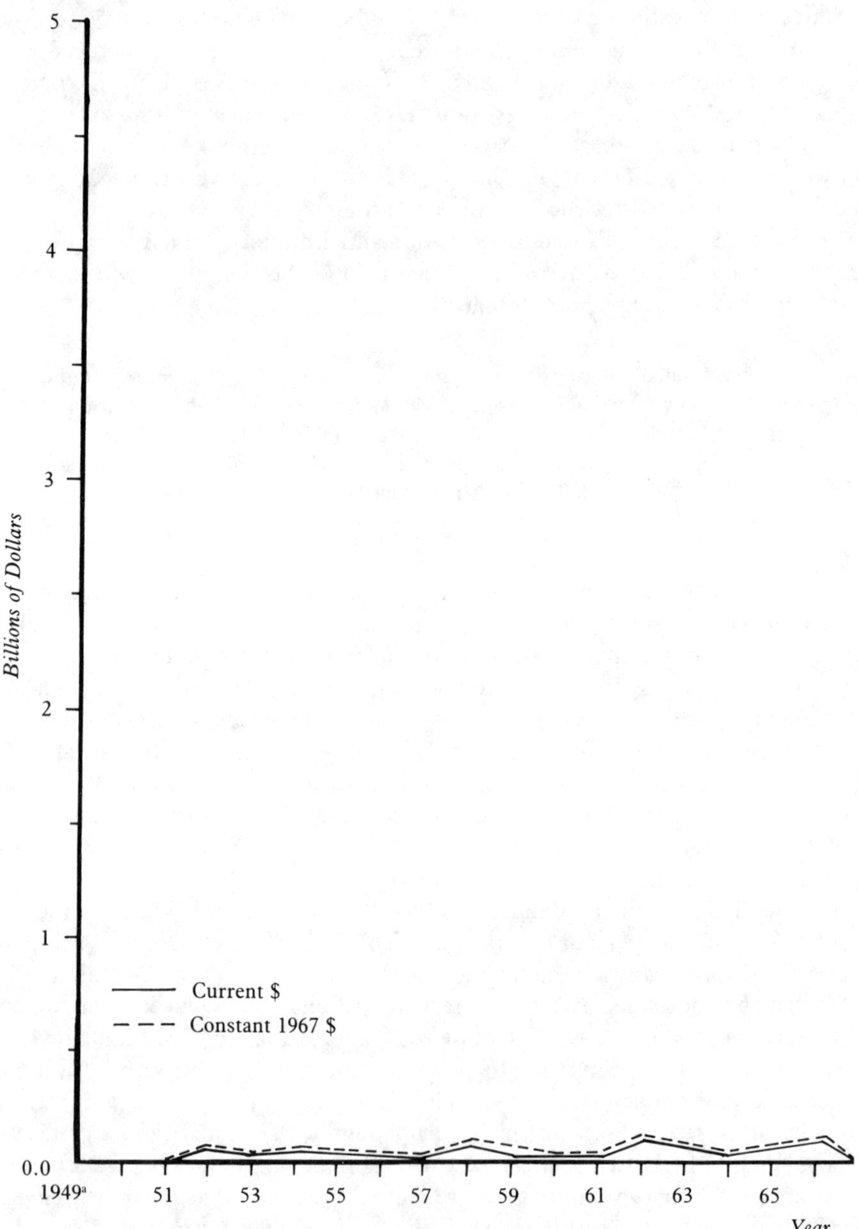

Source: U.S. Agency for International Development, *U.S. Overseas Loans and Grants and Assistance from International Organizations, Obligations and Loan Authorizations,* July 1, 1945–September 30, 1982 (Washington, D.C.: AID, 1983); *U.S. Overseas Loans and Grants from International Organizations, 1983* (Washington, D.C.: AID, 1984).

[a]Export-Import bank loans only

Figure 6–1. U.S. Assistance to Israel 1949–83 (fiscal years)

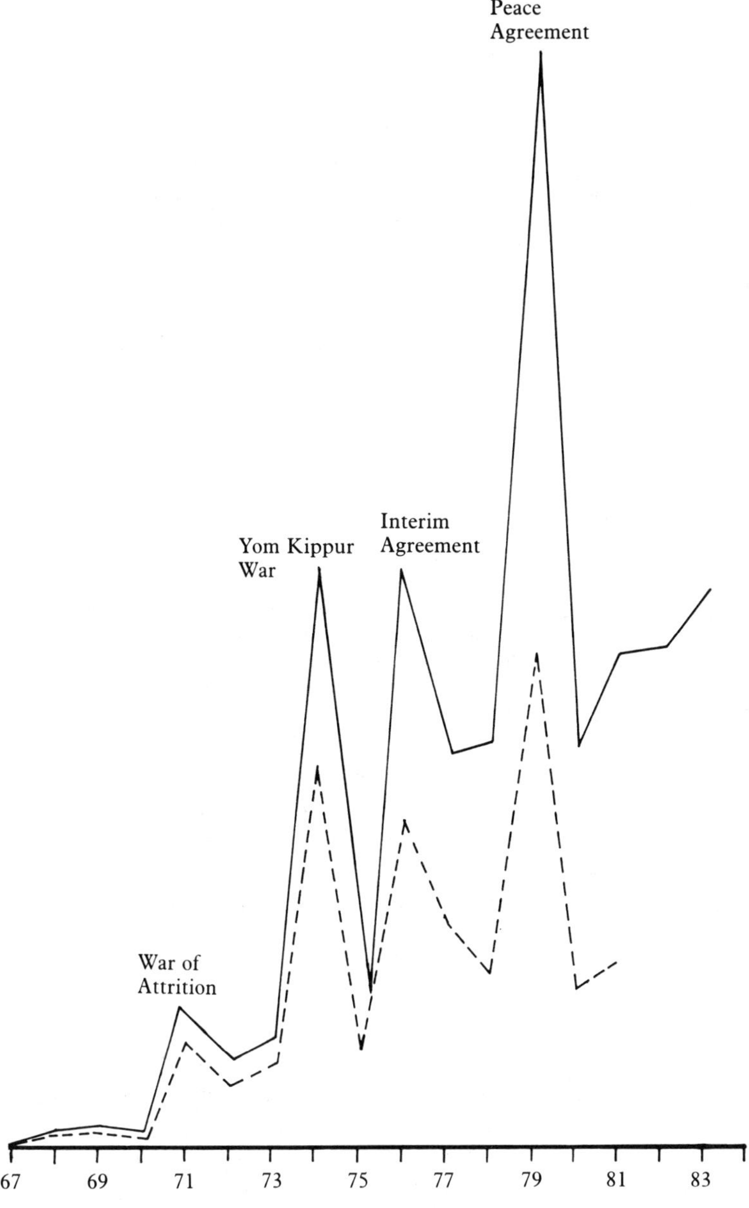

Peace
Agreement
Interim
Agreement
Yom Kippur
War
War of
Attrition
67
69
71
73
75
77
79
81
83

Table 6–1
Attitudes toward U.S. Military Aid

Questions

(a) Do you favor or oppose *giving* military aid to other nations?

(b) Do you favor or oppose our *selling* military equipment to other nations?

(c) Do you favor or oppose the U.S. giving military supplies to nations friendly to the U.S.?

(d) Do you support or oppose military assistance to those countries trying to defend themselves?

Q	*Date*	*Poll*	*Favor*	*Oppose*	*D.K.*
(a)	Dec. '74	Harris	22%	65%	13%
(a)	Nov. '82	Gallup-Chicago	28	63	9
(b)	Feb. '75	Harris	35	53	12
(b)	Mar. '78	NBC	43	47	10
(b)	Aug. '81	NBC	27	52	21
(b)	Nov. '82	Gallup-Chicago	39	53	8
(c)	July '81	Harris	37	59	4
(d)	Aug. '83	Sindlinger-Heritage	46	31	23

Sources: Harris: Seymour Martin Lipset and William Schneider, *Israel and the Jews in American Public Opinion,* 21; *Index to International Public Opinion 1981–82,* 304. Gallup-Chicago: *American Public Opinion and U.S. Foreign Policy 1983,* 26. NBC: *NBC News Poll,* March 21–22, 1978, released on March 23, 1978. August 10–11, 1981. Sindlinger and Heritage: *The Heritage Foundation News,* September 16, 1983.

attitudes toward foreign aid in general. Foreign aid was never popular in American public opinion and became even less popular during and after the war in Vietnam and Southeast Asia.[27] When it was presented in the context of government spending, almost seven out of ten Americans opted for reduction, or even termination, of aid.[28] Polls conducted for the Chicago Council on Foreign Relations found in 1974, 1978, and 1982 that economic and military aid has been the least favored federal program and that the public supports cuts in such allocations.

Since most U.S. aid to Israel is military, it is interesting to identify the general pattern of public opinion on this specific type of aid. Table 6–1 indicates considerable opposition to military aid. The sales of American equipment was also opposed, but by somewhat lower ratios.[29] Only question (d), which included a bias leading to a positive answer (aid to countries trying to defend themselves), produced a positive result. This result is interesting, since Israel has usually been perceived as a country trying to defend itself through its own armed forces.

Since American aid to Israel was rather small until the Six-Day War, no polls were conducted to measure how Americans felt about it. Since 1967, however, the aid issue has appeared in many general and specific polls. Because military aid has comprised most of the American aid to Israel, most polls

Table 6–2
Attitudes toward Levels of Aid to Israel

Question

(a) In view of the situation in the Middle East, do you feel the U.S. should increase its present aid (military or economic and military) to Israel, continue it at the same level as now or cut it back?

Date	*Poll*	*Increase*	*Same Level*	*Increase + Same Level*	*Cut (Decrease)*	*D.K.*
Jan. '75	Yenkelovich	9%	36%	45%	41%	14%
Mar. '77	Yankelovich	10	49	59	26	15
Feb. '81	Yankelovich	10	47	57	23	20
Aug. '81	Penn-Schoen	20	51	71	22	8
May '82	Penn-Schoen	20	52	72	22	7
Nov. '82	Roper	8	42	50	35	14

Question

(b) How do you feel about U.S. military aid to Israel, do you think we're giving too much military aid, not enough military aid, or do you think the U.S. is giving about the right amount of military aid to Israel?

Date	*Poll*	*Not Enough*	*Right Amount*	*Not Enough + Right Amount*	*Too Much*	*D.K.*
Mar. '78	NBC	6%	47%	53%	31%	16%
Dec. '79	NBC	5	38	43	38	19
Aug. '81	NBC	7	42	49	37	14
Oct. '81	*WP*-ABC	16	44	60	28	12
Jan. '82	NBC	7	49	56	30	14
Aug. '82	NBC	6	43	49	36	15

Sources: Yankelovich: Geraldine Rosenfield, *Similarities and Differences Between Recent Polls of American Opinion Regarding Israel and the Jews* (New York: American Jewish Committee, Information and Research Services, June 1975), 5; Gregory Martire and Ruth Clark, *Anti-Semitism in the United States* (New York: Praeger, 1982), 78. Penn and Schoen: General Survey Tracking, No. 244, 357, May 1982. *WP*-ABC: *WP*-ABC News Poll, October 14–18, 1981. Roper: *Roper Reports*, November 1982. NBC: *NBC News Poll*, March 23, 1978, and August 11, 1982.

yielded opinions on arms supplies. Only a few referred to the total aid package and regularly dealt in terms of scope—sufficient, too small, or too large.

The general pattern in table 6–2 is very positive. On the average, Americans said, by a ratio of two to one, that aid should be either increased or kept at the same level. This pattern differs considerably from the one found in table 6–1. However, it should be noted that it is one thing to sympathize with the general idea of aid and another to support specific aid programs. In September 1975, for example, following the conclusion of the interim agreement between Israel and Egypt and the revelations about the U.S. aid commitments to both

Table 6–3
Attitudes toward Military Aid to Israel

Question

(a) Do you think the U.S. was right in sending planes and other military supplies to Israel, or do you think we should have taken a different course? (Harris)

Date	*Right in Sending*	*Different Course*	*D.K., Not Sure*
June '67	35%	39%	26%
Sep. '67	42	36	22
Oct. '73	46	34	20
Mar. '78	48	36	16

Question

(b) Do you favor or oppose sending Israel what it needs in the way of military hardware? (Harris)

Date	*Favor*	*Oppose*	*D.K.*
Dec. '74	66%	24%	10%
Jan. '76	65	23	12
July '80	73	15	12

Israel and Egypt (over $2 billion each), the Gannett News Service poll found that 64 percent opposed aid to Israel "in the range of $2.5 billion," and 24 percent approved of it.[30] No similar question was asked about the aid commitment to Egypt.

Further polls employed more specific questions about U.S. military aid to Israel, and the results varied accordingly. One question presented a choice between approval of aid and an unspecified, vague policy. Harris posed question (a) in table 6–3 immediately after the Six-Day War, during the Yom Kippur War, and in March 1978. Responses to question (a) reveal a steady increase in the number of respondents who said the United States was right to send planes and other military supplies to Israel. Only in June 1967 was the score slightly negative for Israel, and it is probable that after the decisive Israeli victory, the public did not discern a need for U.S. military aid to Israel.

Responses to questions (b) and (c) in table 6–3 indicate substantial support for military aid to Israel, from 62 to 75 percent. Question (b) mentions Israel's needs, and question (c) refers to extensive Russian military supplies to its Arab allies in the Middle East. These formulations tended to elicit a highly positive response toward Israel.

Question (d) examines attitudes toward military aid to Israel within the context of war. On one hand, because of the question's wording, we might expect stronger support for aid. On the other hand, aid during war might be

Table 6–3 continued

Question

(c) As you know, the U.S. has sent planes, tanks, artillery and other weapons to arm Israel. The Russians have sent similar supplies to Egypt and Syria. In general, with the Russians arming Egypt and Syria, do you think the U.S. is right or wrong to send Israel the military supplies it needs?" (Harris)[a]

Date	*Right*	*Wrong*	*D.K., Not Sure*
Jan. '75	65%	21%	14%
Mar. '75	64	18	18
May '75	62	18	20
May '76	65	23	12
Mar. '78	68	19	13
July '80	75	15	10

Question

(d) If war broke out again in the Middle East between the Arabs and Israel, would you favor or oppose the U.S. continuing to send military supplies as they are needed, but not troops or personnel, to help Israel? (Harris)

Date	*Favor*	*Oppose*	*Not Sure*
Dec. '74	66%	24%	10%
Jan. '76	64	25	11
July '80	73	18	9

Sources: (a) Connie de Boer, "The Polls: Attitudes Toward the Arab-Israeli Conflict," *Public Opinion Quarterly* 47(Spring 1984): 128; Lipset and Schneider, 10, 15; *Washington Post,* April 10, 1978. (b) *Jerusalem Post,* October 3, 1980. (c) *The Harris Survey,* April 10, 1975; de Boer, 128; *New York Post,* April 10, 1978. Louis Harris and Associates, Study No. 804011 (August 1980), 34. (d) *How Americans Feel about Israel,* 45.

[a]In the polls of 1978 and 1980, "Egypt" was replaced by "Iraq."

seen as a prelude to direct U.S. military involvement, an option many Americans have rejected since America's involvement in Vietnam. Question (d) asks for opinions on U.S. military supplies to Israel in the event of war but explicitly rules out the dispatching of troops. This formulation yielded favorable scores for Israel, from 64 to 73 percent. These results are very similar to those found in the responses to questions (b) and (c).

The preceding data reveal substantial support in American public opinion on military aid to Israel. This result is even more impressive when it is contrasted to the highly negative general attitudes toward military aid. At this point, it should be interesting to discover how Americans felt about military aid to U.S. Arab allies in the Middle East and how these feelings compare with those on military assistance to Israel.

Comparative Opinions on Aid to Israel

Enormous U.S. assistance to several Arab countries, such as Jordan, Saudi Arabia, and Egypt, received little attention in public opinion polls. Questions concerning this assistance were asked infrequently and usually only in connection with highly controversial deals, such as the AWACS sale, or with package deals in which both Israel and American Arab allies were involved.

Following the Israeli-Egyptian interim agreement (September 1975), Egypt requested and received weapons from the United States. In January 1976, the CBS-*NYT* poll presented a national sample with the following question: "In addition to military aid to Israel do you agree that the U.S. should sell arms to Egypt in order to play a more even-handed role in the Middle East?" The sample disagreed with this proposal by 59 to 21 percent.[31] Similar results were obtained in response to a question on the delivery of military arms to Jordan. In the May 1982 Penn and Schoen survey, the public opposed weapons sales to Jordan by a majority of 66 to 21 percent. A similar percentage, 62 versus 21 percent, rejected, in an August 1983 Roper poll, the sale of arms and weapons to Saudi Arabia.[32]

In May 1981, Roper asked for opinions on the supply of U.S. weapons to several pro-American Arab countries: "There has been a lot of discussion lately about ways to protect U.S. interests in the Persian Gulf oil region. Here is a list of possible steps the U.S. could take. For each would you tell me if you favor it strongly, generally favor it, generally oppose it, or oppose it strongly: supply advanced military planes to Saudi Arabia, Egypt and other moderate Arab countries in the Persian Gulf area."[33] Only 8 percent of the sample strongly favored this policy, and exactly twice as many respondents strongly opposed it. Overall, the opponents outscored the supporters by a 48 to 32 percent plurality.

The most controversial American arms deal with an Arab country was the 1981 AWACS deal with Saudi Arabia. The AWACS system is the most sophisticated early warning and command system in the world. Saudi Arabia had earlier acquired F-15 combat jets and, coupled with AWACS, the two systems could be unbeatable. The Reagan administration strongly defended the AWACS deal with Saudi Arabia, but Israel strongly opposed it; Congress has similar reservations. A major battle emerged between the Congress, which had to approve the deal, and the administration. Reagan was forced to exert tremendous pressure on Republican senators, who finally agreed to the deal. What was the attitude of public opinion toward the AWACS deal?

In October 1981, Harris asked: "All in all do you favor or oppose the sale of AWACS to Saudi Arabia?" A close plurality of 48 to 42 percent opposed the deal. However, at the same time, the *Los Angeles Times* also examined opinions on the AWACS deal, but included in the question the Israeli reservations: "President Reagan has proposed that the United States sell five early warning radar planes and a package of other sophisticated military equipment to Saudi Arabia. Neighboring Israel says that the sale of these airplanes called AWACS, for Airborne Warning and Control Systems, would threaten their national security. Do you approve or disapprove of Reagan's plan to sell AWACS planes to Saudi Arabia?" In response to this question, the public opposed the deal by a majority of 56 to 29 percent. In May 1982, Penn and Schoen used a general question similar to that used by Harris on attitudes held during the AWACS debate: "Did you favor or oppose the sale of the advance weapon detection system called AWACS to Saudi Arabia last year?" The response to this question again found substantial opposition to the deal by a majority of 60 to 30 percent. These results indicate that public opinion opposed the AWACS deal by a ratio of two to one.

Data cited earlier suggest that military aid to Israel was much more popular in the United States than was similar aid to American Arab allies in the Middle East. How, then, did the public react to a package deal that proposed the sale of weapons to both Israel and the pro-American Arab countries or to polls that included, in a single question or sequence, military aid to both Israel and the Arab countries?

In January 1975, the Yankelovich organization asked a national sample the following question: "Do you favor selling arms and military equipment to both Israel and the Arabs, just Israel, just Arabs, or neither?"[34] The majority of respondents (63 percent) favored selling arms to neither side; 14 percent favored selling arms to both; and an identical percentage favored selling arms to Israel. No one favored selling to the Arabs. Thus, a total of 28 percent supported military aid to Israel—a very low figure in contrast to the results in table 6–3.

On three separate occasions—1968, 1973, and 1978—Gallup conducted surveys on the U.S. supply of arms and material to Israel and the Arabs. Responses to question (a) in table 6–4 indicate substantial opposition to the proposition, although opposition to the supply of arms to the Arab side was far greater than opposition to the supply of arms to Israel. Again, the negative results for Israel in table 6–4 are opposite from those recorded in table 6–3, in which "military aid" was presented in relation only to Israel.

Another interesting example of this phenomenon is the distribution of opinions on Carter's 1978 package deal. At the beginning of 1978, President Carter submitted to the Congress a package deal for the sale of combat aircraft to Israel (75 F-16s and 15 F-15s), Egypt (50 F-5Es), and Saudi Arabia (60 F-15s). Obviously, Carter wished to use the popularity of military aid to Israel on Capitol Hill to gain approval for the much less popular military aid to U.S. Arab allies in the Middle East.[35] Congress resented this tactic. In March 1978, when the package deal was being hotly debated in public forums and in the Congress, Gallup found opposition to the U.S. supply of arms to Israel by a majority of 56 to 31 percent, yet the supply of arms to the Arabs was opposed

Table 6–4
Opinions of U.S. Arms Sales and Supplies to Israel and the Arabs

Question

(a) Do you think the U.S. should supply arms and material to Israel/the Arabs? (Gallup)

	Israel			*Arabs*		
Date	*Yes*	*No*	*D.K.*	*Yes*	*No*	*D.K.*
July '68	24%	59%	17%	3%	79%	18%
Oct. '73	37	49	14	2	85	13
Mar. '78	31	56	13	16	72	12

Question

(b) President Carter wants to go ahead with the sale of military aircraft to Israel, Saudi Arabia and Egypt for $4.8 billion. He wants to sell Israel 15 F-15s and 75 F-16s, the most modern jet planes the United States produces. Egypt would receive 50 F-5Es, which are effective short-range fighter bombers. Saudi Arabia would receive 60 F-15s, a sophisticated long-range fighter. The President wants to sell all of the planes as one package: either all three countries receive their planes or none receive them. Do you favor or oppose this U.S. sale of military planes to Israel, Egypt and Saudi Arabia?

	NBC, Feb. '78		*Harris, Apr. '78*	
Country	*Favor*	*Oppose*	*Favor*	*Oppose*
Israel	24%	63%	28%	64%
Egypt	21	66	20	71
Saudi Arabia	17	69	18	73
All countries	—	—	26	66

Sources: (a) Michael W. Suleiman, "American Public Support of Middle Eastern Countries: 1939–1979," in M. Hudson and R. Wolfe, eds., *The American Media and the Arabs* (Washington, D.C.: Georgetown University, Center for Contemporary Arab Studies, 1980), 32. (b) de Boer, 129, *NBC News Poll*, February 23, 1978.

by an even higher majority of 72 to 16 percent (see question (a) in table 6–4). NBC News and Harris asked specific questions on the package deal. The second part of table 6–4 indicates that the public opposed the package deal by a substantial ratio. Respondent opposition to the deal with Israel was the weakest, with Saudi Arabia the strongest; the Egyptian rating falls closer to that of Saudi Arabia.

These data suggest that when a question proposes military aid to both Israel and the Arabs, the results for both sides, but more for Israel, are substantially lower in contrast to results of questions that deal separately with each entity. It is likely that many Americans oppose the idea of two neighbors fighting each other with the same American-made weapons.

Thus far, American opinions on military aid to Israel have been discussed in an Israeli and an Arab-Israeli context, but it is useful to examine these opinions within a setting of comparative views on American military aid to U.S. allies in the Middle East and elsewhere around the world. In October 1974, the Yankelovich organization listed a number of countries and asked a representative sample of Americans whether they thought the United States should send arms to each. Responses to question (a) in table 6–5 show that opponents of military assistance to Israel outnumbered supporters by a margin of 57 to 31 percent. Compared to the other nine countries, Israel received the highest rate of support. In this poll, military aid to NATO members such as Italy, Greece, and Turkey was opposed by much larger ratios. This finding was also present in the scores of U.S. Arab allies in the Middle East—Jordan and Saudi Arabia. Saudi Arabia ranked last on the list.

Responses to question (b) in table 6–5 were recorded a decade later, but still indicate similar results. Arms sales to Israel were opposed by a plurality of 37 to 46 percent, with 10 percent expressing mixed feelings. Yet Israel occupied the fourth place on the list, behind England, West Germany, and Mexico, which were not included in the Yankelovich list of October 1974. Israel's rating was also higher than that of Japan, a close U.S. ally. As in the Yankelovich poll, the other two Middle Eastern countries, Iran and Saudi Arabia, lagged far behind Israel.

Opinions on Dispatching Troops to Israel in Times of Crisis

Another major aspect of the aid issue is the concept of direct military intervention on behalf of Israel in potentially critical situations. In general, American military involvement abroad has always been a highly controversial issue in U.S. public opinion. This attitude was present in the American approach to the establishment of Israel. Chapter 1 reveals that Americans were reluctant to support the dispatching of American troops to help enforce the 1947 U.N. partition resolution, and chapter 4 demonstrates the strong reservations in American public opinion on the peacemaking mission of U.S. troops in Lebanon from 1982 to 1984. The public even had reservations on the clearer and more genuine peacemaking mission of Americans during the Egyptian-Israeli peacemaking process.

In September 1975, Israel agreed to withdraw from strategic areas in the Sinai Peninsula as part of the interim agreement with Egypt. This withdrawal hinged on, among other factors, the construction and maintenance of early-warning stations in the Sinai Desert by the United States. About 200 radar technicians were required to carry out this task. The Ford administration agreed to build these stations and asked Congress to approve the necessary

Table 6–5
Attitudes toward the Sale of Weapons to Israel and Other Countries, 1974 and 1983

Question

(a) The U.S. sends arms and military equipment to a number of foreign countries. Do you personally feel that the U.S. should or should not send arms to . . . ? (Yankelovich, 1974)

Rank Order	*Country*	*Should*	*Should Not*	*D.K., Not Sure*
1	Israel	31%	57%	12%
2	South Vietnam	28	62	10
3	South Korea	28	61	11
4	Italy	20	69	11
5	Greece	18	70	12
6	Ireland	16	72	12
7	Jordan	15	72	13
8	Turkey	14	74	12
9	Yugoslavia	14	73	13
10	Saudi Arabia	12	77	11

Question

(b) You may have differing opinions about selling arms and weapons to certain specific countries. Here is a list of some different countries. (Card shown respondent) Would you go down that list and for each one tell me whether you think the United States should or should not sell them arms? (Roper, 1983)

Rank Order	*Country*	*Should sell arms*	*Mixed Feelings*	*Shouldn't sell arms*	*D.K.*
1	England	66%	4%	24%	6%
2	West Germany	45	6	40	8
3	Mexico	42	8	42	8
4	Israel	37	10	46	7
5	Japan	35	7	50	7
6	Anti-Russian Forces in Afghanistan	30	7	53	10
7	Taiwan	29	10	53	9
8	China	21	11	61	8
9	El Salvador	21	9	62	8
10	Saudi Arabia	21	8	62	9
11	Yugoslavia	17	9	62	12
12	Anti-government Forces in Nicaragua	14	9	65	12
13	Iran	6	4	83	6

Sources: Geraldine Rosenfield, *Attitudes of the American Public Toward Israel and American Jews* (New York: American Jewish Committee, Information and Research Services, December 1974, mimeographed), 8. (b) *Roper Reports,* August 1983, 49.

financing. Public opinion was not enthusiastic about this American involvement. Gallup found that 43 percent of the public supported this action and 41 percent opposed it.[36] The Gannett News poll asked a national sample whether Congress should approve of the dispatching of American technicians to the Sinai Desert and found a plurality of only 41 to 38 percent in favor of the plan.[37] These results are interesting because the issue here was American involvement in a peacemaking process, using technicians rather than military advisers or personnel; yet the public clearly expressed reservations even about this role.[38] It could be that in this case the involvement itself, rather than its nature or purpose, determined the direction of the opinions.[39]

The lack of public support for the peacekeeping mission in the Sinai Peninsula might have been related to the traumatic American failures in Vietnam. In 1975, South Vietnam ceased to exist, and the United States completely withdrew from that area in a less-than-honorable manner. The memories of the involvement in Vietnam were still fresh, and the mere suggestion of dispatching American advisers or technicians to a conflict-ridden area, such as the Middle East, probably evoked the Vietnam association. (It should be recalled that the involvement in Southeast Asia also began with the dispatching of a few advisers.) Thus, in the second half of the 1970s, American public opinion was very sensitive to any kind of military involvement abroad.[40] In February 1969, for example, the CBS-*NYT* poll posed the issue of military involvement abroad in the following manner: "Aside from an attack on the United States, is there any other situation when you might approve sending American troops to fight overseas?" Of those who offered an opinion, 69 percent said there was no other situation.[41]

A willingness and readiness to assist an ally in times of crisis is the ultimate test of a credible alliance. This test is especially relevant to a stand occasionally taken by American politicians, policymakers, and scholars who advise Israel to make important concessions to the Arabs that entail substantial security risks in return for American guarantees.[42] "Guarantees," in this context, implies a willingness to commit troops in cases of serious threats to Israel's survival, such as a massive Arab invasion.

Israel has never counted on the assistance of U.S. troops in crisis situations and has never sought direct military intervention on its behalf. On the contrary, the major tenet of Israel's political-strategic doctrine has always been total self-reliance on the IDF for meeting any military challenge.[43] Israeli leaders of all political beliefs and ideologies continually and consistently have asked solely for weapons of sufficient quantity and quality to defend their country. Moshe Dayan expressed this view on the CBS television program "60 Minutes" on April 13, 1971: "I would like you to sell us arms, to help us in the political field. I don't want you to fight for us, because once you will be getting killed for us, you won't like us very much." Menachem Begin asserted the same principle in March 1978, when he said: "We don't want even one American soldier to fight our battles. . . . We can sustain our independence. From time to time we need some tools."[44] Still the issue remains: To what extent can Israel depend on the American public to support the sending of American troops to Israel should a highly adverse situation arise?

From 1967 to 1970, and also in 1975, Gallup raised the question of military involvement in a context of options available to the United States in dealing with Israel and the Middle East. He asked those who had heard or read about the troubles between Israel and the Arab nations in the Middle East, "What would you like to see the U.S. government do about this situation?" One of the options given was the dispatching of troops (see table 2–3). Table 2–3 shows that, within that particular choice of options, a plurality (in most years, the majority) preferred to maintain outside the conflict. Between 10 and 16 percent of the respondents preferred that the United States grant Israel economic and military aid. In the highly critical, dangerous situation of June 1967, in a poll taken the day after the Six-Day War broke out, when Israel's ability to withstand the Arab armies was still in question, only 5 percent favored direct American military intervention in the form of troops (at other times, a mere 1 to 2 percent supported this form of aid).

The relatively high percentage of those who chose the stay-out option and the low percentage of those who preferred the send-troops option have several explanations that are related to both the methodology and the substance of the survey options. The choice of answers in table 2–3 was especially rich and included diplomatic options such as "negotiate for peace" or "work through the U.N." These were naturally more popular than military involvement in the eyes of many respondents. The stay-out option appeared first on the list and probably attracted many respondents. This option might have also reflected the growing disillusionment in the American performance in Vietnam.

In table 2–3, "sending troops" was given as only one of many options for dealing with the Arab-Israeli conflict. When the choice of responses was restricted, the number of those who supported direct involvement on behalf of Israel grew substantially. In December 1970, following the Egyptian-Israeli War of Attrition, the *Newsweek*-Gallup poll presented a national sample two questions on American assistance to Israel in crisis situations. The respondents were given a choice of three possible answers: "send troops," "send equipment," and "stay out." The first question was related to an event that occurred during the War of Attrition, when Israeli pilots engaged Russian pilots and shot down five of them.[45]

The question was presented in the following way: "What should the U.S. do if Russian pilots in Egypt engaged Israelis in direct combat?" The largest number of respondents (44 percent) preferred that the United States stay out; 34 percent supported delivery of equipment to Israel; and 11 percent chose the send-troops option.[46] The second question omitted the Russians and read: "What should the U.S. do if Israel seemed in danger of being overrun by Arab armies?" The response to this question was very similar to the one given to the first question. Forty-two percent preferred the stay-out option; 32 percent supported sending equipment; and 14 percent approved of sending troops.

In July 1977, Roper used a similar structure and asked: "What should the United States do in case of a war between Israel and the Arab countries?" Three options were provided: "take no sides," "support Israel with arms and economic aid," and "send troops." Roper's results were very similar to those of the second question in the *Newsweek*-Gallup poll—42 percent preferred to "take no sides," 34 percent were in favor of economic and military aid, and 16 percent supported "sending troops."[47] In comparison to the responses in table 2–3, the results of the *Newsweek*-Gallup and Roper polls were much more favorable to Israel. In these polls, considerably fewer Americans (42 percent) advocated the stay-out policy, and many more (between 14 and 16 percent) favored the send-troops option.

Comparative Opinions on Sending Troops to Israel

As in the question of military aid, the issue of American military involvement on behalf of Israel in hypothetical threatening situations appeared in a comparison of Israel with other American allies. Table 6–6 shows Israel in the lower part of a 12-nation list, with only 9 to 12 percent of the samples favoring the sending of American troops to defend it against a potential attack of Communist or Communist-backed forces. On the other hand, in all three polls, Israel received the highest percentages in the "send supplies" column.

Bruce Russett and Miroslav Nincic were surprised by the low percentage of Americans who were willing to commit American troops to Israel in case of Communist aggression. In a study of variables determining public willingness to send U.S. troops abroad, they had predicted that a much higher percentage (25) would support sending troops to aid Israel.[48] According to their first explanation, this result might have been caused by the phrasing of the question in the 1969 poll. In this poll, the question dealing with Israel was different from that used for all other countries. The phrase "if it looked as though Israel would be overrun by the Arabs with Russian help" could have been perceived by Americans as less threatening than the phrase "being attacked by Communist-backed forces," which was employed for all of the other countries (table 6–6). This explanation is weak, however, and the results of the 1971 and 1975 surveys were not that much higher than those of 1969.

A further explanation might be more convincing. The circumstances in table 6–6 were presented in a hypothetical context. But in some cases, it was only a remote possibility that U.S. involvement would be necessary, as in the case of Canada and Mexico, while in others, such as Israel, this need could

Table 6–6
Preferred U.S. Response in the Event a Nation Is Attacked by Communist-Backed Forces

Questions

(a) If (*country*) were invaded by outside Communist forces would you favor American action with U.S. armed forces, military and economic aid or stay out? (*Time*-Harris, 1969)

(b) In the event a nation is attacked by Communist-backed forces, there are several things the U.S. can do about it. As I read the name of each country, tell me what action you would want to see us take if that nation is actually attacked—send American troops or send military supplies but not send American troops or refuse to get involved. (Gallup, 1971, 1975)

	Send Troops			*Send Supplies*			*Stay Out*			*Don't Know*		
Country[a]	*1969*	*1971*	*1975*	*1969*	*1971*	*1975*	*1969*	*1971*	*1975*	*1969*	*1971*	*1975*
Canada	57%	—	57%	22%	—	19%	11%	—	14%	10%	—	10%
Mexico	52	45	42	24	26	25	13	19	23	11	10	10
England	—	37	37	—	33	30	—	19	24	—	11	9
Philippines	30	—	29	17	—	34	19	—	26	34	—	11
W. Germany	38	28	27	21	41	32	28	22	33	13	9	8
Japan	27	17	16	15	34	35	21	38	40	37	11	9
Brazil	34	16	15	18	36	33	28	33	39	20	15	13
Israel	9	11	12	35	44	42	39	33	37	17	12	9
Thailand	25	11	10	15	36	32	37	38	46	23	15	12
Turkey	—	10	9	—	36	29	—	37	49	—	17	13
Taiwan	26	11	8	15	30	27	36	45	54	23	14	11

Sources: (a) *Time*, May 2, 1969, 20–21. (b) *New York Times*, May 11, 1975.

[a]Ranking was done according to the "send troops" column for 1975.

have been seen as significantly more plausible. After all, within a period of just 6 years, between 1967 and 1973, Israel fought three major wars against the Arabs (the Six-Day War, the War of Attrition, and the Yom Kippur War) and only the first was won decisively. The Soviet Union was heavily involved in these wars and assumed combat roles during the War of Attrition. The polls measuring attitudes toward possible U.S. military involvement in the Middle East were conducted during this period, and their results could have been affected by the likelihood and frequency of Arab-Israeli wars. In addition, the proximity of a country increases support for military intervention. Therefore, it is not surprising to find that Canada and Mexico appeared at the top of the list in table 6–6.

The third group of questions and responses yielded much higher rates of support for the dispatching of American troops to help Israel. Table 6–7 shows results of polls conducted from 1967 until 1985. All these polls presented the respondents with only one choice—favoring or opposing U.S. military involvement on behalf of Israel, besides a "do not know" option. All questions provided a hypothetical context of extreme danger to the Jewish state. The three polls conducted by Harris in 1971 and 1973 mentioned the Soviet factor. Most of the polls presented various circumstances around the world that might justify sending U.S. troops to Israel, including an Arab invasion. All results in table 6–7 were negative, but by different ratios.

The lowest rates and the largest negative ratios in table 6–7 were obtained in July and November 1978, when Egypt and Israel were involved in intensive peace negotiations. The November 1978 poll was conducted after the conclusion of the Camp David summit conference and the signing of the two frameworks for peace in the Middle East. Perhaps the successful peace process rendered an Arab invasion of Israel less probable in American eyes, hence the low support for U.S. intervention.

The highest rates of support for direct American military involvement on behalf of Israel were recorded in December 1979 and February 1980 (*Newsweek*-Gallup). The reasons for these results are fairly clear. They appeared in a period of dramatic change in U.S. policy on military involvement abroad.[49] This change came about following the fall of the Shah of Iran, the Soviet invasion of Afghanistan, and the hostage crisis in Tehran. Immediately after these events, Carter, in his 1980 State of the Union address, announced a new American doctrine for the Middle East. The Carter doctrine defined "red lines" in the Persian Gulf and expressed an American determination to defend its interests and those of its allies in the Middle East by all means, including military force.[50] The dramatic events in the northern tier of the Middle East accentuated the importance of Israel to the United States as a stable and strong democratic country, and this image could have contributed to the relatively high rates of December 1979 and February 1980.

The difference of 8 percent (in the "favor" column for February 1980)

Table 6–7
Attitudes toward Sending Troops to Israel in the Event of Arab Invasion, 1967–85

Question

There has been some discussion about the circumstances that might justify using U.S. troops in other parts of the world. I'd like to ask your opinion about several different situations. Would you favor or oppose the use of U.S. troops if Arab forces invaded Israel?

Date	*Poll*	*Favor*	*Oppose*	*D.K.*
June '67	Harris	24%	56%	20%
Jan. '71	Harris[a]	39	44	17
July '71	Harris[a]	25	52	23
Dec. '73	Harris[a]	34	51	15
Dec. '74	Harris-Chicago[b]	27	50	23
Jan. '75	Harris	23	55	22
Aug. '75	Caddell[c]	24	57	19
July '78	Roper	21	65	14
Nov. '78	Gallup-Chicago	22	63	15
Dec. '79	*Newsweek*-Gallup	40	49	11
Feb. '80	Roper	35	47	18
Feb. '80	*Newsweek*-Gallup	43	47	10
Oct. '80	*Newsweek*-Gallup	29	57	14
Feb. '81	Roper	26	58	16
July '81	Roper	28	61	11
Nov. '82	Gallup-Chicago	30	70	—
Nov. '83	Roper	37	47	16
Mar. '85	*Newsweek*-Gallup	35	50	15

Sources: Harris: "American Public Opinion," *American Jewish Year Book* 69(1968), 199; Seymour M. Lipset and William Schneider, "Carter vs. Israel What the Polls Reveal," 64 *Commentary* (November 1977): 24. Harris-Chicago, Roper (1978–81): *Public Opinion* 3(February–March 1980): 26; 4(December–January 1982): 45. *Newsweek*-Gallup: *Newsweek*, December 17, 1979; October 27, 1980; April 15, 1985; Gallup-Chicago: John E. Rielly, ed., *American Public Opinion and U.S. Foreign Policy, 1983*, 31. Caddell: Lipset and Schneider, 23; Roper (1983): *Public Opinion* 7(April–May 1984): 35.

[a]The question in 1971 and 1973 was: "Suppose it looked as though the Arabs with the help of the Russians were going to take over Israel in the Middle East. Would you favor or oppose sending U.S. troops to keep Israel from being taken over?" In the 1975 poll, the Russians were omitted.

[b]Poll commissioned for the Chicago Council on Foreign Relations.

[c]The question solicited opinions on "sending troops to protect Israel."

between the *Newsweek*-Gallup and Roper polls is too high for the standard statistical deviation and cannot be explained. The results of November 1982 found in the survey Gallup conducted for the Chicago Council on Foreign Relations are also interesting. These results were obtained after the highly controversial and debated Israeli war in Lebanon. Yet despite the war, the figure in the "favor" column was the highest since February 1980. But the figure in the "oppose" column was also the highest for the entire period. It appears that the war sharpened the division in U.S. public opinion on that issue.

The data in table 6–7 were extracted from surveys on American attitudes toward U.S. military involvement on behalf of various countries in various hypothetical circumstances. Therefore, it should be interesting to compare the results for Israel with the results for other countries and events when the choice of answers is restricted to "favor" and "oppose." Table 6–8 presents this comparison.

Table 6–8 indicates that the highest rates of approval were accorded to situations in which the Soviet Union attacked America's most important allies—Western Europe and Japan. In 1978, the majority of Americans approved U.S. military involvement only in response to a Soviet invasion of Western Europe. In 1982, the majority also supported the use of American troops against possible Soviet invasion of Japan. In 1983, a majority favored U.S. military intervention in case Cuban troops were involved in a Communist takeover in a Central American country. In all other hypothetical circumstances, the majority opposed American military involvement, including situations defined as threatening to vital U.S. interests. For example, in 1978, only 36 percent, and in 1982, 39 percent, approved of the use of American troops in response to the Arabs cutting off the supply of oil in America. Involvement on behalf of Israel was ranked in the middle of the list. The use of troops to counter an Iranian invasion of Saudi Arabia or a North Korean invasion of South Korea received lower rates of approval.

Table 6–8 indicates that, in general, from 1978 to 1983, Americans were more willing to use military force overseas.[51] The polls registered substantial increases in the number of Americans (8 and 11 percent, respectively) ready to approve of the use of troops in the event the Arabs invaded Israel. Only in the first two situations—Soviet aggression in the Gallup poll and the Cuban intervention in the Roper poll—were there greater increases. Several other surveys revealed a change in American attitudes toward defense spending and military involvement.[52] This change was caused by a combination of several developments that included the end of détente, the Soviet invasion of Afghanistan, the Solidarity crisis in Poland, the revolution in Iran, the hostage crisis, and the election of Reagan to the presidency in 1980. These and other events reversed the post-Vietnam tendency to minimize the role of military force in American foreign policy.[53] Table 6–8 indicates that Americans are still selective

Table 6–8
Opinions on U.S. Military Response to Crisis Situations

Question

There has been some discussion about the circumstances that might justify using U.S. troops in other parts of the world. I'd like to ask your opinion about several situations. Would you favor or oppose the use of U.S. troops if . . . (Gallup Poll for the Chicago Council on Foreign Relations, and Roper)

	Gallup 1978		*Gallup 1982*			*Roper 1981*		*Roper 1983*		
Situations	*Favor*	*Oppose*	*Favor*	*Oppose*	*Change*	*Favor*	*Oppose*	*Favor*	*Oppose*	*Change*
Soviets invade Western Europe	54%	46%	65%	35%	+11%	51%	35%	61%	30%	+10%
Soviets invade Japan	42	58	51	49	+ 9	—	—	—	—	—
Arabs cut off oil to U.S.	36	64	39	61	+ 3	39[a]	45[a]	—	—	—
Soviets invade Poland	—	—	31	69	—	23	58	28	58	+ 5
Arabs invade Israel	22	78	30	70	+ 8	26	58	37	47	+11
Iran invades Saudi Arabia	—	—	25	75	—	22	64	26	55	+ 4
Saudi Araba invaded by Mideast country										
N. Korea invades S. Korea	21	79	22	78	+ 1	20	63	27	56	+ 7
Soviets invade China										
China invades Taiwan	20	80	18	82	− 2	—	—	—	—	—
Cuban troops help in a Communist takeover in Central America	—	—	—	—	—	42	42	56	31	+14

Sources: Gallup: *American Public Opinion and U.S. Foreign Policy, 1983*, p. 31. Roper: Benson, "The Polls: U.S. Military Intervention," 593; and "Opinion Roundup," *Public Opinion* 7(April–May 1984): 35.

[a]Scores for February 1980.

about U.S. involvement abroad and that the increase in the willingness to use force has applied only in certain circumstances and to specific countries, which at times include Israel.[54]

Attitudes toward Aid as a Means of Pressure

In 1985, U.S. aid to Israel accounted for about 12 percent of the Israeli government budget. Since the early 1980s, the United States has subsidized between one-fourth and one-third of Israel's defense spending. This growth in American aid to Israel since 1973 and the crucial importance of this aid to the Israeli economy have made Israel more dependent on the United States. This dependence has given the United States some leverage over Israel.[55] Although Vice-President Walter Mondale stated in June 1977, "We do not intend to use our military aid as pressure on Israel," there have been a few cases in which granting, delaying, or withholding military aid was used to exert pressure on Israel.[56]

According to one interpretation, during the 1973 Yom Kippur War, Kissinger stalled on the airlift in order to force a no-win, no-lose situation on both sides. In March 1975, upon Kissinger's recommendation, President Ford announced a reassessment of U.S. policy in the Middle East. Its purpose was to apply pressure on Israel to make concessions to Egypt as part of the interim agreement, by delaying the processing of the new Israeli request for weapons.[57] No public opinion polls were conducted on this subtle application of pressure on Israel, but on May 21, 1975, 76 senators wrote a letter to President Ford protesting this action:

> We believe that preserving the peace requires that Israel obtain a level of military and economic support adequate to deter a renewal of war by Israel's neighbors. *Withholding military equipment from Israel would be dangerous, discouraging accommodation by Israel's neighbors and encouraging a resort to force.*[58] (emphasis added)

This letter limited the Ford-Kissinger intention to use military aid as an effective means of pressure against Israel. Furthermore, the letter reflected public opinion on this matter. Polls taken by Gallup and Harris in April and May 1975 found substantial support for military aid to Israel. The Gallup results were 54 versus 37 percent in favor of military aid (see table 6–6) and those of Harris were 62 versus 18 in favor of military aid (see question (c) in table 6–3). Ironically, perhaps, the "carrots" of aid, not the "sticks," contributed to the changes in the Israeli positions that finally led, in late August, to the signing of the 1975 interim agreement. In a special U.S.-Israeli Memorandum of Agreement, which was an integral part of the interim agreement, the United States made the following pledge:

> The U.S. Government will make every effort to be fully responsive, within the limits of its resources and Congressional authorization and appropriation, on an ongoing and long term basis, to Israel's military equipment and other defensive requirements, to its energy requirements and to its economic needs.[59]

In a statement delivered on September 16, Kissinger announced that in this commitment, the administration was responsive to the letter of the 76 senators. He also added, "In the present context our aid takes on new significance; it is central to our policy and vital to the chances for a lasting peace in the Middle East."[60]

In subsequent years, pollsters asked direct and specific questions about actual or potential uses of aid as a means of pressure on Israel in only a few exceptional cases. They can be classified into two distinct categories. The first includes questions that solicit opinions on possible cuts in American aid to make Israel do something. The second category includes questions that sought opinions on sanctions taken by the Reagan administration against Israel, probably with the intention of deterring Israel from taking actions that precipitated the punishment.

A question asked by an NBC News poll in March 1978 is a typical example of queries included in the first category. It read: "Do you agree or disagree with the following statement: The U.S. should cut off all aid to Israel unless Israel signs a peace agreement with her neighbors." This question was asked after a major breakdown in the Israeli-Egyptian peace talks, which probably affected the distribution of opinions—42 percent agreed with the statement and 46 percent disagreed.[61]

A CBS-*NYT* poll of congressmen revealed, in April 1982, opposition of 53 to 30 percent to the use of "U.S. arms sales to Israel as a way of bringing pressure on it to negotiate with the Palestinians."[62] The preceding examples present straightforward statements, but a question on the use of aid as a means of pressure, which appeared in the *Newsweek*-Gallup poll of September 1982, suggested a misleading context. The question was, "Do you think U.S. aid to Israel should be suspended or reduced in order to force a pullout of Israeli forces from Lebanon?"[63] The response was 50 versus 38 percent in favor of suspension; but the circumstances of the time (the massacre in Beirut) and the formulation of the question—as if the United States wanted Israel to pull out and the only issue was whether to cut aid for this purpose—led to the outcome in favor of pressure.

As mentioned earlier, pollsters employed questions that sought opinions on the actual suspension of aid to Israel as a means of punishment. In response to the 1981 Israeli attacks on the Iraqi nuclear reactor and the PLO headquarters in Beirut, the Reagan administration suspended delivery of F-16 combat airplanes to Israel. A *Newsweek*-Gallup poll asked whether this suspension should continue and received a 61 to 30 percent affirmative response.[64] But a year later, under similar circumstances, an NBC News poll found a close plurality of 46 to 44 percent opposing reduction in military aid to Israel.[65]

To gain a better understanding of the preceding results, it would be useful to compare them with responses to other questions dealing with aid to Israel asked at approximately the same time. In March 1978, for example, the NBC poll found only a close plurality opposing the use of aid as a means of pressuring Israel into "signing a peace agreement," presumably one that it could not accept. But at the same time, a much higher percentage, 68 versus 19 percent, supported military aid to Israel (see question (c) in table 6–3). In July 1981, the *Newsweek*-Gallup poll found support for the continuing suspension of the F-16 delivery, but almost at the same time, a poll by Penn and Schoen found that 71 percent supported either an increase in aid or maintenance at the same level. In this poll, only 22 percent thought aid to Israel should be decreased (see question (a) in table 6–2).

The paucity of data on the issue of aid as a means of pressure permits only tentative inferences. First, American public opinion has distinguished between the basic American aid commitment to Israel and use of this aid to pressure Israel. It has favored the first and has had reservations about the second. The public seemed to oppose the use of aid as a means of extracting concessions from Israel to the Arabs but tended to agree with American punitive action taken in extreme controversial cases of tension and disagreement between the two countries.

Conclusions

The magnitude of the economic and military aid the United States has extended to Israel in the last decade is certainly unique. Laufer, who studied this subject, concluded that "the secret of Israel's success remains the continued support for Israel in American public opinion, and the effective articulation of this support by the organized Jewish community in relation to the administration and particularly the Congress."[66] The main finding of this chapter is that general sympathy for Israel in American public opinion has indeed been translated into support for U.S. assistance to Israel and that this support is even more impressive in the light of American opinions on foreign aid in general.

Polls on American military aid to Israel yielded rates of support ranging from 75 to 24 percent. Tables 6–2 through 6–6 indicate that polls conducted at the same time yielded very different results. Two polls conducted in October 1973 (question (a) in table 6–3 and question (a) in table 6–4) produced opposite results. Polls conducted within a period of 3 months (November 1974 to January 1975) found rates of support for military aid to Israel ranging from 66 to 28 percent (see tables 6–3, 6–4, and 6–5). In a single poll taken in January 1975, Yankelovich asked two different questions and received very different results. Four polls taken in March 1978 also produced very different results (see question (b) in table 6–2; questions (a) and (c) in table 6–3; and question (a) in table 6–4). It seems, then, that the phrasing of questions and answers, contexts, and information affected the distribution of responses. Support for aid to Israel was the strongest in responses to questions that emphasized Soviet military aid to Arab countries, Arab aggression, and blackmail or Communist threats. Support for aid was the weakest in response to questions that mentioned supply of arms and material to both Israel and the Arabs or a price tag.

Lipset and Schneider, who investigated polls on aid to Israel, found another interesting phenomenon.[67] Whenever aid to Israel appeared in polls on Israel or the Arab-Israeli conflict, it received much greater support than it did in polls that examined the same issue in a context of American aid to other countries. They argued that foreign aid in general was not popular in American public opinion; therefore, when aid to Israel was mentioned in this context, it received relatively lower rates of support. In other polls dealing only with Israel or the Arab-Israeli conflict, the same issue received greater support. Data collected in this chapter indicate that of 41 responses to questions on aid to Israel, the supporters outnumbered the opponents in 33. Despite the variation in results, the American public has strongly supported economic and military assistance to Israel.

Results of polls on the issue of dispatching U.S. troops to aid Israel in a hypothetical critical situation also varied considerably. This variation is again probably related to the framing of questions.[68] When military involvement was presented as one of many options available to the United States in the Middle East, it received relatively little support—between 1 and 2 percent (table 2–3). When the public was offered three choices—supply weapons, send troops, or stay out—the send-troops option was approved by 9 to 16 percent of the respondents. Finally, when only one choice was given—favoring or opposing the dispatching of troops—this option received support in the range of 21 to 43 percent (table 6–7). The main conclusion of this reaction is that the public has been hesitant in its support for direct American military intervention on behalf of Israel, even in critical situations. However, according to the polls, the public showed little enthusiasm for U.S. military involvement anywhere. In addition, most experts on this issue agreed that "the willingness of the public to aid in the defense of a country varied almost directly with the proximity of that country to the U.S."[69] Thus, direct involvement on behalf of Mexico and Canada received much more support than involvement on behalf of other U.S. allies, including Israel. It should also be noted that opinions on hypothetical situations may not necessarily be consistent with actual, critical situations. American public opinion supported all cases of U.S. military involvement abroad since World War II, including the involvement in Vietnam until the war became too long, costly, purposeless, and controversial.[70]

The last section of this chapter demonstrates that the public was quite divided on the issue of employing aid to dictate policies to Israel. The public has generally opposed reduction or suspension of aid in an attempt to extract concessions from Israel to the Arabs but supported Reagan's withholding of arms supplies to Israel in the very few cases of high tension and disagreement between the two countries.

Although presidents may favor providing economic and military aid to American allies, the Congress must authorize all aid programs and therefore plays a key role in the shaping of the U.S. aid policy. An examination of the congressional role in the processing of aid to Israel shows an interesting aberration.[71] In general, the Congress has been very critical of U.S. aid programs and has thoroughly scrutinized them. In the case of Israel, it has shown more leniency. Moreover, on many occasions it has added funds to the original presidential requests by as much as 30 percent or has improved the terms and conditions of the aid—for example, favoring grants over loans. The Congress has also initiated special aid programs for Israel.[72]

The congressional actions on aid to Israel could not have been possible without strong general support for Israel and specific support for aid to Israel in American public opinion.[73] The relative popularity of aid to Israel can be appreciated only if it is compared to the relative unpopularity of aid in general and aid to specific countries in particular. Apparently, this finding was known to several presidents and policymakers who used aid to Israel as a vehicle for obtaining congressional approval for aid to other, less popular countries or for the entire foreign aid bill.

Notes

1. George Liska, *The New Statecraft: Foreign Aid in American Foreign Policy* (Chicago: University of Chicago Press, 1960); and Robert Wendzel, *International Politics* (New York: Wiley, 1981), 250–63.

2. U.S. Agency for International Development, *U.S. Overseas Loans and Grants and Assistance from International Organizations, Obligations and Loan Authorizations,* July 1, 1945–September 30, 1982 (Washington, D.C.: AID, 1983).

3. Cecil V. Crabb, Jr., and Pat M. Holt, *Invitation to Struggle: Congress, the President and Foreign Policy* (Washington, D.C.: Congressional Quarterly Press, 1980), 41–43; and Michael K. O'Leary, *The Politics of American Foreign Aid* (New York: Atherton, 1967).

4. John D. Montgomery, *Foreign Aid in International Politics* (Englewood Cliffs, N.J.: Prentice-Hall, 1967), chs. 1, 2; and Joan M. Nelson, *AID, Influence, and Foreign Policy* (New York: Macmillan, 1968).

5. On security assistance and its problems, see Caesar Sereseres, "U.S. Military Assistance to Nonindustrial Nations," in Ellen Stern, ed., *The Limits of Military Intervention* (Beverly Hills, Calif.: Sage, 1977), 216–19; and Ernest Graves and Steven A. Hildreth, eds., *U.S. Security Assistance, The Political Process* (Lexington, Mass.: Lexington Books, 1984.)

6. Bruce W. McDaniel, "American Technical Assistance and Economic Aid in Israel," *Middle Eastern Affairs* 6(October 1955): 303–18.

7. John Felton, "Reagan Will Weigh Huge Boost in Aid to Israel," *Congressional Quarterly* (December 29, 1984): 3159.

8. For a survey of U.S. aid to Israel since 1948, see Leopold Yehuda Laufer, *U.S. Aid to Israel: Problems and Perspectives*, Policy Oriented Publications No. 7 (Jerusalem: Leonard Davis Institute for International Relations, U.S.-Israel Project, May 1983). See also Clyde R. Mark, *Foreign Assistance to the State of Israel: A Compilation of Basic Data* (Washington, D.C.: Library of Congress, Congressional Research Service, 1976).

9. See Shlomo Slonim, "The 1948 American Embargo on Arms to Palestine," *Political Science Quarterly* 94(Fall 1979): 495–514.

10. Mordechai Gazit, *Israeli Military Procurement from the U.S.* Policy Oriented Publications No. 8 (Jerusalem: Leonard Davis Institute for International Relations, U.S.-Israel Project, May 1983), 15-24.

11. Paul Jabber, *Not By War Alone* (Berkeley: University of California Press, 1981), ch. 4.

12. Jon D. Glassman, *Arms for the Arabs: The Soviet Union and War in the Middle East* (Baltimore: Johns Hopkins University Press, 1975), ch. 2.

13. Sylvia F. Crosbie, *A Tacit Alliance: France and Israel from Suez to the Six Day War* (Princeton, N.J.: Princeton University Press, 1974).

14. Mordechai Gazit, *President Kennedy's Policy Toward the Arab States and Israel* (Tel Aviv: Tel Aviv University, Shiloah Center for Middle Eastern and African Studies, 1983), 41-46.

15. On Nixon's arms policy toward Israel, see Lewis Sorley, *Arms Transfer Under Nixon* (Lexington: University Press of Kentucky, 1983), ch. 4.

16. U.S. Senate, Committee on Foreign Relations, *Arms Sales Package to Saudi Arabia, Hearings*, 97th Cong., parts 1, 2, October 1, 5, 6, 14 and 15, 1981 (Washington, D.C.: Government Printing Office, 1981).

17. *New York Times*, February 17, 1982.

18. Israel lost about 800 tanks and 100 fighter aircraft. See Chaim Herzog, *The Arab-Israeli Wars* (London: Arms and Armour Press, 1982), 306, 310–11; and Netanel Lorch, *One Long War* (Jerusalem: Keter, 1976), 212.

19. Marvin Feuerwerger, "The Emergency Security Assistance Act of 1973 and American-Israeli Relations," *Midstream* 20(August-September 1974): 20-38.

20. Roger F. Pajak, "The Effectiveness of Soviet Arms Aid Diplomacy in the Third World," in Robert H. Donaldson, ed., *The Soviet Union in the Third World: Successes and Failures* (Boulder, Colo.: Westview Press, 1981), 393; and Roger E. Kanet

and Rajam M. Menon, "Soviet Policy Toward the Third World," in Donald R. Kelley, ed., *Soviet Politics in the Brezhnev Era* (New York: Praeger, 1980), 235–66.

21. U.S. Arms Control and Disarmament Agency, *World Military Expenditures and Arms Transfers, 1985* (Washington, D.C.: Government Printing Office, August 1985), 134.

22. Paul Rivlin, "The Burden of Israel's Defence," *Survival* 20(July-August 1978): 146–54.

23. See Anne Hessing Cahn, "U.S. Arms to the Middle East, 1967-1976: A. Critical Examination," in Milton Leitenberg and Gabriel Sheffer, eds., *Great Power Intervention in the Middle East* (New York: Pergamon, 1979), 101–33.

24. AIPAC memorandum, January 1985.

25. Bernard Reich, *The United States and Israel: Influence in the Special Relationship* (New York: Praeger, 1984), 150.

26. Steven L. Spiegel, "Israel as a Strategic Asset," *Commentary* 75(June 1983): 51–55.

27. Ralph B. Levering, *The Public and American Foreign Policy, 1918–1978* (New York: Morrow, 1978), 137–38; O'Leary, *The Politics of American Foreign Aid*, ch. 3; Paul Laudicina, *World Poverty and Development: A Survey of American Opinion* (Washington, D.C.: 1973); and Richard Dawson, *Public Opinion and Contemporary Disarray* (New York: Harper & Row, 1973), 29-33.

28. Lloyd A. Free and Hadley Cantril, *The Political Beliefs of Americans: A Study of Public Opinion* (New York: Simon and Schuster, 1968), 72–75.

29. However, a sample of leaders that was included in the poll for the Chicago Council on Foreign Relations sharply disagreed with the general-public sample on this issue: 60 percent supported military aid, and 67 percent supported sales of military equipment. John E. Rielly, ed., *American Public Opinion and U.S. Foreign Policy 1983.* (Chicago: Chicago Council on Foreign Relations, 1983), 27. See also Walter Slocombe, et al., *The Pursuit of National Security, Defense and the Military Balance* (Washington, D.C.: Potomac Associates, May 1976), 33-34.

30. *Jerusalem Post*, September 8, 1975.

31. Cited and analyzed in Seymour Martin Lipset and William Schneider, *Israel and the Jews in American Public Opinion* (New York: American Jewish Committee, 1977, Mimeographed) 23.

32. Steven J. Rosen and Yosef I. Abramowitz, *How Americans Feel About Israel*, AIPAC Papers on U.S.-Israel Relations, No. 10 (Washington, D.C.: American Israel Public Affairs Committee, 1984), 23.

33. This and the other questions on the AWACS deal are cited in ibid., 43, 25.

34. Geraldine Rosenfield, *Similarities and Differences Between Recent Polls of American Opinion Regarding Israel and the Jews*, No. 75.185.2 (New York: American Jewish Committee, Information and Research Services, June 1975).

35. Reich, *The U.S. and Israel*, 62, 167; and Seth P. Tillman, *The United States in the Middle East: Interests and Obstacles* (Bloomington: Indiana University Press, 1982), 98-106.

36. George Gallup, *The Gallup Poll: Public Opinion, 1972-1977*, vol. I (Wilmington, Del.: Scholarly Resources, 1981), 568.

37. *Christian Science Monitor*, September 9, 1975.

38. Gallup established a correlation between opposition to the U.S. peacekeeping role and the estimate of the likelihood of war in the Middle East. A majority of those who envisioned a new war also opposed the peacekeeping role.

39. It is interesting to note that a sample of participants in the "Great Decisions" foreign policy discussion program of the Foreign Policy Association approved, in May 1976, the dispatching of U.S. technicians to the Sinai by a majority of 66 to 21 percent; see *FPA Outreacher* (July 1976).

40. Bruce Russett, "The Americans' Retreat From World Power," *Political Science Quarterly* 90(Spring 1975): 1-22. Michael Ruskin attributed the shift to isolationism to generational differences in "From Pearl Harbor to Vietnam: Shifting Generational Paradigms," *Political Science Quarterly* 89(Fall 1974): 563-588; but this explanation was contradicted in Ole Holsti and James Rosenau, "Does Where You Stand Depend on When You Were Born?" *Public Opinion Quarterly* 44(Spring 1980): 1-22. Holsti and Rosenau also argued against the tendency to use simple labels such as "hawk" or "dove" in the attempt to characterize American attitudes toward military involvement abroad; see their article "Cold War Axioms in the Post Vietnam Era," in Ole Holsti, Randolph Siverson, and Alexander George, eds., *Change in the International System* (Boulder, Colo.: Westview Press, 1980).

41. John Benson, "The Polls: U.S. Military Intervention," *Public Opinion Quarterly* 46(Winter 1982): 592.

42. See, for example, the suggestion of Senator William Fulbright, *Congressional Record*, Senate, August 24, 1970, 29805. See also Mark A. Bruzonsky, *A U.S. Guarantee for Israel* (Washington, D.C.: Georgetown University, Center for Strategic and International Studies, 1976); and Richard Ullman, "Alliance with Israel," *Foreign Policy* 19(Summer 1975): 18-33.

43. Michael Handel, *Israel's Political Military Doctrine* (Cambridge: Harvard University, Center for International Affairs, Occasional Papers Series, 1974); and Efraim Inbar, "Israeli Strategic Thinking after 1973," *Journal of Strategic Studies* 6(March 1983): 36-59.

44. Both statements are cited in Reich, *The United States and Israel*, 209–10.

45. Yaacov Bar-Siman-Tov, *The Israeli-Egyptian War of Attrition, 1969-1970* (New York: Columbia University Press, 1980), 169.

46. *Newsweek*, December 14, 1970.

47. Cited in Lipset and Schneider, "Carter vs. Israel: What the Polls Reveal," *Commentary* 64(November 1977): 23-24.

48. Bruce Russett and Miroslav Nincic, "American Opinion on the Use of Military Force Abroad," *Political Science Quarterly* 91(Fall 1976): 422.

49. See Charles W. Kegley, Jr., and Eugene R. Wittkopf, "The Reagan Administration's World View," *Orbis* 26(Spring 1982): 232–35.

50. For the text of Carter's speech, see *Public Papers of the Presidents of the U.S.: Jimmy Carter, 1980-1981*, (Washington, D.C.: Government Printing Office, 1981), 197.

51. For a cautious interpretation of this finding, see John E. Rielly, "American Opinion: Continuity Not Reaganism," *Foreign Policy* 50(Spring 1983): 86-104.

52. See, for example, Louis Kriesberg and Ross Klien, "Changes in Public Support for U.S. Military Spending," *Journal of Conflict Resolution* 24(March 1980): 79-111.

53. On this change, see Bruce Russett and Donald R. Deluca, "'Don't Tread on Me': Public Opinion and Foreign Policy in the Eighties," *Political Science Quarterly* 96(Fall 1981): 381–99; Daniel Yankelovich and Larry Kaagan, "Assertive America," *Foreign Affairs* 59(Winter 1980): 696-713.

54. Alvin Richman, "Public Attitudes on Military Power, 1981" *Public Opinion* 4(December 1981–January 1982): 44-46.

55. David Pollock, *The Politics of Pressure: American Arms and Israeli Policy Since the Six Day War* (Westport, Conn.: Greenwood Press, 1982), 185-96.

56. *New York Times,* June 18, 1977.

57. Abraham Ben-Zvi, *Alliance Politics and the Limits of Influence: The Case of the U.S. and Israel, 1975-1983,* Paper No. 24, (Tel Aviv: Tel Aviv University, Jaffe Center for Strategic Studies, April 1984), 12-21.

58. *New York Times,* May 22, 1975.

59. Edward Sheehan, *The Arabs, Israelis, and Kissinger: A Secret History of American Diplomacy in the Middle East* (New York: Crowell, 1976), 253, 256.

60. *The Quest for Peace,* Principal U.S. Public Statements and Related Documents on the Arab-Israeli Peace Process, 1967-1983 (Washington, D.C.: U.S. Department of State, 1984), 64.

61. *NBC News Poll,* March 23, 1978.

62. *New York Times,* April 11, 1982.

63. *Newsweek,* October 4, 1982, 11.

64. *Newsweek,* August 3, 1981, 16.

65. *NBC News Poll,* June 14-16, 1982.

66. Laufer, *U.S. Aid,* 29.

67. Seymour Martin Lipset and William Schneider, "Carter vs. Israel: What the Polls Reveal," 24.

68. For several other methodological problems in polls on military involvement, see John Mueller, "Changes in American Public Attitudes Toward International Involvement," in Stern, ed., *The Limits of Military Intervention,* 323–44; and Richard F. Hamilton, "A Research Note on the Mass Support for 'Tough' Military Initiatives," *American Sociological Review* 33(June 1968): 439–45.

69. Albert H. Cantril and Charles W. Roll, Jr., *Hopes and Fears of the American People* (New York: Universe Books, 1971), 45.

70. See John E. Mueller, *War, Presidents and Public Opinion* (New York: Wiley, 1973).

71. Crabb and Holt, *Invitation to Struggle,* ch. 4.

72. Marvin C. Feuerwerger, *Congress and Israel: Foreign Aid Decision-Making in the House of Representatives, 1969–1976* (Westport, Conn.: Greenwood Press, 1979).

73. John Felton, "Budget Cutting Fervor, Politics, and New Burdens for Foreign Aid Programs," *Congressional Quarterly* (October 25, 1980): 3213.

7
Opinions of American Jewry

Almost every book written on American Jewry includes reference to the significant role of Israel in the lives of American Jews. Similarly, most literature on the history of Israel and subsequent American-Israeli relations includes numerous references to the important contributions of American Jewry to Israel. The two largest Jewish communities of our times have certainly established a unique partnership and a special relationship.

Active Zionism, the movement for return to the ancient homeland and for Jewish nationalism and statehood, has never been popular among American Jews, and American Zionist organizations have never attracted a large membership.[1] Yet from the beginning of the effort to revive Jewish nationalism in Israel, the great majority of American Jews have accorded it their full support. This support was crucial in the critical days of November 1947 and May 1948, when Israel fought for its independence.[2] The birth of Israel had many dramatic effects on American Jews. Although it increased the disintegration and dissolution of most traditional Jewish ideologies, it created a new central focus for Jewish expression and identification.[3]

This chapter sheds light on the attitudes and opinions of American Jews toward Israel and Israel-related issues. The attachment of Jews to their homeland has always been one of the central tenets of Judaism. Without this bond, the attitudes of Jews, including American Jews, to Israel would be difficult to understand. Therefore, this chapter begins with an exploration of the nature and depth of the American-Jewish affinity with Israel.

Since Israel was created by a secular, national movement, would not the more observant and orthodox Jews be less devoted to Israel than are other groups and movements in American Judaism? This is examined in the second section of the chapter. Another issue analyzed is whether *Zionism* is identical to *pro-Israelism*—or whether these terms define two different approaches to Israel.

Chapter 6 discussed the amount of aid the United States has provided Israel over the years. American Jews have also contributed substantial amounts of money to Israel. The fourth section of this chapter presents and examines attitudes toward both governmental and private Jewish aid to Israel. The Arab-Israeli conflict has been a source of constant anxiety to most American Jews. Their opinions on critical issues of the conflict—such as the peacemaking process, the Palestinian question, and the status of Jerusalem—will be discussed in some detail. The chapter concludes with an analysis of an oft-discussed thorny problem—dual loyalty. Has the attachment of American Jews to Israel in any way compromised their loyalty to the United States.

The data for this chapter were collected and integrated from several surveys of American Jews. The design of a Jewish sample for these surveys has not been simple.[4] For example, the U.S. census does not include a question on religion, making it difficult for pollsters to define the exact size and boundaries of the American-Jewish community from which a representative sample could be drawn. Therefore, the first large surveys of Jewish attitudes were conducted in cities in which locating predominantly Jewish areas was relatively easier. The first survey of this kind was commissioned by the American Jewish Committee (AJC) and was conducted by NORC in Baltimore in May 1948, just a few days after the birth of Israel.[5]

A decade later, in 1957 and 1958, the AJC sponsored two surveys of Jews who lived in two typically Jewish-American milieus. The first survey was conducted between January and May 1957 in an industrial city on the East Coast. The real identity of the city was concealed. For the purposes of research, it was called Riverton, a city of 130,000 people, of whom 8,500 were Jews.[6] The second survey was conducted between October 1957 and May 1958 in "Lakeville," a Midwestern suburb of 25,000 people, of whom approximately 8,000 were Jews.[7] Although the sample of 200 Jewish families in Riverton was considered to be analogous to the views of about a third of American Jewry (excluding the Jews of New York), the Lakeville sample of 432 Jews was considered by its authors to be "representing to a greater or lesser extent the experiences of most American Jews."

Two further surveys, conducted in 1968—69 and 1970, targeted a more specific sample, producing a different dimension of American-Jewish attitudes. Charles Liebman investigated the views of rabbis and presidents of synagogues affiliated with the three main movements in American Jewry: Orthodox, Conservative, and Reform.[8] In 1970, Leonard Fein and others conducted a major survey of Reform Jews through a sample of 864 adults and 779 youngsters.[9]

In the early 1980s, the major polling agencies—Harris,[10] Gallup,[11] and Yankelovich[12]—took comprehensive polls of American-Jewish opinion, primarily on issues surrounding the Arab-Israeli conflict. At the same time, Steve M. Cohen and others experimented with an innovative sampling technique—random telephone dialing to persons with distinctive Jewish names (DJN).[13] These experiments produced four national surveys of American Jews—the National Survey of American Jews (NSAJ) in 1981, 1982, 1983, and 1984, under the sponsorship of the AJC.[14] The survey of 1983 included a separate poll of Jewish leaders.[15] Each poll in the NSAJ series included about 650 respondents.

The capsule history of poll-taking on the attitudes of American Jewry exposes a variety of samples and approaches. Nevertheless, several important questions and themes were repeated over time, and they provide a sufficient base for trend analysis.

American-Jewish Attachment to Israel

The first poll of American Jewry on attitudes toward Israel was probably conducted by Elmo Roper in September 1945, barely a few months after World War II. Roper asked a cross-sectional sample of American Jews to state its views on the following proposal:

> A Jewish state in Palestine is a good thing for the Jews and every possible effort should be made to establish Palestine as a Jewish state or commonwealth for those who want to settle there.[16]

About 80 percent of the respondents approved of this statement; 10 percent disapproved. In response to another question in the same survey, more than 80 percent rejected the notion that "Jews are a religious group only and not a nation, and it would be bad for the Jews to try to set up a Jewish state in Palestine or anywhere else."

Roper commented that the decision to support or oppose the establishment of Israel was taken with a high "degree of firmness" and that the supporters "were evenly distributed through all economic levels." About two months later, Gallup found overwhelming support in the American-Jewish community (90 to 10 percent) for the proposal to allow Jews to settle in Palestine.[17] In May 1948, just a few days after the birth of Israel, NORC asked the Jews in Baltimore:

> The Jews have set up a new Jewish state in part of Palestine. Do you approve or disapprove of this action by the Jews?[18]

Ninety percent approved of the establishment of Israel, and a similar percentage also thought that the United States was right to recognize Israel.[19] All of the initial surveys of American-Jewish opinion yielded highly favorable opinions on Israel. By overwhelming majorities of 90 to 10 percent, American Jews supported the establishment of Israel, Jewish immigration to Israel, the Israeli

Table 7–1
Feelings toward Israel, 1957–83

A. General Feelings

Date	*Poll*	*Favorable, Pro-Israel*	*Unfavorable, Anti-Israel*	*Neutral*	*(n)*
1957	Riverton	94%	5%		(200)
1972	Herman	91	9	—	(269)
1981	Yankelovich	96	4	—	(174)
1981	NSAJ	93	1	6	(673)
1982	NSAJ	88	1	11	(500)
1983	NSAJ	91	3	6	(640)

B. Feeling a Personal Sense of Loss If Israel Were Destroyed

Date	*Poll*	*Yes*	*No*	*Not Sure*	*(n)*
1957	Lakeville	90%	10%	—	(432)
1975	Harris	94	6	—	NA
1981[a]	NSAJ	83	13	5	(673)
1982[a]	NSAJ	83	9	8	(500)
1983[a]	NSAJ	77	10	13	(640)

Sources: For surveys presented in this and the remaining tables in this chapter, consult notes 5 through 14. Further survey scores will be cited as necessary. Herman: Simon N. Herman, *Jewish Identity, A Social Psychological Perspective* (Beverly Hills, Calif.: Sage, 1977), 213.

[a]Results for 1981, 1982 and 1983 were obtained in response to the following: "If Israel were destroyed I would feel as if I had suffered the *greatest* personal tragedy of my life."

Declaration of Independence, and the decision by President Truman to recognize Israel immediately after its birth.

Since the establishment of Israel, American Jewry has held highly favorable feelings toward it. Results of various polls on this question have been remarkably consistent. All but one of the scores for favorable feelings toward Israel in table 7–1 rank above 90 percent. The breakdown of the last score for 1983 shows an enormous affinity to Israel, among both the Jewish public and the leaders of the Jewish community. Of the 91 percent expressing favorable feelings toward Israel, 43 percent said that they were *very* pro-Israel, and 48 percent were pro-Israel. The combined score for all the remaining categories—neutral, anti-Israel, and very anti-Israel—was less than 10 percent.[20]

Since its inception, Israel has faced a large, hostile Arab world; this in turn, has generated American-Jewish concern about the state's ability to survive. In a 1981 Yankelovich survey, 93 percent of the respondents said that "the continuation of Israel as a Jewish state is important," and only 5 percent held the opposite opinion.[21] A better and perhaps more dramatic illustration of Israel's importance to American Jews is seen in the response to a query posing the hypothetical destruction of Israel. Results to question (b) in table 7–1 indicate that the great majority of American Jews would feel a great personal loss if Israel were destroyed. It should be noted that ratings of 83 and 77 percent, respectively, for 1981–82 and 1983 were achieved in response to the description of the loss of Israel as the "greatest personal tragedy" in the respondent's life.

In May–June 1967, the hypothetical situation of table 7–1 turned suddenly into a frightening reality. Many books and numerous articles were written on the reactions of world Jewry, particularly of American Jewry, to the Six-Day War.[22] Most described accounts of personal experiences, emphasizing themes of fear, anger, anxiety, and the memory of the Holocaust. The enormous Jewish activity in the United States on behalf of Israel during the crisis and war of 1967, the outpouring of volunteers and money, and the political campaign testified better than any public opinion poll to the strong attachment of American Jews to Israel.[23] The polls taken after the war basically reflected the concern and action of American Jewry on behalf of Israel.

Marshal Sklare, one of the authors of the 1957–58 Lakeville studies, returned to Lakeville in the early months of 1968 "to learn something about the response [of American Jewry] to the Israeli crisis, to the war, and to its aftermath."[24] Sklare called this mission "a reconnaissance effort." He was able to interview only 17 residents of Lakeville, 11 of whom were among the 432 persons of the original sample. Moreover, the socioeconomic structure of Lakeville did not make it the type of community "where one would look for a maximum response to the Six-Day War." Therefore, according to Sklare, "If we find that a given impact occurred in Lakeville, it would be fair to infer that this impact was at least as strong in the country at large."

Despite these obvious limitations, Sklare's "reconnaissance mission" yielded several interesting results. He found that during the crisis, most of the respondents were very concerned about the survival of Israel. They strongly supported the Israeli position and increased their financial contributions to the state. The decisive Israeli victory relieved them of tension and anxiety, giving them a sense of pride and confidence. These feelings were shared even by self—proclaimed anti-Zionists. On the other hand, most of the respondents did not reveal any eagerness to visit Israel, and to Sklare's surprise, they did not show greater philanthropic or political support for various efforts on behalf of Israel, at least as compared with the original 1957 results.[25]

At the same time, Simon Herman was investigating the Jewish identity of American-Jewish students studying in Israel. These students, personally experiencing the intense events of the war, were obviously subjected to different pressures from those of their counterparts in the United States. Nevertheless, the Herman findings on their reactions could illuminate another dimension in the American-Jewish bond to Israel. The following statement, which Herman cited, well represented the students' feelings:

> I'd say the biggest impact of the Six-Day War on me was the realization (the knowledge was there before June 1967) that the destruction of Israel meant the end of our one sign of hope in modern Jewish existence. American Jews couldn't live without Israel.[26]

Herman also found that 87 percent of the respondents indicated that they had been reminded of the Holocaust during the Six-Day War.

Although the foregoing studies dealt with feelings and opinions of specific groups in the American-Jewish community, they all produced similar results, indicating a basic attachment to Israel and its fate. This is supported by the actual behavior of American Jews during the Six-Day War and by the numerous accounts of individual experiences. Similar attitudes and behavior emerged during the 1973 Yom Kippur War.[27] Therefore, it could be argued that both critical wars tested and demonstrated the depth of the American-Jewish commitment to Israel's survival.

Religious Observance and Ethnic Identification with Israel

Undoubtedly, part of the American-Jewish attachment to Israel is rooted in religion and ethnic identity. This section explores whether various degrees of religious observance and affiliation with various movements in American Judaism have influenced attitudes toward Israel. In the Lakeville survey of 1957–58, the respondents were asked to rank qualities of the "good" Jew. One of the suggested qualities was defined as "support Israel." The same item appeared in the 1970 comprehensive survey of Reform Jews. The results of the two surveys are reported in table 7–2. Both surveys reveal that American Jewry accorded considerable importance to the support of Israel in their perception of the "good" Jew.

The results in table 7–2 should be interpreted with caution. The Lakeville study was based on a limited regional sample, whereas the survey of Reform Jews was based on a national sample. Second, the Lakeville survey included members of all three streams of American Judaism, whereas the survey of Reform Jews was limited to only one group. Finally, 13 years passed between the surveys. Because of these disparities, it is difficult to ascertain the causes of the variations between the two surveys.

Nevertheless, table 7–2 demonstrates that in 1970, the percentage of respondents who thought support to Israel is essential to being a good Jew was substantially higher than in 1957. Eighty-two percent in 1970, compared to 68

Table 7–2
Support for Israel and for Zionism

	Support Israel		*Support Zionism*	
	Lakeville	*Reform Jews*	*Lakeville*	*Reform Jews*
Percentage who believe that to be a "good" Jew, the item:				
Is essential	21%	37%	7%	13%
Is desirable	47	45	23	30
Makes no difference	32	17	59	49
Is essential not to do	0	1	9	8
Rank order of item of 22 total items	14	5	17	16
Rank order of item of 14 items of specifically Jewish content	7	2	9	9

Polls: Lakeville, $n = 432$; Reform Jews, $n = 864$.
Source: Leonard J. Fein, *Reform Is a Verb: Notes on Reform and Reforming Jews* (New York: Union of American Hebrew Congregations, 1972), 69.

percent in 1957, thought that supporting Israel is either essential or desirable for a good Jew. In addition, in the Lakeville survey, support of Israel was ranked far lower in comparison to other items. In 1957, it ranked fourteenth out of 22 items; in the 1970 survey, it ranked fifth. Moreover, among the items of specifically Jewish content, such as belonging to a synagogue, attending services on the high holidays, and marrying within the Jewish faith, "support Israel" was ranked seventh in 1957 and second in 1970.

On the basis of these results, it could be argued that since 1970, Israel has moved to the top of the list of American-Jewish priorities. According to the authors of the 1970 survey, the drama of the Six-Day War and the 1969–70 War of Attrition contributed to this shift in opinion. Moreover, in the 1983 National Survey of American Jews, 78 percent of the public and 90 percent of the Jewish leaders agreed with the statement, "Caring about Israel is a very important part of my being a Jew."

Since Israel was established by a secular, national movement, one would assume that Orthodox Jews would not be especially attached to the state. In fact, a few extremely Orthodox minority zealots within American Jewry, such as the Neturei Karta, even opposed the establishment of Israel on religious and historical grounds. These groups are still very hostile to the Jewish state and criticize its domestic and foreign affairs. However, the vast majority of Orthodox Jews in America, who originally might have felt that establishment of Israel should be initiated only by God, have become reconciled to the fact that Israel is a state and extend it their full support.

According to several surveys of American Jewry, the Orthodox have been the most attached and committed to Israel. The 1948 Baltimore poll found that although the level of commitment to Jewish life did not affect the direction of attitudes toward Israel, it did affect the intensity of these attitudes. Therefore, although an identical percentage of those who expressed a high level of commitment and those who expressed a low level of commitment to Jewish life (90) agreed that "it was right for the U.S. to recognize the new Jewish state in Palestine," but 60 percent of the former group and only 46 percent of the latter group agreed that "the U.S. government should send arms and ammunition to help the Jews in Palestine." On the basis of this and other findings, the authors of the Baltimore study concluded:

> Thus, it is apparent that merely being Jewish was enough to evoke pro-Israel sympathies; however, it is equally apparent that something more was generally needed to transform these sympathies into active involvement with and support for Israel. A firm attachment to Jewish life and the sharing of strong sentiments and feelings about Jewishness played an important part in producing this involvement and support.[28]

The 1957 Lakeville study also established a clear correlation between religious observance and support for Israel. High involvement in synagogue life, frequent attendance at the synagogue, and a high level of home observance produced higher levels of support for Israel.[29] In 1968 and 1969, surveys of rabbinical leaders and synagogue officials of the three major movements in American Judaism yielded further evidence for the correlation between religious observance and identification with Israel. According to these surveys, the more orthodox rabbis and leaders identified much more strongly with Israel than the nonorthodox.[30]

The Harris survey of July 1980 and the 1981 National Survey of American Jews provided additional information on the correlation between religious observance and support of Israel. Harris found that Orthodox Jews, far more than other Jewish groups, admired Prime Minister Begin and supported his policies in the Arab-Israeli conflict. Steven M. Cohen distinguishes four levels of ritual observance: secular, minimal, moderate, and observant. In his 1981 poll, he found that the more observant Jews were much more concerned about Israel and expressed considerably more support for its foreign policy than did the other groups.[31] In addition, whereas 58 percent of the "observant" group reported they had visited Israel, only 21 percent of the "secular" group made the same claim.

The relationship between levels of religious observance and identification with Israel was examined in several surveys from 1948. The empirical evidence shows that the more orthodox Jews exhibited higher levels of commitment to Israel. More than the less observant Jews, they saw Israel as a spiritual center for the entire Jewish people. They were more prepared to immigrate to Israel, which they visited more frequently. Finally, Orthodox Jews were more supportive of Israel's foreign policy and American aid and action on behalf of Israel.

Zionism versus Pro-Israelism

The preceding data and discussions reveal a strong emotional, religious, and ethnic attachment of American Jews to Israel. Do these findings also indicate that most American Jews have become Zionists? Norman Podhoretz, the editor of *Commentary,* said in a much-quoted statement, "If Zionism means supporting the idea of a sovereign Jewish state in Palestine, then most American Jews have been Zionist since the end of World War II."[32] But does the concept of Zionism signify just the support of a "sovereign Jewish state"? David Sidorsky observed that American Judaism rejects both Zionist and non-Zionist ideologies and added:

> Support of Israel in a non-ideological way that is without a philosophy of Jewish history or a coherent set of principles, but with a sense of moral purpose and pragmatic policies, has become a major aspect of the American Jewish consensus. The obvious question to put to the thesis is whether the distinction between pro-Israel consensus and a Zionist ideology is a distinction without a difference.[33]

Sidorsky did not provide a direct answer to his question, but others did. Simon Herman and Chaim Waxman argued that there is a major difference between Zionism and pro-Israelism. Herman explained that "a Zionist ideology represents an all-encompassing approach to the problems of the Jewish people," not just positive attitudes toward Israel or an ever-readiness to immigrate to Israel.[34] Waxman added that from a true Zionist perspective, Israel is the spiritual and cultural center of Judaism: "A Zionist is one for whom Israel plays a central role in his own personal life, in his sense of identity and very existence."[35] By contrast, according to Waxman, a pro-Israeli American Jew is one "who lives in the United States and who supports Israel economically, politically, and even emotionally, but whose primary source of Jewish identification is derived from, and oriented to, the American Jewish community." Even if these theoretical distinctions are accepted, do they exist in the mind of American Jews?

In the 1983 National Survey of American Jews, 39 percent of the public and 50 percent of the leaders identified themselves as Zionists. In addition, several major non-Zionist Jewish-American organizations joined the Jewish

Agency and the World Zionist Organization.[36] These views and actions were probably a measure of protest against the attempts of the Arab bloc, Communists, and Third World countries to delegitimize Israel via the denunciation of Zionism. This attempt culminated in November 1975, when the U.N. General Assembly adopted a resolution that equated Zionism with racism.[37] This resolution was seen by Jews everywhere as a direct assault not only on Israel but also on world Jewry. Thus, during the middle and late 1970s, generally favorable statements about Zionism did not provide an accurate measure of the true feelings of American Jewry toward Zionism.

Several surveys of American-Jewish opinion show that American Jews have not equated support of Israel with support of Zionism. Table 7–2 demonstrates a substantial difference between the ranking of "support Israel" and "support Zionism" as essential or desirable for a "good" Jew. Although the 1970 survey of Reform Jews showed a greater number of respondents who considered supporting Zionism as essential or desirable in being a "good" Jew (43 percent as compared to 30 percent in 1957), the ranking of the item in terms of importance was nearly identical in both surveys.

Classical Zionism defines the conditions of the Jews in the Diaspora as permanently insecure and consequently requiring immigration and settlement in Israel. But American Jews have never accepted these assumptions. In the 1948 Baltimore study, only 5 percent of the respondents said that they would like to immigrate to Israel. The Riverton survey identified 7 percent who expressed an interest in moving to Israel. Recent results are slightly higher, but they do not alter the basic trend. In the 1981 NSAJ, only 12 percent of the respondents agreed with the statement, "Each American Jew should give serious thought to settling in Israel." Eighty-two percent disagreed with this statement. The 1983 NSAJ reported that only 17 percent of American Jewry "ever seriously considered living in Israel."

All the pieces of data conclude that although a great majority of American Jews are attached to Israel and think it should be supported, only a minority consider themselves Zionists, and an even smaller minority are prepared to settle in Israel. From this evidence and analysis, it is clear that American Jews distinguish between Zionism and pro-Israelism. They are mainly pro-Israel, not Zionists, and they hold these views for a variety of reasons, including the need to protect their religio-ethnic identity.[38]

Opinions on Economic and Military Assistance

The extensive economic assistance that American Jewry has extended to Israel over the years has probably been one of the most impressive measures of American-Jewish attachment to Israel.[39] All the surveys of American Jewry have shown overwhelming majorities who wanted and expected both the U.S. government and American Jewry to aid Israel. In the 1948 Baltimore survey, 76 percent supported American aid to Israel, but a much greater majority (95 percent) said that American Jews should assist Israel even if the U.S. government did not. These results are hardly surprising in view of the traditional Jewish norms of contributing and helping at both the individual and communal levels.

The 1948 survey also examined respondents' preferences for various types of aid, from both the government and American Jewry. Most respondents preferred American-Jewish over U.S.-official aid to Israel. The highest rates of support were given to assistance in the form of money (91 percent) and food and clothing (93 percent). The lowest support was given to the sending of soldiers, although about half still expected American Jews to volunteer for military service on behalf of Israel. Only about a quarter expected the U.S. government to take military action on behalf of Israel. These results reflected the reservations of the general public about direct U.S. military intervention in the Arab-Israeli conflict and the weariness that Americans felt from World War II.

The 1957–58 Lakeville survey also yielded substantial support for Jewish economic aid to Israel. The respondents were asked to review six different types of possible Jewish support of Israel.[40] One of them was "raising money for Israel," of which 93 percent of the sample approved.

In the July 1980 Harris survey, 83 percent of the respondents said that they had given financial contributions to "an organization which supports Israel." In the 1981 NSAJ survey, almost half of the respondents said that they had contributed directly to "Israeli educational or charitable institutions." The same survey in 1983 found 34 percent of the respondents reporting that they had "given the UJA $100 or more in the last twelve months." Perhaps the best example of Jewish financial contributions to Israel was found in a Harris survey (1974–75) in which 87 versus 7 percent felt that "Jews who live in the U.S. have special obligations to support Israel with funds and other aid."[41] However, it should be noted that contributions rise substantially in times of war, but from 1976 to 1981, they drastically declined. The total amount in 1984 was less than that collected annually from 1969 to 1978, after adjustment to U.S. inflation.

As mentioned earlier, Israel has requested and received growing amounts of economic and military aid from the United States since 1970. These high levels have been fully supported by American Jewry. Table 7–3 presents results of several surveys that have been conducted on the aid issue since 1971. Various kinds of questions yielded support for official U.S. aid in the range of 91 to 96 percent. Moreover, as shown in the responses to questions (h) and (i) in table 7–3, almost half of American Jewry approved of America's assistance

Table 7–3
Jewish Opinion on U.S. Economic and Military Assistance

Date	*Poll*	*Statement*	*Yes*	*No*	*D.K., N.O.*
Feb. '71	*Newsweek*-Gallup	(a) The U.S. should help Israel with diplomatic support and military equipment.	95%	2%	3%
Jan. '75 July '80	Harris Harris	(b)(c) Agree-disagree: U.S. sending military support and supplies to Israel	96 96	2 2	2 2
Feb. '81	Yankelovich	(d) The U.S. should increase (continue at same level, cut back) military aid to Israel: increase and continue = yes, cut = no.	93	2	5
Feb. '81	Yankelovich	(e) The continuation of U.S. support to Israel is important.	95	2	3
Dec. '81 June '83	NSAJ NSAJ	(f)(g) U.S. support for Israel is in America's interest.	93 91	2 3	5 6
Feb. '71	*Newsweek*-Gallup	(h) U.S. should help Israel with diplomatic support and military equipment, even at the risk of becoming involved in a war.	49	32	19
July '80	Harris	(i) If it looked as though Israel were going to be overrun by the Arabs in another war, the U.S. should be willing to send troops to support Israel.	56	27	17

Sources: (a) (h) *Newsweek*, March 1, 1971. 43. For sources of the other statements see notes 10, 12, and 14.

to Israel, even at the risk of the United States becoming involved in a Middle East war, and more than half supported the dispatching of American troops to defend Israel in case of extreme danger.

American Jewry has provided Israel with extensive aid since 1948. Jewish attitudes toward this aspect of the relations between American Jews and Israel have been highly favorable. This may be attributed to a genuine concern for Israel's security needs and possibly to perceived obligations to contribute to Israel's well-being.

Attitudes toward the Arab-Israeli Conflict

The American-Jewish community has been concerned with the Arab-Israeli conflict since Israel's inception in 1948. This concern grew in times of crisis and war, and it was channeled into massive support for Israel. Though American Jews have generally agreed with fundamental Israeli positions in the conflict, they have, since the early 1980s, indicated some reservations about certain policies, especially those that have also generated controversy in Israel.

Throughout the 1950s, one of the fundamental obstacles in the Arab-Israeli conflict was the failure of successive efforts, including those of the United States, toward conflict resolution. These attempts failed mostly because of the Arab refusal to recognize Israel or to negotiate with its government. Most American Jews accepted this assessment. In 1953 and 1955, 67 and 69 percent, respectively, cited only the Arabs as the catalysts in the Arab-Israeli conflict.[42] During the 1956 war, 7 percent of American Jewry blamed Israel for the Arab-Israeli conflict, and about three-quarters blamed the Arabs. After the 1957 Israeli withdrawal from the Sinai Desert, the percentage of Jews blaming Israel dropped to 2 percent, and the percentage of those who blamed the Arabs rose by 7 percent to 83 percent.

The highly emotional reactions of American Jewry to the Six-Day War have already been discussed. These reactions found expression in various polls conducted immediately after the war. Harris asked the American public, "Who do you think has more right on their side, the Arabs or Israel?" The answer of the Jewish sample overwhelmingly favored Israel; 99 percent said that Israel had more right on its side.[43] The same percentage of respondents also expressed sympathy for Israel.

Interest in Peace

Most American Jews have always believed in Israel's interest in establishing peace with its Arab neighbors. This belief was compounded by Israel's conduct during the peace process with Egypt. When asked, in July 1980, whether "Israel really wants peace with Egypt," 80 percent of the Jewish sample felt that Israel very much wanted a peace agreement with Egypt, and 75 percent and 50 percent, respectively, felt that Israel very much wanted such an agreement with Jordan and Syria. In several polls between 1974 and 1980, Harris asked American Jews whether the leadership of Israel and the Arab countries was "reasonable and will work for a just peace settlement." Between 89 percent (in 1974) and 87 percent (in 1980) agreed with this statement.[44]

The 1981 and 1982 NSAJ used the "hawkish-dovish" prism to solicit views from American Jews regarding Israel's basic policy in the Arab-Israeli conflict. The question was "In general, do you think Israel's policies in its dispute with the Arabs have been too hawkish, too dovish or about right, not too hawkish or too dovish?" About three-quarters of the respondents (74 percent in 1981 and 77 percent in 1982) felt that Israel's policies were neither hawkish nor dovish. Twenty-three percent in 1981 and 19 percent in 1982 thought such policies too hawkish, and 3 percent in 1981 and 4 percent in 1982 saw them as too dovish. These results indicate general support for Israeli foreign policy and, perhaps, an appreciation for Israel's interest in peace.

The preceding data and analysis deal only with general perceptions. The following discussion, however, examines whether Jewish-American attitudes have remained supportive on specific issues, such as the role of the PLO in the peacemaking process, solutions to the Palestinian question, and the status of Jerusalem.

The Palestinian Question

The Palestinian problem has become an important subject in many recent surveys of American Jewish opinion. Most questions in this category focus on two issues: Israel-PLO negotiations and the establishment of an independent Palestinian state on the West Bank.

Table 7–4 indicates that the issue of Israel-PLO negotiations was approached by pollsters from two different angles. The first question presented the official Israeli position in this matter and asked the respondents to evaluate it. The second question described a hypothetical situation, with the answer conditional on one or two major changes in PLO ideology: recognition of Israel and renunciation of terrorism. A comparison of the answers to the two questions reveals a distinct contrast. So long as the PLO adhered to the goals stated in its National Convenant and employed terrorism, American Jewry overwhelmingly supported the Israeli refusal to negotiate with PLO representatives. However, as responses to the second question indicate, if the PLO had recognized Israel and renounced terrorism, a sizable majority of American Jews and Jewish leaders would have been ready to support PLO-Israeli talks.

A similar picture emerges in the attitudes toward the establishment of a Palestinian state. The second part of table 7–4 shows that when the issue of an independent Palestinian state was presented in a general context with a strong pro-Palestinian bias, as in question (a), almost half of the respondents supported the idea. However, the addition of the PLO and information about Israel's security needs yielded a totally different outcome. The introduction of Arafat and the PLO created enormous opposition to a Palestinian state (86 to 6 percent). Question (c) gave the respondents a choice between Israeli annexation and the establishment of a Palestinian state. On two different occasions, American Jews preferred Israeli annexation—in 1980, by a substantial ratio. Question (d) includes references to both Palestinian rights and Israel's security needs, but different samples produced mixed results.[45]

Part of the confusion in opinions on this important issue is most likely a result of the subject's objective complexity, but another reason could be the contrast between the wishes and the realistic expectations of those interviewed. In the July 1980 Harris survey, a 59 to 25 percent plurality agreed with the statement: "There must be a way to guarantee Israel's security and also give the Palestinians an independent state on the West Bank." However, despite the emphasis on "There must be a way," American Jewry has shown skepticism toward possible future relations between Israel and an independent Palestinian state. In the same Harris survey, 63 percent agreed with the following

Table 7–4
Jewish Opinion on the Palestinian Question, 1980–84

A. Israel-PLO Negotiations

Questions

(a) Israel is right in refusing to negotiate with the PLO (because it is a terrorist organization that wants to destroy Israel).

(b) Israel should talk with the PLO if the PLO recognizes Israel (and renounces terrorism).

Q	*Date*	*Poll*	*Yes*	*No*	*D.K., N.O.*	*(n)*
(a)	July '80	Harris	90%	7%	3%	(1,030)
(a)	Feb. '81	Yankelovich	62	28	10	(174)
(a)	Dec. '81	NSAJ	74	18	8	(673)
(a)	Aug. '81	NSAJ	76	15	9	(640)
(b)	July '80	Harris	53	34	13	(1,030)
(b)	Sep. '81	*Newsweek*-Gallup	69	23	8	(522)
(b)	Aug. '82	NSAJ	66	23	10	(500)
(b)	June '83	NSAJ	70	17	13	(640)
(b)	Mar. '84	AJYLS	66	24	9	(756)

B. Palestinian State

Questions

(a) The Palestinian people are now homeless and deserve their own independent state, just as the Jews deserved a homeland after World War II.

(b) Arafat and the PLO should be given the West Bank and allowed to form an independent Palestinian State.

(c) If the alternatives are permanent Israeli annexation of the West Bank or an independent Palestinian state, then an independent Palestinian State is preferable.

(d) Palestinians have a right to a homeland on the West Bank and Gaza, so long as it doesn't threaten Israel.

Q	*Date*	*Poll*	*Context*	*For*	*Against*	*D.K.*
(a)	July '80	Harris	General rights	49%	36%	15%
(b)	July '80	Harris	Under PLO	6	86	8
(c)	July '80	Harris	Israeli security	20	54	26
(c)	Dec. '81	NSAJ	Israeli security	28	42	30
(d)	June '83	NSAJ	Rights and Israel	48	26	27
(d)	Mar. '84	AJYLS	Security	34	46	19

Sources: AJYLS: Deborah Lipstadt, Charles Pruitt, and Jonathan Woocher "What They Think: The 1984 American Jewish Young Leadership Survey," *Moment* 9(June 1984): 13–17. For sources of other questions, consult notes 10 through 14.

statement: "If the West Bank became an independent Palestinian state, the Russians would soon use it as a launching pad for them to destroy Israel and to take over the entire oil-rich Middle East." A similar percentage (64 versus 11 percent) agreed with the following statement, which was presented in the 1981 NSAJ: "If the West Bank became an independent Palestinian state, it would probably be used as a launching pad to endanger Israel." These findings indicate that about two-thirds of American Jews feared that an independent Palestinian state would threaten Israel's security. Indeed, the February 1981 Yankelovich survey found that 71 versus 17 percent of the Jewish sample agreed that the "Israeli attitudes toward a Palestinian state on the West Bank are reasonable." These findings also correlate with the fact that 42 percent in the 1983 NSAJ, 44 percent in the 1984 NSAJ, and 48 percent in the 1984 American Jewish Young Leadership Survey, agreed with the statement that Israel should maintain permanent control over the West Bank.

So far, the discussion of attitudes toward a possible solution to the Palestinian question has been restricted to the independent-state option. But other ideas were suggested, and their relative popularity in contrast to the independent-state option was examined by the *Newsweek*-Gallup poll of September 1981 and September 1982. In both polls, the independent-state solution attracted the least support (9 percent in 1981 and 7 percent in 1982) when it appeared within the context of other proposals. This was true for the period before and after the 1982 Israeli war in Lebanon, and it should be noted that the poll of September 1982 was conducted immediately following the tragic massacre in Sabra and Shatila. The *Newsweek*-Gallup polls indicate that the majority of American Jews—61 percent in 1981 and 58 percent in 1982—favored Israeli sovereignty over the West Bank, with or without civil control by local Palestinians.

The preceding results demonstrate a possible pattern of Jewish views on the Palestinian issue. It seems that a considerable segment of American Jewry opposed the establishment of an independent Palestinian state on the West Bank and Israeli-PLO negotiations. They preferred Israeli control over the West Bank, primarily because of concern for Israeli security needs. Although many American Jews were prepared to revise their views on the conditions that the PLO change its ideology and tactics and Israeli security needs be met, they were quite skeptical about the prospects for such changes and accommodations.

Jerusalem

Jerusalem has always occupied a special place in Jewish history, and apparently there is a strong consensus, both in Israel and in world Jewry, about its fate. According to this consensus, Jerusalem should remain unified under Israeli sovereignty and control, and Israel should protect and enact special provisions for Christian and Muslim holy places similar to those accorded foreign embassies.

In his poll of July 1980, Harris examined Jewish opinions on three possible proposals for the future of Jerusalem.[46] A substantial majority (82 versus 7 percent) rejected a proposal calling for the redivision of the city and the return of the eastern side to Arab control. A majority of 72 to 14 percent rejected the proposal to internationalize the city, but a majority of 66 to 21 percent supported the Israeli position, which asserts control over the entire city while granting special provisions for the holy sites. The February 1981 Yankelovich poll also found overwhelming support for Israel's right to make Jerusalem its capital (74 versus 14 percent).

Begin's Policies

Interest in the Arab-Israeli conflict has not been confined solely to issues. Arab personalities such as Nasser, Sadat, Hussein, and Assad and Israeli leaders Ben-Gurion, Meir, Dayan, and Begin have also played significant roles in peace and war. Among these notables, the leadership and style of one Israeli leader, Begin, became a source of considerable controversy inside and outside the American Jewish community.[47]

Begin's role in Middle Eastern issues appeared in several surveys, some of which were accompanied by news articles. At times, these articles were rather sensational. For example, on September 14, 1981, *Newsweek* published the results of a poll on the opinions of American Jews toward Begin and his policies under the title, "A Poll: Jewish Misgivings about Begin." The accompanying story was entitled, "Dilemma for U.S. Jews." In the *Newsweek*-Gallup poll, American Jews were asked whether Begin's policies hurt support for Israel in the United States. This question was repeated by the same poll in September 1982 and by another poll in 1983.

Table 7–5 indicates that the majority of American Jews—a rather substantial majority in 1982—felt that Begin's policies indeed hurt support for Israel in the United States. The 1983 NSAJ placed Begin's favorability rating at 31 percent, in fourth place on a list of six Israeli leaders. (However, Begin's rate was identical to the score of incumbent Israeli Prime Minister Shimon Peres, then chairman of the opposition Labor party.[48]) Table 7–5 also shows that in response to a question (b), concerning possible effects of Begin's policies on Israel, 35 percent of the American-Jewish public stated that those policies had damaged Israel. When the same issue was formulated in positive terms, as in question (c), the results were favorable to Begin.

In any case, it appears that Begin was not popular in the eyes of American Jewry. Was this because of his policies? Did it have any effect on this group's attitudes toward Israel? A close look at the *Newsweek*-Gallup poll of Septem-

Table 7–5
Opinions on Begin's Policies

Questions

(a) Do you think Israeli Prime Minister Begin's policies are *hurting* support for Israel in the United States?

(b) The policies of Menachem Begin and his government have *damaged* Israel.

(c) The policies of the Begin government *strengthened* Israel.

Q	*Date*	*Poll*	*Yes*	*No*	*D.K.*
(a)	Sep. '81	*Newsweek*-Gallup	53%	34%	13%
(a)	Sep. '82	*Newsweek*-Gallup	78	12	10
(a)	June '83	NSAJ	50	22	28
(b)	June '83	NSAJ	35	38	27
(c)	Mar. '84	AJYLS	48	24	28

Sources: See the relevant sources in table 7–4.

ber 1981 reveals that a clear majority of American Jews supported Begin's policies. In response to a question on the West Bank, a majority of 61 percent supported the proposal for Israeli sovereignty with or without Palestinian autonomy. Sixty-nine versus 19 percent of the respondents thought that the 1981 Israeli bombing of the PLO headquarters in Beirut was justified, "although it caused extensive civilian casualties." So far as attitudes toward Israel are concerned, when asked if they were more or less sympathetic to Israel than they were 5 years ago, only 11 percent of respondents said that they were less sympathetic; 87 percent said either that they had not changed their sympathy for Israel or that they were more sympathetic. Furthermore, when asked about financial contributions to Israel, only 3 percent of American Jews stated that they had decreased them; 70 percent said that they had contributed the same amount as they had for the last 5 years; and almost a quarter of the respondents claimed to have increased their financial support.

Basic agreement with Begin's strategies, with some reservations about several of his specific policies, was also found in the July 1980 Harris survey. For example, only a 44 to 42 percent plurality of American Jews rejected the following statement: "By advocating and allowing more Jewish settlements on the West Bank, he [Begin]is making it almost impossible to get a peace settlement." On the other hand, an overwhelming majority of 90 to 4 percent credited Begin with proving at Camp David that "he is capable of making concessions that can lead to a peace settlement when he agreed to give back Sinai to Egypt." American Jews rejected the charge that Begin "seems too inflexible, unbending, and unchangeable for people to really believe he really wants peace" by a majority of 66 to 25 percent.

A comparison of answers to various queries about Begin's policies shows an interesting inconsistency. Many American Jews thought that Begin damaged support for Israel in the United States, yet they have continued to back most of his policies—presumably, the same policies that were described as harmful to Israel in the United States. Earl Raab provided an explanation for this finding by arguing that American Jews were not primarily uneasy about the substance of Begin's policies or actions but were more concerned with the *effects* of the policies on the image of Israel in America: "In other words, while the Jews did not themselves become less sympathetic, they believed other Americans had."[49] If this was the case, the results of earlier chapters show that many American Jews have misperceived the general American opinions on the Arab-Israeli conflict.

Effects of the 1982 War in Lebanon

Begin's policy on the Arab-Israeli conflict became more controversial during the 1982 Israeli war in Lebanon. Many articles that appeared during the war carried prominent headlines describing a serious rift between Israel and American Jewry over the war and its conduct.[50] This description grew even more intense after the massacre of Palestinian refugees by Christian Phalangists in Sabra and Shatila. But as Raab suggested, by August 1982, the main breach did not exist *between* American Jewry and Israel but rather was *inside* each of these communities.[51]

Unfortunately, few empirical data are available on the attitudes of American Jewry toward the war in Lebanon. The two polls that were conducted on the war—one early in September 1982 by Steven M. Cohen for the American Jewish Committee, the other in late September 1982 (immediately after the massacre) by Gallup for *Newsweek*—did not include a direct question on the overall Israeli operation.[52] Cohen found that 49 percent of the sample agreed that "Israel was right to have sent its military forces into West Beirut to try to expel the PLO military forces." Another 27 percent agreed that "Israel should have attacked and destroyed the PLO military forces in West Beirut." Only 5 percent said that "Israel should have never gone into Lebanon in the first place."

When asked to compare their sympathy for Israel in August 1982 with their feelings a year earlier, 42 percent of American Jews said that they were more sympathetic, 48 percent did not identify any change, and only 10 percent said that they were less sympathetic. "Palestinians" was then substituted for "Israel" in the same question; in this case, 8 percent of American Jews were more sympathetic and 42 percent were less sympathetic.

Immediately after the massacre in Beirut, Gallup asked both Jews and non-Jews about their sympathies for Israel. In this instance, 33 percent of the Jewish sample were more sympathetic, 36 percent were less sympathetic, and 31 percent did not report any change. These results could have been influenced by the Sabra and Shatila massacres, since a majority of American Jews (65 percent) said that Israel had been at least partially responsible for the massacre. Another interesting result was the opposition of 75 percent of the respondents to any suspension or reduction in U.S. aid to force a pullout of the Israeli forces from Lebanon. Furthermore, Jewish views on a central relevant issue—the Palestinian question and the fate of the West Bank—changed only slightly after the war. Fifty-eight percent, as opposed to 61 percent in 1981, now supported Israeli sovereignty over the West Bank, and 7 percent, as opposed to 9 percent in 1981, supported the establishment of a Palestinian state on the West Bank (see table 7–4).

The lack of consensus in American Jewry about the Israeli war in Lebanon brought to the fore the question of whether to publicly voice criticism of Israeli policy and action or to keep it within the Jewish community for possibly quieter exchanges. This is not a simple question, since harsh criticism of Israel in America could be effectively used against Israel and American Jewry. In three of the four NSAJ and AJYLS polls conducted on this issue between 1981 and 1984, the majority of American Jews disagreed with the statement that they "should not criticize Israel's policies publicly."[53] The only exception to this trend was registered during the 1982 war in Lebanon, when 49 percent versus 43 percent disagreed with the statement. These results may indicate that American Jewry is more reluctant to criticize Israel publicly in times of war or crisis.

Pressure on Israel

The United States has, in the past, applied various kinds of pressure on Israel to affect its policy. Such pressure was clearly evinced during the peacemaking process.[54] However, American Jewry has strongly opposed this pressure. In July 1980, when Harris presented the statement, "Israel only seems to want to make peace concessions when the U.S. puts pressure on it to agree to peace terms," 66 versus 25 percent rejected it. Responses to questions that focused on a specific issue also revealed strong opposition to the use of American pressure on Israel.

By a majority of 89 to 6 percent, American Jews rejected the use of pressure on Israel "to give back all the Arab occupied land." The August 1982 NSAJ found a majority of 69 to 17 percent opposing pressure on Israel to be "more conciliatory in dealings with the Palestinians." Logically, there could be a correlation between attitudes toward a specific issue and attitudes toward American pressure on that issue. For example, respondents who feel that Israel should not relinquish all the territory it has occupied since 1967 would naturally tend to oppose American pressure on Israel to do so. On the other hand, individuals might be in favor of Israeli withdrawal from all of the occupied territories but, for various reasons, would oppose pressure on Israel to take this action. Unfortunately, no suitable data are available to ascertain a possible correlation between opinions on the issues and attitudes toward U.S. pressure in connection with these issues.

In conclusion, it could be argued that most American Jews believe in Israel's sincere interest in peace and approve of its main policies and actions in the Arab-Israeli conflict. American Jewry supported the Israeli positions on Jerusalem and the Palestinian question. However, in contrast to other Arab-Israeli wars, the 1982 war in Lebanon was not unanimously supported, and many Jews had reservations about Begin's style. Finally, most American Jews strongly opposed American pressure on Israel in connection with its stand in the Arab-Israeli conflict. These attitudes probably stem from genuine concern for the security of Israel and from general trust in Israeli leaders and their judgments about the course of the Arab-Israeli conflict.

The Dual-Loyalty Issue

The dual-loyalty issue remains sensitive and has been used against the Jews by anti-Semites throughout modern and earlier periods. The establishment of Israel and the strong attachment of American Jewry to the Jewish state has further raised and intensified this issue.[55] The point in question is to what degree if any, the existence of Israel and the strong attachment of American Jewry to the state have affected the obligations and commitments of American Jews to America. Several surveys of American Jewry failed to find any perceptions of conflict in loyalties. The authors of the 1948 Baltimore survey concluded:

> Thus, for most Jews Israel and the United States stood for two different kinds of commitments and ties, neither of which clashed with the other and both of which were essential to their total image of themselves as American Jews. However, should they be faced with a situation where they would have to choose between the two countries—a situation which they were anxious to avoid—loyalty to the U.S. would prevail.[56]

This assessment has been corroborated by several recent surveys. For example, the 1981 and 1983 National Survey of American Jews asked the respondents for their opinions on the following statement: "There are times when my devotion to Israel comes into conflict with my devotion to America." In 1981, 72 percent of the sample disagreed with this statement and 25 percent agreed. In 1983, 65 percent disagreed and 24 percent agreed. The Yankelovich survey of February 1981 presented its Jewish sample with an extreme hypothetical situation by asking: "If the United States and Israel ever broke off relations, with whom do you think most American Jews would side in the dispute?" Forty-three percent said that most American Jews would side with the United States, 26 percent selected Israel, 14 percent both, and 17 percent neither.[57]

A substantial majority of American Jews did not view their close ties with Israel as detrimental to American interests. In April 1980, Gallup asked the following question: "Is it good or bad for the U.S. that many American Jews have close ties to Israel or doesn't it matter one way or the other?" Forty-five percent of the Jewish sample said that such ties were good for America; 43 percent said it did not matter one way or the other; and only about 10 percent said that it was bad for the United States.[58]

A great majority of American Jews denied any conflict of loyalties in the foregoing surveys. Likewise, in the Gallup survey of August 1979, 86 percent of the Jewish respondents rejected the statement: "Most American Jews are more loyal to Israel than to the U.S." Only about 14 percent agreed with the statement.[59] The Yankelovich survey of February 1981 asked: "Do you think that most Jewish people in the country feel closer to the U.S. or Israel?" Seventy percent claimed that most American Jews feel closer to the United States, and 18 percent thought of themselves as close to both the United States and Israel.[60]

Although the great majority of American Jews rejected the notion that they were more loyal or closer to Israel than to the United States, they believed that most non-Jewish Americans believed otherwise. In the Harris survey of July 1980, a majority of the Jewish respondents (51 versus 38 percent) thought that most non-Jews feel that "Jews are more loyal to Israel than to America." However, when non-Jews were asked for their opinions on the same statement, a plurality of only 41 to 30 percent took the view that Jews are more loyal to Israel.

Since 1964, the question of Jewish loyalty to the U.S. and Israel has been examined as part of an ongoing effort to measure anti-Semitism in the United States.[61] A trend analysis of the results shows a fluctuation between 25 and 37 percent (figure 7–1).[62] The gap between the two responses in figure 7–1 can be used to gauge the "level of suspected loyalties." Larger gaps mean less suspicion, and smaller gaps mean more serious suspicion of dual loyalties. Figure 7–1 reveals that fluctuations in the results were registered during periods of change in relations between America and Israel. When these relations were good, fewer Americans had reason to suspect the loyalty of American Jews. However, when the two nations ran into disputes, greater numbers of America's gentiles believed that Jews were more loyal to Israel. Thus, as figure 7–1 shows, the narrowest ratios between those who agreed and those who disagreed with the statement were recorded in April 1974 and at the beginning of 1983; the largest gaps were registered in August 1979 and January 1984. The energy crisis following the Yom Kippur War took a full swing in 1974, and this development might have been linked to the 1974 result. The Israeli war in Lebanon and the Israeli rejection of the Reagan plan for peace in the

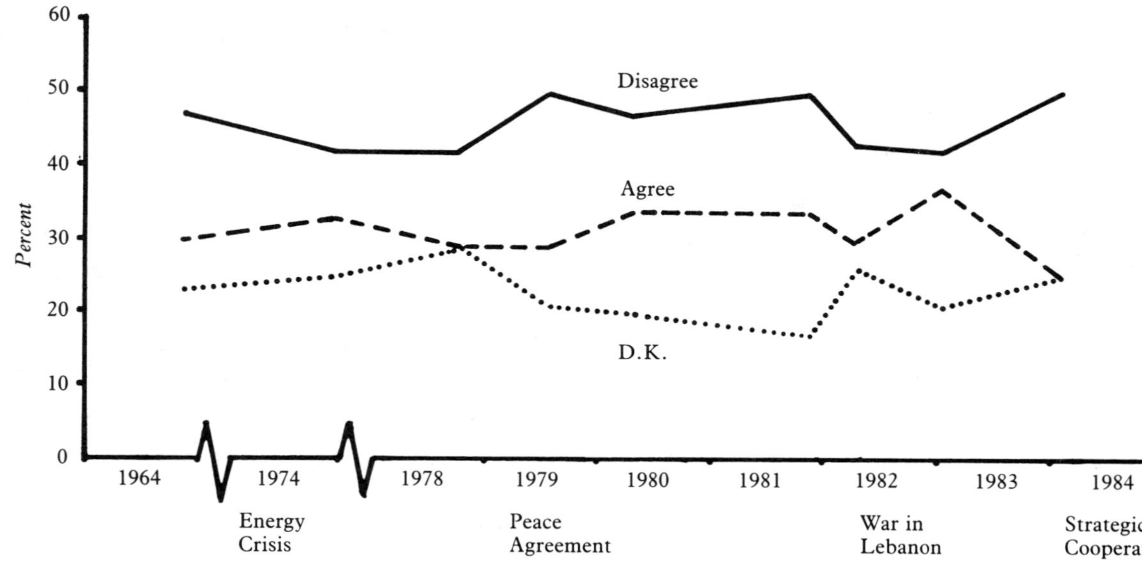

Sources: Geraldine Rosenfield, "The Polls: Attitudes Toward American Jews," *Public Opinion Quarterly* 46(Fall 1982): 431–43; and *The American Jewish Committee's January 1984 Poll* (New York: American Jewish Committee, Information and Research Services, February 1984, mimeographed).

Figure 7–1. Loyalties of American Jews as Seen by non-Jews.
Question: Please tell me whether you agree or disagree with the following statement: most American Jews are more loyal to Israel than to the U.S.

Middle East might be linked to the closest ratio ever recorded on this issue—42 to 37 percent. In January 1984, American-Israeli relations had improved, and this development might have triggered the largest gap ever recorded on the loyalty index—50 to 25 percent. Thus, in a single year, Americans completely reversed their views on the loyalty of American Jews. This remarkable finding is another indication of the intense political relations that developed between Israel and the U.S. government at the beginning of the 1980s.[63]

Conclusions

The first polls conducted on the attitudes of American Jewry toward Israel were limited both in methodology (sampling) and in substance. Later surveys were more comprehensive but were still restricted to specific geographic areas or to certain religious movements in American Judaism. Recent surveys, however, have been based on more sophisticated samples of American Jewry and have dealt with almost all aspects of Jewish life in America and in relation to Israel. It appears that the recent, relatively intensive polling of the American-Jewish community has reflected a growing interest of the Jewish community and of American society in the opinions of American Jews concerning both internal issues and Middle Eastern affairs. Dramatic and controversial moves toward both peacemaking and violence in the Middle East have only strengthened this interest.

Despite the limitations of the data base on the attitudes of American Jewry toward Israel, it is still possible to identify several major trends, one of which clearly shows that American Jewry has been strongly attached to Israel. Most American Jews are concerned with the survival and well-being of Israel and have heavily supported it both politically and economically. The bulk of American Jewry has not considered itself Zionist in the classical meaning of the term, however, and only a few American Jews express the wish to settle in Israel. Still, the great majority of American Jewry is in line with the larger American consensus on the high levels of economic and military aid the U.S. government has provided Israel, primarily on the grounds that it serves both American and Israeli interests.

American Jews have traditionally supported basic Israeli positions and strategies in the Arab-Israeli conflict. They mobilized to assist Israel during times of war and crisis and were enthusiastic about the prospects for a comprehensive Arab-Israeli peace that were opened by Sadat. The attitudes toward the status of Jerusalem have been in full accordance with the consensus in Israel and among world Jewry. This consensus calls for a united Jerusalem under Israeli sovereignty, with special provisions for the holy places of Islam and Christianity. The approach to the Palestinian problem has been more complex. American Jewry has supported the Israeli opposition to negotiations with the PLO and the establishment of an independent Palestinian state on the West Bank, but it is ready to revise these opinions if the PLO changes its ideology and tactics and if the establishment of a Palestinian state no longer threatens the security of Israel. Contrary to popular impressions, the changes in the Israeli government, and especially the historic change of 1977, apparently have not influenced the basic attitudes of American Jewry toward Israel and the Arab-Israeli conflict.

The question of dual loyalty arose after the establishment of Israel. It appeared in one of the first polls on Israel and has been present in every major survey concerning anti-Semitism in the United States since 1964. The results illustrate that most American Jews do not perceive any conflict between their loyalties to the United States and Israel but presume that most non-Jewish Americans do perceive such a conflict among Jews; therefore, they have been concerned about it. The polls reveal that the majority of non-Jews in America have not questioned the loyalties of Jews to the United States, but approximately one-third of non-Jews still suspect Jewish loyalties.[64]

Unfortunately, few data have been generated on the distribution of attitudes toward Israel and the Arab-Israeli conflict among-various strata of American Jewry. Sufficient data to warrant trend analysis were available from only one variable—religious observance. Higher commitments to Jewish observance at the synagogue or at home were correlated with higher levels of pro-Israelism. Limited data on the effects of other sociodemographic factors were produced in the recent NSAJ and AJYLS polls. Steven Cohen found, in his NSAJ of 1981, that older and less educated respondents were more concerned about Israel and more supportive of Israel's policies than were younger and more highly educated respondents.[65] He also found that left-wing liberals were more critical of Israeli policy than were liberal and conservative American Jews. However, the difference in the pro-Israel rate of the liberals (66 percent) and the conservatives (70 percent) was just 4 percent, and after all, these two groups constitute the great majority of American Jews.[66] The 1984 AJYLS survey found that young Jewish leaders possessed the sociodemographic characteristics of Republicans, but they adhered to liberal views and supported the policies of the Israeli Likud-led government more than did the leaders' sample of Steven M. Cohen in his NSAJ.

Figure 7–2 describes and illustrates possible sources and explanations of Jewish attitudes and actions as they relate to Israel and the Arab-Israeli conflict. The most dramatic evidence for the top left box in the figure was found in answers to a question about the hypothetical destruction of Israel. More than 80 percent of American Jews said that they would feel a great personal loss if Israel were destroyed. The strong concern and care for Israel can probably be attributed to religious tenets as well as to the memory of the Holocaust and to the place of Israel in the efforts of American Jews to maintain their

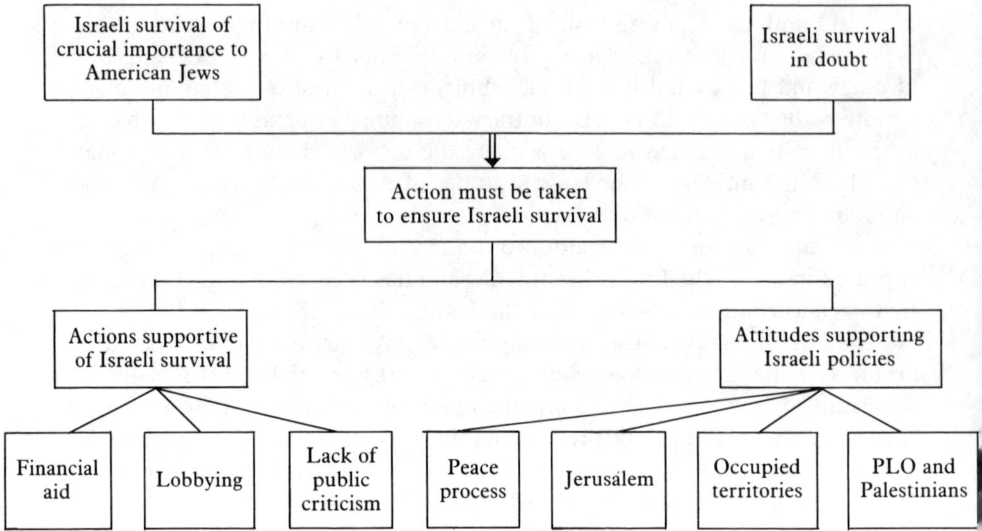

Figure 7–2. The Dynamics of Jewish Attitudes toward Israel

ethnic identity. Lucy Dawidowicz interpreted the reactions of American Jews to the Six-Day War:

> American Jews have been afflicted with a deep sense of guilt. With the passage of time, their very survival when millions of other Jews were murdered and even worse, their failure to rescue more than a minuscule number of European Jews have increasingly tormented them.[67]

Obviously, older Jews have been influenced by the Holocaust more than younger Jews, for whom it has been but a chapter of Jewish history. But when Greenberg reflected on the impact of the Holocaust on American Jewry, he did not distinguish between young and old. He argued:

> Since American Jews perceived that if Israel were to be destroyed, they themselves would become highly vulnerable, there is a much stronger tendency to see the fate of both communities as inseparable.[68]

Although the evidence overwhelmingly indicates that the existence of Israel has been crucial for American Jews, they have been concerned about the future of Israel. In the 1981 NSAJ, only 12 percent of American Jews agreed with the statement that Israel's future is secure. The same survey found that of five major issues or problems that confront American Jews, the security of Israel was rated a very important issue by the highest ratio—69 to 19 percent.

These findings may explain the general Jewish support of major Israeli policies and actions in the Arab-Israeli arena, even at times when these policies were seen as challenging the traditional norms and values of many American Jews (bottom right boxes in figure 7–2). Another expression of the relationship between concern for Israel's survival and reaction to Israel's problems can be found in a number of actions by American Jewry that are intended to strengthen Israel. These include financial aid and lobbying on behalf of Israel (bottom left boxes in figure 7–2). Expressions of favorable attitudes toward Israel might be construed as actions contributing to the Israeli cause. On the one hand, this might contribute to the holding of favorable attitudes; on the other, it might inhibit public criticism of Israel. Generally, there is a dynamic interaction between holding supportive attitudes and taking supportive action, since each influences and reinforces the other.

The most interesting finding of this chapter is the remarkable continuity and stability in the attitudes of American Jewry toward Israel and—to a lesser extent—toward the Arab-Israeli conflict.[69] If the past provides any guidance for the future, American Jews are likely to support Israel so long as the Jewish state is seen as vital to their ethnic survival and as a major vehicle for expressing their Jewishness.

Notes

1. Ben Halpern, "Zion in the Mind of American Jews," in David Sidorsky, ed., *The Future of the Jewish Community in America* (New York: Basic Books, 1973), 22–45; and Henry L. Feingold, *Zion in America: The Jewish Experience from the Colonial Times to the Present* (New York: Twayne, 1974).

2. See Zvi Ganin, *Truman, American Jewry and Israel, 1945-1948* (New York: Holms and Meier, 1979).

3. Marshall Sklare, *America's Jews*, (New York: Random House, 1971) ch. 7; Charles S. Leibman, *The Ambivalent American Jew* (Philadelphia: Jewish Publication Society of America, 1973), ch. 4; and Edward Glick, *The Triangular Connection: America, Israel and American Jews* (London: George Allen and Unwin, 1982).

4. Problems of design and sampling in surveys of American Jewry are discussed in Harold S. Himmelfarb, "Research on American Jewish Identity and Identification: Progress, Pitfalls and Prospects," in M. Sklare, ed., *Understanding American Jewry* (New Brunswick, N.J.: Transaction, 1982), especially 66–73; Samuel C. Heilman, "The Sociology of American Jewry: The Last Ten Years," *Annual Review of Sociology* 8(1982); 135-60; and Egon Mayer, *From Suburb to Shtetl: The Jews of Boro-Park* (Philadelphia: Temple University Press, 1979).

5. Marshall Sklare and Benjamin B. Ringer, "A Study of Jewish Attitudes Toward the State of Israel," in M. Sklare, ed., *The Jews: Social Patterns of an American Group* (Glencoe, Ill.: Free Press, 1958), 437–50.

6. Marshall Sklare and Mark Vosk, *The Riverton Study: How Jews Look at Themselves and Their Neighbors* (New York: American Jewish Committee, May 1957).

7. Marshall Sklare and Joseph Greenblum, *Jewish Identity on the Suburban Frontier* (New York: Basic Books, 1967), ch. 6.

8. Charles Leibman, "The Role of Israel in the Ideology of American Jewry," *Dispersion and Unity* 10(Winter 1970): 19-26.

9. Leonard J. Fein, et al., *Reform Is a Verb: Notes on Reform and Reforming Jews* (New York: Union of American Hebrew Congregations, 1972).

10. In July 1980, Harris conducted a comprehensive survey of both Jews and non-Jews, using for the Jewish part a sample of 1,030 respondents. Louis Harris, *A Study of the Attitudes of the American People and the American Jewish Community Toward Anti-Semitism and the Arab-Israeli Conflict in the Middle East,* Study No. 804011, August 1980.

11. Gallup preferred telephone interviews. In September 1981, for example, he interviewed a sample of 522 Jews and, in August 1982, a national sample of 605 adults and an additional cross section of 258 American Jews. Gallup claimed a margin of error of plus or minus eight percentage points for the September 1981 poll and plus or minus eight percentage points for the August 1982 survey. These margins of error are somewhat larger than those that are accepted for national samples. See *Newsweek,* September 14, 1981, 38, and October 4, 1982, 11.

12. In February 1981, the Yankelovich, Skelly and White firm conducted a major survey of Jews and non-Jews on their beliefs on Israel and other issues. It used a sample of 1,072 adults and a supplemental Jewish sample. In all, the Jewish sample included 174 respondents. For a detailed description of these samples, see appendix C. Also see Gregory Martire and Ruth Clark, *Anti-Semitism in the United States* (New York: Praeger, 1982)

13. The DJN technique is explained in Fred Massarik, "New Approaches to the Study of the American Jew," *Jewish Journal of Sociology* 8(December 1966): 175–91.

14. Steven M. Cohen, "The 1981-1982 National Survey of American Jews," *American Jewish Year Book* 83(1983): 89-110; and "What American Jews Believe," *Moment* 7(July-August 1982): 23-27; The 1982 National Survey of American Jews, Press Release, September 8, 1982; Steven M. Cohen, *Attitudes of American Jews Toward Israel and Israelis: The 1983 National Survey of American Jews and Jewish Communal Leaders* (New York: American Jewish Committee, Institute of Human Relations, 1983):and *The National Survey of American Jews: Political and Social Outlooks* (New York: American Jewish Committee, Institute of Human Relations, 1984). For NSAJ's sample, see appendix D.

15. However, the selection of leaders omitted important Jewish organizations, and the response of the leaders was limited. This and other features of the 1983 NSAJ were criticized by Shmuel Katz in the *Jerusalem Post* on January 6 and February 17, 1984. Cohen answered this criticism in the same newspaper on February 9 and 16, 1984.

16. *American Jewish Year Book* 48(1946-1947): 243–44.

17. George H. Gallup, *The Gallup Poll: Public Opinion, 1935–1971,* vol. I (New York: Random House, 1972), 554.

18. Sklare and Ringer, "A Study of Jewish Attitudes," 440.

19. On the reactions of American Jewry to the establishment of Israel, see Bernard Postal and Henry W. Levy, *And the Hills Shouted for Joy: The Day Israel Was Born* (Philadelphia: Jewish Publication Society of America, 1973); and Stanley Feldstein,

The Land That I Show You: Three Centuries of Jewish Life in America (New York: Anchor Books, 1979), ch. 8.

20. Cohen, *Attitudes*, 34.

21. Martire and Clark, *Anti-Semitism*, 87.

22. On the reactions of American Jewry to the Six-Day War, see, for example, Arthur Hertzberg, "Israel and American Jewry," *Commentary* 44(August 1967): 69-73; and Milton Himmelfarb, "In the Light of Israel's Victory," *Commentary* 44(October 1967): 53-61.

23. The Six-Day War was a turning point in American Jewish financial contributions to Israel. See Abraham J. Karp, *To Give Life: The UJA in the Shaping of the American Jewish Community* (New York: Schocken Books, 1981) ch. 18.

24. Marshall Sklare, "Lakeville and Israel: The Six-Day War and its Aftermath," *Midstream* 14(October 1968) 3-21.

25. The six types of support of Israel were (1) raise money for Israel; (2) seek to influence U.S. foreign policy in favor of Israel; (3) belong to Zionist organizations; (4) give Israeli financial need priority over local Jewish causes; (5) encourage their children to immigrate to Israel; (6) participate personally in the building of Israel through becoming a citizen of Israel. Sklare and Greenblum, *Jewish Identity* 255.

26. Simon N. Herman, *American Students in Israel* (Ithaca, N.Y.: Cornell University Press, 1970), 137.

27. Moshe Davis, ed., *The Yom Kippur War: Israel and the Jewish People* (New York, Arno Press, 1974), 1-93.

28. Sklare and Ringer, "A Study of Jewish Attitudes," 442.

29. Sklare and Greenblum, *Jewish Identity*, 232–33.

30. Charles Leibman, "The Role of Israel in the Ideology of American Jewry," 19-26.

31. Steven M. Cohen, *American Modernity and Jewish Identity* (New York: Tavistock, 1983), 162–63.

32. Norman Podhoretz, "Now, Instant Zionism," *New York Times Magazine*, February 3, 1974, 11.

33. David Sidorsky, "The End of Ideology and American Jewry," *Betfuzot Hagolah*, no. 85/86(Summer 1978): 114.

34. Simon N. Herman, *Jewish Identity: A Social Psychological Perspective* (Beverly Hills, Calif.: Sage, 1977), 121.

35. Chaim I. Waxman, "The Centrality of Israel in American Jewish Life: A Sociological Analysis," *Judaism* 25(Spring 1976): 177.

36. Among them were the world organizations of the three mainstreams of American Judaism: Orthodox, Conservative, and Reform.

37. See Chaim Herzog, *Who Stands Accused? Israel Answers Its Critics* (New York: Random House, 1978), ch. 1; Daniel P. Moynihan, *A Dangerous Place to Live* (Boston: Little, Brown, 1978); Bernard Lewis, "The Anti-Zionist Resolution," *Foreign Affairs* 55(October 1976): 54-64; and S. L. Liskofsky, "U.N. Resolution on Zionism," *American Jewish Year Book* 77(1977): 97–122.

38. Steven M. Cohen distinguishes between classical and modern Zionism, implying that in America the latter is pro-Israelism. He argues that pro-Israelism in the United States emerged from two processes of modernization. The first is the transfor-

mation of political participation into a mass phenomenon. From this perspective, pro-Israelism was a vehicle American Jews used for mass participation in the American political system. However, the vast freedoms of expression, organization, and participation and the melting-pot mechanism threatened the ethnic survival of American Jewry. From this perspective, pro-Israelism was pursued as a principal way to protect the ethnic identity of American Jewry. See Cohen, *American Modernity and Jewish Identity,* 155. See also the interesting analysis of Jonathan S. Woocher, who places Israel as one of the central elements of American "Civil Judaism"; "The Civil Judaism of Communal Leaders," *American Jewish Year Book* 81(1981): 149–69. See also Chaim I. Waxman, *America's Jews in Transition* (Philadelphia: Temple University Press, 1983).

39. See *United Israel Appeal, 1984 Annual Report* (New York, 1985), 18; and Marc Lee Raphael, *A History of the United Jewish Appeal, 1939-1982, Brown Judaic Studies 34 (Providence, R.I.: Brown University, 1982).*

40. See note 25.

41. Quoted in Seymour Martin Lipset and William Schneider, "Carter vs. Israel: What the Polls Reveal," *Commentary* 64(November 1977): 27.

42. The general American public held similar views. See table 1–6.

43. Hazel Erskine, "The Polls: Western Partisanship in the Middle East," *Public Opinion Quarterly* 33(Winter 1969–70): pp 630–31.

44. These results appear in the report on the July 1980 poll; see note 10.

45. The survey of young American Jewish leadership was conducted by Deborah Lipstadt, Charles Pruitt, and Jonathan Woocher in March 1984. Seven hundred fifty-six young leaders participated in the survey. The author would like to thank Professor Lipstadt for making the results of this survey available to him. Selected results of this survey were published in *Moment* 9(June 1984): 13–17.

46. Harris took his poll from July 11 until August 1980. During that period, the Israeli Knesset debated on a special new law for Jerusalem. This law, which was approved by a substantial majority, was designed to enhance the status of Jerusalem as the capital of Israel.

47. For a few examples, see Sidney H. Schwartz, "Jewish Impotence—Jewish Power," *Judaism* 30(Spring 1981): 142–50; Sol Stein, "Menachem Begin vs. the Jewish Lobby," *New York Magazine,* April 24, 1978, 59–63; George E. Gruen, "Solidarity and Dissent in Israel—Diaspora Relations," *Forum* 30–31(Spring-Summer 1978):33–53.

48. The other Israeli leaders were Abba Eban, Yitzhak Rabin, Yitzhak Navon, and Ariel Sharon.

49. Earl Raab, "American Jewish Attitudes on Israel: Consensus and Dissent," *Perspectives* (November 1981):14-15.

50. See, for example, "Being a Jew and an American: Congruence or Conflict," Special Issue, *Judaism* 32(Summer 1983); Mark Helprin, "American Jews and Israel," *New York Times Magazine,* November 7, 1982.

51. Earl Raab, "How American Jews Have Reacted to the War," *Jewish Monthly,* 97(August-September 1982): 40-42. See also his "Is the Jewish Community Split?" *Commentary* 74(November 1982): 21-25.

52. *Newsweek,* October 4, 1982, 11.

53. See notes 14 and 45.

54. See David Pollock, *The Politics of Pressure: American Arms and Israeli Policy Since the Six Day War* (Westport, Conn.: Greenwood Press, 1982).

55. Both American Jewry and Israel were sensitive to this issue. For one of the first interesting communications on this, see Nathaniel Weyl, *The Jew in American Politics* (New Rochelle, N.Y.: Arlington House, 1968), 294.

56. Sklare and Ringer, "A Study of Jewish Attitudes," 445.

57. The comparable results for the non-Jews were siding with the United States, 35 percent; siding with Israel, 31 percent; both, 6 percent; not sure, 28 percent. Martire and Clark, *Anti-Semitism,* 90.

58. Gallup Poll, *The Study of Attitudes Concerning the American Jewish Community,* G08065, May 1980.

59. Gallup Poll, August 1979.

60. Martire and Clark, *Anti-Semitism,* 90.

61. Americans were asked whether they agree or disagree with the statement worded more or less as follows: Most American Jews are more loyal to Israel than to the United States. Disagreement means that Jews are seen as more loyal to the United States. Agreement means that American Jews are probably seen as less than fully loyal. For recent studies on anti-Semitism in America, see Nathan Perlmutter and Ruth A. Perlmutter, *The Real Anti-Semitism in America* (New York: Arbor House, 1982); Harold Quinley and Charles Glock, *Anti-Semitism in America* (New York: Harper & Row, 1979); and Ernest Volkman, *A Legacy of Hate: Anti-Semitism in America* (New York: Franklin Watts, 1982).

62. For detailed data, see Geraldine Rosenfield, "The Polls: Attitudes Toward American Jews," *Public Opinion Quarterly* 46(Fall 1982): 431–43.

63. For an additional work on possible linkages between Israel and anti-Semitism, see William Schneider, *Anti-Semitism and Israel: A Report on American Public Opinion* (New York: American Jewish Committee, December 1978, mimeographed).

64. In his September 1982 poll, Gallup found that 77 percent of American Jewry and 51 percent of the general public thought that anti-Semitism in the United States was likely to increase after the war in Lebanon.

65. Steven M. Cohen, *American Modernity and Jewish Identity* 164-167.

66. In recent years it has been argued that a substantial segment of the American Jewish community has moved from liberalism to the center or even to the right. This impression has been based in part on the increase in the Jewish vote for Republican presidential candidates, but several studies have shown that basically, the majority of Jews still adheres to liberalism. See, for example, Alan M. Fisher, "Jewish Political Shift? Erosion, Yes; Conversion, No," in Seymour Martin Lipset, ed., *Party Coalition in the 1980's* (San Francisco: Institute for Contemporary Studies, 1981), 327-40; and Milton Himmelfarb, "Are Jews Becoming Republican?" *Commentary* 72(August 1981): 27-31.

67. Lucy S. Dawidowicz, "The Arab-Israeli War of 1967—American Public Opinion," *American Jewish Year Book* 69(1968): 203.

68. Irving Greenberg, "The Interaction of Israel and American Jewry After the Holocaust," in M. Davis, ed., *World Jewry and the State of Israel* (New York: Arno Press, 1977), 268.

69. A forecast of possible developments in American-Israeli relations can be found in Donald Feldstein, *The American Jewish Community in the Twenty First Century—A Projection* (New York: American Jewish Congress, March 1984, mimeographed).

8
Sociodemographic Dimensions

The previous chapter explored in some detail the opinions of American Jews toward Israel and the Arab-Israeli conflict. This chapter examines the opinions of other strata in American society on identical issues. The main purpose of this chapter is to discern whether various groups of Americans have differed in their opinions of Israel and the Middle East over time and, if they have, for what reasons?

When conducting surveys, different American pollsters employ different sociodemographic distinctions. The most frequently used categories are sex, age, race, education, region, income, politics, religion, occupation, city size, and labor union membership. There are also varying distinctions within each category. For example, in the *race* category, Roper distinguishes between blacks and whites, Gallup between whites and non-whites, and Harris employs three subcategories: whites, blacks, and hispanics. Similarly, pollsters use various subcategories of age and income. In the *politics* category, several pollsters classify groups by party affiliation: Republicans, Democrats, and independents; others use the ideological criterion and divide the category into conservatives, liberals, and "middle-of-the-roaders." All these different classifications complicate efforts to integrate opinion data into meaningful trends and patterns; therefore, data that could not be reasonably integrated had to be discarded.

The methodology employed in this chapter consists of three elements. The first is presentation and analysis of trends in the distribution of sympathies of various groups for Israel and the Arab nations. The second element outlines and explains possible differences in opinions of a selected list of principal issues, including military aid, the Palestinian problem, U.S. policy, the Israeli-Egyptian peacemaking process, the territorial dimension, and the 1982 Israeli war in Lebanon. The particular questions selected for each issue were deemed to be the most illuminating regarding possible differences among the various groups. As noted in previous chapters, responses to these questions do not necessarily represent the most balanced and bias-free distribution of opinions. They are used here only for the purpose of comparison. The third methodological element is presentation and analysis of special surveys and studies of particular groups, such as blacks, political elites, and church members. The results of these studies, combined with the more standard data, shed light on opinions and attitudes among various sociodemographic groups.

A comparison between the attitudes of two groups in specific samples raises a methodological question, since differences in percentages may be due primarily to sampling error. This question is discussed and explained in appendix B. At this point, it should be noted that in certain percentage distributions in small samples, the sampling error is higher than usual. In addition, results based on fewer than 100 responses must be interpreted with extreme caution.

It is quite obvious that not all Americans follow events in Israel and the Middle East with the same amount of interest. Gallup polls conducted in the early 1980s that gauged American public awareness by sociodemographic breakdown revealed that men are generally much more aware of the Middle East situation than women are, whites more than nonwhites, and the college-educated more than the lesser-educated.[1] In the *income* category, awareness increased with earnings, so that the highest wage-earners are the most aware. Republicans heard or read about the Middle East slightly more than did Democrats and independents. The scores for Protestants and Catholics are almost identical. In summary, it appears that white, college-educated men who are 25 years and older and work in high-income professional and business positions are the most aware of the situation in the Middle East. One of the questions explored in the following pages is whether awareness correlates with particular opinions and attitudes toward this area.

This chapter opens with an exploration of the attitudes and opinions of American blacks. It then analyzes principal socioeconomic factors—education, profession, and income—and their bearing on opinions of Israel and the Arab-Israeli conflict. The chapter then continues with an investigation of possible gender and generation gaps in attitudes toward Israel and the Middle East. The next section compares opinions among different regions of the United States followed by an analysis of attitudes by religious orientation and political outlook. The chapter concludes with opinions of leaders and compares them with the opinions of the general public.

Blacks

The attitudes of American blacks toward Israel and the Arab-Israeli conflict have been shaped by three prisms: relations with American Jews, perceptions of American and Israeli foreign policy, and racial solidarity with the Third World. Relations between American Jews and American blacks have developed between two opposite poles. The first is the pole of minorities. As two large minority communities in the United States, Jews and blacks have held a common interest in fighting all forms of discrimination. The generally liberal outlook of American Jewry also has helped place Jewish leaders at the head of the campaign for civil rights in America. Civil and minority rights occupied a significant place in the post–World War II platforms and activities of the Democratic party; consequently, blacks and Jews found themselves working together in this party.

However, at the other extreme has been the pole of economic and racial antagonism. Blacks have also perceived Jews as whites, landlords, bankers, and merchants—members of the "exploiting economic elite" of the United States. Throughout the 1950s and 1960s, these feelings were mitigated by the common battle for human rights. In the 1970s, however, the black-Jewish coalition disintegrated. Leaders of the two groups disagreed on the campaign for civil rights, frequently clashing over programs such as affirmative action and school integration. Black youth grew radical and challenged the traditional black leadership, which still valued cooperation with American Jews.[2]

Jewish-black differences over domestic issues coincided with the dramatic consequences and effects of the Six-Day War. Even before this war, several black groups perceived the Arabs as the blacks of the Middle East and the Israelis as the whites. They concluded that as American whites discriminated against and exploited American blacks, so the white Israel oppressed the "black" Arabs.[3] This attitude is quite ironic. The Arabs, more than any other inhabitants of the Middle East, have persecuted, oppressed, and enslaved blacks.[4] The perception of Israel as a white nation is also false, since the majority of Israeli Jews are either of Sephardic or of non-European origin.

The occupation of Arab lands in the Six-Day War, the rise of the PLO, and the wide publicity accorded the Palestinian problem since 1967 added another dimension to the attitudes of several black groups toward Israel and the Arab-Israeli conflict. These groups envisioned the Palestinian campaign for national rights as analogous to their campaign for civil rights and the PLO as analogous to their own Southern Christian Leadership Council.[5] This perception was strongly expressed in September 1979, during the Reverend Jesse Jackson's visit to Israel and Lebanon. Jackson met with a pro-PLO group in an Arab suburb of Jerusalem and sang with them "We Shall Overcome."[6] He also met with PLO Chairman Yasser Arafat and endorsed many of his positions toward Israel. The Arabs sensed this anti-Israeli sentiment among Jackson's group, and after his visit to the Middle East contributed substantial sums of money to his Chicago-based organization, PUSH.[7]

During the 1984 Democratic presidential primary elections, Jackson's anti-Israel attitudes were further accentuated by negative remarks directed at American Jews. One particular anti-Semitic slur, given much prominence in the media, sparked both black and Jewish concern toward Jackson's ideology. According to a poll conducted by Harris on April 9, 1984, 58 percent of the black sample agreed with the statement: "My opinion of Jesse Jackson went way down when he made negative remarks about New York Jews." Yet later surveys conducted by CBS News (April 23–26), Gallup (April 25–26), and *WP*-ABC (May 16–22) recorded substantial support for Jackson's candidacy among blacks. Thus, two weeks after Jackson's anti–Jewish attack, most American blacks didn't feel he was anti-Semitic, or that his "blunder" might damage chances for voter support.

One black group, the Black Muslims, has identified with the Arabs since the creation of Israel. By its nature, this group shares religious and cultural similarities with the Arab world and has tended to adopt its extremist views on Israel. The Black Muslims have rejected Israel's right to exist and see Israel as a creation of "American imperialism."[8] One of the present leaders of the Black Muslims movement, Louis Farrakhan, established a close relationship with Qaddafi of Libya and has voiced extremist views on Judaism, the Jewish people and Israel. The Black Muslims are a small group in the American black community, but in recent years, despite religious differences, has allied with other groups, including that of Jesse Jackson's. Nevertheless, results recorded from a survey of American blacks conducted in October 1985 by Market Facts for the Simon Wiesenthal Center indicate that only 29 percent of the 500–person sample expressed favorable attitudes toward Farrakhan. Seventeen percent held unfavorable views and a 53–percent majority held no opinion.[9]

One additional, influencial factor in the attitudes of many American blacks toward Israel has been Israel's standing in the Third World, particularly in Africa. In the 1950s and 1960s Israel established excellent and constructive relations with black Africa, primarily through various programs of technical cooperation. These relations gradually deteriorated after the Six-Day War and even more after the Yom Kippur War. In an effort to delegitimize Israel, the Arab and Communist world instigated a massive propaganda campaign designed to prove a close ideological, economic and military relationship between Israel and South Africa.[10] Israel's relations with South Africa have never differed from those of Britain, France, and the United States, or even from those of most black African and Arab states.[11] Most of these countries maintain commercial relations with South Africa, and Western nations are its chief weapons suppliers. Yet Israel was singled out by the Arabs as the closest and the most important ally of South Africa. These allegations have affected the attitudes of some American blacks toward Israel. To what extent, then, have these various perceptions and beliefs been reflected in the overall opinions Blacks have of Israel?

American blacks are not anti-Israel. In the February 1981 Yankelovich survey, blacks expressed favorable feelings for Israel by a majority of 65 to 35 percent. However, the comparable results for whites were 75 to 25 percent.[12] Furthermore, of the 75–percent favorable group, 35 percent expressed a highly favorable attitude for Israel. The comparable figure for black Ameri-

Table 8–1
Distribution of Sympathies for Israel and the Arab Nations, by Race

		Whites		*Blacks*[a]	
Date	*Poll*	*Israel*	*Arabs*	*Israel*	*Arabs*
Dec. '73	Gallup	53%	7%	27%	8%
Jan. '75	Gallup	46	7	34	12
June '77	Gallup	46	7	23	12
Oct. '79	*L.A. Times*	47	13	47	15
Oct. '80	Gallup	47	11	34	25
Nov. '81	Gallup	50	12	44	14
Mar. '82	*WP*-ABC	50	8	38	18
Nov. '82	Gallup	50	16	34	24
July '83	Gallup	49	11	40	18
Jan. '84	Roper	47	8	29	10
	Average	48	10	35	16

Sources: See the relevant sources in tables 2–1, 3–2 and 4–1.
[a]Gallup distinguished between whites and nonwhites.

cans was 20 percent. Similar differences were recorded in the Gallup favorability rating of Israel conducted in August 1982, during the war in Lebanon.

Examination of the distribution of sympathies for Israel and the Arabs among blacks through an entire decade indicates that blacks have consistently expressed more sympathy toward Israel, most recently by a ratio of three to one (see Table 8–1). However, a comparison between the scores of whites and blacks show that in most cases, blacks sympathized less with Israel and more with the Arabs then did whites. Only in one poll (October 1979) were the differences between these two groups marginal. The largest gaps were recorded after the Yom Kippur War and the war in Lebanon. In the most recent score the differences between whites and blacks are apparent only in the Israeli column.

Surveys conducted in the early 1980s reveal pro–Israeli sentiments among blacks on several key issues. In 1982, more blacks than whites opposed the AWACS sale to Saudi Arabia (67 percent), and the proposed sale of weapons to Jordan (70 percent).[13] At the same time, a clear majority of 77 percent believed that the United States should maintain or increase military aid to Israel. More blacks than whites (86 percent versus 74 percent) also noted that the U.S.-Israel relationship is not close enough, or the right kind of relationship.

As mentioned earlier, several black leaders, particularly Jesse Jackson, adopted a favorable attitude toward the PLO and Arafat. But have the "rank and file" of the American black community also adhered to these sentiments? Two months after Arafat's appearance at the United Nations, the Yankelovich organization examined the perceptions of Americans, including black Americans, of the PLO and Israel. Those who had heard of the PLO (52 percent) were asked to choose the most applicable characteristics of the organization. Similar percentages of black and whites agreed that the PLO was "backward," "undemocratic," "anti-U.S.," and "pro-Communist."[14] However, twice as many Blacks as whites felt that the PLO was "freedom loving," and a lesser percentage characterized it as a "terrorist organization."

Several years later, in August 1979, immediately after the PLO-Young affair, the *Newsweek*-Gallup poll asked a representative sample of 523 blacks: "Do you consider the PLO mainly a terrorist group or is it more like an American civil-rights organization, or don't you have an opinion?"[15] The analogy between the PLO and an American civil-rights organization was not only biased but also unfounded because the PLO's fight is for national, not civil, rights. The majority of respondents probably recognized this disparity and selected the "no opinion" answer; 27 percent chose the civil-rights analogy, and 16 percent cited the PLO as a terrorist group.

During another controversial event, the 1982 Israeli war in Lebanon, Harris examined the distribution of American sympathies for Israel versus the PLO. He found that while whites sympathized more with Israel by a majority of 63 to 1 percent, American blacks sympathized more with Israel only by a plurality of 44 to 29 percent.[16]

Another controversial issue related to the PLO is the Israeli and American position on negotiations with this organization. In the Yankelovich survey of January 1975, the general public, by a close plurality of 36 to 29 percent stated that Israel was wrong in refusing to negotiate with the PLO. Blacks held the same view by a similar plurality of 34 to 27 percent. However, in the case of U.S. negotiations with the PLO, whites took a different stance than did blacks, preferring that Washington not conduct talks with the PLO.[17] Therefore, when Andrew Young met with the PLO representative at the United Nations in violation of an official American pledge and consequently was forced to resign, blacks looked on this incident from a very different angle than did whites and the general public.[18] While whites *disapproved* of the Young meetings with the PLO representative by a 54 to 33 percent majority, blacks *approved* of the action by a clear majority of 62 to 17 percent.[19]

Whites also disapproved of other black leaders' taking up the cause of the PLO by a majority of 62 to 20 percent, but blacks held the opposite view by a 44 to 26 percent plurality. Whites rejected the notion that Young lost his job because of Israeli and Jewish pressure, but blacks were equally divided on this issue. Both groups agreed, however, that the PLO did not benefit from the Young affair.

The results from blacks for the entire Young-PLO affair must be interpreted with great caution. Young was one of the most prominent black leaders in the United States, and his appointment to the U.N. post was viewed by American blacks as a major step toward genuine black participation in the

United States government. It could well be that the aforementioned black views of the Young affair stemmed from concern about Young and black involvement in government, not from any firmly held beliefs about the issue that led to Young's resignation.

Finally, on the issue of an independent Palestinian state, American blacks favored neither the Israeli nor the PLO position. The 1979 *Newsweek*-Gallup survey of American blacks included the following question:

> The PLO has fought for many years with Israel for the establishment of a new homeland for the Palestinians. Israel says that such a Palestinian state would be a threat to its security. Do you think the U.S. should favor the PLO on this issue, favor Israel on this issue or remain neutral?

The escape clause of neutrality may have prevented a clear-cut response, since it was selected by 68 percent of the respondents. Ten percent favored the PLO position, and 7 percent favored the Israeli position on this issue.

The data and analysis in this section reveal that blacks generally support Israel. Blacks hold favorable opinions toward the state, sympathize more with Israelis than with Arabs and oppose military aid to Arab nations. Comparatively, however, blacks have expressed less sympathy for Israel than have whites. Like all Americans they held some reservations about the PLO and its policies, but still expressed a somewhat more favorable opinion of that organization than did whites.

Socioeconomic Factors

Public opinion research has demonstrated that socioeconomic factors—such as education, occupation, and income—create certain attitude structures. Americans who are well educated, hold professional, white-collar, or business positions, and earn from a medium to a high income tend to be more interested in public affairs, especially foreign affairs, and hold firmer and more consistent opinions than the less educated and those who work in less well-paid positions. This section examines possible correlations between education, occupation, and income and opinions of Israel and the Arab-Israeli conflict. Since education determines occupation and income to a large extent, it is examined first.

Education

Most public opinion polls distinguish among three levels of education: grade school, high school, and college. Some include a fourth level—graduate school. Table 8–2 presents results of polls on sympathies for Israel and the Arab nations by the three standard educational levels.

The first part of table 8–2 indicates that a much greater percentage of

Table 8–2
Sympathies for Israel and the Arab Nations, by Socioeconomic Levels

A. Educational Level

	Grade School		High School		College	
Date	*Israel*	*Arabs*	*Israel*	*Arabs*	*Israel*	*Arabs*
June '67	50%	7%	50%	3%	69%	5%
Jan. '69	39	3	49	4	59	9
Dec. '73	42	7	48	7	58	9
Jan. '75	33	3	43	8	51	11
June '77	27	5	43	7	52	10
Oct. '79	38	11	47	12	55	14
Aug. '81	28	5	44	10	50	13
July '83	37	13	49	11	53	12
Jan. '84	36	6	42	7	52	10
Average	37	7	46	8	55	10

B. Occupation

	Non-Labor		Blue-Collar, Manual		White-Collar, Clerical Sales		Professional, Business	
Date	*Israel*	*Arabs*	*Israel*	*Arabs*	*Israel*	*Arabs*	*Israel*	*Arabs*
June '67	49%	4%	52%	3%	62%	2%	64%	4%
Oct. '72	46	8	41	12	45	12	53	10
Aug. '81	32	9	47	10	42	14	49	13
Jan. '84	—	—	39	9	49	6	55	11
Average	42	7	45	8	49	8	55	9

C. Income Level[a]

Date	Low		Low-Middle		Middle		Upper-Middle		High	
	Israel	*Arabs*	*Israel*	*Arabs*	*Israel*	*Arabs*	*Israel*	*Arabs*	*Israel*	*Arabs*
June '67	51%	6%	49%	5%	45%	3%	62%	4%	63%	3%
Jan. '69	42	5	41	6	44	5	55	5	56	7
Dec. '73	37	12	45	7	52	5	58	6	59	7
Apr. '75	29	8	26	6	38	8	43	7	47	9
Mar. '79	26	8	28	10	37	8	36	13	35	15
Aug. '81	37	7	45	6	43	12	45	14	49	14
July '83	43	8	48	15	46	13	55	10	57	14
Jan. '84	37	7	45	8	46	7	—	—	49	11
Average	38	8	41	8	44	8	50	8	52	10

Sources: Each poll in this table was conducted by Gallup, with the exception of January 1984, which was conducted by Roper. See the relevant sources in tables 2–1, 3–2 and 4–1.

[a]1983 Income *Gallup:* low, under $7,000; low-middle, $7,000–$14,999; middle, $15,000–19,999; upper-middle, $20,000–$39,000; high, $40,000 and over.

respondents with a college education sympathized with either Israel or the Arabs. In 1967, 74 percent of the college graduates sympathized with one side or the other; only 57 percent of the grade school graduates had strong opinions. In 1984, 62 percent of the college graduates chose sides, but the equivalent number of grade school graduates was only 42 percent.

In each poll in table 8–2, the majority of college graduates sympathized more with Israel. The percentage of those who held he same view at the grade school level was much lower—around the upper thirties. During the last decade, fluctuations in the Israeli and Arab scores in both the college and high school columns grew much smaller than those of the less educated. The Israeli scores at the college level wavered between 50 and 58 percent; those at the high school level, between 42 and 49 percent; but a wide gap of between 27 and 42 percent was recorded for the grade school level.

Table 8–3 presents distributions of results by educational level for various Israeli and Arab Israeli issues. Again, in most scores, the college-educated took positions more often than did those with only a grade school education. As indicated in question (a), support for the establishment of Israel increased with the level of education. Each category disapproved of the Israeli military operation in the Sinai Peninsula in 1956, but several months later the same groups placed the blame for the crisis mainly on Egypt. The culpability of Egypt also increased with the level of education.

The next section in table 8–3 presents various scores of polls on general sentiments toward Israel. In all of these polls, positive attitudes toward Israel substantially increased with the level of education. On the territorial question, the college-educated supported by a much larger ratio the Israeli position ("keep all" and "give back part") and were the least supportive of the Arab

Table 8–3
Attitudes toward Selected Issues, by Education

Date		*Poll*	*Issue*	*Grade School*	*High School*	*College*	*(n)*
			Establishment of Israel				
(a)	Apr. '48	Roper	For U.N. partition resolution	24%	26%	30%	(3,62[illegible]
			Suez-Sinai Crisis (1956)				
(b)	Nov. '56	Gallup	Israeli action in Egypt:				
			Approve	5	12	15	
			Disapprove	38	48	56	
(c)	Apr. '57	Gallup	Blame for the conflict:				
			Israel	9	14	12	
			Egypt	33	41	54	
			General Feelings toward Israel				
(d)	Aug. '75	Caddel	Israelis "like Americans"	37	49	59	

Table 8–3 continued

Date		Poll	Issue	Grade School	High School	College	(n)
(e)	Aug. '76	Gallup	Favorability rating	55	62	77	
(f)	Mar. '77	NA	Israel friendly or ally of U.S.	34	46	75	
(g)	Feb. '81	Yankelovich	Favorable attitudes	68	71	80	(1,072)
(h)	Aug. '82	Gallup	Favorability rating	52	54	63	
			Territories				
(i)	Oct. '77	Gallup	Israel should:				
			Give back part	26	33	47	
			Give back all	17	12	11	
			Keep all	18	27	27	
			Peacemaking				
(j)	Apr. '78	CBS-NYT	Israel made too many and enough concessions	31	31	36	(1,417)
(k)	Dec. '78	Harris	Israel more right in talks breakdown	30	34	30	(1,498)
(l)	Mar. '79	Gallup	Israel doing all to bring peace	23	23	31	
			Military Aid				
(m)	Oct. '73	Gallup	Favor supply of arms to Israel	32	35	44	
(n)	Dec. '74	Harris	Favor military aid	58	66	69	
(o)	Jan. '75	Yankelovich	Favor aid	43	46	51	(1,468)
(p)	Feb. '81	Roper	Favor use of U.S. troops if Arabs invade Israel	12	17	30	(2,000)
			PLO and Palestinians				
(q)	Mar. '79	Gallup	Favor Palestinian nation	22	33	47	
(r)	Aug. '79	Harris	Young-PLO meeting:				
			Right	20	38	39	(1,201)
			Wrong	55	45	53	
(s)	June '82	Harris	Sympathize more:				
			With Israel	48	57	66	(1,255)
			With PLO	14	18	14	
			War in Lebanon				
(t)	July '82	Harris	Justified	33	39	52	(1,250)
			Unjustified	26	38	35	
			Israel-U.S. Ally				
(u)	Jan. '84	Roper	Reliable	46	51	61	(1,994)
			Not reliable	21	27	22	

Sources: (a) See sources in table 1–2. (b) Ch. 1, note 70. (c) Table 1–6. (d)(f) Lipset and Schneider, *Israel and the Jews in American Public Opinion*. (e) Table 2–2. (g) Note 12. (h) *Gallup Report*, September 1982, 24. (i) Table 2–5. (j) *New York Times*, April 14, 1978. (k) *ABC News-Harris Survey*, January 1979. (l)(q) *Gallup Opinion Index*, March 1979, 16. (m) Table 6–4. (n) Table 6–3. (o) Table 6–2. (p) Table 6–7. (r) Note 19. (s)(t) Note 16. (u) *Roper Reports*, February 1984, 19.

stand ("give back all"). No significant differences were found in the responses of the three groups to questions on the peacemaking process.

Support for aid to Israel also increased with the level of education. In various surveys of American attitudes toward foreign aid, college-educated Americans supported aid much more than did the less educated and the general public. Responses to the questions on aid in table 8–3 confirm this tendency. Polls conducted on the PLO and the Palestinians reveal more support among the college-educated for a Palestinian nation if the alternative is "to continue to live as they do now." At the same time, the Young-PLO meeting was rejected by the three groups—mostly by the grade school and college graduates. The sympathy scores for the PLO were similar among the three groups, but sympathy for Israel slightly increased with higher education. Although the high school graduates barely justified the Israeli War in Lebanon (by one percentage point), the college graduates justified Israel's move by a majority of 52 to 35 percent. Finally, in 1984, positive evaluation of Israel's reliability as an American ally also increased with education.

On the basis of the evidence in tables 8–2 and 8–3, it could be said that Americans with college education sympathize more with Israel than do less-educated Americans.[20] The college-educated held more favorable feelings for Israel, have perceived it as an American ally, supported military aid, and justified Israel's military action and its policy on the territorial issue more than did the less educated. However, college-educated respondents also held opinions on certain aspects of the Palestinian problem that were opposed by both the United States and Israeli governments.

Occupation

Most American pollsters divide occupations into four categories: professional and business; white-collar, clerical, and sales; blue-collar and manual work; and the non–labor force, which includes farmers. Education determines occupation to a large extent, and it is quite common to find a greater percentage of college graduates among Americans in professional and business jobs than among blue-collar workers. The point in question is whether the patterns of attitudes by educational levels also correlates with the opinions of various occupational groups.

The second part of table 8–2 indicates that sympathy for Israel has remained strong among all four occupational groups but strongest in the professional and business column. Responses from each group to questions (g) and (h) in table 8–3 are similar, but during the 1982 war in Lebanon, the favorability rating for Israel among Americans in professional and business occupations was higher (63 percent) than that registered for the other three groups (between 52 and 55 percent). On the territorial issue, support for Israel clearly increases with occupational levels, but the most favorable attitudes toward

Israel's positions in the peacemaking process were recorded in the white-collar column, with the next highest results appearing in the professional and business column. Professional and business people mostly supported the establishment of a Palestinian nation if the alternative would be the continuation of the status quo in the Palestinian refugee camps (question (q) in table 8–3). But Americans in professional and business positions held very negative opinions of the PLO and justified the Israeli war in Lebanon by a much larger ratio (54 to 34 percent) than did the other occupational groups. Finally, the identical group perceived Israel as a reliable U.S. ally by the largest ratio (62 to 22 percent). The comparable score for the blue-collar group was 49 to 27 percent.

Income

Pollsters have employed between five and seven different categories of income when conducting national surveys. Inflation has also confused income classification. What was considered "high income" in the early 1970s fell to "medium income" in the mid-1980s. Thus, for the purpose of comparison, it is necessary to construct brackets of income classified by words, not figures. Five categories are suggested, ranging from low to high income. The standard comparable 1983 figures for each category in the Gallup polls are listed in the income portion of table 8–2.

Table 8–2 indicates that in most polls conducted since 1967, sympathy for Israel has risen with income levels, whereas sympathy for the Arab countries has remained similar among all the income groups. Trend analysis shows that with the exclusion of the record scores of the Six-Day War (June 1967), the 1969 scores recorded in the Israeli column are similar among all the groups to the scores recorded in July 1983. On the other hand, in the higher income bracket, sympathy for the Arabs doubled. Even so, Israel's score surpassed that of the Arabs in 1983 in the higher and lower income brackets by ratios of four and five to one.

During the 1982 war in Lebanon, the highest favorability rating for Israel (question (h) in table 8–3) was recorded in the two highest income brackets (59 percent). The lowest rating (47 percent) was recorded in the low income bracket. However, the difference between the results in the low-middle and the high income categories was only eight percentage points. Responses to other questions on specific issues suggest a similar pattern. The distribution of responses to the question on the war in Lebanon (question (t) in table 8–3) yielded an interesting finding. Respondents in the lowest income level said that the Israeli operation was unjustified by a 37 to 30 percent plurality, but respondents from the remaining categories felt that the war was justified, with those in the low-middle and the high income categories giving the highest approval ratings (45 to 35 percent and 50 to 30 percent, respectively).

Polls on various levels of education, occupation, and income point to a clear pattern of opinions on Israel and the Arab-Israeli conflict. First, the college-educated who work in business, professional, and white-collar jobs and who also earn a medium to high income chose sides and took a position more than those in the other groups. In other words, the percentages in the "don't know" column for these groups were smaller than those for the other groups in the same column. The evidence gathered in this section suggests that general sympathy for Israel and support for most of its stands are strongest among the well educated, well employed, and well paid. This pattern has held over time and spans a great variety of issues.

Gender and Generation Gaps

Several studies of public opinion, especially those conducted since the final stages of America's involvement in Vietnam, revealed stronger criticism and reservations about American policy and military aid to South Vietnam from women and young adults than from other groups in American society.[21] This attitude affected, to a certain degree, the overall approach of women and young adults to foreign affairs and American foreign policy.

In the past 15 years, Arab-Israeli relations have been marred by several major wars and other less intensive acts of violence. The United States has extended substantial military aid to Israel and to its Arab allies in the Middle East. To what extent, then, have the characteristics of the Arab-Israeli conflict and the fundamental aversion of women and young adults to violence affected the opinions these groups have of Israel?

Gender Gaps

The first part of table 8–4 presents distributions of sympathies for Israel and Arab nations among men and women from 1967; it reveals only slight differences in the scores of the two groups. In eight of the eleven polls, the differences in the Israeli column averaged between one and two percentage points. In only one poll (November 1982), conducted during the Israeli war in Lebanon, was the difference greater than 3 percent. In general, so far as sympathies are concerned, no differences were recorded in the opinions of women and men. Both groups overwhelmingly sympathized with Israel.

The scores in the first part of table 8–5 confirm the general pattern of table 8–4. Both groups held identical degrees of favorable feelings for Israel, but during the war in Lebanon, men more than women rated Israel favorably (see the aberrant sympathy score for November 1982 in table 8–4). On the issue of basic U.S. policy, women supported Israel more than men, but men were slightly more pro-Israel on the territorial issue and the peacemaking pro-

Table 8–4
Sympathies for Israel and the Arab Nations, by Gender and Age

Gender

	Men		*Women*	
Date	*Israel*	*Arabs*	*Israel*	*Arabs*
Jan. '67	56%	4%	55%	4%
Jan. '69	48	5	50	6
Apr. '75	38	9	36	6
June '77	44	10	43	5
Apr. '78	38	12	39	10
Mar. '79	33	10	35	10
Oct. '80	47	15	44	12
Aug. '81	45	11	43	10
Nov. '82	52	18	45	16
Jan. '83	48	14	51	10
Jan. '84	45	10	43	6
Average	45	11	44	9

Age

	21–29		*30–49*		*50 and over*	
Date	*Israel*	*Arabs*	*Israel*	*Arabs*	*Israel*	*Arabs*
June '67	67%	1%	54%	3%	54%	6%
Jan. '69	55	5	48	6	47	5

	18–24		*25–29*		*30–49*		*50 and over*	
Date	*Israel*	*Arabs*	*Israel*	*Arabs*	*Israel*	*Arabs*	*Israel*	*Arabs*
Dec. '73	46%	5%	48%	8%	53%	6%	48%	9%
Jan. '75	55	12	47	13	43	7	38	5
Oct. '77	—	—	47	13	46	10	44	10
Mar. '79	35	9	33	7	36	11	32	14
Aug. '81	54	12	40	14	49	9	36	11

	18–24		*25–34*		*35–49*		*50 and over*	
Date	*Israel*	*Arabs*	*Israel*	*Arabs*	*Israel*	*Arabs*	*Israel*	*Arabs*
Jan. '83	46%	13%	55%	11%	53%	12%	47%	11%
July '83	64	7	48	14	48	12	41	13

Sources: See the relevant sources in tables 2–1, 3–2, and 4–1.

Table 8–5
Attitudes toward Selected Issues, by Gender

	Date	*Poll*	*Issue*	*Men*	*Women*	*(n)*
			General Feelings toward Israel			
(a)	Feb. '81	Yankelovich	Favorable feelings	73%	73%	(1,072)
(b)	Aug. '82	Gallup	Favorability rating	61	51	
			Basic U.S. Policy			
(c)	Aug. '79	Gallup	U.S. should			
			Give strongest support to Israel	35	41	(1,555)
			Pay more attention to Arabs	31	20	
			Territories			
(d)	June '77	Gallup	Israel should			
			Give back part	33	36	
			Give back all	20	13	
			Keep all	27	21	
			Peacemaking			
(e)	Dec. '78	Harris	Israel more right in talks breakdown	32	29	(1,498)
(f)	Mar. '79	Gallup	Israel doing all to bring.peace	28	22	
			Military Aid			
(g)	Oct. '73	Gallup	Favor supply of arms to Israel	45	29	
(h)	Apr. '75	Gallup	Favor supplies & troops to Israel	56	51	(1,599)
(i)	Feb. '81	Roper	Favor use of U.S. troops if Arabs invade Israel	30	22	
			PLO and Palestinians			
(j)	Mar. '79	Gallup	Favor Palestinian nation	42	33	
(k)	Nov. 79	CBS-*NYT*	Favor U.S. talks with PLO	48	36	(1,385
(l)	June '82	Harris	Sympathize more with			
			Israel	68	54	(1,255
			PLO	13	18	
			Israeli War in Lebanon			
(m)	July '82	Harris	Justified	56	34	(1,250
			Unjustified	32	39	
			U.S. Involvement in Lebanon			
(n)	Oct. '83	CBS-*NYT*	Approve of sending Marines to Beirut	55	41	(1,09
			Israel-U.S. Ally			
(o)	Jan. '84	Roper	Reliable	60	48	(1,99
			Not reliable	22	25	
			TWA Hostage Crisis			
(p)	June '85	*WP*-ABC	Approve of Reagan's handling of crisis	64	52	(1,01
(q)	June '85	*WP*-ABC	Israel doing all to resolve crisis	28	20	

Sources: (c) The Gallup Poll, Study No. G0 79167-H, conducted for the American Jewish Committee, Se tember 1979. (h) Table 6–6. (n) Table 4–6. (p) Table 4–2 (q) Table 4–9. For sources of remaining questio see sources cited in table 8–3.

cess. Higher percentages of men also favored military aid, but women, much more than men, supported the Israeli positions on talks with the PLO and a Palestinian nation.

Results for the last four issues in table 8–5 reveal a more discernible pattern. Men, much more than women, justified Israel's military operation in Lebanon, approved of the U.S. military involvement in Beirut, perceived Israel as a reliable American ally, and approved of Reagan's handling of the TWA hostage crisis. They also felt that Israel was doing all it could to resolve the hostage crisis.

The preceding data and analysis suggest that American men and women have generally held similar views on Israel and Arab-Israeli issues. In one area, however—military aid, military operations, and counterterrorism—men, more than women, have expressed stronger support of Israel. These results correlate with findings of general studies on the distribution of opinions between men and women on military aid and the use of force. However, opinions in this area have not affected women's overall attitudes toward Israel or Israel-related issues.

Generation Gaps

It has been argued that the Holocaust created a worldwide wave of sympathy for Jews and was a significant factor contributing to the highly favorable and positive attitudes of Americans toward the creation and survival of the Jewish state. Further, it has been asserted that those who heard of or were directly exposed to the horrors of the Holocaust are more likely to support Israel than are younger Americans, untouched by this tragedy in Jewish history. This hypothesis is tested against public opinion data in table 8–4.

Pollsters have in the past employed different categories of age groups, making comparisons across various issues and over time very difficult and often impossible. Therefore, the data in the second panel in table 8–4 are somewhat fractured, though nevertheless sufficient to establish some partial patterns. Table 8–4 indicates that young adults—Americans between 18 and 24—have consistently sympathized with Israel more than have other age groups, sometimes by substantial margins. On only two occasions, the Yom Kippur War and the war in Lebanon, did older age groups sympathize more with Israel than did young adults. In the most recent survey, the score for the 18- to 24-year-old age group is substantially more pro-Israel than are the scores recorded from the other three groups.

Responses to questions on favorability rating (questions (a) and (b) in table 8–5) indicate similar results for all age groups. Support for both Israel and the Arabs was the highest recorded in young adults' answers to question (c), concerning U.S. policy, but Israel still surpassed the Arabs by 12 percentage points. Young adults, more than other age groups, also supported Israel's position on the territorial issue. Only slight differences appeared between the opinions of all age groups on Israel's peace efforts, but again, young adults, much more than older Americans, supported U.S. military aid to Israel and the use of U.S. troops to aid Israel in the event of an Arab invasion (question (i) in table 8–5). Slight differences appeared in responses to the question on the concept of a Palestinian nation. Young adults were the least critical of the Young-PLO meeting and, during the war in Lebanon, expressed a relatively high rate of sympathy for the PLO. They were also closely divided on the justification of this war.

The distribution of opinions on Israel among the various age groups in the United States reveal that young adults, more than any other age groups, have sympathized with Israel and have supported its policies and the granting of U.S. aid to that country. The data clearly negate the hypothesis that exposure to the Holocaust correlates with higher rates of pro-Israelism. On the contrary, young adults, for whom the Holocaust is a chapter in history, have remained more supportive of Israel than have those who lived through World War II. Both women and young adults criticized Israel during periods of war, but unlike women, the young demonstrated a surprising amount of support for U.S. military aid to Israel.

Sociogeographic Factors

The United States is a large nation composed of several distinct regions that differ considerably in lifestyle, culture, climate, and economic and social conditions. The demographic structure of these various regions is also in a constant state of flux. In recent years, more and more Americans have migrated from the Northeast to the "sunbelt" in the South and West. This section examines the distribution of opinions on Israel and the Arab-Israeli conflict not only among the four major regions of the United States—East, Midwest, South, and West—but also among different community sizes—from large cities to rural areas.

Table 8–6 reveals that sympathies for Israel are predominant in all four regions. However, the highest average pro-Israel ratio was found in western scores and the lowest in eastern scores. Data analysis since 1975 reveals the following trends: in the East sympathy for Israel declined and sympathy for the Arabs increased. Increases were recorded in both the Israeli and the Arab columns in the Midwest. Sympathy increased for Israel and remained unchanged in the South for the Arabs, and the distribution of sympathy in the West remained stable, changing only slightly. The 1982 Israeli war in Lebanon prompted an increase in the number of respondents that chose sides in all regions (November 1982). But a poll conducted 8 months later indicates that while the scores in the Israeli column remained almost constant across all the

Table 8–6

Sympathies for Israel and the Arab Nations, by Region and Community Size

Region

	East		*Midwest*		*South*		*West*	
Date	*Israel*	*Arabs*	*Israel*	*Arabs*	*Israel*	*Arabs*	*Israel*	*Arabs*
June '67	50%	3%	54%	4%	65%	4%	57%	5%
Jan. '69	47	6	50	4	48	6	54	4
Jan. '75	47	8	41	8	39	7	50	7
June '77	41	8	42	9	43	6	51	7
Sep. '78	39	13	37	10	44	9	51	9
Jan. '79	38	17	34	14	43	12	48	13
Aug. '81	37	15	47	8	48	9	42	13
Nov. '82	43	18	47	18	51	15	54	18
July '83	42	19	48	12	50	9	52	8
Jan. '84	44	8	42	10	40	7	54	6
Average	43	11	44	10	47	8	51	9

Community Size

	1,000,000+		*500,000–999,000*		*50,000–499,000*		*2,500–49,000*		*2,500*	
Date	*Israel*	*Arabs*	*Israel*	*Arabs*	*Israel*	*Arabs*	*Israel*	*Arabs*	*Israel*	*Arabs*
June '67	54%	5%	56%	4%	65%	3%	52%	5%	49%	4%
Jan. '69	52	3	52	7	48	4	51	6	47	3
Oct. '77	39	17	39	16	49	9	49	10	49	5
Mar. '79	33	10	29	15	30	14	40	11	36	9
Aug. '81	38	14	41	12	49	12	45	7	43	10
Average	43	10	43	11	48	8	47	8	45	6

Sources: Each poll in this table was conducted by Gallup, with the exception of January 1984, which was conducted by Roper. See the relevant sources in Tables 2–1, 3–2 and 4–1.

regions, the Arabs' score remained the same only in the East. In other regions, especially in the West and South, the Arabs' score declined considerably.

Responses to questions on favorability between the regions (questions (a) and (b) in table 8–5) indicate a variation of seven percentage points in response to the first question and ten percentage points in response to the second. The highest scores were registered in the South and East, but the second highest responses to the two questions appear in the West column. The highest score for Israel in response to question (c), on basic U.S. policy, appeared in the South and the second highest in the West. The lowest score for Israel and the highest for the Arabs appears in the East column.

The widest support for Israel on the territorial issue was found in the West, with 70 percent supporting Israel's stand. The majority of respondents in the East agreed with Israel's position, but by the lowest ratio for all four regions—58 to 16 percent. The question on Israel's peace policy yielded similar results in all four regions. Majorities of respondents in each region, except the Midwest, support U.S. military aid to Israel, but the widest support was recorded in the East. Southern and midwestern respondents favored the establishment of a Palestinian nation less than did respondents in the West and East, and respondents in each region sympathized much more with Israel than with the PLO and, by similar ratios, justified the 1982 Israeli military operation in Lebanon.

Definitions of community size usually appear in two forms: verbal—cities, suburbs, towns, and rural; and quantitative—the population of each community, ranging from less than 2,500 to over one million. The second part of table 8–6, which employs the quantitative criterion, reveals an interesting transition in the distribution of sympathies in different communities. Until 1977, only slight differences existed among various community sizes. Since 1977, however, the highest rates of sympathy for Israel and the lowest for the Arabs have been registered in small towns and rural areas.

The preceding data and analysis suggest only slight differences in the distribution of opinions on Israel among the major regions of the United States and in different American communities. It appears, however, that in the last decade, the highest pro-Israeli sentiments have been found in the West and the lowest in the East. In terms of community size, identical pro-Israel sentiments were strongest in small cities and towns.

Religious Orientations

Attitudes of American clergy and their congregations toward Israel and the Arab-Israeli conflict have gained considerable prominence in recent years.[22] On one hand, the National Council of Churches has continually questioned the legitimacy of Israel and has supported the PLO and the extremist Arab positions toward Israel. On the other hand, evangelical and fundamentalist Christians under the leadership of the Reverend Jerry Falwell have expressed highly pro-Israeli sentiments and have strongly supported Israel's policies and actions in the Arab-Israeli conflict.[23] Reverend Falwell frequently visits Israel and has met the prime minister and members of the cabinet. The fundamentalists are close to Ronald Reagan, worked for his election and reelection, and during his tenure have repeatedly appealed to him to adopt pro-Israeli stands.[24]

In earlier years, the pro-Israeli positions of the fundamentalists probably would have surprised American scholars and public figures. In 1966, for example, Charles Glock and Rodney Stark argued that orthodox Christian beliefs contributed substantially to anti-Semitism.[25] Anti-Semitism means anti-Jewishness, and since Israel is a Jewish state, according to Glock and Stark, highly orthodox Christians should demonstrate more anti-Israeli sentiment than the nonreligious or those of other Christian dominations. However, various surveys conducted in the 1970s indicate that if religious orientations have at all affected attitudes toward Israel, then the more orthodox have been more rather than less pro-Israel.

A study of rural America conducted during the 1973 Yom Kippur War examined the possible effects of church membership on attitudes toward economic and military aid to Israel.[26] The study found that church members supported economic and military aid to Israel more than did non-church members. However, no significant differences were found between the attitudes of the less religious and the more religious respondents toward the same issue. The survey of rural America also found a strong, positive correlation between religious orthodoxy and the belief that Israel represents fulfillment of Biblical prophecy. This belief may well have conditioned other responses of the religious toward Israel.

The Harris survey of 1974 also reveals that the more religious respondents among most of the Christian denominations sympathized more with Israel and more emphatically supported American aid to Israel than did the nonreligious, who expressed relatively less support for Israel.[27] Most surveys on American attitudes toward Israel do not provide detailed, specific data on the various Christian denominations. If information is available, it breaks down into the two main streams of Christianity—Protestants and Catholics. Alfred Hero, Jr., found that until the 1967 Six-Day War, Protestants and Catholics held similar, positive, opinions of Israel.[28] Table 8–7 presents data on the distribution of sympathies for Israel and the Arabs between Protestants and Catholics.

According to table 8–7, both groups consistently sympathized more with Israel by substantial ratios. With the exception of one case (a survey conducted during the 1982 war in Lebanon), Protestants sympathized with Israel more than did Catholics. In 1948, similar percentages of the two groups sympathized with Israel, but the number of Catholics who expressed sympathy for the Ar-

Table 8–7
Protestant and Catholic Sympathies for Israel and the Arab Nations

		Protestants		*Catholics*	
Date	*Poll*	*Israel*	*Arabs*	*Israel*	*Arabs*
June '48	NORC	34%	12%	31%	22%
June '67	Gallup	54	5	53	2
Jan. '69	Gallup	50	4	44	7
Mar. '70	Gallup	45	2	34	6
Dec. '73	Gallup	50	7	47	10
Dec. '74	Harris	58	5	47	9
Apr. '75	Gallup	36	7	35	11
Dec. '77	Gallup	37	7	33	11
Mar. '78	Gallup	38	10	32	13
Oct. '79	*L.A. Times*	50	11	44	15
Oct. '80	Gallup	49	12	41	14
Aug. '81	Gallup	46	10	37	12
July '82	Gallup	41	12	41	12
Jan. '83	Gallup	52	10	43	16
Jan. '84	Roper	44	9	38	13
	Average	46	8	40	11

Sources: See the relevant sources in Tables 1–5, 2–1, 3–2 and 4–1.

abs was double the number of Protestants who held the same view. Twenty years later, however, during the Six-Day War, the scores for Protestants and Catholics were very similar in both columns. Slight differences between the two groups also appeared during the Yom Kippur War and the 1982 war in Lebanon, but otherwise the Protestants demonstrated higher rates of pro-Israeli sentiment than did the Catholics.

The pattern in table 8–7 is consistent with responses to various questions on Israel and the Arab-Israeli conflict. The Protestants' attitudes have been more pro-Israel than have those of the Catholics. In 1957, for example, both groups mostly cited Egypt for instigating the Suez-Sinai crisis, but Protestants held this view by a larger ratio (41 to 11 percent) than did Catholics (38 to 15 percent). By similar ratios, both religious groups supported military aid to Israel, but responses to questions on the PLO and Palestinians reveal relatively wider differences, with the Protestants adopting a much more pro-Israeli approach than the Catholics.

The main reason for the slightly stronger pro-Israeli stand of the Protestants may stem from historical and ideological characteristics. Like the Jews, Protestants suffered from discrimination and oppression on religious grounds and were forced to move from one place to another in search of religious freedom.[29] Also, Catholics are considered more doctrinaire than Protestants and obedient to the Pope in the Vatican.[30] Since the establishment of Israel, successive Popes have been unsympathetic to the Jewish state and have occasionally criticized its policy.[31] Generally, however, it appears that pro-Israelism in the United States does have its roots in religious affiliations. Schneider illustrates this phenomenon by quoting a devout Southern fundamentalist. When asked why she supported Israel even though she had never met a Jew, she answered, "I have prayed to the God of Israel all my life."[32]

Political Outlooks

Traditionally, Democrats and liberals have been considered more pro-Israel than Republicans and conservatives. Democratic presidents, such as Truman and Johnson, were described as more friendly and committed to Israel than Republican presidents, such as Eisenhower. This perception was based on ideological orientations, domestic politics, and historical events. Democrats and liberals have supported active American involvement in world affairs, whereas Republicans have favored selected involvement. Most American Jews have voted for Democratic candidates and have been active in the Democratic party, whereas Republicans have been thought of as closer to the interests of the pro-Arab oil companies.[33] In general, the platforms of the Democrats have been more pro-Israel than those of the Republicans. Finally, although President Truman supported the establishment of Israel and President Johnson defended the Israeli action during the 1967 Six-Day War, President Eisenhower is remembered for his criticism, threats, and pressure on Israel throughout the 1956 Suez-Sinai crisis and war.

These traditional characteristics altered dramatically in the 1970s. The right and left, conservatives and liberals, were replaced by the "new left," the "new right," and the "neoconservatives." The new left and the new liberals criticized Israel for retaining the occupied territories and for refusing to negotiate with the PLO on the concept of a Palestinian state in the West Bank. The neoconservatives, however, supported Israel for its role in the campaign against communist expansionism in the Middle East.

In the 1972 presidential elections, for the first time in the post–World War II era, more than a third of American Jews voted for the Republican candidate, Richard Nixon.[34] A slightly higher percentage voted for Reagan in the 1980 and the 1984 presidential elections. The big-party platforms on Israel and Middle Eastern issues grew very similar in substance and tone. Republican presidents Nixon and Reagan were perceived by large segments of American society as more supportive of Israel than was Jimmy Carter, the only Democratic president in the 1970s and most of the 1980s.

Public opinion polls have always explored the views of Republicans, Dem-

Table 8–8
Sympathies for Israel and the Arab Nations, by Political Outlook

	Republicans		*Democrats*	
Date	*Israel*	*Arabs*	*Israel*	*Arabs*
Jan. '67	56%	4%	57%	4%
Feb. '69	52	5	52	4
Jan. '75	47	6	42	6
June '77	50	7	41	8
Apr. '78	39	13	38	9
Jan. '79	43	19	41	11
Aug. '81	48	10	43	13
Nov. '82	53	18	52	15
Jan. '83	53	11	47	13
July '83	53	11	47	13
Jan. '84	55	8	42	9
Average	50	10	46	9

Sources: Each poll in this table was conducted by Gallup with the exception of January 1984 which was conducted by Roper. See the relevant sources in tables 2–1, 3–2 and 4–1.

ocrats, and independents on domestic and foreign issues. They have also occasionally asked respondents to identify themselves along ideological lines as conservatives, moderates, or liberals. However, because of the ideological transformations in the American political system, these labels grew vague and became loaded with different interpretations. Data for both types of political differentiations were collected, and wherever possible a comparison was made between the scores of the two classifications.

Table 8–8 indicates that Republicans and Democrats alike have expressed much more sympathy for Israel than for the Arabs. The average Republican pro-Israel score is 50 percent; for the Democrats, 46 percent. The average pro-Arab score for both parties is only about 10 percent. However, although in the late 1960s the Democrats were slightly more pro-Israel than the Republicans, in the 1970s and 1980s the Republicans' pro-Israel sentiments surpassed those of the Democrats.

Table 8–9 arrays results spanning various issues by political outlooks. Responses to the first question reveal only slight differences among the groups in the two classifications. But during the 1982 war in Lebanon, Republicans expressed more favorable feelings for Israel than did Democrats and independents. The second response in table 8–9 reveals the distribution of opinions on the manner in which President Eisenhower handled the Suez-Sinai crisis. Scores show that responses followed party affiliations; the Republicans were satisfied with his conduct, but the Democrats were not.

Slight differences were recorded in responses to the question concerning basic United States policy and the territorial issue, but Democrats and independents opposed more strongly than Republicans the notion that the United States should press Israel to return the West Bank to assure the flow of oil to the United States. When the identical question was examined along the conservative-liberal dichotomy, the differences among the three groups were much smaller. The three political segments held similar views about the Israeli position in the peacemaking process and American military aid to Israel, but they differed substantially on the AWACS deal with Saudi Arabia. Republicans supported the deal much more than the other groups did, probably as a result of President Reagan's insistence on its approval by Congress.

Similar percentages of various political affiliations supported the establishment of a Palestinian nation when the alternative was that the Palestinians continue to live in refugee camps. Responses to questions on hypothetical and actual U.S. meetings with the PLO reveal that Republican respondents criticized Young's talks with the PLO more than did Democrats and independents. But Democrats and Republicans held similar negative views on the basic issue of U.S. talks with the PLO, whereas independents expressed the opposite view. In 1984, Republicans more than Democrats and independents perceived Israel as a reliable U.S. ally, and on the final issue—Israel's conduct during the June 1985 TWA hostage crisis—Democrats were the most critical of Israel and, as expected, the least satisfied with Reagan's handling of the incident.

The preceding data and analysis suggest that, in general, the various political factions in the United States have expressed similar views on Israel and Arab–Israeli issues. Where differences do exist, they usually reveal that Republicans are slightly more pro-Israel than other major political groups. Respondent evaluations of presidential conduct in Arab-Israeli affairs follow party affiliation; therefore, Republicans, much more than Democrats, have been satisfied with the performance of Republican presidents, including policies and actions taken in the Arab-Israeli conflict.

Leaders and the General Public

The final section of this chapter presents the opinions of leaders and offers a comparison between their attitudes and those of the general public. It is based on several recent surveys of various leadership groups. Definitions of elite and leadership groups have varied in different polls. The Harris and Gallup polls conducted for the Chicago Council on Foreign Relations included a leadership sample drawn from "prominent individuals in government, international business, labor, academia, the mass media, religious institutions, private foreign policy organizations and special interest groups."[35] However, the publications

Table 8–9
Attitudes toward Selected Issues, by Political Outlook

	Date	*Poll*	*Issue*	*Repub.*	*Dem.*	*Ind.*	*Cons.*	*Mod.*	*Lib.*
			General Feelings toward Israel						
(a)	Feb. '81	Yankelovich	Favorable feelings	74%	73%	79%	74%	74%	73%
(b)	Aug. '82	Gallup	Favorability rating	62	55	52			
			Suez-Sinai War						
(c)	Apr. '57	Gallup	Satisfied with Eisenhower's handling of crisis	66	37	48			
			U.S. Basic Policy						
(d)	Sep. '79	Gallup	The U.S. should						
			Give strongest support to Israel	41	37	39			
			Pay more attention to Arabs	26	24	27			
			Territories						
(e)	June '77	Gallup	Israel should:						
			Give back part	32	34	39			
			Give back all	17	17	14			
			Keep all	29	22	23			
(f)	Nov. '79	Harris	Israel should give back West Bank to assure oil flow						
			Favor	26	31	32	29	30	35
			Oppose	39	51	54	57	53	54
			Peacemaking						
(g)	Dec. '78	Harris	Israel more right in talks breakdown	32	30	28	34	28	33
(h)	Mar. '79	Gallup	Israel doing all to bring peace	27	27	22			
			Military Aid						
(i)	Oct. '73	Gallup	Favor supply of arms to Israel	42	35	37			
(j)	Apr. '75	Gallup	Favor supplies & troops to Israel	55	52	58			
(k)	Nov. '81	Harris	Favor AWACS to Saudi Arabia	56	35	42	—	43	31
(l)	Feb. '81	Roper	Favor use of U.S. troops if Arabs invade Israel	29	25	25	28	25	25

			PLO and Palestinians						
(m)	Mar. '79	Gallup	Favor Palestinian nation	34	39	37			
(n)	Aug. '79	Harris	Young-PLO meeting:						
			Right				32	37	50
			Wrong				60	50	39
(o)	Dec. '79	Yankelovich	U.S. should						
			Negotiate with PLO				30	34	44
			Not negotiate with PLO				42	44	38
(p)	June '82	Harris	Sympathize more with						
			Israel	69	54	64	67	60	57
			PLO	14	18	15	13	16	21
			War in Lebanon						
(q)	July '82	Harris	Justified	48	42	45	45	47	47
			Unjustified	34	36	40	36	36	40
			Israel-U.S. Ally						
(r)	Jan. '84	Roper	Reliable	60	52	52	55	54	56
			Not reliable	24	24	26	23	24	24
			TWA Hostage Crisis						
(s)	June '85	*WP*-ABC	Approve of Reagan's handling of crisis	74	48	56			
(t)	June '85	*WP*-ABC	Israel doing all to resolve crisis	26	19	27			

Sources: (c) Ch. 1, note 73. (f) *ABC News-Harris Survey*, November 6, 1979. (k) Ch. 6, note 33.For sources of the remaining questions, see sources cited in tables 8–3 and 8–5.

of the council do not provide information on the methodology used to define the leadership community from which the samples were drawn.

In May 1975, the Foreign Policy Association (FPA) conducted a survey of approximately 60,000 participants in its "Great Decisions" foreign policy discussion programs.[36] The highest number of ballots, 7,547, were received in response to nine questions on the Middle East and the Arab-Israeli conflict. According to the authors of the FPA report, the participants in the "Great Decisions" program "constitute a specific segment of the total American public, ranking higher in education, occupation and income than the average citizen and taking a more than average interest in foreign affairs."

Further polls of leadership groups were conducted by the Council on Foreign Relations (CFR), and these are the most precise in defining *leaders* for this study.[37] Included were the 2,100 members of the national council and 3,600 members of the council's committees in 37 U.S. cities. Council members were characterized as those who hold "prominent positions in their communities and are among opinion leaders across the country in matters of foreign affairs."

Polls conducted for the Chicago Council on Foreign Relations examined sympathies of leaders and the general public for Israel and the Arab countries. In each poll (1974, 1978, and 1982), leaders sympathized more with Israel by slightly higher ratios than those recorded for the general public. In 1982, for example, the leaders' score was 51 to 19 percent in favor of Israel and the public's was 48 to 17 percent.

Table 8–10 arrays responses to identical questions on Israel and the Arab-Israeli conflict that were addressed to national samples of the general public and leaders. Responses indicate that a much greater percentage of leaders noted that they would be "very upset" if Israel were destroyed and felt that the "U.S. has a vital interest in Israel." Substantial differences were also recorded in attitudes toward aid. The leaders, more than the public, favored aid to Israel and the notion of sending U.S. technicians to the Sinai Desert. Furthermore, by a larger than two-to-one ratio, the leaders noted that they would approve of the sending of U.S. troops to help Israel in the event of an Arab invasion. In the 1982 CFR survey, 54 percent of the national council sample and 60 percent of the council-committees samples expressed the same view.

In December 1974, the leadership sample, more than the public sample, stated that the official Israeli peace policy was reasonable. But similar rates of support for a Palestinian nation were recorded from the leaders and public samples in September–November 1982. The leaders' approval rating of the Israeli War in Lebanon was just 6 percent higher than that of the general public.

The 1976 FPA and the 1980 CFR polls of leadership groups also found substantial agreement regarding the American role in the peacemaking pro-

Table 8–10
Leaders' versus General Public's Opinions on Selected Issues

Date	*Poll*	*Issue*	*Leaders (n)*	*General Public (n)*
		General Feelings toward Israel		
Dec. '74	Harris	Will be "very upset" if Israel is overrun	65% (491)	44% (3,377)
Nov. '78	Gallup	U.S. has a vital interest in Israel	91 (366)	78 (1,546)
Nov. '82	Gallup	U.S. has a vital interest in Israel	92 (341)	75 (1,546)
		Military Aid		
Dec. '74	Harris	Support military aid to Israel	65	44
Sep. '75 May '76	Gallup FPA	Approve of sending U.S. technicians to Sinai	69 (7,547)	43
Dec. '74	Harris	Dissaprove of cutting aid to Israel to get Arab oil	93	64
Nov. '82	Gallup	Send troops if Arabs invade Israel	70	30
Dec. '82	CFR	Send troops if Israel's existence in genuinely endangered	60 (1,644)	—
		Arab-Israeli Issues		
Dec. '74	Harris	Israeli leadership reasonable in seeking peace settlement	77	57
ep. '82 Dec. '82	*Newsweek*-Gallup CFR	Support Palestinian state	22 (1,621)	23 (605)
Nov. '82	Gallup	Approve Israel operation in Lebanon	27 (341)	21 (1,546)

ources: Notes 35 to 38; *Newsweek,* October 4, 1982, 11.

cess. In the 1976 poll, majorities of respondents (74 versus 16 percent) supported the "reconvening of the Geneva Conference." Several years later, when the United States successfully completed a peace agreement between Israel and Egypt and moved away from the Geneva Conference concept, 84 versus 12 percent of the 1980 CFR poll agreed that "the U.S. should maintain its current course of working with both Egypt and Israel to solve the Palestinian issue, and should work to maintain good relations with both Israel and the Arab nations."[38]

The preceding analysis is based on general surveys of leaders and "elites," but further data are available on the opinions of several *specific* groups. In 1976, the *Washington Post* and the Harvard Center for International Affairs jointly conducted a survey of 2,565 leaders in eight areas of American life.[39] The survey included an interesting question concerning Israel. Respondents were asked to agree or disagree with the following statement: "The U.S. has a moral obligation to prevent the destruction of Israel." The percentages of those who agreed with this statement among each "elite" group are as follows, in descending order: Seventy percent of the political elite and 67 percent of the media elite supported Israel. The black elite followed with 64 percent, a somewhat surprising result in view of the data and analysis presented earlier in this chapter. Next on the list are the feminists, with 63 percent. This score is also somewhat inconsistent, given the earlier evidence that women generally oppose military aid to Israel. The score for the intellectual elite is 62 percent; for the farm elite, 59 percent; for business people, 57 percent; and for youth 54 percent. These scores indicate that among each elite group, majorities (from 54 to 70 percent) felt that the United States has a moral obligation to prevent the destruction of Israel.

In the winter of 1979–80, S. Robert Lichter pursued the same question with a sample of media elite and business executives.[40] The media elite population was defined as "individuals having substantive input into news and public affairs content at the media outlets most influential in forming opinion within other national elites"; it included 235 respondents. The business executive population was defined as "the top and middle management of seven Fortune 500 corporations drawn from all major sectors of the economy"; it included 216 respondents. Lichter found a 72-percent support rate for U.S. defense of Israel among the media elite, compared to 67 percent in the 1976 study, and a 61-percent support rate for Israel among the business elite, compared to 57 percent in the 1976 *Washington Post*-Harvard study. Both in 1976 and the 1980 scores reveal strong pro-Israeli sentiments among significant leadership groups.

The data accumulated in this section suggest a high level of support for Israel among leadership and elite groups, extending well beyond the levels of support found among the general public. This finding is compatible with the principal pattern of opinions revealed in the previous sections. Elite and leadership groups generally originate in the upper socioeconomic strata of the United States, and as demonstrated earlier in this chapter, well-educated, well-employed, and well-paid Americans have expressed stronger pro-Israeli sentiments than have those in other American socioeconomic strata.

Another explanation of the "elite" attitudes toward Israel might be related to the disproportionate Jewish representation in the leadership samples. Jews constituted 7 percent of the 1976 *Washington Post*-Harvard leadership sample and 9.8 percent of the 1982 sample of the Council on Foreign Relations and the Council's committees on foreign relations. These percentages are between two and five times higher than the percentage of Jews in the general U.S. population. As clearly revealed in chapter 7, American Jews are strongly attached to Israel, and their substantial representation in the elite samples might have contributed to the highly positive attitudes of the elite and leadership groups toward Israel.

Conclusions

The data and analysis in this chapter provide insights into the distribution of opinions on Israel and the Arab-Israeli conflict among various groups in American society. Consistently strong pro-Israeli sentiments were found among each stratum of American society. But, specific groups have been found to be more pro-Israel and less pro-Arab than others. The strongest support for Israel was found among the following: whites; the well-educated, well-employed, and well paid; men and young adults; those who live in the western United States and in small cities and towns; Protestants; and Republicans.

The data further indicate a possible correlation between level of awareness of the situation in the Middle East and a relatively high level of pro-Israelism. The most knowledgeable groups were indeed found to express the most support for Israel and its stands in the Arab-Israeli conflict. Other data suggest a link between various sociodemographic variables and attitudes toward Israel and Arab nations. Young adults, for example, are better educated than ever and have also been affected by the general national tilt toward conservatism; these changes may account for their positive attitudes toward Israel. The least support for Israel was recorded in the eastern section of the United States and in metropolitan areas. This finding might be attributed to the disproportionate representation of blacks, catholics, and the less-educated in the East and major cities.

Ran Lachman suggests that certain combinations of sociodemographic characteristics may explain variations in attitudes toward Israel.[41] He employed two surveys (NORC 1974, 1975) to compare American sympathy and support for Israel versus Egypt. In 1974, the strongest support for Israel was found among Methodists, other Protestants, and people of no religion with 12 or more years of education. In 1975, the identical attitude was recorded among the upper and middle class, non-Christians, and the working and lower class with good education. Lachman argues that people with different backgrounds may hold similar views and that one variable, such as education, could override all others. Thus, as indicated by his examples and the data in this chapter, education and related socioeconomic variables have had the greatest impact on the distribution of Americans' opinions on Israel.

Finally, evidence gathered in this chapter also demonstrates that opinions of certain segments in the American society—such as blacks, Christians, and businessmen—toward Israel are affected by their relations with American Jewry. A triangular relationship might exist wherein positive relations with American Jews lead to favorable attitudes toward Israel. Conversely, sour relations and negative perceptions of American Jews could lead to unfavorable attitudes toward Israel. This phenomenon confirms one of the most important roles

American Jews play in the formation of the Israeli image in American public opinion.

Notes

1. See for example, *The Gallup Report,* August 1981, 43; *The Gallup Opinion Index,* March 1979, 15; and George Gallup, *The Gallup Poll: Public Opinion, 1972–1977,* Vol. II (Wilmington, Del.: Scholarly Resources, 1981), 1120, 1220.

2. Ben Halpern, *Jews and Blacks: The Classic American Minorities* (New York: Herder and Herder, 1971); and Joseph R. Washington, ed., *Jews in Black Perspective: A Dialogue* (Toronto: Fairleigh Dickinson University Press, 1984); and William Schneider, "Rising Black Consciousness May Mean More Hostility to Jews and Israel," *National Journal* (May 5, 1984): 890–891.

3. Susan Glass, "US Blacks on Israel," *Patterns of Prejudice* 9(November-December 1975): 10–14; and Balfour Brickner, "Jewish Youth, Israel and the Third World," *Reconstructionist* 36(April 1970): 7–13.

4. Zoe Marsh and G.W. Kingsnorth, *An Introduction to The History of East Africa* (Cambridge: Cambridge University Press, 1965), 33; and Bayard Rustin, "American Negroes and Israel," *Crisis: A Record of the Darker Races* 81(April 1974), p. 116.

5. Jack C. Miller, "Black Viewpoints on the Mid-East Conflict," *Journal of Palestine Studies* 10(Winter 1981): 37–49.

6. Charles Silberman, "Jesse (Jackson) and the Jews," *New Republic* (December 29, 1979): 12–14 and Richard Yaffe, "Bombs Kill Israelis As Blacks, Arafat Sing to (we shall) 'Overcome,'" *Jewish Week and American Examiner,* September 30, 1979.

7. In December 1979, for example, Jackson received a sum of $10,000 from Libya. At the beginning of 1980, he received $200,000 from the Arab League. The Arab League also contributed $100,000 to one of Jackson's affiliates—Push For Excellence. See *New York Times,* October 17, 1979; *Wall Street Journal,* December 2, 1983; and *New York Times,* February 5, 1984.

8. Robert G. Weisbord and Arthur Stein, "Black Nationalism and the Arab-Israeli Conflict," *Patterns of Prejudice* 3(November-December 1969): 3–5.

9. *A National Survey of Black Americans* (Los Angeles: The Simon Wiesenthal Center, December, 1985).

10. See for example, Richard P. Stevens and Abdelwahab M. Elmessiri, *Israel and South Africa* (New York: New World Press, 1976).

11. See Michael Curtis, "Africa, Israel and the Middle East," *Middle East Review* 17(Summer 1975): 5–22; Ethan A. Nadelmann, "Israel and Black Africa: A Rapprochement?" *Journal of Modern African Studies* 19(June 1981): 183–219; and *Israel Versus Apartheid* (Jerusalem: Israel-Africa Friendship Society, 1985).

12. Gregory Martire and Ruth Clark, *Anti-Semitism in the United States* (New York: Praeger, 1982), 84.

13. Yosef I. Abramowitz, "A History of Brotherhood: Blacks and Jews," *The Daily Free Press,* October 15, 1984.

14. See George E. Gruen, "Arab Petropower and American Public Opinion," *Middle East Review* 7(Winter 1975–76): 36.

15. *The Gallup Report,* September 1979, 28.

16. Elizabeth Hastings and Philip Hastings, eds., *Index to International Public Opinion, 1982–1983* (Westport, Conn.: Greenwood Press, 1984) 231. See also "Blacks and the Israeli War," *New York Amsterdam News,* September 4, 1982.

17. *New York Times,* November 8, 1979.

18. See chapter 5 and Carl Gershman, "The Andrew Young Affair," *Commentary* 68(November 1979); 25–33.

19. This and subsequent data are cited in the *Index to International Public Opinion, 1979–1980,* 101, 179.

20. Several studies have found that support for Israel slightly declines at the post-graduate level. See, for example, William Schneider, *Anti-Semitism and Israel: A Report on American Public Opinion* (New York: American Jewish Committee, December 1978, Mimeographed), 77–79.

21. Sidney Verba, et al., "Public Opinion and the War in Vietnam," *American Political Science Review* 61(June 1967): 317–33; Roger B. Handberg, Jr., "The 'Vietnam Analogy': Student Attitudes on War," *Public Opinion Quarterly* 36(Winter 1972–1973): 612–15; and Graham T. Allison, "Cool it: The Foreign Policy of Young America," *Foreign Policy* 1(Winter 1970–71): 148–60.

22. For historical background see, Yonah Malachy, *American Fundamentalism and Israel: The Relation of Fundamentalist Churches to Zionism and the State of Israel* (Jerusalem: Hebrew University of Jerusalem, Institute of Contemporary Jewry, 1978).

23. Merrill Simon, *Jerry Falwell and the Jews* (New York: Jonathan David, 1984).

24. Ruth W. Mouly, "Israel: Darling of the Religious Right," *Humanist* 42(May-June 1982): 5–11.

25. Charles Y. Glock and Rodney Stark, *Christian Beliefs and Anti-Semitism* (New York: Harper & Row, 1966). For an interesting critique of this study, see Roy Lotz, "Another Look at the Orthodoxy—Anti-Semitism Nexus," *Review of Religious Research* 18(Winter 1977): 132–33.

26. Kenyon N. Griffin, John C. Martin, and Oliver Walter, "Religious Roots and Rural Americans' Support for Israel During the October War," *Journal of Palestine Studies* 6(Autumn 1976): 104–14.

27. See Schneider, *Anti-Semitism and Israel,* 100–109.

28. Alfred O. Hero, Jr., *American Religious Groups View Foreign Policy: Trends in Rank and File Opinion, 1937–1969* (Durham, N.C.: Duke University Press, 1973).

29. Hertzel Fishman, *American Protestantism and a Jewish State* (Detroit: Wayne State University Press, 1973).

30. For the attitudes of the Catholic press toward Israel, see Esther Y. Feldblum, *The American Catholic Press and the Jewish State, 1917–1959* (New York: Ktav, 1977).

31. Robert F. Drinan, *Honor the Promise: America's Commitment to Israel* (Garden City, N.Y.: Doubleday, 1977), 63–67.

32. Schneider, *Anti-Semitism and Israel,* 109.

33. Stephen D. Isaacs, *Jews and American Politics* (Garden City, N.Y.: Doubleday, 1974).

34. Mark R. Levy and Micahel S. Kramer, *The Ethnic Factor* (New York: Simon and Schuster, 1972); and *WP*-ABC exit polls, *Washington Post,* November 8, 1984.

35. John E. Rielly, *American Public Opinion and U.S. Foreign Policy, 1983,* (Chicago: Chicago Council on Foreign Relations, 1983), 2.

36. "Great Decisions '76 Opinion Ballots," *FPA-Outreacher* (July 1976): 1.

37. Rolland Bushner, ed., "US Policy and The Middle East," an opinion survey among members of the Council on Foreign Relations and of the Committees on Foreign Relations in 37 cities. (Council On Foreign Relations, December 1982, mimeographed).

38. *New Directions in US Foreign Policy,* results of a survey cosponsored by th International Management and Development Institute and the Council on Foreign Relations, December 1980, 5.

39. Barry Sussman, *Elites in America* (Washington, D.C.: Washington Post, 1976).

40. S. Robert Lichter, "Media Support for Israel: A Survey of Leading Journalists," in William C. Adams, ed., *Television Coverage of the Middle East* (Norwood, N.J.: Ablex, 1981), 40–52.

41. Ran Lachman, "American Attitudes Towards Israel: The Social Composition of Respondents in Public Opinion Polls," *Jewish Journal of Sociology* 20(December 1978): 149–63.

9
Conclusion

Judging from the frequency and scope of poll-taking, Israeli and Arab-Israeli issues have increasingly been treated as domestic issues in the United States. The public and media generally accord only limited attention to foreign events, but Israel is an exception. This book has uncovered and analyzed in depth a wealth of opinion data, which reveals a relatively high level of awareness of Israel and the Middle East among Americans.

In recent years, an average of 80 percent of the public claim that they have heard or read about events in the Middle East. In contrast, in a national sample conducted in 1984, several weeks after the U.S. invasion of Grenada, only 58 percent stated that they had heard or read about the crisis in the United States' backyard—the civil war in Nicaragua.[1] Although public awareness does not necessarily indicate knowledge, surveys reveal that Americans know more about Israel and the Middle East than about other foreign affairs.[2] According to a *WP*-ABC poll conducted more than three years after the Camp David summit, 45 percent of a national sample correctly identified the countries involved in the conference besides the United States.[3] When the United States and the USSR signed the hotly debated, much publicized SALT II agreement, a CBS-*NYT* poll found that only 30 percent of a national sample correctly identified the United States and the USSR as the parties to the treaty.[4] In the January 1984 *WP*-ABC poll, only 25 percent of a national sample correctly identified the United States–backed faction in Nicaragua—the rebels. Twenty-seven percent thought that the United States backed the Sandanista government.

Polling history on the Middle East suggests two major turning points: the Six-Day War of 1967 and the 1977 Arab-Israeli peace negotiations. The first polls on Israel were conducted prior to its inception but, until the 1967 war, appeared sporadically and only in times of war and crisis. After the Six-Day War, polls were conducted with more regularity but were limited in scope and depth. Following the dramatic events of 1977 (Carter's strategy, Begin's victory, and Sadat's visit to Jerusalem), polls have been conducted on a regular basis and have encompassed a wider range of subjects and issues.

This final chapter summarizes long-term trends in American public opinion on Israel and the Arab-Israeli conflict. It provides several observations on methodological and ethical problems that characterize certain polls and interpretations of results, and it analyzes and evaluates various opinion sources. The chapter concludes with a few comments on the possible effects of American public opinion on U.S. policy toward Israel and the parties involved in the Arab-Israeli dispute.

Opinion Trends: Israel

General American feelings for Israel have remained consistently favorable since the inception of the Jewish state in 1948. Various polls, utilizing different methods and measurements, have revealed relatively high percentages of national samples stating that Israel is a close, strong, or reliable ally of the United States. This pattern has remained constant even in times of tension and disagreement between the two governments and during controversial events, such as the 1982 Israeli war in Lebanon. During this unpopular war, Gallup found that a majority of 55 percent of a national sample held favorable attitudes toward Israel.[5] Simultaneously, Harris found that 73 percent of his national sample felt that Israel is a close ally or friendly to the United States.[6]

Several surveys have employed questions that reflect the depth of public sentiments on Israel. The February 1981 Yankelovich comprehensive survey found that 73 percent of the sample expressed favorable feelings for Israel, with 32 percent of this group holding highly favorable attitudes.[7] The same survey also revealed that half of the respondents believed that "the continuation of Israel as a Jewish state is important." Further evidence found in the Harris survey disclosed that in 1974, 44 versus 37 percent of the non-Jewish sample said that it would be "very upset if Israel were overrun by the Arabs in another war in the Middle East." Since 1974, this percentage has increased. In 1976, it stood at 50 to 36 percent; in 1980, it grew to 56 versus 33 percent.[8]

Between 1975 and 1982, the Yankelovich poll examined the general Israeli image in the United States by suggesting that respondents select among a variety of descriptions that depicted Israel and its citizens. The polls reveal only slight variations over the years.[9] In 1982, clear majorities perceived Israel as "freedom loving" (83 percent); "modern" (78 percent); "pro-U.S." (77 percent); "democratic" (74 percent); "reasonable people" (72 percent); and "anti-Communist (86 percent). It should be noted that these scores were recorded shortly after the highly controversial war in Lebanon, and particularly after the Israeli rejection of Reagan's peace initiative and the tragic massacre at Sabra and Shatila.

Additional data and information on the Israeli image in the United States are obtained from surveys that compare characterizations of Arabs and Is-

Table 9–1
Images of Israelis and Arabs

Question

Does each word apply more to the Arabs or more to the Israelis?

	More to Israelis	*More to Arabs*	*To Both Equally*	*To Neither*	*Don't Know*
Peaceful	41%	7%	9%	24%	19%
Honest	39	6	13	18	25
Intelligent	39	8	26	5	21
Like Americans	50	5	8	17	21
Friendly	46	6	15	11	23
Backward	6	47	7	15	25
Underdeveloped	9	47	10	10	25
Poor	21	34	9	15	22
Greedy	9	41	20	7	23
Arrogant	11	37	19	7	26
Moderate	31	8	10	21	30
Developing	33	20	21	3	24
Barbaric	4	38	8	23	28

Source: The Cambridge Report, Summer 1975, 180.

raelis. In the summer of 1975, Caddell presented respondents with a list of images and asked whether they applied more to Israel or to the Arabs. At this time, American-Israeli relations were at a low ebb; Kissinger blamed the Israeli government for his failure to achieve an interim agreement, and President Ford announced a policy of reassessment of American-Israeli relations. Yet according to table 9–1, Israel's general image in American public opinion was highly favorable, in both absolute and relative terms. Majorities of Americans (figures for "more to Israelis" and "to both equally" in table 9–1) perceived Israel as "peaceful," "honest," "intelligent," "like Americans," "friendly," and "developing." Very few Americans ascribed those characteristics "more to Arabs." Rather, majorities of Americans perceived the Arabs as "backward," "underdeveloped," "greedy," and "arrogant."

Despite the frequent altercations between the U.S. and Israeli governments from 1975 to 1980, a poll conducted in the fall of 1980 yielded similar, positive results.[10] Israelis were described as "intelligent and competent" (66 percent); "brave" (65 percent); "religious" (75 percent); "friendly" (43 percent); and "persecuted and exploited" (37 percent). In contrast, a large percentage of respondents characterized the Arabs as "rich" (72 percent); "dress strangely" (58 percent); "mistreat women" (51 percent); and "warlike, bloodthirsty" (50 percent).

The favorable American public opinion of Israel and its positive image is evidenced by the attitudes toward U.S. economic and military aid to the Jewish state. Americans have consistently expressed reservations about U.S. foreign aid, favoring cuts and limitations in levels and budgets. However, as demonstrated in chapter 6, most Americans strongly support U.S. economic and military aid to Israel. This support is remarkable when contrasted to the public's support of similar aid to other U.S. allies, particularly Arab allies in the Middle East.

Americans do object, however, to military aid that entails direct involvement on behalf of Israel in actual or hypothetical threatening situations. Chapter 1 revealed that throughout the Israeli War of Independence, Americans opposed direct U.S. military involvement on behalf of Israel by substantial ratios. They favored American participation in a United Nations force only, or as part of a joint mission of the big powers (table 1–4.). Similar results were recorded during the uncertain days of the 1967 crisis and war. Since 1967, pollsters have employed questions on direct military involvement, mostly as part of an ongoing gauge of attitudes toward the use of American forces abroad. Although Americans opposed dispatching American troops to assist Israel in the event of an Arab invasion, they did express relatively higher rates of support of military commitment to Israel when this thesis was placed in a comparative setting.

Opinion Trends: Arab-Israeli Conflict

General American sentiments for Israel within the context of the Arab-Israeli conflict are well demonstrated by the sympathy index. Figure 9–1 presents long-term trends in the distribution of American sympathies for Israel and the Arab nations from 1947 to 1984. The figure indicates that since the establishment of Israel, Americans have consistently sympathized more with Israel than with the Arabs. Throughout the Israeli War of Independence and the mid-1950s, the differences between the two sides were relatively small. Furthermore, a substantial number of Americans chose to remain neutral. Since 1967, however, the American public has regularly expressed more sympathy for Israel by a margin of at least four to one. In times of war and crisis, such as the Six-Day War, the War of Attrition, and even the initial phases of the war in Lebanon, this ratio grew to as high as 14 to 1. The lowest sympathy scores for Israel since 1967, 32–33 percent, were recorded twice—once in February 1978, following a major breakdown in the Israeli-Egyptian peacemaking process, and again in September 1982, immediately after the massacre at Sabra and Shatila. This finding indicates that at least one-third of the American public has consistently supported Israel, even under the most adverse circumstances.

Examination of long-term trends in figure 9–1 reveals that from the 1967 Six-Day War to the end of the 1970 War of Attrition, sympathy scores accorded to Arab nations were exceptionally low. Since the Yom Kippur War, however, these rates returned to those of the late 1940s and mid-1950s. The trends also reveal that, with the exceptions of breakdowns in the peace talks and the 1982 massacre in Sabra and Shatila, decreases in the pro-Israel scores were not paralleled by increases in the pro-Arab scores. The sympathy index is clearly very sensitive to major events and developments in the Middle East. Since 1977, the region has undergone a series of peacemaking processes and violent events, which are clearly reflected in the fluctuation of sympathy scores. The Gallup scores represent the views of those who had heard or read about the Middle East, and the Roper results, presented in figure 9–1 for the period from 1977 to 1984, reflect the views of the general public. A comparison between the two poll trends indicates lower scores for both Israel and the Arabs and more moderate fluctuations in the Roper poll. The Roper results also reveal an average pro-Israel margin of four to one.

Arab-Israeli relations have been marred by periodic outbursts of violence and war. Since the establishment of Israel, at least one large confrontation has been waged between this country and its Arab neighbors each decade. The War of Independence, the 1967 Six-Day War, and the 1973 Yom Kippur War were initiated by the Arabs, whereas Israel instigated the 1956 Suez-Sinai campaign and the 1982 war in Lebanon. Were the attitudes of Americans toward these occurrences affected by the identity of the perpetrators? Were they more negative and critical of the party perceived as responsible for the outbreak of the war? Only partial data are available on this issue. For example, polls were not conducted on American attitudes toward the 1948 Israeli War of Independence, and in later years, more questions were devoted to the Israeli offensives than to those of the Arabs. In the 1967 war, questions gauging attitudes employed the terms *right* and *wrong*. Forty-six percent stated that Israel had more right on its side; only 4 percent said the same of the Arabs. Questions concerning other uses of force included the terms *approve-disapprove* and *justified-unjustified*. The latter measure was employed in more instances and therefore is used for a comparative trend analysis.

Table 9–2 arrays responses to questions on the justification of major and limited uses of force in the Arab-Israeli conflict. The table reveals public criticism of the party perceived as most responsible for the major wars (1956, 1973, 1982), except in the case of the aware group's attitudes toward the war in Lebanon. The most unjust use of force, in terms of relative ratios, is ascribed to the Arab attack on Israel during the Yom Kippur War. It is interesting that Americans were more closely divided on the highly controversial 1982 Israeli war in Lebanon than on the 1956 Israeli military operation in the Sinai Peninsula.

Opinions on the justification of limited uses of force were asked only in

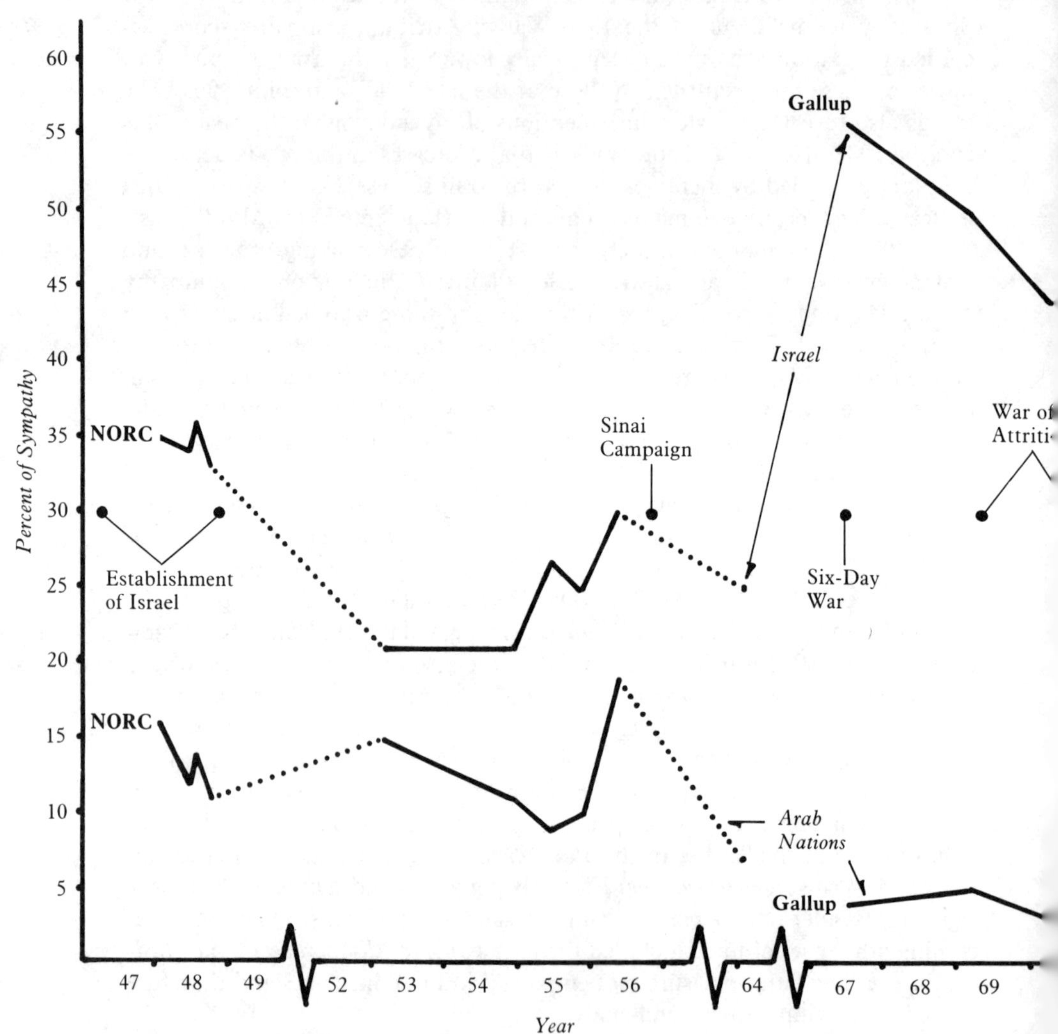

Figure 9–1. American Sympathies for Israel and the Arab Nations, 1947–84

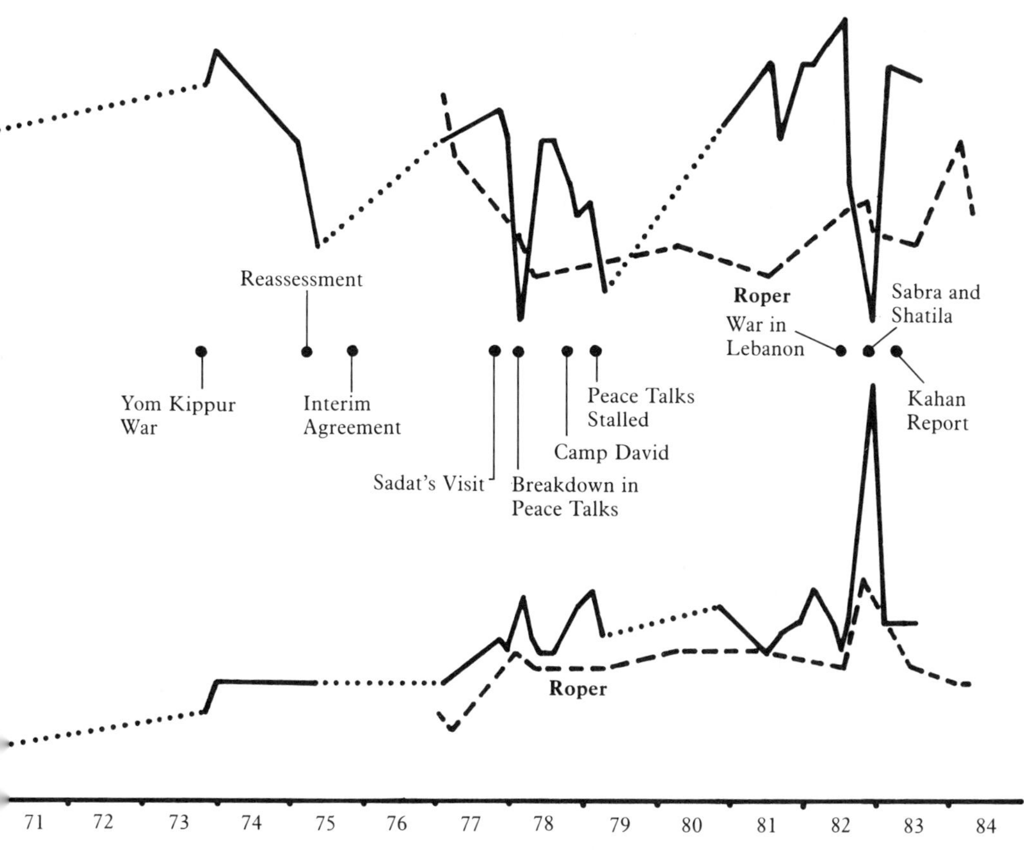

Insufficient data
Reassessment
Roper
Sabra and Shatila
War in Lebanon
Yom Kippur War
Interim Agreement
Peace Talks Stalled
Kahan Report
Camp David
Sadat's Visit
Breakdown in Peace Talks
Roper
71
72
73
74
75
76
77
78
79
80
81
82
83
84

Table 9–2
Opinions on Uses of Force in the Arab-Israeli Conflict

Date		*Poll*	*Issue*	*Justified*	*Not Justified*	*D.K.*
(a)	Nov. '56	NORC	Sending Israeli Army into Egyptian Territory	26%	40%	34%
(b)	Dec. '73	Harris	Arab surprise attack on Israel	24	49	27
(c)	Mar. '78	Harris	"Litani Operation" in Lebanon	47	40	13
(d)	Mar. '78	NBC	(aware group)	50	35	15
(e)	June '81	R.H. Buskin	Attack on Iraqi nuclear reactor	31	38	31
(f)	June '81	CBS	(aware group)	39	39	22
(g)	July '81	*Newsweek*-Gallup	Bombing of PLO positions in Beirut	31	50	19
(h)	July '81	Penn and Shoen		49	29	22
(i)	Aug. '82	*WP*-ABC	Israel's invasion of Lebanon	37	41	22
			(aware group)	52	38	10

Sources: (a) Ch. 1, note 70. (b) Ch. 3, note 25. (c) Ch. 3, note 61. (d) Ch. 3, note 62. (e) Ch. 4, note 10. (f) *CBS News Poll*, June 22–27, 1981, questions 31a and 31b..(g) Ch. 4, note 11. (h) Ch. 4, note 12. (i) Table 4–4.

reference to Israel and resulted in mixed responses. The 1978 Litani operation against the PLO bases in South Lebanon was considered justified by a close plurality of 47 to 40 percent, but the attack on the Iraqi nuclear reactor was deemed unjustified by a plurality of 38 to 31 percent. The two contradictory responses given to the Israeli bombing of PLO headquarters in Beirut were most likely a result of survey question formation.[11] The *Newsweek*-Gallup question emphasized the civilian casualties of the bombing, whereas the Penn and Schoen question included the PLO terrorist attacks that preceded the Israeli action.

Another interesting finding in table 9–2 is the discrepancy between the responses of the general public and of those who claimed they had heard or read about events in the Middle East. On three separate occasions (the Litani operation, the Iraqi nuclear reactor attack, and the war in Lebanon) the aware group justified much more than the general public the Israeli use of force. In the most recent case of the war in Lebanon, the general public perceived it as unjustified by a close plurality, but the aware group said that it was justified, by a majority of 52 to 38 percent. It is possible that the differences between the general public and the attentive public are related to the basic perception of events. It is probable that the attentive group, more than the general, placed events and Israeli actions within a larger historical context, which plays a major role in the comprehensive formation of its opinions.

Following the Yom Kippur War, President Sadat concluded that Israel could not be subdued by force and, therefore, adopted a diplomatic offensive that culminated in the 1979 Egyptian-Israeli peace agreement. Sadat's visit to Jerusalem in November 1977 not only made him an instant hero in the eyes of the American public and media but also favorably altered the Egyptian image in the United States. Prior to his visit, the Egyptian and the generally hostile Arab approach to Israel were perceived as unjustified and unreasonable. Conversely, Israel's conditions for peace—such as direct negotiations, recognition, security guarantees, and border alterations—were viewed as reasonable and justified. Sadat's visit to Jerusalem and his offer to negotiate peace directly with Israel reversed this basic matrix. The positive public perception of the Egyptian interest in peace is exemplified by larger segments of the American public viewing Egypt as a close ally and friendly to the United States. Chapter 3 further demonstrated that Sadat's and Egypt's peace efforts and intentions were rated higher than those of Prime Minister Begin. Yet the improvement in the Egyptian image did not come at the expense of the overall Israeli image.

The Egyptian-Israeli peace agreement changed Egypt's image in the United States. The standing and image of the Arab world as a whole, however, remained unaltered. This result was probably due to the constant criticism of Sadat's peace policy across the Arab world, even among U.S. Arab allies, such as Saudi Arabia and Jordan. The positive ratings of Egypt declined after the murder of Sadat in October 1981 and since then have not been modified.

Recognition and acceptance of Israel by her Arab neighbors poses one central, thorny problem in the Arab-Israeli dispute; another is the Palestinian question. In recent years, this question has frequently appeared in polls and has received widespread attention. Surveys reveal general sympathy for the Palestinians but substantial criticism of the PLO and Arafat. The public clearly distinguishes between the Palestinians and the PLO and deplores the PLO's actions against Israel, Jews, and Americans.

Despite the condemnation of the PLO, Americans are unsure about whether Israel or the United States should conduct negotiations with its leaders. Responses to questions on hypothetical talks yielded mixed results, but clear majorities criticized the actual, covert talks of Ambassador Andrew Young with the United Nations PLO representative in 1979. In terms of solutions to the Palestinian problem, the public was dissatisfied with the conditions in the refugee camps but unclear about whether the solution lay in autonomy, the creation of an independent state, or an entity linked to Jordan. Regardless, the majority of Americans believe that a possible solution depends mainly on Palestinian willingness to negotiate a peace agreement with Israel and assurance of adequate security guarantees for it in the West Bank. The polls reveal, however, that Americans are pessimistic about the prospects of a solution along these lines.

Methodology and Manipulation of Polls

Pollsters have generally concentrated on the more controversial issues in American-Israeli relations and the Arab-Israeli dispute. Prime Minister Golda Meir was probably extremely popular in American public opinion, whereas President Nasser was very unpopular, but polls were not conducted at the time to test this hypothesis. In contrast, polls *were* conducted on the relative popularity of Prime Minister Begin and President Sadat, possibly because pollsters sensed a sensational outcome—in favor of Sadat. Likewise, no questions were asked on the reliability of Israel as an American ally in the early 1970s, when the two nations closely cooperated on many strategic issues. However, numerous questions of this nature were posed in the late 1970s and the early 1980s, when various disagreements emerged between the two allies.

Examination of American surveys on the Middle East reveal a fundamental enigma in the derivation of question wording and context. Polls conducted on the establishment of a Palestinian state yielded rates of support ranging from 11 to 71 percent (table 5–7), and polls on American military aid to Israel yielded rates of support ranging from 24 to 75 percent (tables 6–3, 6–4). Polls on the legitimacy of the 1982 Israeli war in Lebanon produced both negative rates of 29 to 63 percent and positive rates of 61 to 28 percent (table 4–4). The large variations in all of these responses were traced to the incongruity of question wording and context.

Also, variations in the selection and context of answers were responsible for large differences in responses to questions on hypothetical American military involvement on behalf of Israel in situations of extreme danger. When military involvement was presented as one of many options available to the United States in the Middle East, including diplomatic alternatives, it received very little support—between 1 and 5 percent (table 2–3). However, when respondents were offered a choice of three options—supply weapons, send troops, and stay out—the send-troops option was approved by 9 to 12 percent (table 6–6). Finally, when only one choice was available—favor or oppose the dispatching of troops—it received support in the range of 21 to 43 percent (table 6–7).

Large variations in responses may occasionally cause deliberate or unintentional manipulations of results. Scholars, commentators, or politicians may exploit only selective results that support certain statements or arguments. In 1981, Mark A. Bruzonsky wrote an article in defense of a Palestinian state in the West Bank. He cited the responses given to question (a) in table 5–7 (from the July 1980 Harris poll on the Middle East), claiming that "Palestinian nationalism has achieved a rather remarkable following [in] the U.S. in recent years."[12] But table 5–7 demonstrates that other questions in the identical Harris survey and in similar polls yielded opposite responses.

Another intriguing finding shows that, over time, pollsters have altered their approaches toward various issues. For example, from the 1967 Six-Day War until 1977, survey questions dealt with the "occupied territories" in terms of whether these territories should be returned or retained by Israel (tables 2–5, 2–6). Since 1977, however, pollsters—probably following Carter's statement favoring a "national home" for the Palestinians and the return of the Sinai Peninsula to Egypt—have employed questions implying that the return of the territories is a moot point and that the only remaining issues are to whom they should be returned (Jordan or the PLO), for which purpose (autonomous Palestinian state or Jordanian entity), and under what circumstances.

Polls conducted by or for the mass media raise problems of omission and selective reporting. Between March 3 and 8, 1982, the *WP*-ABC News poll conducted a major survey that included 12 questions concerning Israel and the Middle East.[13] The original report on the results of this survey was titled, "Americans Still Support Israelis Strongly over Arabs." The report was accompanied by three pages of statistics and concluded that "despite the widely publicized disagreements between Israel and America in recent months, the American public strongly backs the state of Israel." The "disagreements" referred to the fierce battle over the AWACS deal with Saudi Arabia, the de facto annexation of the Golan Heights, and the suspension of the American-Israeli memorandum of strategic cooperation.

ABC News aired the poll's principal results fairly objectively on March 10, 1982, but the *Washington Post* chose not to publish them. When confronted with the omission, an editorial source at the newspaper ironically claimed that the poll dealt "with issues most people don't think about," and "numbers by themselves are not always helpful."[14] The identical issues were cited frequently in the *Washington Post*, however, and had appeared in earlier polls. Furthermore, although it is true that numbers by themselves are not always helpful, it is difficult to understand why they were not helpful in this particular case. It is possible that the *Post* did not publish the March 1982 results of its own poll because the findings were incompatible with the newspaper's general negative approach to Prime Minister Begin and Israel.[15]

While the *Washington Post* omitted an entire poll, *Newsweek* omitted a particular significant result from a poll it commissioned from Gallup in July 1981. This omission was discovered when results were published by the same magazine more than a year later. The *Newsweek* issue of August 3, 1981, included a lengthy article about the Israeli-PLO war in Lebanon (pages 14–17), accompanied by a report on results of a special poll on the Arab-Israeli conflict conducted by Gallup for *Newsweek* between July 22 and 23, 1981. The poll included a question on the distribution of American sympathies for Israel and the Arab nations. Responses revealed that compared to the answers given to the same question in the previous Gallup Poll (October 1980), Israel had gained four percentage points and the Arabs had lost three (tables 3–2, 4–1). This result, incompatible with the thrust of the *Newsweek* article about the alleged erosion in the American attitude toward Israel, was omitted.

The October 4, 1982, issue of *Newsweek* included a lengthy report on a poll conducted for the magazine by Gallup on September 22 and 23, 1982, shortly after the much-publicized massacre at Sabra and Shatila. The report was titled, "Newsweek Poll—Israel Loses Ground." The first result in the report compared the distribution of responses to the question on American sympathies for Israel and the Arabs in September 1982 with those obtained in the July 1981 survey. Although the comparison demonstrated a substantial slippage in the Israeli rating, it also revealed the omission of the July 1981 score from the original poll report. This finding may suggest that when a particular score is incompatible with the essence of an article in a magazine or newspaper, it is simply omitted. However, when the identical result or score fits the story line, it is resurrected and even accorded prominent saliency. On the basis of existing evidence, it is difficult to ascertain whether total omission or selective reporting is exceptional or typical of the media's analysis of their own polls.

Sources of Opinions

Numerous forces participate in the formation of public opinion. This section examines four such forces on the basis of data accumulated for this book: the presidency, opinion leaders, the mass media, and special interest and lobby groups. Because of data limitations and the absence of adequate methodology, the following examination offers only tentative inferences.

Votes in the United States carry equal weight, but this is not necessarily true in the case of opinions. The opinions of certain individuals may carry more weight than the opinions of others. The *public* consists of several hierarchical strata.[16] At the top of the pyramid are the opinion leaders, with the president acting as principal actuator among them. Below are "elite" groups and the attentive public—individuals who keep abreast of events, read newspapers, and participate in the political process. At the base of the pyramid is the general or mass public. The formation of public opinion consists of intricate interactions among these strata.

The American president holds the greatest potential for shaping public opinion. Ralph Levering suggests that "most Americans, having limited knowledge about foreign affairs, usually look to their president and other public officials for guidance in foreign affairs."[17] Although the Arab-Israeli conflict is extremely complex, the public is more familiar with it than with other foreign issues. Thus, it is interesting to identify possible correlations between the president's opinions and those of the public.

Data analysis reveals that the position of the president on Israel and the Arab-Israeli conflict generally correlates with that of public opinion. Since the end of World War II, most American presidents have strongly supported Israel and its stands on the Arab-Israeli dispute. Polls conducted throughout this period indicate similar public opinion, even during adverse situations between the two allies. Two presidents, Eisenhower and Carter, voiced strong criticism of general and specific Israeli policies. In 1956, President Eisenhower strongly criticized the joint British-French-Israeli military operation in the Sinai Desert and Egypt. Twenty years later, President Carter cited Israel for the breakdowns in the peacemaking talks with Egypt and criticized various policies of Prime Minister Begin. Polls conducted during both of these periods indicate similar critical public positions. Thus, it appears that public opinion follows the president's basic approach to Israel in periods of both harmony and disagreement.

According to Rosenau, other opinion leaders or opinion makers active in the opinion formation process are "all members of the society who occupy positions which enable them regularly to transmit, either locally or nationally, opinions about any issue to unknown persons outside their occupational field or about more than one class of issues to unknown professional colleagues."[18] Opinion makers, then, are politicians, government officials, academics, commentators, heads of civic organizations, corporate executives, and religious leaders. Chapter 8, which examines the attitudes of these opinion leaders toward Israel and the Middle East, reveals that they have consistently held highly favorable opinions of Israel.

Next on the pyramid is the attentive public. It comprises a small segment of the mass public and is disproportionately represented among the more affluent and well-educated strata of American society. Judging on the basis of only one component of the attentive public (general awareness as self-identified by the members of national samples), it is clear that this public is relatively large and knowledgeable about issues concerning Israel and the Middle East. This book has demonstrated that on a wide range of issues, the attentive public, more than the general public, has expressed more favorable attitudes toward Israel and has supported its policies in the Arab-Israeli conflict. The attentive public is the prime target of opinion leaders. If this group is persuaded to adopt a favorable opinion on a particular policy, leaders assume that they have obtained complete public support. Indeed, an empirical study of the attentive public revealed that it serves as an important link between public opinion and public policy.[19]

The role of the mass media in the shaping of public opinion is yet to be fully exposed, but it is clear that the media serve as an opinion transmitter from leaders to the public and back. Furthermore, they regularly express their own opinions on issues, which in turn affect both leaders and public opinion. A decision to cover or ignore an issue in a limited or extensive fashion also affects the potential of public awareness and debate.[20]

Throughout the last decade, Israel and the Arab-Israeli dispute have proved to be a principal source of news to the American media. Most American television networks and news publications maintain permanent bureaus in Israel; reporting from there and the Middle East is considered a highly prestigious assignment. In general, it appears that from the early 1970s, the American media diverged from their fundamental approach toward Israel and Arab-Israeli issues. Prior to the Yom Kippur War, this approach was more favorable to Israel than to its Arab adversaries. Since 1973, and particularly after Begin's victory and Sadat's visit to Jerusalem in 1977, the media have adopted a more balanced approach, at times criticizing Israel more than the Arab nations. The critical approach reached its peak in the 1982 Israeli war in Lebanon.

The media's coverage of the war and other events, such as the 1985 TWA hostage crisis, was very controversial and led to a wave of negative articles and reports. The libel suit that former Israeli Defense Minister Ariel Sharon brought against *Time* magazine, proving its publication of a false report, also raised questions concerning the credibility of news coverage on Arab-Israeli issues. It is interesting that on December 12, 1983, the same magazine published a lengthy report on the credibility of the American media titled, "Journalism Under Fire." The report cited results of polls conducted by NORC that indicated a sharp decline in the public's confidence in the press since 1975.

The role played by the media in the molding of public opinion on Israel and the Arab-Israeli conflict has not been sufficiently investigated. One study found a correlation between coverage of Israel and Arab-Israeli issues in the prestige press from 1966 to 1974 and rates of sympathy for the two sides.[21] The study found alterations in both the Israeli and Arab images in the prestige press after the Yom Kippur War. The image of Israel had deteriorated, while that of the Arab nations had improved. These findings correlated with changes in the distribution of American sympathies for the parties in the dispute. On the other hand, as demonstrated in chapter 4, the American media, particularly the prestige press, were very critical of Israel's offensive in Lebanon and portrayed the PLO and the Palestinians in a favorable light, most noticeably after the Sabra and Shatila massacres. Yet public opinion remained relatively balanced, and after the war, the Israeli image returned to prewar levels, whereas the image of the Arabs remained negative.

The final sources of public opinion on Israel and the Arab-Israeli conflict are the numerous pro-Israel and pro-Arab interest groups. Israel is mostly supported by the American Jewish community, labor federations, and Christian groups; the Arabs are supported by Americans of Arab origin, oil companies, several major corporations, and anti-Jewish sects. The American-Jewish community is extremely well organized and is active in American politics.[22] Chapter 7 clearly demonstrated the significant role Israel plays in the life of American Jewry, revealing a continuing support for most Israeli positions in the Arab-Israeli dispute. The attitudes of American Jewry and other pro-Israeli interest groups have been actualized in the performance of the highly efficient Israeli lobby. This lobby wields considerable power on Capitol Hill and is perceived as an extremely influential political organization.[23] In recent years, the Arab lobby has increased its activity and has improved its organization, but as suggested by Christopher Madison, this has not adversely affected the Israeli lobby.[24] Madison further asserts that the effectiveness of the pro-Arab lobby is limited because it is perceived as more anti-Israel than pro-Arab.

Pro-Israel and pro-Arab interest groups and lobbies are very active in American politics, but the relationship between their activities and subsequent public opinion is unclear. Are special-interest and lobby groups influential because they shape public opinion, reflect public sentiment, or are able to convince politicians and officials to act as opinion makers in defense of a particular approach? Studies of the relationship between pro-Israeli and pro-Arab interest groups and American public opinion from 1966 to 1977 did not produce conclusive evidence to this effect.[25] Only in a general sense did levels of public support for Israel and the Arab states appear to be related to levels of pro-Israel and pro-Arab interest group activities over time. Pro-Israel groups have been more active than pro-Arab groups, and as demonstrated in this book, public opinion has been consistently more supportive of Israel.

The sources of Israel's strength in American public opinion can be traced to the positions of most American presidents since the end of World War II. To a lesser degree, they can be viewed in the attitudes of opinion leaders and the attentive public. The relative weight of the media and the activities of special-interest groups cannot be ascertained on the basis of existing data. It appears, however, that the role of the media is smaller than most people believe; this may be partially attributed to the public's declining confidence in the media.

Public Opinion and Policymaking

Bernard C. Cohen identified a continuum of opinion effects on policymakers ranging from "effective constraints" through "nominal and ineffective constraints" to "positive nonconstraints."[26] The first type includes opinions or opinion circumstances that "direct officials into policies which run counter to their own preferences." At the other extreme are opinions that encourage officials to proceed with a policy they have already adopted or that give them a free hand to choose whichever course they prefer. Cohen also suggests that different types of opinions may have different effects on policymaking.

This book has demonstrated that American public opinion has had some effect on U.S. policy in the Middle East and on certain critical Israeli policies. In Cohen's terms, American public opinion on the establishment of Israel was supportive of Truman's stand but opposed the views of his secretaries of state and defense. For Truman, public opinion served as positive nonconstraint; for his secretaries, it was an effective constraint. The wave of sympathy for Israel that emerged after the Six-Day War enabled President Johnson to formulate principles for conflict resolution that rejected the Arab demands for unconditional withdrawal. Instead, it required negotiations and recognition of Israel in return for withdrawal from the occupied territories. On the other hand, negative public opinion softened the Ford-Kissinger reassessment, a punitive policy against Israel.

At different stages of the Israeli-Egyptian peacemaking process, Carter was concerned with the effects of a breakdown on his standing in public opinion. Consequently, he was more hesitant in his actions. Carter realized that favorable public opinion was important for Israel, possibly as an effective constraint on Begin's positions. Begin, on the other hand, contemplated the use of American public opinion against Carter's pressure. It appears that in contrast to other Israeli governments, the Begin government did not consider American public opinion a prevailing factor in the Israeli decision-making process.

Throughout the June 1967 crisis, Israel delayed its offensive until it was certain that American public opinion would support a war against the Arabs. Also, hours before the outbreak of the Yom Kippur War, the Israeli government considered and rejected a request from the IDF to preempt the imminent Arab attack with an air strike, fearing possible adverse effects on American public opinion. Kissinger held the same view and warned against a preemption. Finally, negative American public opinion forced the Peres government to release Shiite prisoners during the TWA hostage crisis. In each of these cases, American public opinion served an an effective constraint on Israeli policymakers.

Most Arab countries, including American allies, are closed societies. Therefore, American public opinion plays only a limited role, if any, in their decision making. However, Arab leaders, especially President Sadat, have felt that in view of the importance accorded U.S. public opinion in Israel, that public opinion might be employed to apply pressure on Israel. Incumbent Israeli President Chaim Herzog offered an observation on this issue:

> President Sadat directed his entire strategy primarily towards U.S. public opinion and with an eye to the U.S. administration. He concentrated on the

> U.S. media, his assumption being that as long as the resulting exposure continued, any hold or difficulty would be solved by a parallel increase of American pressure on Israel.[27]

The United States is a superpower that has global responsibilities and diverse national interests in the Middle East. These responsibilities cannot always accommodate Israeli national interests, which are much narrower and limited. The two countries share common ideological and strategic goals in the Middle East but occasionally differ on the available means to achieve them. Thus, although both countries genuinely seek a reasonable solution to the Arab-Israeli conflict, they have occasionally differed on particular contents and procedures that should be employed to achieve peace. These disagreements are also debated in the media and in public forums.

The U.S. government criticized Israel for various uses of force, for unilateral actions in the conflict, and for major breakdowns in the Egyptian-Israeli peacemaking process. The public has held similar reservations, but polls reveal that they have been short-lived. This pattern was evident in the Israeli war in Lebanon, particularly during and after the massacre in Sabra and Shatila. For a brief period of time, the public criticized Israel and expressed considerable sympathy for the Arabs and Palestinians, but after several weeks, public opinion returned to its traditional patterns. Despite the highly controversial nature of the war in Lebanon, the base of support for Israel was not adversely affected. A similar pattern emerged during the 1985 TWA hostage crisis and subsequent events.

These findings could shed light on the depth of opinions on Israel in the United States. It has been suggested that as the Holocaust becomes more distant in time and as criticism of Israel mounts in the United States and elsewhere, the Israeli image could tarnish and public support for that state might diminish. The polls have refuted this hypothesis. Despite periodic alterations, the basic trends have remained remarkably stable, and the base of support for Israel has remained remarkably solid. American-Israeli relations have been characterized by a special relationship that has transcended various politicians and conditions in both nations and in the Middle East. Public opinion is one of the major keys to this relationship.

Notes

1. *WP*-ABC Poll, January 12–17, 1984; *Washington Post*, January 20, 1984.
2. See data and observations about the knowledge of Americans about foreign affairs in Lloyd A. Free and Hadley Cantril, *The Political Beliefs of Americans: A Study of Public Opinion* (New York: Simon and Schuster, 1968), 59.
3. *WP*-ABC Poll, No. 0114Y, March 1982, Question 59.

4. *New York Times,* November 8, 1979.

5. *Gallup Report,* September 1982, 21.

6. *USA Today,* November 11, 1982; see also table 4–5.

7. Gregory Martire and Ruth Clark, *Anti-Semitism in the U.S.* (New York: Praeger, 1982), 84.

8. Louis Harris and Associates, *A Study of the Attitudes of the American People and the American Jewish Community Toward Anti-Semitism and the Arab-Israeli Conflict in the Middle East,* Study No. 804011 (August 1980), 5.

9. Yankelovich, Skelly and White, Inc., *Trend Data: Image of Israel,* October 1982, 11.

10. Shelley Slade, "The Image of the Arab in America: Analysis of a Poll on American Attitudes," *Middle East Journal* 35(Spring 1981): 147.

11. See chapter 4.

12. Mark A. Bruzonsky, "America's Palestinian Predicament: Fallacies and Possibilities," *International Security* 6(Summer 1981): 97.

13. *WP*-ABC Poll, No. 0114Y, March 1982.

14. See the article by Joseph Polakoff in *Jewish Week* (Washington, D.C.), April 8–14, 1982, 6.

15. See Douglas J. Feith, "Israel, the Post and the Shaft," *Middle East Review* 12(Summer-Fall 1980): 62–66; and Leonore Siegelman, "The Strange Case of the Washington Post," in Julian J. Landau, ed., *The Media: Freedom, or Responsibility—The War in Lebanon, 1982: A Case Study* (Jerusalem: B.A.L. Mass Communications, 1984), 321–24.

16. This original observation was made by Gabriel A. Almond, *The American People and Foreign Policy* (New York: Praeger, 1960).

17. Ralph B. Levering, *The Public and American Foreign Policy, 1918–1978* (New York: Morrow, 1978), 31.

18. James N. Rosenau, *Public Opinion and Foreign Policy* (New York: Random House, 1961), 45.

19. Donald J. Devine, *The Attentive Public: Polyarchial Democracy* (Chicago: Rand McNally, 1970).

20. James B. Lemert, *Does Mass Communication Change Public Opinion After All?* (Chicago: Nelson Hall, 1981), ch. 6.

21. Janice Monti Belkaoui, "Images of Arabs and Israelis in the Prestige Press, 1966–1974," *Journalism Quarterly* 55(Winter 1978): 732–38.

22. Daniel Elazar, *Community and Polity: The Organizational Dynamics of American Jewry* (Philadelphia: Jewish Publication Society of America, 1976).

23. See I.L. Kenen, *Israel's Defense Line: Her Friends and Foes in Washington* (Buffalo, N.Y.: Prometheus Books, 1981).

24. Christopher Madison, "Arab-American Lobby Fights Rearguard Battle to Influence U.S. Mideast Policy," *National Journal* (August 31, 1985): 1934–1939.

25. Robert H. Trice, "Foreign Policy Interest Groups, Mass Public Opinion and the Arab-Israeli Dispute," *Western Political Quarterly* 31(June 1978): 238–52.

26. Bernard C. Cohen, *The Public's Impact on Foreign Policy* (Boston: Little, Brown, 1973), 135–37.

27. Chaim Herzog, *Who Stands Accused? Israel Answers Its Critics* (New York: Random House, 1978), 212–13.

Appendix A: A Note on Sources

Research for this book drew on various types of sources. The first includes collections of poll results. George Gallup published results of polls he had conducted from 1935 to 1971 in three volumes: *The Gallup Polls: Public Opinion, 1935–1971* (New York: Random House, 1972). Results of the Gallup polls from 1972 to 1977 were published in two additional volumes: *The Gallup Poll: Public Opinion, 1972–1977* (Wilmington, Del.: Scholarly Resources, 1981). Since 1980, Elizabeth H. Hastings and Philip Hastings have edited an annual collection of polls, including polls on the Middle East, entitled *Index to International Public Opinion* (Westport, Conn.: Greenwood Press). However, this collection primarily includes polls conducted by Louis Harris. Thus far, five volumes have been published in this series.

On two separate occasions, the *Public Opinion Quarterly* has published collections of polling data on the Middle East. The first, collected by Hazel Erskine and published in the winter 1969–70 issue, covers the period from 1948 to 1969. The second, covering the period from 1970 to 1982, was collected by Connie de Boer and published in the spring 1983 issue. These collections present only selective and partial data. Finally, Steven J. Rosen and Yosef I. Abramowitz published a collection of polls on Israel conducted from 1967 to 1983: *How Americans Feel About Israel* (Washington, D.C.: AIPAC Papers on U.S.-Israel Relations, No. 10, 1984).

The second type of sources includes reports of polling agencies on current surveys, such as the *Roper Reports,* the *Gallup Opinion Index* or the *Gallup Report International, The Harris Survey,* the reports of the ABC News-Harris Survey or those of the ABC News-*Washington Post* poll, and NORC's "World Opinion Update." Current periodical results of polls were also published in the 1950s in "The Quarter's Polls" section of the *Public Opinion Quarterly.* In recent years, *Public Opinion* has published a similar section, entitled "Opinion Roundup."

Since the establishment of Israel, the American Jewish Committee (AJC) has commissioned surveys of American public opinion on Israel and the Arab-

Israeli conflict. The results of these surveys were published in memorandum format, with limited circulation, and in the AJC's annual publication: *American Jewish Year Book*. From time to time, the AJC also publishes collections of polls on the Middle East. A collection of this nature on the 1982 war in Lebanon was published by Geraldine Rosenfield in the 1984 volume.

Every four years since 1975, the Chicago Council on Foreign Relations has commissioned an extensive and comprehensive survey of opinions on U.S. foreign policy. These surveys include several questions on Israel and the Middle East and also cover general subjects, such as economic and military aid. Thus far, the council has published three surveys (1975, 1979, and 1983), that were used in the preparation of this study.

The next source consists of special comprehensive surveys of opinions on Israel and the Middle East. Harris, for example, conducted a survey of this nature in July 1980 for Edgar Bronfman, who was then the acting chairman of the World Jewish Congress. In February 1981, Yankelovich, Skelly and White, Inc., conducted a major survey of opinions on American Jews and Israel for the AJC. The survey was later published in book form: Gregory Martire and Ruth Clark, *Anti-Semitism in the United States* (New York: Praeger, 1982).

Finally, two unpublished manuscripts—Seymour Martin Lipset and William Schneider, *Israel and the Jews in American Public Opinion* (New York: American Jewish Committee, 1977); and William Schneider, *Anti-Semitism and Israel: A Report on American Public Opinion* (New York: American Jewish Committee, December, 1978)—include a wealth of data and information on American public opinion on Israel and the Arab-Israeli conflict.

Appendix B: The Gallup Sample

Design of the Sample

The design of the sample used by the Gallup Poll for its standard surveys of public opinion is that of a replicated area probability sample down to the block level in the case of urban areas and to segments of townships in the case of rural areas.

After stratifying the nation geographically (New England, Middle Atlantic, East Central, West Central, South Mountain, and Pacific Coast), and by size of community (Central cities of population 1,000,000 and over, 250,000 to 999,999, and 50,000 to 249,999; the urbanized areas of all these central cities as a single stratum; cities of 2,500 to 49,999; rural villages, and rural open county areas), in order to insure conformity of the sample with the 1980 Census distribution of the population, over 350 different sampling locations or areas are selected on a mathematically random basis from within cities, towns and counties which have in turn been selected on a mathematically random basis.

The interviewers have no choice whatsoever concerning the part of the city, town or county in which they conduct their interviews. Approximately five interviews are conducted in each randomly selected sampling point. Interviewers are given maps of the area to which they are assigned and they are required to follow a specified travel pattern on contacting households. At each occupied dwelling unit, interviewers are instructed to select respondents by following a prescribed systematic method.

Within each occupied dwelling unit or household reached, the interviewer asks to speak to the youngest man 18 or older at home, or if no man is at home, the oldest woman 18 or older. This method of selection within the household has been developed empirically to produce an age distribution by men and women separately which compares closely with the age distribution

From *Gallup Political Index*, (October 1965), The Gallup Organization, Inc., Technical Appendix, Go 79167-H (September 1979), and *Gallup Report*, 241 (October 1985), 31–32.

of the population. It increases the probability of selecting younger men, who are at home who tend to be under-represented if given an equal chance of being drawn from among those at home. The method of selection among those at home within the household is not strictly at random, but it is systematic and objective. Interviewing is conducted at times when adults, in general, are most likely to be at home, which means on weekends or if on weekdays, after 4:00 P.M. for women and after 6:00 P.M. for men. This procedure is followed until the assigned numbers of interviews with male and female adults have been completed.

After the survey data have been collected and processed, the demographic characteristics of survey respondents are balanced to match the latest U.S. Census Bureau estimates of the adult population's demographic characteristics. The data are also weighted by the probability of finding individual respondents at home. These weighting procedures ensure the representativeness of the sample. Allowance for persons not at home is made by a "times-at-home" weighting procedure rather than by "call backs."[a] This procedure is one standard method for reducing the sample bias that would otherwise result from under-representation in the sample of persons who are difficult to find at home.

Since this sampling procedure is designed to produce a sample which approximates the adult civilian population (18 and older) living in private households (that is, excluding those in prisons and hospitals, hotels, religious and educational institutions and on military reservations), the survey results can be applied to this population for the purpose of projecting percentages into numbers of people. The manner in which the sample is drawn also produces a sample which approximates the population of private households in the United States. Therefore, survey results can also be projected in terms of numbers of households.

Sampling Error

In interpreting survey results, it should be borne in mind that all sample surveys are subject to sampling error, that is, the extent to which the results may differ from what would be obtained if the whole population surveyed had been interviewed. The size of such sampling error depends largely on the number of interviews.

The following tables may be used in estimating the sampling error of any percentage in this report. The computed allowances have taken into account

[a]A. Politz and W. Simmons, "An Attempt to Get the 'Not at Homes' into the Sample Without Callbacks," *Journal of the American Statistical Association* 44 (March 1949), pp. 9–31.

the effect of the sample design upon sampling error. They may be interpreted as indicating the range (plus or minus the figure shown) within which the results of repeated samplings in the same time period could be expected to vary, 95 percent of the time, assuming the same sampling procedure, the same interviewers, and the same questionnaire.

The first table shows how much allowance should be made for the sampling error of a percentage:

Recommended Allowance for Sampling Error of a Percentage

	Percentage Points (at 95 in 100 confidence level) Sample Size*						
	1,500	*1,000*	*750*	*600*	*400*	*200*	*100*
Percentages near 10	2	2	3	3	4	5	7
Percentages near 20	2	3	4	4	5	7	9
Percentages near 30	3	4	4	4	6	8	10
Percentages near 40	3	4	4	5	6	8	11
Percentages near 50	3	4	4	5	6	8	11
Percentages near 60	3	4	4	5	6	8	11
Percentages near 70	3	4	4	4	6	8	10
Percentages near 80	2	3	4	4	5	7	9
Percentages near 90	2	2	3	3	4	5	7

*The chances are 95 in 100 that the sampling error is not larger than the figures shown.

The table would be used in the following manner: Let us say a reported percentage is 33 for a group which includes 1,500 respondents. Then we go to row "percentages near 30" in the table and go across to the column headed "1,500." The number at this point is 3, which means that the 33 percent obtained in the sample is subject to a sampling error of plus or minus 3 points. Another way of saying it is that very probably (95 chances out of 100) the average of repeated samplings would be somewhere between 30 and 36, with the most likely figure the 33 obtained.

In comparing survey results in two samples, such as, for example, men and women, the question arises as to how large must a difference between them be before one can be reasonably sure that it reflects a real difference. In the tables below, the number of points which must be allowed for in such comparisons is indicated.

Two tables are provided. One is for percentages near 20 or 80; the other for percentages near 50. For percentages in between, the error to be allowed for is between that shown in the two tables:

Recommended Allowance for Sampling Error of the Difference

	*Percentage Points (at 95 in 100 confidence level)**			
	Percentages near 20 or percentages near 80			
TABLE A *Size of Sample*	*750*	*600*	*400*	*200*
750	5			
600	5	6		
400	6	6	7	
200	8	8	8	10
	Percentages near 50			
TABLE B *Size of Sample*	*750*	*600*	*400*	*200*
750	6			
600	7	7		
400	7	8	8	
200	10	10	10	12

*The chances are 95 in 100 that the sampling error is not larger than the figures shown.

Here is an example of how the tables would be used: Let us say that 50 percent of men respond a certain way and 40 percent of women respond that way also, for a difference of 10 percentage points between them. Can we say with any assurance that the 10-point difference reflects a real difference between men and women on the question? The sample contains approximately 750 men and 750 women.

Since the percentages are near 50, we consult Table B, and since the two samples are about 750 persons each, we look for the number in the column headed "750" which is also in the row designated "750." We find the number 6 here. This means that the allowance for error should be 6 points, and that in concluding that the percentage among men is somewhere between 4 and 16 points higher than the percentage among women we should be wrong only about 5 percent of the time. In other words, we can conclude with considerable confidence that a difference exists in the direction observed and that it amounts to at least 4 percentage points.

If in another case, men's reponses amount to 22 percent, say, and women's 24 percent, we consult Table A because these percentages are near 20. We look in the column headed "750" and see that the number is 5. Obviously, then, the 2-point difference is inconclusive.

Appendix C: The Yankelovich, Skelly and White Sample

This study's sample was designed to accomplish several objectives: represent the population of the contiguous United States ages 18 years and older; maximize the efficiency and accuracy of the sample by utilizing a series of innovative but proven sampling techniques; utilize the latest population data available; adequately represent the Jewish and Black population of the United States while maintaining the integrity of the national sample data reported.

The objectives were accomplished through the use of two independent but integrated samples: 1. the General Public sample, comprising, 1,072 interviews, was designed to be representative of the population ages 18 years and older; 2. the Jewish/Black (supplemental) sample, comprising 143 interviews, was designed to be representative of these groups. The two samples were integrated by statistical weighting so that the data reported are representative of the population of the contiguous United States ages 18 years and older with the Jewish/Black segment of that population being representative of that supplemental group in the contiguous United States.

The General Public Sample

The data used in implementing this sample were total final population statistics for states and Standard Metropolitan Statistical Areas as compiled in the 1970 Census of the United States, and updated by Yankelovich, Skelly and White, Inc., to reflect the population as of December 31, 1974. These data reported on the population of: each of the states and the District of Columbia; the counties within the states (and county subdivisions in New England); all incorporated places with 1,000 or more population; the Standard Metropolitan

From Gregory Martire and Ruth Clark, *Anti-Semitism in the United States* (New York: Praeger, 1982), pp. 120–121.

Statistical Areas (SMSA); the central city and noncentral city population distribution within each SMSA; the counties (or portions of counties in New England) falling within each SMSA.

Choosing Cluster Points

The total population of the United States was stratified by the nine standard Census Divisions: New England; Middle Atlantic; East North Central; West North Central; South Atlantic; East South Central; West South Central; Mountain; West; and within the nine divisions by Metropolitan (SMSA) and non-Metropolitan Area. The nine Metropolitan Area strata were then ordered by size of population, specific SMSA's were ordered by size of population within each divisional stratum, and counties (or county subdivisions) were ordered by size of population within each SMSA.

Having ordered the population in this manner, 135 primary sampling units were obtained. Selection from the arrays was on the basis of fixed intervals with random starting points. The interval used for the selection of non-Metropolitan clusters reflected the fact that these clusters would be represented at one-half their normal weight. A weighting procedure was utilized to bring these clusters back to their true representation.

Choosing Starting Points in the Supplemental Samples

The cluster points for the Jewish/Black supplemental samples were based on extending those clusters of the general sample that had yielded two or more interviews with members of the respective groups.

Respondent Selection in the Supplemental Samples

As in the general sample, interviewers in the supplemental samples followed a set of detailed and specific standard instructions for proceeding through the assigned cluster from that starting point. These route-selection procedures were described in great detail in the sampling instructions. Respondent selection in households along the route followed a number of specific procedures designed to minimize the effect of sex-skewed sample execution. In order to determine eligibility for the Jewish sample, potential respondents were screened on a number of questions including items bearing on the observation of religious holidays. Within each eligible household, the eligible respondent

(18 years of age or older) was selected by a random selection process. Once a respondent was designated, there was no substitution of this eligible household member. Only *one* interview per household was completed.

Appendix D: The 1983 National Survey of American Jews and Jewish Communal Leaders

Sampling and Data Collection

As noted, this study consists of two surveys, one of a representative nationwide sample of American Jews, the other of board members of five prominent Jewish communal organizations.

The public sample survey data collection was conducted by A.B. Data Corporation of Milwaukee, a firm that conducts direct marketing campaigns of Jewish communities. In the last year, A.B. Data compiled approximately 80,000 Distinctive Jewish Names (DJN) which it applied against lists of the country's 70 million telephone subscribers to yield well over a million households with a high probability of containing a Jewish member. Using this list, the survey was initially sent (in June, 1983) to a sample of 1600 households. About a quarter of these, in turn, were ineligible or unreachable (non-Jewish, deceased, moved with no forwarding address, etc.). Of the remaining 1200 or so, about half ($N = 640$) eventually returned the questionnaire. Many had received as many as five mailings: an introductory letter, the first questionnaire, a postcard reminder, a second and a third questionnaire, as well as a follow up reminder phone call. The survey's last respondents replied in late July 1983.

Previous research has compared DJN and non-DJN Jews drawn from random samples secured through Random Digit Dialing and other high-cost techniques. That research found few differences, all of which were minor and in conflicting directions, between Jews with Distinctive Jewish Names and those without such names. In other words, it is safe to assume that DJNs are neither more nor less Jewishly committed than non-DJN Jews. The selectivity in returning mail questionnaires might well pose a greater problem. Previous research on returned-mail questionnaires indicated lower response rates among

---

From Steven M. Cohen, *Attitudes of American Jews Toward Israel and Israelis, The 1983 National Survey of American Jews and Jewish Communal Leaders* (New York: American Jewish Committee, Institute on American Jewish-Israeli Relations, 1983), pp. 1, 2, 29–30.

the lesser educated, the geographically mobile, the elderly, and those with less interest in the subject matter. However, a comparison of this survey's respondents with those of more sophisticated (and costly) Jewish population studies revealed only small differences (see below). Slightly more of the present respondents are married; they are slightly more affluent, more Israel-oriented, and more denominationally affiliated than the others. In general, the differences between them and respondents in other studies total about 5% or less.

The leadership sample consists of board members from five national organizations: the American Jewish Committee, the American Jewish Congress, the Anti-Defamation League of B'nai B'rith, the International B'nai B'rith, and the United Jewish Appeal. Again, about half of the eligible respondents returned the questionnaire ($N = 272$). Results below are reported collectively for the five organizations.

Demographic and Social Characteristics

The method of data collection used in this study—mailing questionnaires to Jews with Distinctive Jewish Names nationwide—offers an important advantage over other methods: it is extraordinarily low-cost. Its principal disadvantage, though, is that it may produce biased, or somewhat unrepresentative results. To determine the extent to which this sample is indeed representative of American Jewry, the following table compares selected social and demographic characteristics of the 1983 National Survey of American Jews with the largest recent survey of American Jews, the 1981 Greater New York Jewish Population Study conducted by Paul Ritterband and myself for New York's UJA Federation. This study interviewed over 4,500 Jews living in eight counties containing about a third of all American Jewry.

In many respects the two samples are, if not virtually identical, quite similar. The median age, proportion of households married, the household size and many of the ritual activities are very close. The national sample reported slightly higher income, owing in part to inflation over the last two years, and in part to the higher concentration of working-class Jews in New York, relative to the rest of the country. For similar reasons, educational attainment in the national sample was also higher.

The national sample does appear to over-represent Orthodox and Conservative Jews, and as a consequence it may under-represent the Reform or unaffiliated. In part, these differences are due to the slightly greater motivation of more Jewishly committed individuals to complete and return the study. In contrast, the friendship results point in the opposite direction: fewer of the

Social and Demographic Characteristics

	1983 Public	*1981 Greater N.Y.;*[a]	1983 Leaders
Median Age	48	49	58
% Married	70	65	90
Mean Household Size	2.6	2.5	2.6
% B.A.	62	53	90
Median Income	$37,000	$31,000	$135,000[b]
Denomination			
Orthodox	15	13	8
Conservative	44	36	34
Reform	29	29	50
Other	12	23	8
	100	100	100
Seder	89	90	95
Chanukah Candles	77	76	81
Yom Kippur Fast	59	68	61
Sabbath Candles	34	37	42
Separate Dishes	22	30	16
Christmas Tree	11	—	12
% 3 Closest Friends Jewish	61	70	79
% Currently intermarried (of those married)	17	11	4

[a] Paul Ritterband and Steven M. Cohen, 1981–4 Greater N.Y. Jewish Population Study, Federation of Jewish Philanthropies of N.Y.

[b] Approximate calculation, 69% of the leaders reported incomes in excess of $100,000.

national respondents (61% versus 70%) reported only Jewish close friends than did respondents in the New York study.

In sum, then, some characteristics of the national sample differ in small measure from the standard for representativeness derived from the more sophisticated and more costly New York study. However, none of these differences are large enough to seriously impugn the substantive inferences drawn in this study.

Selected Bibliography

Public Opinion

Abramson, Paul. *Political Attitudes in America: Formation and Change*. San Francisco: Freeman, 1983.

Adams, William C. "Middle East Meets West: Surveying American Attitudes." *Public Opinion* 5(April–May 1982): 51–55.

———. "Blaming Israel For Begin." *Public Opinion* 5(October–November 1982): 51–55.

Bard, Mitchell. "Israel's Standing in American Public Opinion." *Commentary* 80(October 1985): 58–60.

Bennett, Walter Lance. *Public Opinion in American Politics*. New York: Harcourt Brace Jovanovich, 1980.

Benson, John M. "The Polls: U.S. Military Intervention."*Public Opinion Quarterly* 46(Winter 1982): 592–98.

de Boer, Connie. "The Polls: Attitudes Toward The Arab-Israeli Conflict." *Public Opinion Quarterly* 47(Spring 1983): 121–31.

Bogart, Leo. *Silent Politics: Polls and the Awareness of Public Opinion*. New York: Wiley, 1972.

Cantril, Albert H., ed. *Polling on the Issues*. Cabin John, Md.: Seven Locks Press, 1980.

Cantril, Albert H., and Charles W. Roll, Jr. *Hopes and Fears of the American People*. New York: Universe Books, 1971.

Cohen, Bernard C. *The Public's Impact on Foreign Policy*. Boston: Little, Brown, 1973.

Cohen, Steven M. *American Modernity and Jewish Identity* (New York: Tavistock, 1983).

Dawson, Richard E. *Public Opinion and Contemporary Disarray*. New York: Harper & Row, 1973.

Devine, Donald J. *The Attentive Public: Polyarchial Democracy*. Chicago: Rand McNally, 1970.

Erikson, Robert S. and Norman R. Luttbeg. *American Public Opinion: Its Origins, Content and Impact*. New York: Wiley, 1973.

Erskine, Hazel. "The Polls: Western Partisanship in the Middle East." *Public Opinion Quarterly* 33(Winter 1969–1970): 627–40.

Everson, David H. *Public Opinion and Interest Groups in American Politics*. New York: Watts, 1982.

Free, Lloyd A., and Hadley Cantril. *The Political Beliefs of Americans: A Study of Public Opinion*. New York: Simon and Schuster, 1968.

Gallup, George H. *The Sophisticated Poll Watcher's Guide*. Princeton, N.J.: Princeton University Press, 1972.

———. *The Gallup Poll: Public Opinion, 1935–1971* (3 vols.). New York: Random House, 1972.

———. *The Gallup Poll: Public Opinion, 1972–1977* (2 vols). Wilmington, Del.: Scholarly Resources, 1978.

Garnham, David. "The Oil Crisis and U.S. Attitudes Toward Israel." In Naiem A. Sherbiny and Mark Tessler, eds., *Arab Oil: Impact on the Arab Countries and Global Implications*. New York: Praeger, 1976.

Gilboa, Eytan. "Trends in American Attitudes Toward the PLO and the Palestinians." *Political Communication and Persuasion* 3(1985): 45–67.

———. "Effects of the War in Lebanon on American Attitudes Toward Israel and the Arab-Israeli Conflict." *Middle East Review* 18(Fall 1985): 30–43.

———. *Israel in the Mind of American Jews: Public Opinion Trends and Analysis*. Research Report No. 4. London: Institute of Jewish Affairs, March 1986.

———. "Attitudes of American Jews Toward Israel: Trends over Time," in David Singer and Milton Himmelfarb, eds. *American Jewish Year Book*. 86(1986): 110–25.

Griffin, Kenyon N., J.C. Martin, and O. Walter. "Religious Roots and Rural Americans' Support For Israel During the October War." *Journal of Palestine Studies* 6(Autumn 1976): 104–14.

Gruen, George E. "Public Opinion and Israel." *Commentary* 57(March 1974): 14–24.

———. "Arab Petropower and American Public Opinion." *Middle East Review* 7(Winter 1975–76): 33–39.

Harris, Louis. "Oil or Israel." *New York Times Magazine*, April 6, 1975, 21–22, 34.

Hastings, Elizabeth H., and Philip Hastings, eds. *Index to International Public Opinion*. Vol. 1, 1978–79; Vol. 2, 1979–80; Vol. 3, 1980–1981; Vol. 4, 1981–82; Vol. 5, 1982–83. Westport, Conn: Greenwood Press, 1980, 1982, 1984.

Hennessy, Bernard C. *Public Opinion*. Belmont, Calif.: Wadsworth, 1965.

Hero, Alfred O., Jr. *American Religious Groups View Foreign Policy: Trends in Rank-and-File Opinion, 1937–1969*. Durham, N.C.: Duke University Press, 1973.

Janowitz, Morris, and Paul Hirsch, eds. *Reader in Public Opinion and Mass Communication*. New York: Free Press, 1981.

Kohut, Andrew. "American Opinion on Shifting Sands." *Public Opinion* 1(May–June 1978): 15–18.

Lachman, Ran. "American Attitudes Towards Israel: The Social Composition of Respondents in Public Opinion Polls." *Jewish Journal of Sociology* 20(December 1978): 149–63.

Laqueur, Walter. "Israel, The Arabs and World Opinion." *Commentary* 44(August 1967): 49–59.

Levering, Ralph B. *The Public and American Foreign Policy, 1918-1978*. New York: Morrow, 1978.

Lipset, Seymour Martin. "The Wavering Polls." *Public Interest* 43(Spring 1976): 70–89.

———. "The Polls on the Middle East." *Middle East Review* 11(Fall 1978): 24–30.

Lipset, Seymour Martin, and William Schneider. *Israel and the Jews in American Public Opinion*. New York: American Jewish Committee, Mimeographed., 1977.

———. "Carter vs. Israel: What the Polls Reveal." *Commentary* 64(November 1977): 21–29.

Martire, Gregory, and Ruth Clark. *Anti-Semitism in the United States*. New York: Praeger, 1982.

Mueller, John E. *War, Presidents, and Public Opinion*. New York: Wiley, 1973.

———. "Changes in American Public Attitudes Toward International Involvement." In Ellen Stern, ed. *The Limits of Military Intervention*. Beverly Hills, Calif.: Sage, 1977.

Nes, David. "American Public Opinion and Israel." *Middle East International* 48(June 1974): 12–14.

Nincic, Miroslav, and Bruce Russett. "The Effect of Similarity and Interest on Attitudes Toward Foreign Countries." *Public Opinion Quarterly* 43(Spring 1979): 68–78.

Raab, Earl. "Is Israel Losing Popular Support? The Evidence of the Polls." *Commentary* 57(January 1974): 26–29.

———. "American Jewish Attitudes on Israel: Consensus and Dissent." *Perspectives* (November 1981): 1–22.

Rielly, John E., ed. *American Public Opinion and U.S. Foreign Policy, 1975*. Chicago: Chicago Council on Foreign Relations, 1975.

———. *American Public Opinion and U.S. Foreign Policy, 1979*. Chicago: Chicago Council on Foreign Relations, 1979.

———. *American Public Opinion and U.S. Foreign Policy, 1983*. Chicago: Chicago Council on Foreign Relations, 1983.

———. "American Opinion: Continuity, Not Reaganism." *Foreign Policy* 50(Spring 1983): 85–104.

Robinson, John, and R. Meadow. *Polls Apart*. Cabin John, Md.: Seven Locks Press, 1982.

Roll, Charles W., Jr., and Albert H. Cantril. *Polls: Their Use and Misuse in Politics*. Cabin John, Md.: Seven Locks Press, 1980.

Rosen, Steven, J. and Yosef I. Abramowitz. *How Americans Feel About Israel*, AIPAC Papers on U.S.-Israel Relations, No. 10. Washington, D.C.: American Israel Public Affairs Committee, 1984.

Rosenfield, Geraldine. "The Polls: Attitudes Toward American Jews." *Public Opinion Quarterly* 46(Fall 1982): 431–43.

———. "US Public Opinion Polls and the Lebanon War." *American Jewish Year Book* 84(1984): 105–16.

Russett, Bruce, and Donald R. Deluca. "'Don't Tread On Me': Public Opinion and Foreign Policy in the Eighties." *Political Science Quarterly* 96(Fall 1981): 381–99.

Russett, Bruce, and Miroslav Nincic. "American Opinion on the Use of Military Force Abroad." *Political Science Quarterly* 91(Fall 1976): 411–31.

Schneider, William. *Anti-Semitism and Israel: A Report on American Public Opinion*.

New York: American Jewish Committee, December 1978. Mimeographed.

———. "Is Israel Losing Public Support?" *Politics Today* (March–April 1979): 14–16.

Schuman, Howard, and Stanley Presser. *Questions and Answers in Attitude Surveys, Experiments on Question Form, Wording and Context.* New York: Academic Press, 1981.

Sklare, Marshall, and Joseph Greenblum. *Jewish Identity on the Suburban Frontier.* New York: Basic Books, 1967.

Sklare, Marshall, and Benjamin Ringer. "A Study of Jewish Attitudes Toward the State of Israel." In M. Sklare, ed., *The Jews: Social Patterns of an American Group.* Glencoe, Ill.: Free Press, 1958.

Slade, Shelley. "The Image of the Arab in America: Analysis of a Poll on American Attitudes." *Middle East Journal* 35(Spring 1981): 143–162.

Stember, Charles H. "The Impact of Israel on American Attitudes." In Charles H. Stember et al., *Jews in the Mind of America.* New York: Basic Books, 1966.

Suleiman, Michael W. "National Stereotypes as Weapons in the Arab–Israeli Conflict." *Journal of Palestine Studies* 3(Spring 1974): 109–21.

———. "American Public Support of Middle Eastern Countries: 1939–1979." In Michael Hudson and Ronald G. Wolfe, eds., *The American Media and the Arabs.* Washington D.C.: Georgetown University, Center for Contemporary Arab Studies, 1980.

Sussman, Barry. *Elites in America.* Washington D.C.: Washington Post, 1976.

Trice, Robert H. "Foreign Policy Interest Groups, Mass Public Opinion and the Arab-Israeli Dispute." *Western Political Quarterly* 31(June 1978): 238–52.

Welch, Susan, and John Comer, eds. *Public Opinion: Its Formation, Measurement and Impact.* Palo Alto, Calif.: Mayfield, 1975.

Wheeler, Michael. *Lies, Damn Lies and Statistics: The Manipulation of Public Opinion in America.* New York: Dell, 1976.

Mass Media

Alexander, Edward. "The Journalists' War Against Israel, Techniques of Distortion, Disorientation and Disinformation." *Encounter* 12(September–October 1982): 87–97.

Asi, Morad. "Arabs, Israelis, and TV News: A Time-Series, Content Analysis." In William C. Adams, ed., *Television Coverage of the Middle East.* Norwood, N.J.: Ablex, 1981.

Bagnied, Magda, and Steven M. Schneider. "Sadat Goes to Jerusalem: Televised Images, Themes and Agenda." In William C. Adams, ed., *Television Coverage of the Middle East.* Norwood, N.J.: Ablex, 1981.

Bar-Illan, David. "Israel, the Hostages, and the Networks." *Commentary* 80(September 1985): 33–37.

Belkaoui, Janice Monti. "Images of Arabs and Israelis in the Prestige Press, 1966–1974." *Journalism Quarterly* 55(Winter 1978): 732–38, 799.

Chafets, Ze'ev. *Double Vision: How the Press Distorts America's View of the Middle East.* New York: Morrow, 1985.

Cohen, Yoel, and Jacob Reuveny. *The Lebanon War and Western News Media*, Research Report No. 6-7. London: Institute of Jewish Affairs, July 1984.

Daugherty, David, and Michael Warden. "Prestige Press Editorial Treatment of the Mideast During 11 Crisis Years." *Journalism Quarterly* 56(Winter 1979): 776–82.

Feith, Douglas J. "Israel, the Post, and the Shaft." *Middle East Review* 12(Summer–Fall 1980): 62–66.

Feldblum, Esther Y. *The American Catholic Press and the Jewish State, 1917–1959.* New York: Ktav, 1977.

Gervasi, Frank. *Media Coverage: The War in Lebanon.* Washington D.C.: Center for International Security, 1982.

Gordon, Avishag H. "The Middle East October 1973 War as Reported by the American Networks." *International Problems* 14(Fall 1975): 76–85.

Graber, Doris A. *Mass Media and American Politics.* Second Edition. Washington D.C.: Congressional Quarterly Press, 1984.

Hershman, Robert, and Henry L. Griggs, Jr. "American Television News and the Middle East." *Middle East Journal* 35(Autumn 1981): 481–91.

Hudson, Michael C, and Ronald G. Wolfe, eds. *The American Media and the Arabs.* Washington, D.C.: Georgetown University, Center for Contemporary Arab Studies, 1980.

Isaac, Rael Jean. "Time Against Israel." *New Republic* (October 18, 1980): 18–23.

Kalb, Marvin, Ted Koppel, and John Scali. "The Networks and Foreign News Coverage." *Washington Quarterly* 5(Spring 1982): 39–51.

Karetzky, Stephen. *The Cannons of Journalism: The New York Times Propaganda War Against Israel.* Stanford, Calif.: O'Keefe, 1984.

Landau, Julian, ed. *The Media: Freedom or Responsibility—The War in Lebanon, 1982: A Case Study.* Jerusalem: B.A.L. Mass Communications, 1984.

Lemert, James B. *Does Mass Communication Change Public Opinion After All? A New Approach to Effects Analysis.* Chicago: Nelson Hall, 1981.

Lichter, S. Robert. "Media Support for Israel: A Survey of Leading Journalists." In William C. Adams, ed., *Television Coverage of the Middle East.* Norwood, N.J.: Ablex, 1981.

Miller, Mark Crispin. "Strategies of Containment: How TV Covers Wars." *New Republic* (November 29, 1982): 26–33.

Mishra, V. M. "News From The Middle East in Five US Media." *Journalism Quarterly* 56(Summer 1979): 374–378.

Morris, Roger. "Beirut-and the Press-Under Siege." *Columbia Journalism Review* 21(November–December 1982): 23–33.

Muravchik, Joshua. "Misreporting Lebanon." *Policy Review* 23(Winter 1983): 11–66.

Paletz, David, and Robert Entman. *Media, Power, Politics.* New York: Free Press, 1981.

Pipes, Daniel. "The Media and the Middle East." *Commentary* 77(June 1984): 29–34.

Roper, Burns W. "Polls and Politics: The Media and the Polls." *Public Opinion* 3(February–March 1980): 46–47.

Spragens, William C., with Carole Ann Terwood. "Camp David and the Networks:

Reflections on Coverage of the 1978 Summit." In William C. Adams, ed., *Television Coverage of International Affairs*. Norwood, N.J.: Ablex, 1982.

Terry, Janice. "A Content Analysis of American Newspapers." In Abdeen Jabara and Janice Terry, eds., *The Arab World from Nationalism to Revolution* Wilmette, Ill.: Medina University Press International, 1971.

Terry, Janice, with Gordon Mendenhall. "1973 U.S. Press Coverage on the Middle East." *Journal of Palestine Studies* 4(Autumn 1974): 120–33.

Timmerman, Kenneth R. "How the PLO Terrorized Journalists in Beirut." *Commentary* 75(January 1983): 48–50.

Trice, Robert H. "The American Elite Press and the Arab-Israeli Conflict." *Middle East Journal* 33(Summer 1979): 304–25.

Wagner, Charles H. "Elite American Newspaper Opinion and the Middle East: Commitment vs. Isolation." In Willard A. Beling, ed., *The Middle East: Quest for an American Policy*. Albany: State University of New York Press, 1973.

Walsh, Edward. "Reporting from an Alien Landscape." *Nieman Reports* (Summer 1985): 26–28.

American–Israeli Relations and U.S. Policy in the Middle East

Allen, Harry S., and Ivan Volgyes, eds. *Israel, the Middle East, and U.S. Interests*. New York: Praeger, 1983.

Badeau, John S. *The American Approach to the Arab World*. New York: Harper & Row, 1968.

Bain, Kenneth R. *The March to Zion: United States Policy and the Founding of Israel*. College Station: Texas A&M University Press, 1979.

Beling, William A., ed. *The Middle East: Quest for an American Policy*. Albany: State University of New York Press, 1973.

Ben-Zvi, Abraham. *Alliance Politics and the Limits of Influence: The Case of the U.S. and Israel, 1975–1983*, Paper No. 24. Tel Aviv: Tel Aviv University, Jaffe Center for Strategic Studies, April 1984.

Bryson, Thomas A. *United States–Middle East Diplomatic Relations, 1784–1978: An Annotated Bibliography*. Metuchen, N.J.: Scarecrow Press, 1979.

Cahn, Anne Hessing. "U.S. Arms to the Middle East 1967–1976: A Critical Examination." In Milton Leitenberg and Gabriel Sheffer, eds. *Great Power Intervention in the Middle East*. New York: Pergamon, 1979.

Campbell, John C. *Defense of the Middle East: Problems of American Policy*. New York: Praeger, 1961.

Cohen, Michael J. *Palestine and the Great Powers, 1945–1948*. Princeton, N.J.: Princeton University Press, 1982.

Dowty, Alan. *Middle East Crisis: U.S. Decision-Making in 1958, 1970 and 1973*. Berkeley: University of California Press, 1984.

Drinan, Robert F. *Honor the Promise: America's Commitment to Israel*. Garden City, N.Y.: Doubleday, 1977.

Feuerwerger, Marvin C. *Congress and Israel: Foreign Aid Decision-Making in the House of Representatives, 1969–1976*. Westport, Conn.: Greenwood Press, 1979.

Gazit, Mordechai. *President Kennedy's Policy Toward the Arab States and Israel*. Tel Aviv: Tel Aviv University, Shiloah Center for Middle Eastern and African Studies, 1983.

Grose, Peter. *Israel in the Mind of America*. New York: Knopf, 1983.

Jabber, Paul. *Not By War Alone: Security and Arms Control in The Middle East*. Berkeley: University of California Press, 1981.

Kenen, I.L. *Israel's Defense Line: Her Friends and Foes in Washington*. Buffalo, N.Y.: Prometheus Books, 1981.

Lawson, Fred. "The Reagan Administration in the Middle East." *Merip Reports* 14(November–December 1984): 27–34.

Mangold, Peter. *Superpower Intervention in the Middle East*. New York: St. Martin's Press, 1978.

Meyer, Gail, E. *Egypt and the U.S., The Formative Years*. Rutherford, N.J.: Fairleigh Dickinson University Press, 1980.

Neff, Donald. *Warriors at Suez: Eisenhower Takes America into the Middle East*. New York: Linden Press, Simon and Schuster, 1981.

Polk, William R. *The United States and the Arab World*. Cambridge: Harvard University Press, 1975.

Pollock, David. *The Politics of Pressure: American Arms and Israeli Policy Since the Six Day War*. Westport, Conn.: Greenwood Press, 1982.

Pranger, Robert J. *American Policy for Peace in the Middle East, 1969–1971: Problems of Principle, Maneuver, and Time*. Washington, D.C.: American Enterprise Institute for Public Policy Research, 1971.

Quandt, William B. *Decade of Decisions: American Policy Toward the Arab-Israeli Conflict, 1967–1976*. Berkeley: University of California Press, 1977.

———. *Camp David: Peacemaking and Politics*. Washington, D.C.: Brookings, 1986.

The Quest for Peace: Principal United States Public Statements and Related Documents on the Arab-Israeli Peace Process, 1967–1983. Washington, D.C.: United States Department of State, 1984.

Reagan, Ronald. *U.S. Involvement in Mideast Peace Effort: "A Moral Imperative."* U.S. Policy Statement Series, September 1, 1982. Washington, D.C.: United States Information Service, 1982.

Reich, Bernard. *Quest for Peace: United States-Israel Relations and the Arab-Israeli Conflict*. New Brunswick, N.J.: Transaction Books, 1977.

———. *The United States and Israel: Influence in the Special Relationship*. New York: Praeger, 1984.

Safran, Nadav. *Israel—The Embattled Ally*. Cambridge, Mass.: Harvard University Press, 1978.

Saunders, Harold. "Arabs and Israelis: A Political Strategy." *Foreign Affairs* 64(Winter 1985–1986): 304–25.

Shadid, Mohammed K. *The United States and the Palestinians*. London: Croom and Helm, 1981.

Shaked, H., and I. Rabinovich, eds. *The Middle East and the United States: Perceptions and Policies*. New Brunswick, N.J.: Transaction Books, 1980.

Sheehan, Edward R.F. *The Arabs, Israelis, and Kissinger: A Secret History of American Diplomacy in the Middle East*. New York: Crowell, 1976.

Sicherman, Harvey. *Broker Or Advocate? The U.S. Role in the Arab-Israeli Dispute, 1973–1978*, Monograph No. 25. Philadelphia: Foreign Policy Research Institute, 1978.

———. "The United States and Israel: A Strategic Divide?" *Orbis* 24(Summer 1980): 381–93.

Spiegel, Steven L. "Israel as a Strategic Asset." *Commentary* 75(June 1983): 51–55.

———. *The Other Arab-Israeli Conflict: Making America's Middle East Policy, from Truman to Reagan*. Chicago: University of Chicago Press, 1985.

Stookey, Robert W. *America and the Arab States: An Uneasy Encounter*. New York: Wiley, 1975.

Tillman, Seth P. *The United States in the Middle East: Interests and Obstacles*. Bloomington: Indiana University Press, 1982.

Toward Peace in the Middle East: Report of a Study Group. Washington, D.C.: Brookings, 1975.

Trice, Robert H. "Congress and the Arab-Israeli Conflict: Support for Israel in the U.S. Senate, 1970–1973." *Political Science Quarterly* 92(Fall 1977): 443–63.

———. *Interest Groups and Foreign Policy Process: U.S. Policy in the Middle East*. Beverly Hills, Calif.: Sage, 1976.

Tschirgi, Dan. *The Politics of Indecision: Origins and Implications of American Involvement with the Palestine Problem*. New York: Praeger, 1983.

Tucker, Robert W. "The Middle East: Carterism Without Carter?" *Commentary* 72(September 1981): 27–36.

Ullman, Richard. "Alliance With Israel." *Foreign Policy* 19(Summer 1975): 18–33.

Wilson, Evan M. *Decison on Palestine: How the U.S. Came to Recognize Israel*. Stanford, Calif.: Hoover Institution Press, 1979.

Israel and the Arab-Israeli Conflict

Abu-Lughod, Ibrahim, ed. *The Arab-Israeli Confrontation of June 1967: An Arab Perspective*. Evanston, Ill.: Northwestern University Press, 1970.

Ajami, Fouad. *The Arab Predicament*. New York: Cambridge University Press, 1981.

Arian, Asher, ed. *The Elections in Israel—1977*. Jerusalem: Academic Press, 1980.

———. *Elections in Israel—1981*. Tel Aviv: Ramot, 1983.

Bailey, Clinton. *Jordan's Palestinian Challenge, 1948–1983: A Political History*. Boulder, Colo.: Westview Press, 1984.

Becker, Jillian. *The PLO: The Rise and Fall of the Palestine Liberation Organization*. London: Weidenfeld and Nicolson, 1984.

Bill, James A., and Carl Leiden. *Politics in the Middle East*. Boston: Little, Brown, 1979.

Bovis, H. Eugene. *The Jerusalem Question, 1917–1968*. Stanford, Calif.: Hoover Institution Press, 1971.

Brecher, Michael. *Decisions in Israel's Foreign Policy*. New Haven: Yale University Press, 1975.

Bulloch, John. *The Making of a War: The Middle East From 1967 to 1973*. London: Longman, 1974.
Carter, Jimmy. *The Blood of Abraham*. Boston: Houghton Mifflin, 1985.
Cobban, Helena. *The Palestinian Liberation Organization: People, Power, and Politics*. Cambridge: Cambridge University Press, 1984.
Cohen, Saul B. *Jerusalem Undivided*. New York: Herzl Press, 1980.
Dupuy, Trevor N. *Elusive Victory: The Arab-Israeli Wars, 1947–1974*. New York: Harper & Row, 1978.
Eytan, Walter. *The First Ten Years: A Diplomatic History of Israel*. New York: Simon and Schuster, 1958.
Friedlander, Melvin A. *Sadat and Begin: The Domestic Politics of Peacemaking*. Boulder, Colo.: Westview Press, 1983.
Gabriel, Richard A. *Operation Peace for Galilee: The Israeli-PLO War in Lebanon*. New York: Hill and Wang, 1984.
Grose, Peter. *A Changing Israel*. New York: Vintage, 1985.
Harkabi, Y. *The Palestinian Covenant and Its Meaning*. London: Vallentine, Mitchell, 1979.
———. *Arab Strategies and Israel's Response*. New York: Free Press, 1977.
Heikal, Mohamed. *The Road to Ramadan*. New York: Quadrangle, 1975.
Herzog, Chaim. *The War of Atonement: October 1973*. Boston: Little, Brown, 1975.
———. *The Arab-Israeli Wars: War and Peace in the Middle East*. London: Arms and Armour Press, 1982.
Heller, Mark. *A Palestinian State: The Implications for Israel*. Cambridge: Harvard University Press, 1983.
Israeli, Raphael. *The PLO in Lebanon*. London: Weidenfeld and Nicolson, 1983.
Jureidini, Paul, and R.D. McLaurin. *Beyond Camp David: Emerging Alignments and Leaders in the Middle East*. Syracuse, N.Y.: Syracuse University Press, 1981.
Kerr, Malcolm, ed. *The Elusive Peace in the Middle East*. Albany: State University of New York Press, 1975.
Khalil, Nakhleh, and Clifford A. Wright. *After the Palestine-Israel War: Limits to U.S. and Israeli Policy*. Belmont, Mass.: Institute of Arab Studies, 1983.
Khouri, Fred J. *The Arab-Israeli Dilemma*. Syracuse, N.Y.: Syracuse University Press, 1968.
Laqueur, Walter, ed. *The Israel-Arab Reader*. New York: Bantam Books, 1970.
Medzini, Meron, ed. *Israel's Foreign Relations: Selected Documents, 1947–1974*. Jerusalem: Ministry for Foreign Affairs, 1976.
Neff, Donald. *Warriors for Jerusalem: The Six Days that Changed the Middle East*. New York: Simon and Schuster, 1984.
Penniman, Howard, ed. *Israel at the Polls: The Knesset Elections of 1977*. Washington, D.C.: American Enterprise Institute for Public Policy Research, 1979.
Peters, Joan. *From Time Immemorial: The Origins of the Arab-Jewish Conflict Over Palestine*. New York: Harper & Row, 1984.
Polk, William R. *The Elusive Peace: The Middle East in the Twentieth Century*. London: Croom and Helm, 1979.
Rabinovich, Itamar. *The War for Lebanon, 1970–1983*. Ithaca, N.Y.: Cornell University Press, 1984.

Rubin, Barry. *The Arab States and the Palestine Conflict.* Syracuse, N.Y.: Syracuse University Press, 1981.
Sachar, Howard M. *A History of Israel.* New York: Knopf, 1976.
———. *Egypt and Israel.* New York: Marek, 1981.
Said, Edward W. *The Question of Palestine.* London: Routledge and Kegan Paul, 1980.
Safran, Nadav. *From War to War: The Arab-Israeli Confrontation, 1948–1967.* New York: Pegasus, 1969.
Sandler, Shmuel, and Hillel Frisch. *Israel, the Palestinians, and the West Bank.* Lexington, Mass.: Lexington Books, 1984.
Silver, Eric. *Begin: A Biography.* London: Weidenfeld and Nicolson, 1984.
Stein, Janice Gross, and Raymond Tanter. *Rational Decision Making: Israel's Security Choices, 1967.* Columbus: Ohio State University Press, 1980.
Stock, Ernest. *Israel on the Road to Sinai, 1949–1956.* Ithaca, N.Y.: Cornell University Press, 1967.
Touval, Saadia. *The Peace Brokers: Mediators in The Arab-Israeli Conflict.* Princeton, N.J.: Princeton University Press, 1982.
Udovitch, A.L., ed. *The Middle East: Oil, Conflict and Hope.* Lexington, Mass.: Lexington Books, 1976.
Wagner, Abraham R. *Crisis Decision-Making: Israel's Experience in 1967 and 1973.* New York: Praeger, 1974.
Yodfat, Aryeh, and Yuval A. Ohanna. *PLO: Strategy, and Politics.* London: Croom and Helm, 1981.

Memoirs

Ben-Gurion, David. *The Restored State of Israel.* Tel Aviv: Am Oved, 1969.
Brzezinski, Zbigniew. *Power and Principle: Memoirs of the National Security Adviser, 1977–1981.* New York: Farrar, Straus and Giroux, 1983.
Carter, Jimmy. *Keeping Faith: Memoirs of a President.* New York: Bantam Books, 1982.
Dayan, Moshe. *The Diary of the Sinai Campaign.* New York: Schocken, 1967.
———. *Story of My Life.* London: Sphere Books, 1977.
———. *Breakthrough: A Personal Account of the Egypt-Israel Peace Negotiations.* London: Weidenfeld and Nicolson, 1981.
Eban, Abba. *Abba Eban: An Autobiography.* New York: Random House, 1977.
Eisenhower, Dwight D. *Mandate for Change, 1953–1956 The White House Years.* New York: Signet, 1965.
Ford, Gerald R. *A Time to Heal.* New York: Harper & Row, 1979.
Haig, Alexander M., Jr. *Caveat: Realism, Reagan, and Foreign Policy.* London: Weidenfeld and Nicolson, 1984.
Johnson, Lyndon Baines. *The Vantage Point: Perspectives of the Presidency, 1963–1969.* New York: Holt, Rinehart & Winston, 1971.
Kissinger, Henry. *White House Years.* Boston: Little, Brown, 1979.
———. *Years of Upheaval.* Boston: Little, Brown, 1982.
Meir, Golda. *My Life.* New York: G.P. Putnam, 1975.

Nixon, Richard M. *The Memoirs of Richard Nixon.* London: Sidgwick and Jackson, 1978.

Rabin, Yitzhak. *The Rabin Memoirs.* Jerusalem: Steimatzky, 1979.

el-Sadat, Anwar. *In Search of Identity: An Autobiography.* New York: Harper & Row, 1978.

el-Shazly, Saad. *The Crossing of the Suez.* San Francisco: American Mideast Research, 1980.

Truman, Harry S. *Years of Trial and Hope: Memoirs by Harry S. Truman.* New York: Signet, 1965.

Vance, Cyrus. *Hard Choices: Critical Years in America's Foreign Policy.* New York: Simon and Schuster, 1983.

Weizman, Ezer. *The Battle for Peace.* New York: Bantam, 1981.

Weizmann, Chaim. *Trial and Error.* New York: Harper and Brothers, 1949.

Index

About the Author

Dr. Eytan Gilboa lectures on international and Middle Eastern politics and international communications at the Hebrew University of Jerusalem. He also teaches at the National Defense College of the Israeli Army. Since 1974, he has appeared regularly as a commentator on Israeli radio and television, and has edited and produced numerous programs. In addition, Dr. Gilboa has served as consultant to the Israeli ministries of Foreign Affairs and Defense.

Dr. Gilboa graduated summa cum laude from the Hebrew University and received his M.A. and Ph.D degrees in government from Harvard University, where he also served as teaching fellow and associate of the Center for International Affairs. He has traveled and lectured extensively in the United States and Europe and has been a visiting professor at Georgetown University, Tufts University, and the Free University of Berlin.

Dr. Gilboa is author and editor of several books and monographs, including *Simulation of Conflict and Conflict Resolution in the Middle East* (The Magnes Press of the Hebrew University, 1980); *The Arab-Israeli Conflict—Sources, Structure and Prospects for Resolution* (Ministry of Defense Publishing House, 1981); and *International Relations: The Evolution of a Discipline* (London: Croom Helm, forthcoming). He has contributed to many scholarly publications, including *The Yale Review*, *Journal of Peace Research*, *Political Communication and Persuasion*, *Journal of Applied Behavioral Science*, *International Journal of Political Education*, *Middle East Review* and *Public Opinion.*

About the Author